D&D Verlag I Bonn, Germany

www.dunddverlag.de

ISBN (Print): 978-3-945102-54-1

ISBN (eBook): 978-3-945102-55-8

Book & Cover Design: multimedia & more

1st Edition: April 2020

For Anna and our children

Table of Contents

11 Debugging & Testing

12 Build, Deploy & Publish

Bonus: Ionic and other frameworks

Preface

How do I get to write this book?

“Ionic 5 - Creating awesome apps for Android, iOS, Desktop and Web” is my third book about the excellent Ionic framework for developing mobile apps. My own search for specialized literature on this topic was sobering: the few things there are to be found in the book trade are outdated. That's when I realized: the book I'm looking for has yet to be written!

Just like my first books “Ionic 5” addresses new or emerging software developers who previously had little or nothing to do with programming apps or worked with other tools and frameworks and want to build really cool apps in a simple way. If you feel addressed, this book is for you!

The book spans from the idea of the popular app framework Ionic and its installation to the realization of a complete app including its publication in Google Play and Apple's App Store. It offers you a comprehensive introduction to Ionic. With in-depth background knowledge, for example, on Angular, Cordova or JavaScript, I'll hold myself back; there is already good literature about it. A small exception is the second chapter "Angular Essentials", in which I briefly describe the essential concepts and structures of Angular. The one who would like to know more, I'll offer further links in suitable places.

For each chapter I dedicate an own aspect of Ionic and gradually add new functionalities to an initially simple app called "BoB Tours". If you accompany me, at the end of this book, you not only learned to know and use the most important features of Ionic, but also understood how it works in context. With that you finally have the necessary knowledge to be able to develop your own awesome apps with Ionic.

If you find a chapter less exciting or want to skip for any other reason, you can download the source code of a chapter from the book's website (see "The book's website" on page 20) and continue working on the following chapter.

I would like to thank ...

... Ben Sperry and Max Lynch, who started their "Drifty Co." business in 2012 with ambitious goals, but probably didn't even suspect that in 2014 their Ionic frameworks would be one of the most popular cross-platform mobile development technology stacks in the world. Without this amazing success story, there wouldn't be countless awesome apps and even this book.

... Simon Grimm for his great project "Ionic Academy" (https://ionicacademy.com), whose visit I highly recommend to any new Ionite.

... Paul Halliday, Josh Morony, Max Schwarzmüller, Jorge Vegara, Sani Yusuf and all the other passionate authors of excellent Ionic tutorials.

... the team of the GFU Cyrus AG in Cologne, Germany, which was infected by my enthusiasm for Ionic and spontaneously integrated me into their seminar program with this topic.

... the readers of my books for the precious feedback that motivated me to stay tuned.

... you and all other readers of this book. Feel free to give me precious feedback this time, too.

... finally and emphatically with my loved ones for their patience and consideration when I worked hours and hours on this book and for their amazing leniency, when I talked about Ionic, Apps & Co. no less often and always long lectured. What they have left behind them, you as a reader can now look forward to ;-)

Bonn in April 2020

Andreas Dormann

1 Introduction

1.1 The idea behind Ionic

The creators of Ionic didn't reinvent the wheel. The made it even rounder!

The Ionic framework with its functions and components gives us a clear direction to a straightforward app development for Android, iOS and the web – and – if you like it – for the desktop and Windows 10 Universal, too. Ionic itself takes mainly established and very well proven frameworks and forges it together to a powerful Software Development Kit (SDK).

Let me shortly introduce the most important frameworks and modules under the hood of Ionic:

Angular

Angular (formerly known as AngularJS) is a JavaScript framework for creating single page web applications. It is developed by a community of individuals and companies, led by Google, and published as open source software.

Angular has data binding as an automatic way of updating the view, controllers to manage the DOM, directives to establish new HTML syntax, reusable components, form validation and much more.

Ionic has a specific `@ionic/angular` package that helps with integration with Angular. In the chapter "Angular Essentials" (starting from page 25) I describe the most important concepts of this powerful framework.

More about Angular you can find here:

- https://angular.io

App-Scripts

When `ionic serve` or `ionic cordova run` are invoked, it ultimately calls Node Package Manager (npm) scripts. These npm scripts call the `@ionic/app-scripts` library to execute the build process.

Out of the box, Ionic starters have been preconfigured with great defaults for building fast apps, including:

- Multi-core processing tasks in parallel for faster builds
- In-memory file transpiling and bundling
- Transpiling source code to ES5 JavaScript
- Ahead of Time (AoT) template compiling
- Just in Time (JiT) template compiling
- Template inlining for JiT builds
- Bundling modules for faster runtime execution
- Tree-shaking unused components and dead-code removal
- Generating CSS from bundled component Sass files
- Auto-prefixing vendor CSS prefixes
- Minifying JavaScript files
- Compressing CSS files
- Copying src static assets to www
- Linting source files
- Watching source files for live-reloading

Just the bullet list above is a little overwhelming, and each task requires quite a bit of development time just to get started. Ionic App Script's intention is to make it easier to complete common tasks so developers can focus on building their app, rather than building build scripts.

More about App-Scripts you can find here:

▶ https://github.com/ionic-team/ionic-app-scripts

Autoprefixer

Autoprefixer is a tool that adds vendor-specific-prefixes to hand-written Sass/CSS code. This ensures that standardized CSS rules you write will be applied across all supporting browsers. Let's have a look at an example.

You write:

```
.example {
    display: grid;
    transition: all .5s;
    user-select: none;
    background: linear-gradient(to bottom, white, black);
}
```

Autoprefixer parses this code and generates:

```
.example {
    display: -ms-grid;
    display: grid;
    -webkit-transition: all .5s;
    -o-transition: all .5s;
    transition: all .5s;
    -webkit-user-select: none;
       -moz-user-select: none;
        -ms-user-select: none;
            user-select: none;
    background: -webkit-gradient(linear, left top,
                      left bottom, from(white), to(black));
    background: -webkit-linear-gradient(top, white, black);
    background: -o-linear-gradient(top, white, black);
    background: linear-gradient(to bottom, white, black);
}
```

More about Autoprefixer you can find here:

- https://github.com/postcss/autoprefixer#browsers

Closure Compiler

Google's Closure Compiler is a tool for making JavaScript download and run faster. Instead of compiling from a source language to machine code, it compiles from JavaScript to better JavaScript. It parses your JavaScript, analyzes it, removes dead code and rewrites and minimizes what's left. It also checks syntax, variable references and types, and warns about common JavaScript pitfalls.

What are the benefits of using Closure Compiler?

- Efficiency. The Closure Compiler reduces the size of your JavaScript files and makes them more efficient, helping your application to load faster and reducing your bandwidth needs.
- Code checking. The Closure Compiler provides warnings for illegal JavaScript and warnings for potentially dangerous operations, helping you to produce JavaScript that is less buggy and easier to maintain.

More about Google's Closure Compiler you can find here:

► https://developers.google.com/closure/compiler/

Cordova and Capacitor

Apache Cordova (formerly PhoneGap) generates on the base of standard web technologies (HTML5, CSS3 and JavaScript) mobile/hybrid apps for many platforms. It enables wrapping up of CSS, HTML, and JavaScript code depending upon the platform of the device.

It extends the features of HTML and JavaScript to work with the device. The resulting applications are hybrid, meaning that they are neither truly native mobile application (because all layout rendering is done via Web views instead of the platform's native UI framework) nor purely Web-based (because they are not just Web apps, but are packaged as apps for distribution and have access to native device APIs).

Ionic apps use Cordova plugins to provide near-hardware functionalities like camera, accelerometer or geolocation. Ionic calls its curated set of Cordova plugins Ionic Native. I dedicated the chapter 9 to the topic "Ionic Native" (starting on page 393).

Capacitor is Ionic's "spiritual successor" to Cordova, focused entirely on enabling modern web apps to run on all major platforms with ease. I've dedicated a section in the bonus chapter to Capacitor (starting from page 565).

More about Cordova and Capacitor you can find here:

- https://ionicframework.com/docs/native/
- https://capacitor.ionicframework.com/
- https://cordova.apache.org

Git

Git is a free and open source distributed version control system for managing code. It allows development teams to contribute code to the same project without causing code conflicts.

Git is easy to learn and has a tiny footprint with fast performance. It outclasses SCM tools like Subversion, CVS, Perforce, and ClearCase with features like cheap local branching, convenient staging areas, and multiple workflows.

Git works directly with Ionic Appflow (see "12.9 Ionic Appflow" on page 553). Appflow uses your code base as the source of truth for Deploy and Package builds. In order for Appflow to access your code, you can choose to integrate directly using a hosting service like Github or Bitbucket, or you can push your code directly to Appflow.

More about Git and related topics you can find here:

- https://git-scm.com
- https://git-scm.com/book/en/v2
- https://github.com
- https://bitbucket.org

Node.js

Node.js is a runtime environment that allows JavaScript to be written on the server-side. In addition to being used for web services, node is often used to build developer tools, such as the Ionic CLI.

With Node.js you can also realize web servers. Node.js runs in the JavaScript runtime environment "V8", originally developed for Google Chrome, and provides a resource-efficient architecture that enables a particularly large number of concurrent network connections.

Let's have a look at an HTTP server version of a hello world program in Node.js using `text/html` as Content-Type header and port `3000`:

```
var http = require('http');

http.createServer(function (req, res) {
  res.writeHead(200, {
    'Content-Type': 'text/html'
  });
  res.write('Hallo Welt');
  res.end();
}).listen(3000);
```

On the Web you'll find interesting tutorials on full-stack projects, which were realized with Firebase or MongoDB as backend, a Node.js server as middleware and Ionic as frontend, for example (see link below).

More about Node.js and related topics you can find here:

- https://nodejs.org
- https://www.joshmorony.com/integrating-an-ionic-application-with-a-nodejs-backend/

Stencil (new)

Stencil is a Web Component compiler built by the Ionic Framework team to help build faster, more capable components that work across all major frameworks.

Web components are a set of web platform APIs that allow you to create new custom, reusable, encapsulated HTML tags to use in web pages and web apps. They are based on existing web standards.

Stencil combines the concepts of popular frameworks into a simple build-time tool.

Stencil takes features such as

- Virtual DOM
- Async rendering (inspired by React Fiber)
- Reactive data-binding
- TypeScript
- JSX

and then generates standards-based Web Components with these features baked in. Especially for Progressive Web Apps as a rapidly growing target for web developers the approach of Web Components leads to a big improvement in performance, latency and code size. So Ionic apps, based on Web Components, run well on fast and slow networks, across a diversity of platforms and devices.

More about Stencil you can find here:

▶ https://stenciljs.com

▶ https://github.com/ionic-team/stencil

TypeScript

TypeScript is a superset of JavaScript, which means it gives you JavaScript, along with a number of extra features such as type declarations and interfaces. Although Ionic is built with TypeScript, using it to build an Ionic app is completely optional - but recommended.

The first publicly available version of TypeScript was released in 2012 after two years of development by Microsoft in version 0.8. Shortly after the language was announced, it was praised by Miguel de Icaza. However, he complained that there were no other development environments apart from Microsoft Visual Studio, which wasn't available for Linux and MacOS in 2013. Since 2013 there was plug-in support for Eclipse. Meanwhile, a variety of text editors and development environments support TypeScript. These include Emacs, vim, Sublime Text, WebStorm, Atom and Microsoft's own Visual Studio Code editor. The latter I'll use in this book to develop Ionic apps.

TypeScript doesn't render JavaScript a static typed language, but allows *strong typing*. With this, variables and methods can be typed, whereupon certain errors can be detected even at compile time.

The basic types in TypeScript are: `Any`, `Array`, `Boolean`, `Enum`, `Never`, `Null`, `Number`, `Object`, `String`, `Tuple`, `Undefined`, `Void`.

More about TypeScript you can find here:

- https://www.typescriptlang.org
- http://www.typescriptlang.org/docs/handbook/basic-types.html

Webpack

Webpack bundles together JavaScript modules and other assets. It can be used to create single or multiple "chunks" that are only loaded when needed. Webpack can be used to take many files and dependencies and bundle them into one file, or other types.

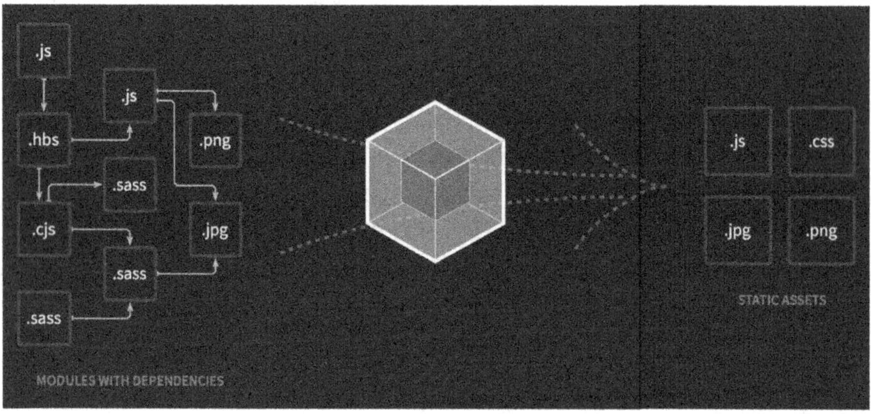

Webpack is designed primarily for JavaScript, but can convert front-end elements such as HTML, CSS, and even images, if the corresponding plug-ins are included.

More about Webpack you can find here:

- https://webpack.js.org

1.2 Installations

Node & npm

First of all make sure to install the latest version of Node.js from

- ► https://nodejs.org

I recommend selecting the LTS version to ensure best compatibility.

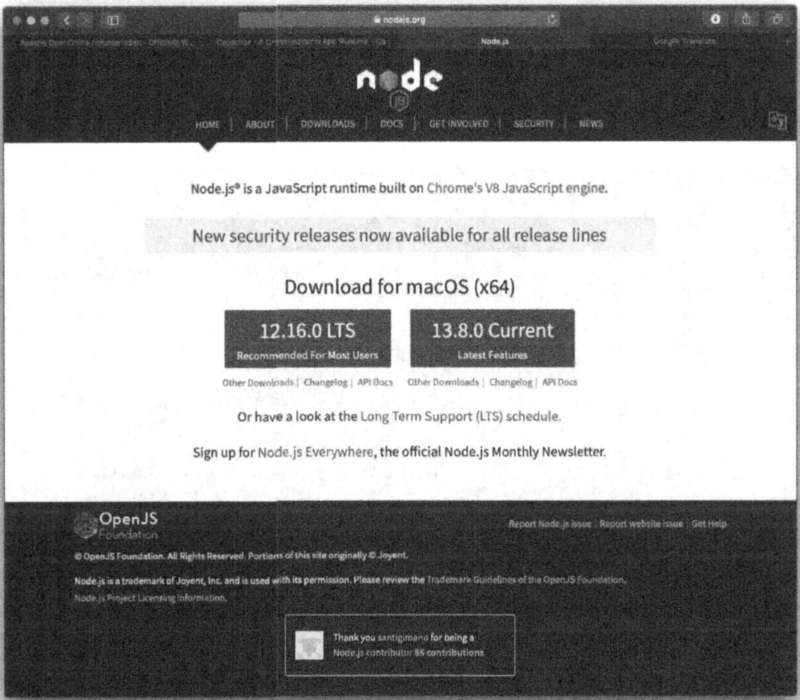

Node is bundled with `npm`, the package manager for JavaScript.

To verify the installation, open a new terminal window and run:

```
$ node -version
$ npm --version
```

Ionic CLI

Now we install the Ionic command-line utility (CLI). It supports us with a bunch of dev tools and help options to create and develop our applications. Install the Ionic CLI globally with **npm**:

```
$ npm install -g @ionic/cli
```

Note: The `-g` means it is a global install. For Window's it's recommended to open an Admin command prompt. Mac/Linux users should use `sudo` for installation.

In the course of this book we will get to know the most important commands of the Ionic CLI. To give you an overview in advance, you can enter the following after installing the CLI in the terminal:

```
$ ionic --help
```

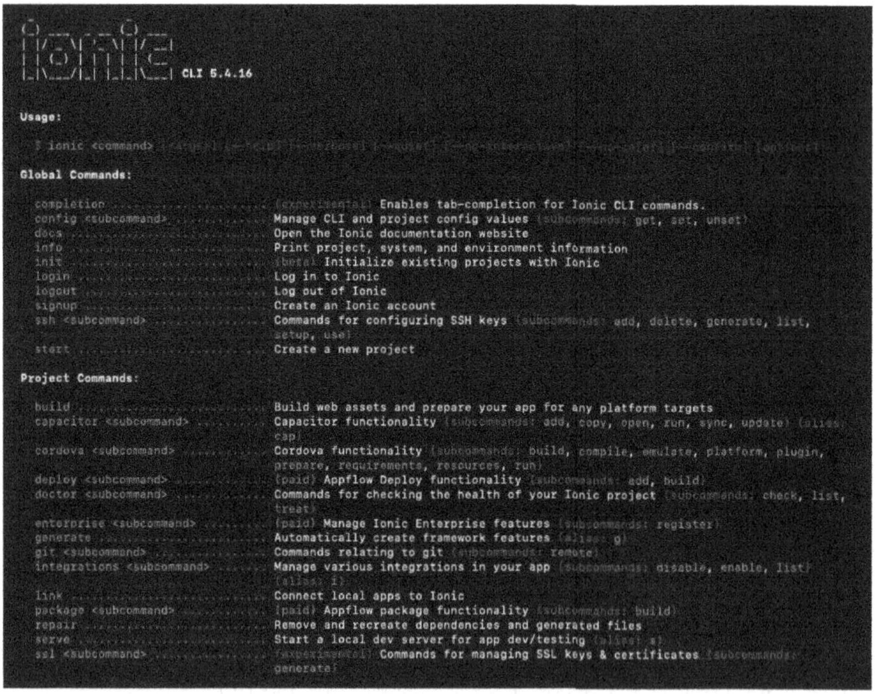

More about the Ionic CLI (including a full command reference) you can find here:

- https://ionicframework.com/docs/cli

Visual Studio Code

Last but not least we install Microsoft's free code editor Visual Studio Code (VSC) from

- ► https://code.visualstudio.com/

It's the Integrated Development Environment (IDE) I use in this book. There are IDE alternatives like the "big" Microsoft Visual Studio, Atom and Eclipse or, of course, Ionic's own new Ionic Studio (https://ionicframework.com/studio).

Since many illustrations and explanations in this book are based on VSC, however, I recommend that you also use VSC if you want to better follow the programming in this book and avoid (visual) deviations.

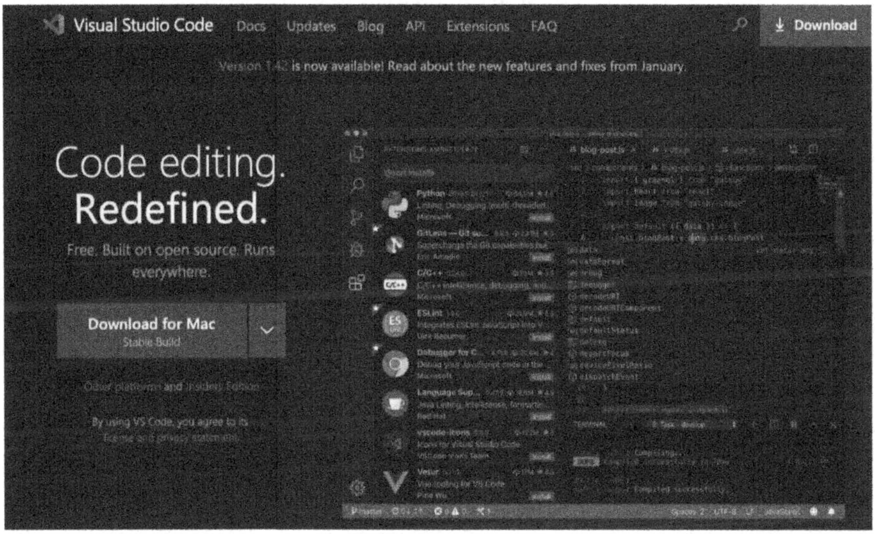

After the installation and the first call of VSC you should activate the integrated terminal (menu `View > Terminal`). So you can code and use the Ionic CLI in one interface.

Google Chrome

For developing you can choose whatever browser you want. But I recommend to use Google Chrome. Its built-in `Developer Tools` will give us great support while developing, debugging and testing Ionic applications.

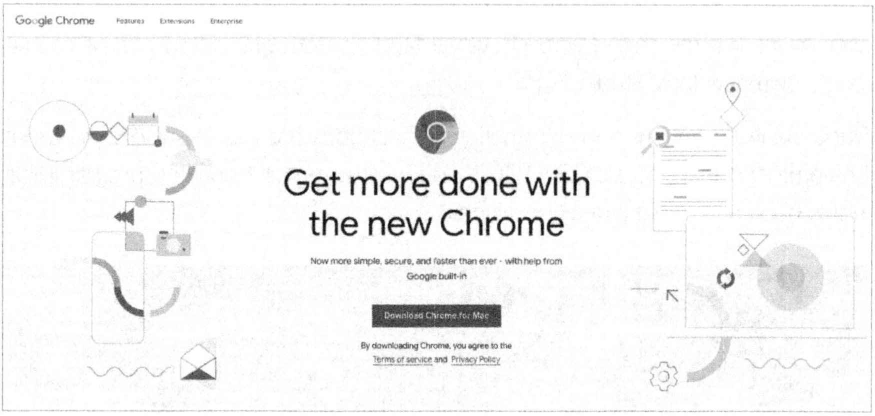

You can install it from

- https://www.google.com/chrome

or use the developer version from

- https://www.google.com/chrome/dev

1.3 How to read this book

The story of this book is all about one big application called „BoB Tours". It begins in chapter 3 („The first app", starting on page 55) and ends in chapter 12 („Build, deploy and publish", starting on page 511). In every chapter you'll learn how to add new components and functionality to the app until it's a real world application.

In chapter 2 („Angular Essentials", starting on page 25) I explain fundamental concepts of Angular, the JavaScript framework, that accompains Ionic by default. If you' re familiar with Angular or if you're eager to start with Ionic directly, you can skip that chapter. But when it comes to the use of Angular structures I recommend Angular newcomers to read the corresponding topics to understand what they are coding there.

The addendum at the end of this book („Ionic and other frameworks", starting on page 561) is for those of you, who want to look at the bigger picture. Since Ionic 4 you aren't be forced to use Angular. There are interesting alternatives like Electron, jQuery, React and Vue. In that chapter I'll take a look at the world beyond Angular and show you how some of these other frameworks fit together with Ionic.

1.4 The book's website

A book like this may become outdated soon. To deal with that I created a website to this book. There you'll find all source code we write in this book – to every chapter the respective development progress – always up to date! You can download it and compare it to your own code or use it as a base to start from whatever chapter you want.

If it happens that you read my book in a few months, install the latest version of Ionic and notice at some point that the code used here for some reason doesn't work, take a look at the forum of the website. If necessary, updated hints are given for each chapter. Otherwise, don't be afraid to post a question in the forum. The reader community and I will do our best to answer as soon as possible.

Here are QR, web address and code to my book's website:

- https://ionic.andreas-dormann.de/

1.5 Our „BoB Tours“ app

So that you can see what you are doing here, I will describe and show you our app, how you - after working through all the chapters - will have developed it yourself at the end of the book.

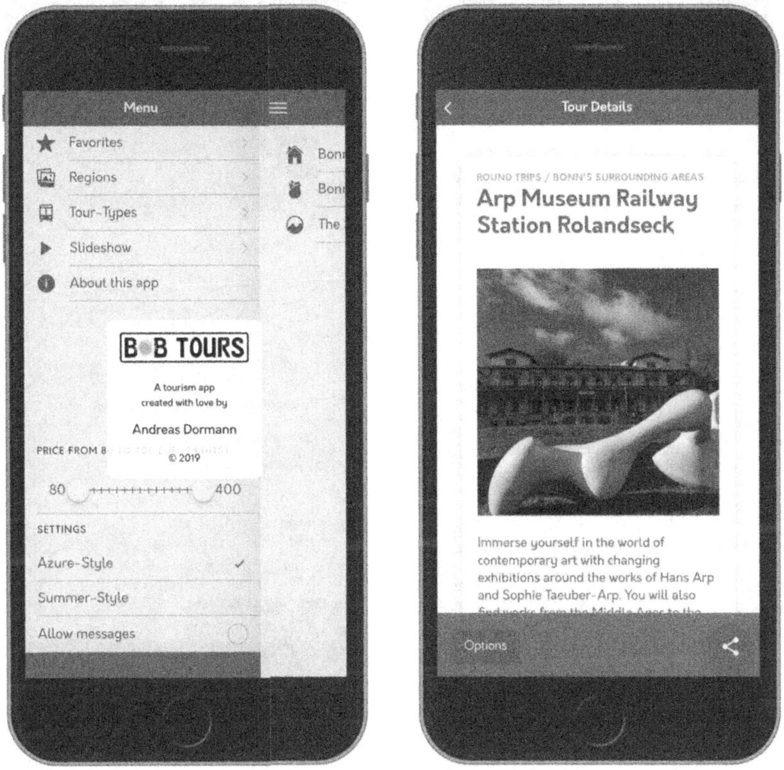

Our app can be characterized as follows: "BoB Tours" is the app of an imaginary tourism company called "Best of Bonn Tours GmbH", in short: "BoB Tours", that offers city tours, biking, hiking and segway trips around my beautiful home of Bonn.

In the app, the tour offer can be searched for regions (e.g., "Bonn City" or "Bonn's Surrounding Areas") and tour types (e.g., "Round Trips" or "Segway Tours") as well as for a price range. If you have found an interesting tour, you can view their details together with a photo and save them as a favorite.

The starting point and the route from the current location to the starting point of each tour can be displayed in a map. Finally, you can formulate and send a booking request directly to the tourism company from the app. Of course the form will be validated.

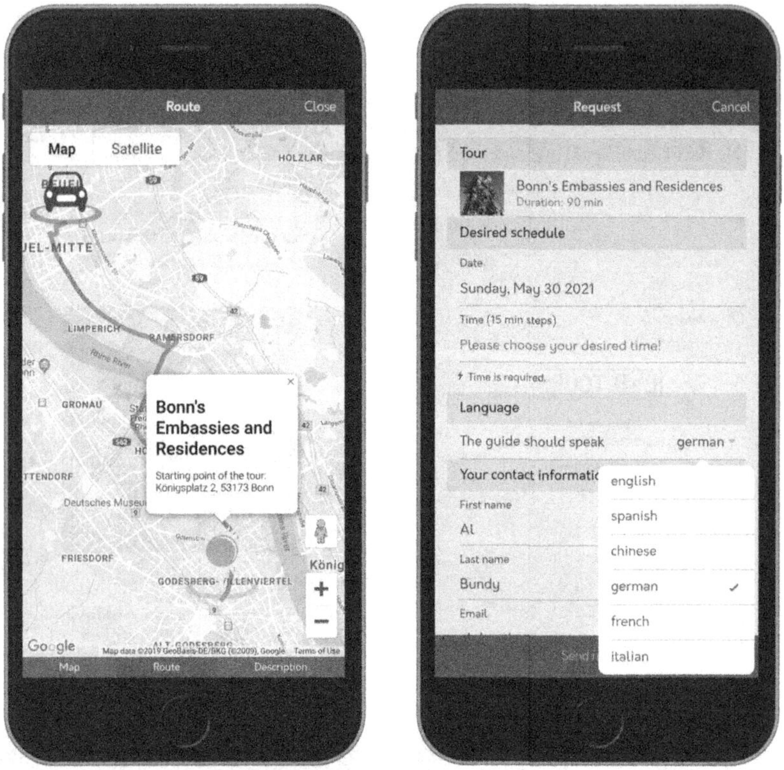

Our app should make a good impression on a smartphone, in the browser and on a tablet as well. Therefore, we will also turn to the aspect of "responsibility".

In the user settings, you can finally switch between different color designs.

You see, the whole thing is already a small real life app. In doing so, we will encounter a number of typical programming situations, as in the real life of an app developer.

Incidentally, I got inspiration for this app from some of the interesting tour offers on bonntouren.de. I can personally recommend the charming owner Soledad Sichert as an excellent tour guide!

If you have completed this book and your app successfully, you should donate you and your loved ones a trip to Germany to Bonn's Rhineland and one of the exciting Bonn tours ;-)

Here you can watch a demo version of "BoB Tours":

► https://ionic.andreas-dormann.de/demo

Summary

In this chapter, you got to know the idea behind Ionic. You now know that Ionic has many specialized single frameworks under its hood.

You also did all the installations necessary to work with Ionic: Node and npm, Ionic CLI, Microsoft Visual Studio Code and Google Chrome with its Dev Tools.

I finally introduced you to the book website and our app "Bob Tours".

2 Angular Essentials

2.1 What is Angular?

Preliminary remarks

Client-side programming has become extremely complex in recent times. The requirements for a web application are now just as high as for a desktop application - if not higher. The desire for a framework that enables the developer to cover all these requirements on the web is thus getting bigger.

Angular is a client-side framework that makes it possible to create web applications. It helps the developer to bring known and new architectural concepts to the client and develop complex applications. The work can be aligned not only on the server, but via JavaScript on the client. The application can fulfill modern architectural concepts by separating the responsibilities and is thus more maintainable and testable.

Ionic uses Angular since Ionic 2 (and its predecessor AngularJS since Ionic 1). Therefore, it makes sense to be proficient in Angular to develop good Ionic apps. We also use Angular with the current Ionic 5 in this book.

It should not go unmentioned that Ionic 5 also cooperates with other frameworks. I have dedicated this topic to the bonus chapter "Ionic and other frameworks" (starting on page 561).

What can Angular do?

Angular was developed with TypeScript (see "1.1 The idea behind Ionic" on page 13) and is aligned to a component-based architecture. It combines modern architectural approaches with the necessary flexibility to master the complex requirements of web applications. By using TypeScript, Angular has similar type security as developers know it from other languages like C# or Java. Nevertheless, Angular isn't tied to TypeScript and allows developers to use JavaScript with ES5 or ES2015/ES6.

Angular is designed for component-based architectures. It separates the responsibilities and the view from the logic. The developer can divide an application so that it becomes maintainable, testable and expandable. The idea is to break the application down into small testable pieces so that the developer paradigms "single-responsibility" and "separation-of-concerns" can be met. Angular helps with many emerging issues such as creating components, data binding to the UI/HTML, transformation of data against the UI with pipes, outsourcing of "work" in services, communication with an API, etc.

Angular makes it possible to communicate with components, feed them with data and receive events from components; it makes components reusable and more isolated. For example, the flexibility to separately develop the view as HTML allows different teams to work on logic, architecture, and design.

In order to achieve the greatest possible flexibility and to be broadly positioned, Angular draws on further projects and their functionality, such as `RxJS`. The integration of third-party libraries is therefore simple and simple, which means you can extend your application to almost any JavaScript library and use its flexibility.

This allows you to create complete applications that are bigger and more powerful than a "normal" website: A web application that has the same rights and obligations (architecture, testability, etc.) as an application in a familiar language, such as the desktop.

In this chapter I describe the most important concepts and structures of Angular, which can be useful for you in the realization of your Ionic Apps.

2.2 Components

With Angular, there is no direct manipulation of the HTML-DOM, but a separation according to the model-view-controller (MVC) pattern: In the view, the developer defines so-called templates that connect static HTML tags with dynamic contents from the controller. This mix allows the framework through custom HTML syntax elements ("directives").

A custom tag in a page is represented by a component class decorated with `@Component`. The selector (see Listing 1) sets the tag name. The template-related template can be specified directly by the web developer as a string in the template property, but this is only possible with very short HTML blocks. Otherwise you refer to a `.html` file with `templateUrl` (see Listing 2).

A component can also have its own CSS specifications (inline or stand-alone file) that apply solely to the submission of this component, unless the developer doesn't explicitly refer to the parent and child components with the additions `:host` or `/deep/`.

In the template for the tour list in Listing 2 you can see a custom tag again with `<TourDetails>`. This is a child component that interacts with the parent component through properties and events. Using the `@Input()` and `@Output()` decorators, the developer must clearly define which properties and events are accessible to other components. For event communication Angular offers its own event emitter.

A component triggers various events throughout its lifecycle that the developer can hook into. Listing 1 shows this with the example of the event `OnInit`, which from the point of view of TypeScript is a class that, like all other types, has to be integrated with `import {OnInit, ...} from '@angular/core'`. Other events are related to data binding (`ngOnChanges`, `ngDoCheck`).

Listing 1: Component class for TourList

```
// Angular library imports
import { Component, OnInit } from '@angular/core';
import { Router } from '@angular/router';
import { Observable } from 'rxjs/Observable';
```

```
// Imports for own classes
import { Tour } from '../Model/Tour'
import { BookingService } from '../Services/BookingService'
import { TourDetails } from '../TourDetails/TourDetails';

@Component({
selector: 'TourList',
templateUrl: 'App/TourList/TourList.html',
providers: [BookingService]
})
export class TourList implements OnInit {

  // Here we inject BookingService and Router
  constructor(private bookingService: BookingService,
              private router: Router) {}

  status: string;
  tours: Tour[];

  ngOnInit() {
    this.bookingService.getAll(data => { // Callback
      this.tours = this.bookingService.tours;
      this.status = this.tours.length + " tours booked.";
    });
  }

  Delete(tour: Tour) {
    this.bookingService.delete(tour); // Call service
    this.status = `Tour ${tour.ID} deleted!`;
  }

  Change(tour: Tour) {
    let link = ['/edit', tour.ID];
    this.router.navigate(link);
  }

  // Event handler for message from child component
  onTourDeleted(tour: Tour) {
    this.status = `Tour ${tour.ID} deleted!`;
    this.tours = this.bookingService.tours;
  }
}
```

Listing 2: Angular template for TourList

```
<ul>
  <li *ngFor="let t of tours;
            let isEven = even;
            let i = index">
    <span [ngClass]="{'text-primary': isEven,
                    'text-info': !isEven}">
      <span class="badge">
        {{i+1}}: Tour #{{t.ID | fixedLenNumber:3}}
      </span>
      <TourDetails [tour]="t"
                   (tourDeletedEvent)="onTourDeleted($event)">
      </TourDetails>
      <button type="info"
              *ngIf="t.FreeSeats > 0"
              (click)="Change(t)">
        Change
      </button>
      <button type="warning"
              [disabled]="t.FreeSeats <= 0"
              (click)="Delete(t)">
        Delete
      </button>
    </span>
  </li>
</ul>
```

Don't worry if this seems very abstract to you. From the next chapter we will create many components (pages) ourselves. And with the help of Ionic, the whole thing will be very easy for you.

Further informations about this topic you can find in the official Angular documentation:

▶ https://angular.io/guide/architecture-components

2.3 Lifecycle Hooks

Ionic 5 uses the Angular Lifecycle Hooks. That's why it makes sense to spend a little time on it to:

- understand the different phases an Angular component (see "2.2 Components", starting from page 27) goes through from being created to being destroyed.
- know how to hook into those phases and run your own code.
- know the order in which the different phases happen and what triggers each phase.

A component in Angular has a lifecycle, a series of different phases that it goes through from "birth to death". We can familiarize ourselves with these different phases to get a pretty fine control of our application. To do this, we add some specific methods to our component class that are called during each of these lifecycle phases. These methods are called *hooks*.

The hooks are executed in this order:

We distinguish between hooks for the component itself (red and blue) and hooks for their children (green).

Hooks for a component

constructor

This is invoked when Angular creates a component or directive by calling `new` on the class.

ngOnChanges

is invoked every time there is a change in one of the input properties of a component.

ngOnInit

is invoked when a component has been initialized. This hook is only called *once* after the first `ngOnChanges`

ngDoCheck

is invoked when the change detector of a component is invoked. It allows us to implement our own change detection algorithm for a component.

ngOnDestroy

This method will be invoked just before Angular destroys a component. Use this hook to unsubscribe Observables (see "2.10 Observables", starting from page 46) and detach event handlers to avoid memory leaks.

Hooks for a component's children

ngAfterContentInit

is invoked after Angular performs any Projection (see "2.6 Content Projection" on page 39) into a components view.

ngAfterContentChecked

is invoked each time the content of the given component has been checked by the change detection mechanism of Angular.

ngAfterViewInit

is invoked when a component's view has been fully initialized.

ngAfterViewChecked

is invoked each time the view of the given component has been checked by the change detection mechanism of Angular.

Code example

In this code I show a typical use of the `constructor` and `ngOnInit` hook. Both will be used regularly throughout this book. They're Angular's bread and butter hooks.

```
import { Component } from '@angular/core';

@Component({
  selector: 'actors-data',
  templateUrl: 'actors-data.html',
})
export class ActorsData {

  myStar;

  constructor() {
    console.log('constructor - My star is $(this.myStar)');
    myStar = 'Julia Roberts';
  }

  ngOnInit() {
    console.log('ngOnInit - My star is $(this.myStar)');
  }

}
```

The following console output would appear in an app:

```
constructor - My star is undefined
ngOnInit - My star is Julia Roberts
```

At the constructor's console log output the property `myStar` is undefined. The value is assigned *after* the console statement. By the time the `ngOnInit` hook is called we can see that the property `myStar` is now set to the given value.

More detailed information about Lifecycle Hooks you can find here:

- https://angular.io/guide/lifecycle-hooks
- https://ionicframework.com/docs/lifecycle/angular

2.4 Dependency Injection

Dependency Injection is a core technique for the development of loosely coupled systems where the parts of the application are assembled at the start of the application.

In a component-based system, or when using a service, the client normally instantiates the server/component/service:

```
class Environment
{
  Client c = new Client();
  c.Process();
}

class Client
{
  public void Operation()
  {
    Service d = new Service();
    d.Action();
  }
}

class Service
{
  public void Action()
  {
    ...
  }
}
```

The disadvantage of this method is

- that the service can't simply be exchanged for another
- that the client can't be tested without the service.

Dependency Injection assumes that the concrete implementation of the service is variable and is passed from the environment to the client, e.g. into the constructor or by passing a property, a method call. Either the type of the service, an instance of the service, or an initialization object describing the service can be passed.

Example: Injection by constructor and a concrete instance

```
class Environment
{
  Client c = new Client(new Service());
  c.Process();
}

class Client
{
  Service d;

  public Client (Service Service)
  {
    d = Service;
  }

  public void Operation()
  {
    d.Action();
  }
}

class Service
{
  public void Action()
  {
    ...
  }
}
```

Further informations about this topic you can find in the official Angular documentation:

- https://angular.io/guide/dependency-injection

2.5 Routing and Lazy Loading

Routes

A route simply defines an URL path and a component to display it's content.

There are three main types of routes that you will use frequently:

- **Eager**. Routes that point to a single component.
- **Lazy**. Routes that point to a module.
- **Redirect**. Routes that redirect to another route.

```
const routes: Routes = [
  // Regular Route
  { path: 'eager', component: MyComponent },

  // Lazy Loaded Route (Page)
  { path: 'lazy', loadChildren:
'./lazy/lazy.module#LazyPageModule' },

    // Redirect
  { path: 'here', redirectTo: 'there', pathMatch: 'full' }
];
```

src/app/app-routing.module.ts

The root configuration for an Ionic application router lives in the `src/app/app-routing.module.ts` file. Here you define your routes. For pages that you generate with the Ionic CLI (`ionic generate page...`) all corresponding routes are defined automatically. For example see the route for a page named `Favorites`:

```
{
  path: 'favorites',
  loadChildren:()=>import('./pages/favorites/favorites.module')
    .then(m => m.FavoritesPageModule)
}
```

It's important to understand the code that is generated. Instead of routing to a component, the route is configured to lazy load a child module (that may contain many components). The basic idea of lazy loading is that it breaks your application down into smaller chunks, and only loads what is necessary at the time. When your application is first loaded, only the components that are necessary to display the first screen need to be loaded. This is especially beneficial for Progressive Web Apps where page load times are critical. This magic is made possible with Webpack Code Splitting.

With lazy loading, your application can boot much faster because it doesn't need to load much – you could have a huge application, with 50 pages, but it could still load just as fast as an application with just 2 pages.

A lazy loaded route renders the `FavoritesPageModule` where the so called `outlet` is defined in the HTML in the `app.component.html`:

```
<ion-router-outlet></ion-router-outlet>
```

When you navigate to the `/favorites` path in the browser, it will render the specific component in the HTML outlet.

Ionic's own router outlet implementation `<ion-router-outlet>` (basically, you just plop the router outlet wherever you want the component for the active route to be displayed) is mostly the same as Angular's `<router-outlet>` except that it will automatically apply the screen transition animations with a "direction" (e.g. a forward navigation will animate the new screen in from the right).

ActivatedRoute

Angular has an `ActivatedRoute` to bring data from one page to another. In other words: an `ActivatedRoute` contains the information about a route associated with a component (page) loaded in an outlet.

Example: Data is sent from a calling page e.g. via HTML like

```
[routerLink]="['/target', data]"
```

and is received by a `target.page.ts` by code like this:

```
import { Component, OnInit } from '@angular/core';
import { ActivatedRoute } from '@angular/router';

@Component({
  selector: 'app-target',
```

```
  templateUrl: './target.page.html',
  styleUrls: ['./target.page.scss'],
})
export class TargetPage implements OnInit {

  incoming_data = null;

  constructor(private activatedRoute: ActivatedRoute) { }

  ngOnInit() {
    this.incoming_data = this.activatedRoute.snapshot.params;
  }

}
```

The Code is shortly explained: An `ActivatedRoute` has to be imported from the `@angular/router` module. To use it it has to be injected via the constructor of the page component. In the `ngOnInit` event we can grab the data e.g. from the `snapshot.params` property of `ActivatedRoute` to bind it to a component variable (`incoming_data`).

There are more properties available in `ActivatedRoute`.

Further informations you can find in the official Angular documentation:

- https://angular.io/api/router/ActivatedRoute

2.6 Content Projection

The easiest way to display a component property is to bind the property name through Content Projection. With Content Projection, you put the property name in the view template, enclosed in double curly braces: {{myStar}}.

Here's an example class:

```
export class PrettyWoman {
  title = 'Pretty Woman';
  actors = ['Julia Roberts', 'Richard Gere', 'Hector
Elizondo'];
  myStar = this.actors[0];
}
```

In HTML you can write:

```
<h1>{{title}}</h1>
<h2>My favorite star is: {{myStar}}</h2>
```

Angular automatically pulls the value of the title and myStar properties from the component and inserts those values into the browser. Angular updates the display when these properties change. More precisely, the redisplay occurs after some kind of asynchronous event related to the view, such as a keystroke, a timer completion, or a response to an HTTP request.

When you bootstrap with the AppComponent class (in main.ts), Angular looks for an <app-root> in the index.html, finds it, instantiates an instance of AppComponent, and renders it inside the <app-root> tag.

Now run the app. It should display the title and star name:

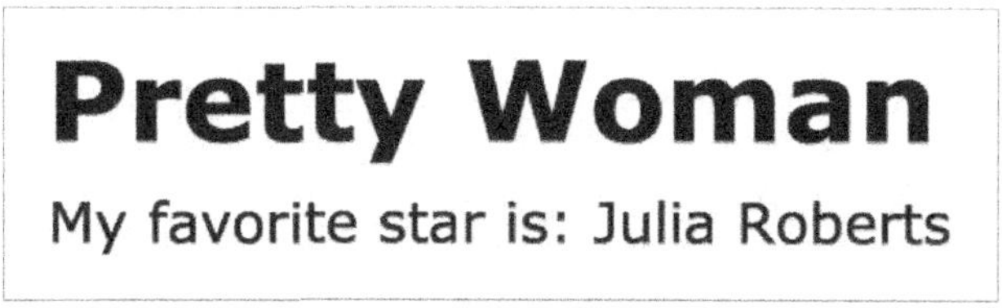

You want to know more about this topic? Then read:

► https://angular.io/guide/displaying-data

2.7 *ngFor

One very often used Angular directive is `ngFor`. It's a "repeater" directive and helps you to iterate through an array of objects.

Remember the example class `PrettyWoman` in the previous division "2.6 Content Projection". Here is a short code example that uses the HTML unordered list with `<ul>` and `<li>` tags and Content Projection for showing a list of actors in "Pretty Woman":

```
<ul>
  <li *ngFor="let actor of actors">
    {{ actor }}
  </li>
</ul>
```

Run the app. It should display the list of actors:

You should never forget the leading asterisk (*) in `*ngFor`. It's an essential part of the syntax.

Further informations about this topic you can find in the Angular documentation:

► https://angular.io/guide/displaying-data

2.8 Pipes

Angular pipes enable data to be transformed and/or formatted in the DOM before rendering (for strings, for example). Often, with regard to the user experience, you don't want to display the data within an app one to one, even in the view. Imagine we have an actor object like this:

```
import { Component } from '@angular/core';

@Component({
  selector: 'actor-data',
  templateUrl: 'actor-data.html',
})
export class ActorData {

  actor = {
    name: 'Julia Roberts',
    birthday: new Date(1967, 10, 28)
  }

}
```

In the HTML file we use Content Projection (see “2.6 Content Projection” on page 39) to display the data:

```
<div>
  <h1>{{actor.name}}</h1>
  <h2>{{actor.birthday}}</h2>
</div>
```

Since the Content Projection in this case uses the `toString()` method in `actor.birthday` and renders the result of it to the view, the following is rendered to the UI:

Julia Roberts

Tue Nov 28 1967 00:00:00 GMT+0100 (Central European Standard Time)

However, our users are not interested in the current time zone or the day of the week. So we just want to show them the date in a common format. In order to implement this formatting as elegantly as possible, Angular offers the possibility to use pipes for this purpose. You use a kind of filter for the Content Projection, which then delivers the result. For this we need a new TypeScript class, which is declared as a pipe with a decorator:

```
import { Pipe, PipeTransform } from '@angular/core';

@Pipe({
  name: 'birthdayFormatPipe'
})
export class BirthdayFormatPipe implements PipeTransform {

  transform(value: Date): any {
    let dd = value.getDate();
    let MM = value.getMonth() + 1;
    let yyyy = value.getFullYear();
    let formattedBirthday = `${dd}.${MM}.${yyyy}`;
    return formattedBirthday;
  }

}
```

Now we have to make the pipe known with our ActorData component module:

```
import { RouterModule } from '@angular/router';
import { NgModule } from '@angular/core';
import { CommonModule } from '@angular/common';
import { FormsModule } from '@angular/forms';
import { ActorData } from './actor-data';
import { BirthdayFormatPipe }
  from './../birthday-format.pipe';

@NgModule({
  imports: [
    ...
  ],
  declarations: [ActorData, BirthdayFormatPipe]
})
export class ActorDataModule {}
```

Now we have to use our pipe in the HTML file. To use a pipe, we need the so-called pipe operator (|):

```
<div>
  <h1>{{actor.name}}</h1>
  <h2>{{actor.birthday | birthdayFormatPipe}}</h2>
</div>
```

The result is then formatted as expected and displayed in our view:

Hint: To prevent problems with `undefined` and/or `null` exceptions, there is the Safe Navigation Operator (also known as the Elvis Operator). This can be used if you are not sure if the property being bound doesn't belong to an object that is `undefined` and/or `null` at the time of rendering. In our example it looks like this:

```
<div>
  <h1>{{actor?.name}}</h1>
  <h2>{{actor?.birthday | birthdayFormatPipe}}</h2>
</div>
```

To be honest: Angular comes with a stock of prefabricated pipes such as `DatePipe`, `UpperCasePipe`, `LowerCasePipe`, `CurrencyPipe`, and `PercentPipe`. They are all available for use in any template. So before writing your own pipes be sure to first check the built-in pipes.

You want to know more about pipes? Then read:

- https://angular.io/guide/pipes
- http://masteringionic.com/blog/2017-08-02-understanding-angular-pipes

2.9 Promises

Promises - what they are and what they do

To make Promises understandable, let's start with a rough description and then go into details and concrete applications. If you can't imagine anything at first under the term Promise, you are not alone. Promises are something like "Callbacks 2.0", advanced functions that are given to other functions that take care of their execution (maybe in the future).

Promise is a pretty apt name. If an asynchronous function returns a Promise, it gives you a promise that this part of the program will be executed. Either this succeeds and the promise is held (`resolve`) or not (`reject`). As a result, we have the opportunity from the outset to simply react to a successful or incorrect execution.

Let's create a simple example with `setTimeout` to simulate a real Promise (like an asynchronous database call):

```
function asyncWriteFanMailToJuliaRoberts() {
  var promise = new Promise((resolve, reject) => {
    setTimeout(() => {
      console.log("Mail sent!");
      if (error) {
        reject();
      } else {
        resolve();
      }
    }, 1000);
  });
  return promise;
}
```

Resolve a Promise

But how do we respond to a `resolve` or a `reject`? To do this, each Promise object has a `then` function, which means something like: If the asynchrony is finished or the promise has been resolved (by `resolve` or `reject`), then execute. For this reason, promises are also often called *thenables*.

This `then` function can handle two callback functions. The first for the success and the second for the case of error.

Our call to `asyncWriteFanMailToJuliaRoberts` now looks like this:

```
asyncWriteFanMailToJuliaRoberts().
  .then((data) => console.log(data))
  .catch((err) => console.error(err));
```

Real world example

Here is a little code snippet, as we'll use it later in our sample app:

```
this.getTours().then(data => {
  this.tours = _.sortBy(data, 'Title');
  this.all_tours = _.sortBy(data, 'Title');
  this.filterTours({lower: 80, upper: 400});
  this.favService.initialize(this.all_tours);
});
```

Without the need to understand the code of the function `getTours()`, you immediately realize that `getTours()` is a Promise function, right? The little word `then` tells it. Once `getTours()` asynchronously and successfully returns data, some more functions (inside the curly brackets) are executed here. All these inner functions can rely on `getTours()` keeping its promise and delivering valid data.

Further informations about Promises you can find here:

- https://codecraft.tv/courses/angular/es6-typescript/promises/

2.10 Observables

An observable is an object that emits events (or notifications). An observer is an object that listens for these events, and does something when an event is received. Together, they create a pattern that can be used for programming asynchronously.

In other words: An observer keeps an eye on things and reacts to possible changes. If another part of the application wants to be informed by the observer about changes to the observable, it can subscribe to it (`subscribe`) and also unsubscribe (`unsubscribe`).

Observables can be abstractly considered simply as data streams. As a result, they can also be used flexibly and, for example, several observables can be linked or combined.

The principle is very similar to the Observer pattern and is called Reactive Programming. Angular uses the observables of the ReactiveX architecture as a basis. Through Microsoft's Microsoft Reactive Extensions, there is a very good implementation in JavaScript and other languages - called `RxJS` for short.

Let's look at a complete example of how observables in Angular (and Ionic) can be used. In the following, the individual sections and functions of the following source code are explained in more detail.

Listing 1: Create an Observable (actors.service.ts)

```
import { Injectable } from '@angular/core';
// Import Observable from RxJs
import { Observable } from 'rxjs';

@Injectable({
  providedIn: 'root'
})
export class ActorsService {

  actors = [{
      id: 1,
      name: 'Julia Roberts',
      birthday: new Date('1967-10-28')
    },
```

```
    {
      id: 2,
      name: 'Richard Gere',
      birthday: new Date('1949-08-31')
    },
    {
      id: 3,
      name: 'Hector Elizondo',
      birthday: new Date('1936-12-22')
  }];

  constructor() { }

  // Create an Observable
  public getActors(): any {
    const actorsObservable = new Observable(observer => {
      setTimeout(() => {
        observer.next(this.actors);
      }, 1000);
    });
    return actorsObservable;
  }

}
```

Listing 2: Define the subscriber (actors-data.ts)

```
import { Component } from '@angular/core';
import { ActorsService } from './services/actors.service';

@Component({
  selector: 'actors-data',
  templateUrl: 'actors-data.html',
})
export class ActorsData {

  actors = [];

  constructor(private actorsService: ActorsService) {}
```

```
  ngOnInit() {
    const actorsObservable = this.actorsService.getActors();
    // Define a Subscriber
    actorsObservable.subscribe((actorsData) => {
      this.actors = actorsData;
    });
  }

}
```

Listing 3: Display the actors (actors-data.html)

```
<div *ngFor="let actor of actors">
  <div class="card">
    <h5 class="card-title">{{ actor.name }}</h5>
    <h6 class="card-subtitle">Actor ID: {{ actor.id }}</h6>
    <p class="card-text">
      Born: {{ actor.birthday | date: 'shortDate' }}
    </p>
  </div>
</div>
```

Explanation to Listing 1:

In a service (`actors.service.ts`) there is an array of actors (this data could also come from a database):

```
actors = [{
      id: 1,
      name: 'Julia Roberts',
      birthday: new Date('1967-10-28')
    },
    {
      id: 2,
      name: 'Richard Gere',
      birthday: new Date('1949-08-31')
    },
    {
      id: 3,
      name: 'Hector Elizondo',
```

```
      birthday: new Date('1936-12-22')
  }];
```

The `getActors()` method creates an observable to read the data.

```
public getActors(): any {
    const actorsObservable = new Observable(observer => {
      setTimeout(() => {
        observer.next(this.actors);
      }, 1000);
    });
    return actorsObservable;
  }
```

The Observable calls the `next` method of its `observer` object to emit data (`this.actors`). To be able to use an Observable, `Observable` is to be imported from the ReactiveX library (`RxJS`):

```
import { Observable } from 'rxjs';
```

Explanation to Listing 2:

The component (`actors-data.ts`) provides an empty array for the actors:

```
actors = [];
```

The component imports the service from Listing 1 with:

```
import { ActorsService } from './services/actors.service';
```

and injects it via its constructor:

```
constructor(private actorsService: ActorsService) {}
```

In `ngOnInit` the service is called and a subscriber is defined who writes the data output by the service to the actor array:

```
ngOnInit() {
  const actorsObservable = this.actorsService.getActors();
  actorsObservable.subscribe((actorsData) => {
    this.actors = actorsData;
  });
}
```

Explanation to Listing 3:

In the HTML file, the array is rendered via an `*ngFor` loop (see "2.7 *ngFor" on page 40) into the view.

The result looks like this:

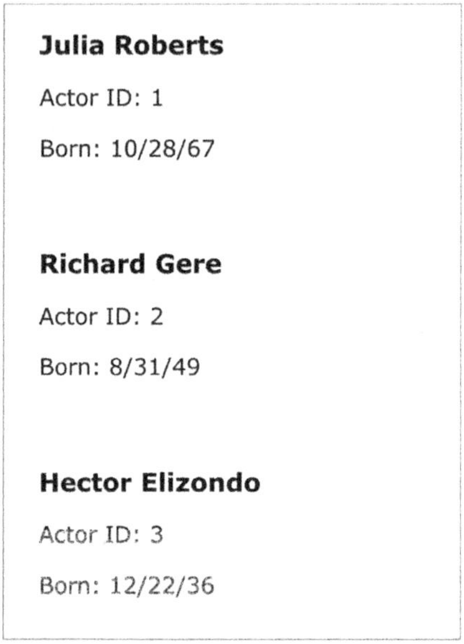

Observables in the real world

You won't always create Observables yourself. Many JavaScript libraries provide their functionality via Observables. A prominent representative of an Observable is `http.get()`, which is provided by the `HttpClient` object from the `@angular/common/http` library.

We use `http.get()` in chapter "5.2 An HTTPClient Service" (starting on page 101) to get data from a database.

Further informations about Observables you can find in the official Angular documentation:

► https://angular.io/guide/observables

2.11 Async / Await

`async/await` is a newer JavaScript syntax to declare an asynchronous function. It is based on Promises, but is much easier to read.

For a basic explanation of Promises, see section "2.9 Promises" on page 44.

`async/await` are the JavaScript keywords that greatly simplify asynchronous programming:

- `async` defines a function as asynchronous.
- `await` is used to wait for the fulfillment of the promise.
  `await` can only be used within an `async` function.

In other words: With this concept, you only use a couple of keywords, but your code will behave as though it is synchronous code. This is a fantastic change. You get the benefits of *async*, with the readability of *sync* (or close to).

An example:

Look at our Promise function from page 44:

```
function asyncWriteFanMailToJuliaRoberts() {
  var promise = new Promise((resolve, reject) => {
    setTimeout(() => {
      console.log("Mail sent!");
      if (error) {
         reject();
      } else {
        resolve();
      }
    }, 1000);
  });
  return promise;
}
```

What if we have more than one Promise before we continue? We can solve it in two ways - *one after the other* or *at the same time*.

One after the other

```
async function() {
  let mail = await asyncWriteFanMailToJuliaRoberts();
  let answer = await asyncReadAnswerFromJuliaRoberts();
  if (answer == 'Hi fan, I want to meet you!') {
    let pretty = await asyncMakeMePrettyForWoman();
    MeetJuliaRoberts();
  }
}
```

The function `asyncReadAnswerFromJuliaRoberts()` can't be executed until the previous function `asyncWriteFanMailToJuliaRoberts()` completed successfully. And only when `asyncReadAnswerFromJuliaRoberts()` could be completed successfully (and Julia wants to meet you), it goes on with the next function and so on.

So the execution time is the sum of the execution times of all promises.. This can lead to big performance problems. So if the Promises are not dependent on each other, they should be executed at the same time.

At the same time

```
async spam_fan_mails() {
  let mail_to_amy = asyncWriteFanMailToAmyYasbeck();
  let mail_to_julia = asyncWriteFanMailToJuliaRoberts();
  let mail_to_laura = asyncWriteFanMailToLauraSanGiacomo();

  let amy = await mail_to_amy;
  let julia = await mail_to_julia;
  let laura = await mail_to_laura;

  console.log('Spammed all fan mails!');
}
```

Here are three Promises running at the same time and `console.log('Spammed all fan mails!')` is waiting for all. The total execution time is the longest execution time of the promises.

Optimists who think that all their favorite actresses want to meet with them can now wait for all answers and finally decide with which woman they want to meet or arrange to meet them all ;-)

async/await in the real world

In our app we will successively develop the following code:

```
async initialize() {
  const loading = await this.loadingCtrl.create({
    message: 'Loading tour data...',
    spinner: 'crescent'
  });
  await loading.present();
  await this.getRegions()
    .then(data => this.regions = data);
  await this.getTourtypes()
    .then(data => this.tourtypes = _.sortBy(data, 'Name'));
  await this.getTours()
    .then(data => {
      this.tours = _.sortBy(data, 'Title');
      this.all_tours = _.sortBy(data, 'Title');
      this.filterTours({lower: 80, upper: 400});
      this.favService.initialize(this.all_tours);
    });
    await loading.dismiss();
}
```

Above you see a function labeled `async` with a whole series of `await` commands in it. This `initialize()` function is part of a service and gets all data from a database by some sub functions. The sub functions are called one after the other. A loading component is displayed during the data retrieval and only dismissed after all data has been loaded.

I hope, you (better) understand this flow logic now.

Summary

In this chapter you met the most important concepts and structures of Angular, which can be useful for you in the realization of your Ionic Apps:

Components, Lifecycle Hooks, Dependency Injection, Routing and Lazy Loading, Content Projection, *ngFor, Pipes, Promises, Observables, Async/Await.

It is particularly important to me that you got to know the concepts of asynchronous data processing. Because they're the backbone of modern apps.

3 The first app

This chapter assumes that you have made all the installations from chapter 1 (see "1.2 Installations", starting on page 15).

Now it's time to start our first app. And with the `start` command you actually create an Ionic app.

3.1 ionic start

Open the terminal and go to the path where you'll want to put your Ionic projects in future.

```
$ cd my/ionic/projects
```

Then write

```
$ ionic start first-app
```

When we execute the command (with Enter), Ionic asks:

```
Pick a framework! □

Please select the JavaScript framework to use for your new app. To
bypass this prompt next time,
supply a value for the --type option.

? Framework: (Use arrow keys)
á Angular | https://angular.io
  React   | https://reactjs.org
```

We accept the preselected Angular Framework with Enter. Ionic now asks:

```
Let's pick the perfect starter template! □

Starter templates are ready-to-go Ionic apps that come packed with
everything you need to build
your app. To bypass this prompt next time, supply template, the sec-
ond argument to ionic start.

? Starter template: (Use arrow keys)
```

```
á tabs         | A starting project with a simple tabbed interface
  sidemenu     | A starting project with a side menu with navigation
in the content area
  blank        | A blank starter project
  my-first-app | An example application that builds a camera with
gallery
  conference   | A kitchen-sink application that shows off all Ionic
has to offer
```

Again we accept the preselection (the tabs template) and press Enter. The creation process continues:

```
Preparing directory ./first-app - done!
4 Downloading and extracting tabs starter - done!

Installing dependencies may take several minutes.

  ──────────────────────────────────────────────────────────────

        Ionic Appflow, the mobile DevOps solution by Ionic

           Continuously build, deploy, and ship apps 
        Focus on building apps while we automate the rest 

                   https://ion.link/appflow  

  ──────────────────────────────────────────────────────────────


> npm i
npm WARN deprecated core-js@2.6.11: core-js@<3 is no longer main-
tained and not recommended for usage due to the number of issues.
Please, upgrade your dependencies to the actual version of core-js@3.
npm WARN deprecated request@2.88.2: request has been deprecated, see
https://github.com/request/request/issues/3142


> fsevents@1.2.11 install /Volumes/Data/Persönlich/Ionic5/code/first-
app/node_modules/@angular/compiler-cli/node_modules/fsevents
> node-gyp rebuild

  SOLINK_MODULE(target) Release/.node
  CXX(target) Release/obj.target/fse/fsevents.o
  SOLINK_MODULE(target) Release/fse.node
```

```
> fsevents@1.2.11 install /Volumes/Data/Persönlich/Ionic5/code/first-
app/node_modules/karma/node_modules/fsevents
> node-gyp rebuild

  SOLINK_MODULE(target) Release/.node
  CXX(target) Release/obj.target/fse/fsevents.o
  SOLINK_MODULE(target) Release/fse.node

> fsevents@1.2.11 install /Volumes/Data/Persönlich/Ionic5/code/first-
app/node_modules/watchpack/node_modules/fsevents
> node-gyp rebuild

  SOLINK_MODULE(target) Release/.node
  CXX(target) Release/obj.target/fse/fsevents.o
  SOLINK_MODULE(target) Release/fse.node

> fsevents@1.2.11 install /Volumes/Data/Persönlich/Ionic5/code/first-
app/node_modules/webpack-dev-server/node_modules/fsevents
> node-gyp rebuild

  SOLINK_MODULE(target) Release/.node
  CXX(target) Release/obj.target/fse/fsevents.o
  SOLINK_MODULE(target) Release/fse.node

> core-js@3.6.4 postinstall
/Volumes/Data/Persönlich/Ionic5/code/first-app/node_modules/@angular-
devkit/build-angular/node_modules/core-js
> node -e "try{require('./postinstall')}catch(e){}"

Thank you for using core-js ( https://github.com/zloirock/core-js )
for polyfilling JavaScript standard library!

The project needs your help! Please consider supporting of core-js on
Open Collective or Patreon:
> https://opencollective.com/core-js
> https://www.patreon.com/zloirock

Also, the author of core-js ( https://github.com/zloirock ) is look-
ing for a good job -)


> core-js@2.6.11 postinstall
/Volumes/Data/Persönlich/Ionic5/code/first-app/node_modules/core-js
> node -e "try{require('./postinstall')}catch(e){}"
```

```
> @angular/cli@8.3.25 postinstall
/Volumes/Data/Persönlich/Ionic5/code/first-
app/node_modules/@angular/cli
> node ./bin/postinstall/script.js

npm notice created a lockfile as package-lock.json. You should commit
this file.
npm WARN ws@7.2.1 requires a peer of bufferutil@^4.0.1 but none is
installed. You must install peer dependencies yourself.
npm WARN ws@7.2.1 requires a peer of utf-8-validate@^5.0.2 but none
is installed. You must install peer dependencies yourself.
npm WARN karma-jasmine-html-reporter@1.5.2 requires a peer of jas-
mine-core@>=3.5 but none is installed. You must install peer
dependencies yourself.

added 1468 packages from 1074 contributors and audited 19143 packages
in 61.874s

25 packages are looking for funding
  run `npm fund` for details

found 0 vulnerabilities

> git init
Initialized empty Git repository in
/Volumes/Data/my/ionic/projects/first-app/.git/
> git add -A
> git commit -m "Initial commit" --no-gpg-sign
[master (root-commit) 4ee8ef2] Initial commit
 Committer: User1 <user1@ionic.andreas-dormann.de>
Your name and email address were configured automatically based
on your username and hostname. Please check that they are accurate.
You can suppress this message by setting them explicitly. Run the
following command and follow the instructions in your editor to edit
your configuration file:

    git config --global --edit

After doing this, you may fix the identity used for this commit with:

    git commit --amend --reset-author

 58 files changed, 14720 insertions(+)
 create mode 100644 .gitignore
 create mode 100644 angular.json
 create mode 100644 browserslist
 create mode 100644 e2e/protractor.conf.js
```

```
 create mode 100644 e2e/src/app.e2e-spec.ts
 create mode 100644 e2e/src/app.po.ts
 create mode 100644 e2e/tsconfig.json
 create mode 100644 ionic.config.json
 create mode 100644 karma.conf.js
 create mode 100644 package-lock.json
 create mode 100644 package.json
 create mode 100644 src/app/app-routing.module.ts
 create mode 100644 src/app/app.component.html
 create mode 100644 src/app/app.component.scss
 create mode 100644 src/app/app.component.spec.ts
 create mode 100644 src/app/app.component.ts
 create mode 100644 src/app/app.module.ts
 create mode 100644 src/app/explore-container/explore-container.com-
ponent.html
 create mode 100644 src/app/explore-container/explore-container.com-
ponent.scss
 create mode 100644 src/app/explore-container/explore-container.com-
ponent.spec.ts
 create mode 100644 src/app/explore-container/explore-container.com-
ponent.ts
 create mode 100644 src/app/explore-container/explore-container.mod-
ule.ts
 create mode 100644 src/app/tab1/tab1.module.ts
 create mode 100644 src/app/tab1/tab1.page.html
 create mode 100644 src/app/tab1/tab1.page.scss
 create mode 100644 src/app/tab1/tab1.page.spec.ts
 create mode 100644 src/app/tab1/tab1.page.ts
 create mode 100644 src/app/tab2/tab2.module.ts
 create mode 100644 src/app/tab2/tab2.page.html
 create mode 100644 src/app/tab2/tab2.page.scss
 create mode 100644 src/app/tab2/tab2.page.spec.ts
 create mode 100644 src/app/tab2/tab2.page.ts
 create mode 100644 src/app/tab3/tab3.module.ts
 create mode 100644 src/app/tab3/tab3.page.html
 create mode 100644 src/app/tab3/tab3.page.scss
 create mode 100644 src/app/tab3/tab3.page.spec.ts
 create mode 100644 src/app/tab3/tab3.page.ts
 create mode 100644 src/app/tabs/tabs-routing.module.ts
 create mode 100644 src/app/tabs/tabs.module.ts
 create mode 100644 src/app/tabs/tabs.page.html
 create mode 100644 src/app/tabs/tabs.page.scss
 create mode 100644 src/app/tabs/tabs.page.spec.ts
 create mode 100644 src/app/tabs/tabs.page.ts
 create mode 100644 src/assets/icon/favicon.png
 create mode 100644 src/assets/shapes.svg
 create mode 100644 src/environments/environment.prod.ts
```

```
 create mode 100644 src/environments/environment.ts
 create mode 100644 src/global.scss
 create mode 100644 src/index.html
 create mode 100644 src/main.ts
 create mode 100644 src/polyfills.ts
 create mode 100644 src/test.ts
 create mode 100644 src/theme/variables.scss
 create mode 100644 src/zone-flags.ts
 create mode 100644 tsconfig.app.json
 create mode 100644 tsconfig.json
 create mode 100644 tsconfig.spec.json
 create mode 100644 tslint.json

[INFO] Next Steps:

       - Go to your newly created project: cd ./first-app
       - Run ionic serve within the app directory to see your app
       - Build features and components: https://ion.link/scaffolding-
docs
       - Run your app on a hardware or virtual device:
https://ion.link/running-docs
```

Perhaps you get a few warnings, e.g. because of deprecated modules. Don't worry. We can ignore them at the moment.

The creation process of our first Ionic application has finished. And as you can see, Ionic has created a lot of files, which we will get to know bit by bit.

In Visual Studio Code (VSC), our app structure looks like this:

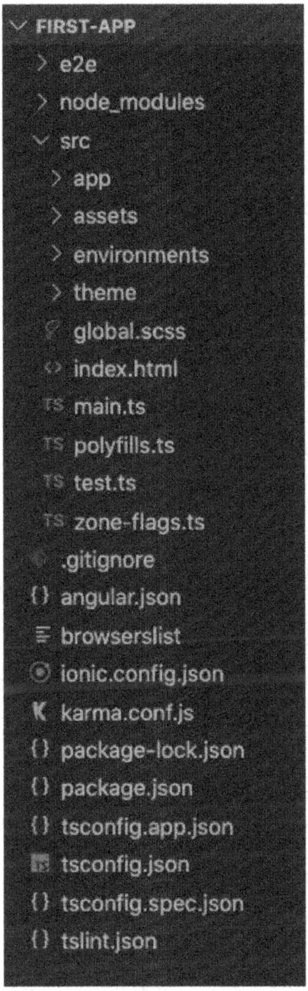

We'll discuss this structure in more detail later (see "3.4 Structure of an Ionic project " starting on page 69). First of all, this first glance should suffice and show that we have just created a complete project framework with all the components required for our first app with the Ionic start command.

That we've really got a working app now, we'll try out immediately.

3.2 ionic serve

To run the new app we change into the app folder with

```
$ cd first-app
```

and then type

```
$ ionic serve
```

Ionic now compiles the project...

```
> ng run app:serve --host=localhost --port=8100
[ng] ъ □wds□: Project is running at http://localhost:8100/webpack-de-
v-server/
[ng] ъ □wds□: webpack output is served from /
[ng] ъ □wds□: 404s will fallback to //index.html
[ng] chunk {common} common.js, common.js.map (common) 30.1 kB  [ren-
dered]
[ng] chunk {core-js-js} core-js-js.js, core-js-js.js.map (core-js-js)
78.7 kB  [rendered]
[ng] chunk {css-shim-978387b1-1e75855f-js} css-shim-978387b1-
1e75855f-js.js, css-shim-978387b1-1e75855f-js.js.map (css-shim-
978387b1-1e75855f-js) 21.9 kB  [rendered]
[ng] chunk {dom-76cc7c7d-0a082895-js} dom-76cc7c7d-0a082895-js.js,
dom-76cc7c7d-0a082895-js.js.map (dom-76cc7c7d-0a082895-js) 19.8 kB
[rendered]
[ng] chunk {dom-js} dom-js.js, dom-js.js.map (dom-js) 20.2 kB  [ren-
dered]
[ng] chunk {focus-visible-70713a0c-js} focus-visible-70713a0c-js.js,
focus-visible-70713a0c-js.js.map (focus-visible-70713a0c-js) 2.15 kB
[rendered]
[ng] chunk {hardware-back-button-5afe3cb0-js} hardware-back-button-
5afe3cb0-js.js, hardware-back-button-5afe3cb0-js.js.map (hard-
ware-back-button-5afe3cb0-js) 2.06 kB  [rendered]
[ng] chunk {input-shims-a4fc53ac-js} input-shims-a4fc53ac-js.js, in-
put-shims-a4fc53ac-js.js.map (input-shims-a4fc53ac-js) 13.5 kB
[rendered]
[ng] chunk {ios-transition-1850e475-js} ios-transition-1850e475-
js.js, ios-transition-1850e475-js.js.map (ios-transition-1850e475-js)
27.8 kB  [rendered]
[ng] chunk {main} main.js, main.js.map (main) 36.4 kB [initial] [ren-
dered]
[ng] chunk {md-transition-083fcf52-js} md-transition-083fcf52-js.js,
md-transition-083fcf52-js.js.map (md-transition-083fcf52-js) 3.91 kB
[rendered]
```

```
[ng] chunk {polyfills} polyfills.js, polyfills.js.map (polyfills) 296
kB [initial] [rendered]
[ng] chunk {runtime} runtime.js, runtime.js.map (runtime) 9.84 kB
[entry] [rendered]
[ng] chunk {shadow-css-4889ae62-23996f3f-js} shadow-css-4889ae62-
23996f3f-js.js, shadow-css-4889ae62-23996f3f-js.js.map (shadow-css-
4889ae62-23996f3f-js) 14.8 kB  [rendered]
[ng] chunk {status-tap-839e1402-js} status-tap-839e1402-js.js, sta-
tus-tap-839e1402-js.js.map (status-tap-839e1402-js) 1.79 kB
[rendered]
[ng] chunk {styles} styles.js, styles.js.map (styles) 115 kB [ini-
tial] [rendered]
[ng] chunk {swipe-back-c7acdfde-js} swipe-back-c7acdfde-js.js, swipe-
back-c7acdfde-js.js.map (swipe-back-c7acdfde-js) 2.68 kB  [rendered]
[ng] chunk {swiper-bundle-ccdaac54-js} swiper-bundle-ccdaac54-js.js,
swiper-bundle-ccdaac54-js.js.map (swiper-bundle-ccdaac54-js) 176 kB
[rendered]
[ng] chunk {tab1-tab1-module} tab1-tab1-module.js, tab1-tab1-mod-
ule.js.map (tab1-tab1-module) 6.03 kB  [rendered]
[ng] chunk {tab2-tab2-module} tab2-tab2-module.js, tab2-tab2-mod-
ule.js.map (tab2-tab2-module) 6.03 kB  [rendered]
[ng] chunk {tab3-tab3-module} tab3-tab3-module.js, tab3-tab3-mod-
ule.js.map (tab3-tab3-module) 6.03 kB  [rendered]
[ng] chunk {tabs-tabs-module} tabs-tabs-module.js, tabs-tabs-mod-
ule.js.map (tabs-tabs-module) 8.58 kB  [rendered]
[ng] chunk {tap-click-606f325e-js} tap-click-606f325e-js.js, tap-
click-606f325e-js.js.map (tap-click-606f325e-js) 6.38 kB  [rendered]
[ng] chunk {vendor} vendor.js, vendor.js.map (vendor) 4.77 MB [ini-
tial] [rendered]
[ng] Date: 2020-02-14T16:06:53.507Z - Hash: 1d933e84f2669667e01a -
Time: 7281ms
[INFO] ... and 77 additional chunks
[ng] ъ □wdm□: Compiled successfully.

[INFO] Development server running!

       Local: http://localhost:8100

       Use Ctrl+C to quit this process

[INFO] Browser window opened to http://localhost:8100!
```

... and creates a build of our first app. It's shown in the (default) browser by running a web server at `http://localhost:8100`. Our first Ionic app runs! That's great, isn't it?

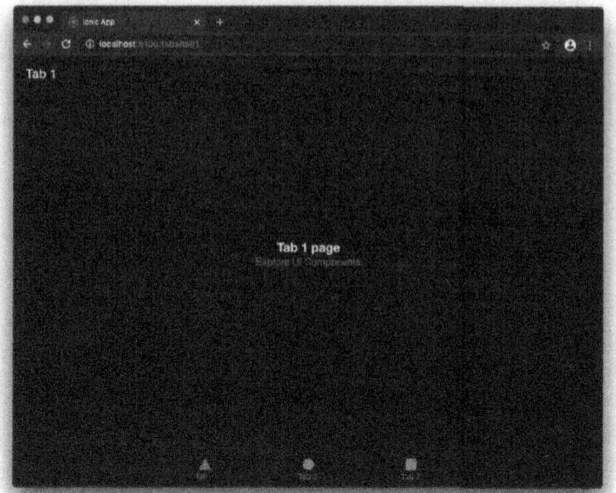

To let our app look like a real app (and not like a website – yeah, of course, it *is* a website) let's activate the developer tools in Google Chrome (CMD+ALT+I). Activate the Device Toolbar by clicking on the Toggle Device Toolbar button in the developer tools header (see picture below). Now you can simulate different mobile devices to see what our app looks like in different environments.

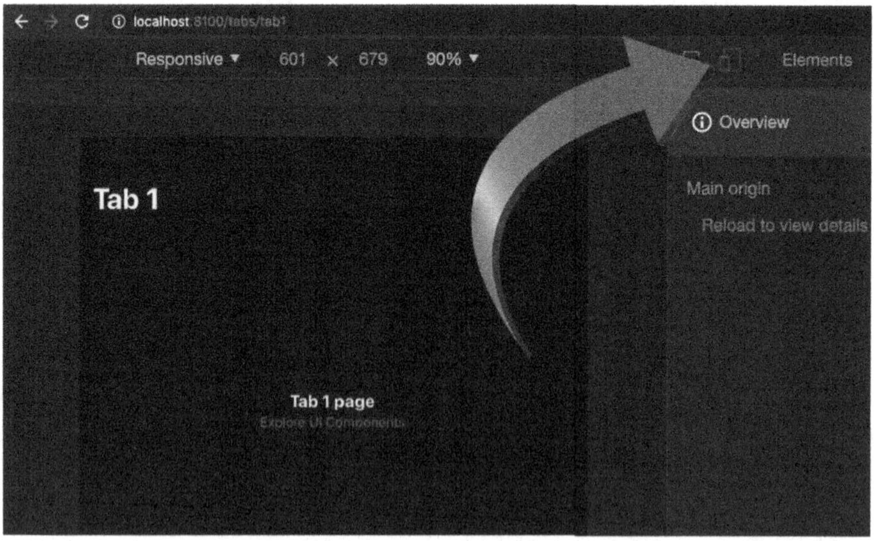

Our first app in an **iPhone 6/7/8 Plus** (left) and **Galaxy S5** (right) view:

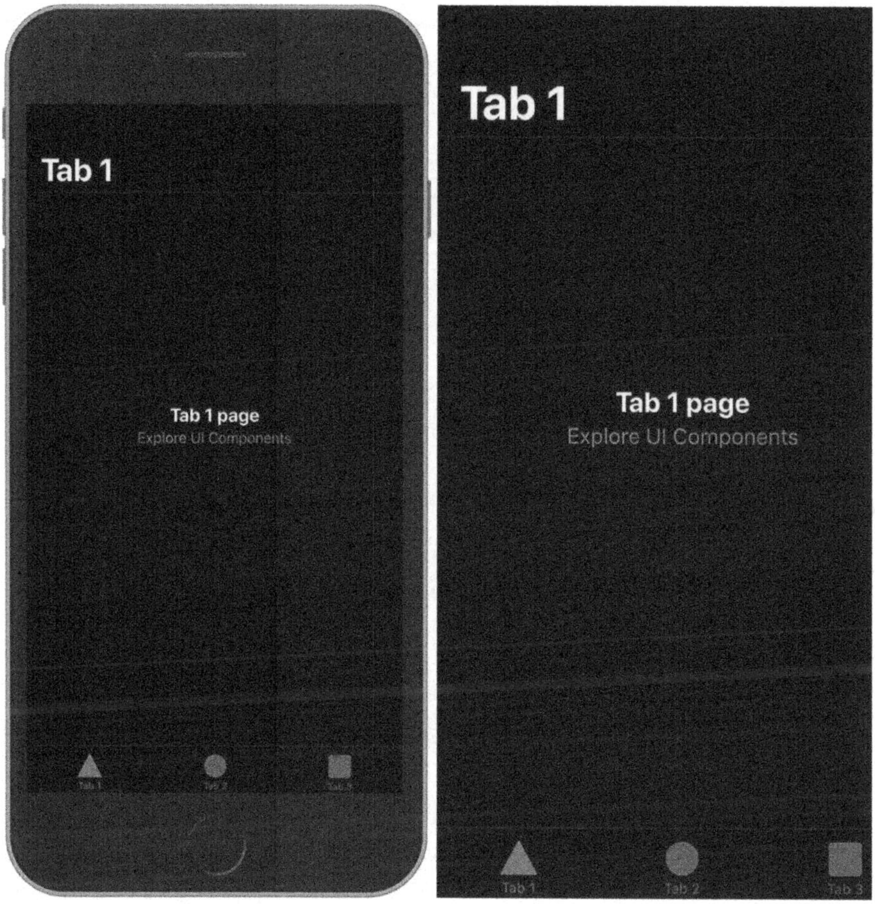

We can even display our app in the format of an *iPad*. This will later become of practical importance if we also make our app suitable for tablet use (see "8.10 UI-Design for Tablets (Split Pane Layout)", starting on page 382).

The Rotate icon in the preview pane of Chrome lets you switch the orientation between *Portrait* and *Landscape*.

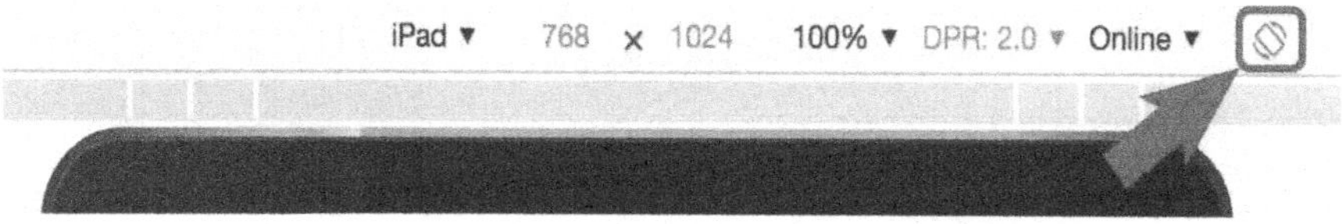

3.3 First coding and Live Reload

Open the `src/app/tab1/tab1.page.html` file in VSC and change the code as shown here in the bold formatted places:

```
<ion-header [translucent]="true">
  <ion-toolbar>
    <ion-title>
      Tab 1
    </ion-title>
  </ion-toolbar>
</ion-header>

<ion-content [fullscreen]="true">
  <ion-header collapse="condense">
    <ion-toolbar>
      <ion-title size="large">Tab 1</ion-title>
    </ion-toolbar>
  </ion-header>

  <app-explore-container name="My first app page, yeah!"></ap-
p-explore-container>
</ion-content>
```

To enjoy the next exciting moment, you should place browser and editor windows next to each other.

Now save the changed code in the editor (`CTRL+S` or `cmd+S`) and pay attention to the contents of the browser window!

Voila! The app has immediately updated itself and implemented your changes immediately. Great, this live reload, right?

In the mood for a really blatant change? Then open the file `src/theme/variables.scss` and change the line

```
@media (prefers-color-scheme: dark) {
```

to

```
@media (prefers-color-scheme: light) {
```

With this small modification you have just radically changed the appearance of the entire app and switched from dark mode to light mode!

Is that cool?

3.4 Structure of an Ionic project

Let's have a look at the structure of our project. We want to get a first overview.

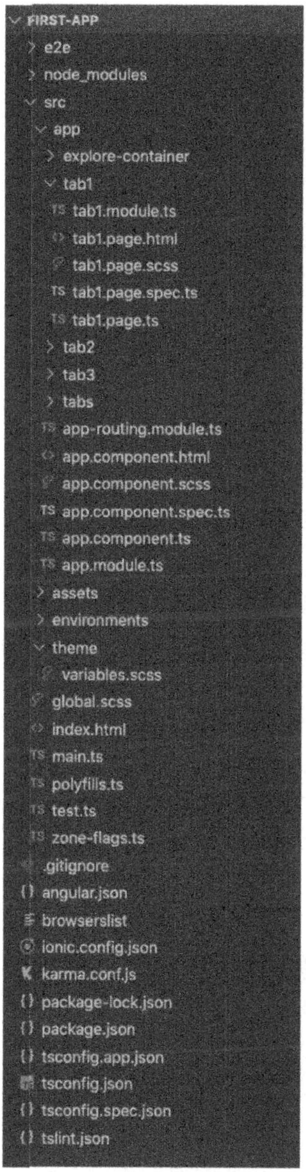

src

In the folder src (source) we will spend most of our development time, as it contains most of the code files that we will be editing. Here we will (soon) also create a whole series of own code files.

app

This is the startup folder of an app. Here or in `app.module.ts` and `app.component.ts` you can place initialization code.

explore-container

Contains a component that is used by this example tabs app.

tab1, tab2, tab3, tabs

These folders contain the individual components, views or pages of an app. Their names can of course be completely different than here. The example of `tab1` shows that one page consists of several files:

- `tab1.module.ts` is the module file of the page with all imports of further required modules.
- `tab1.page.html` contains the HTML code with the visible elements of a page.
- `tab1.page.scss` is a Sass file. In short, Sass is syntactically extended CSS and takes care of style statements for a page.
- `tab1.page.specs` is used for test purposes.
- `tab1.page.ts` is the code behind the UI and our main playground for programming.

app-routing.module.ts, app.component.html, app.component.specs.ts, app.component.ts, app.module.ts

These are the top level files of our app. Their meaning basically corresponds to the individual files on the page level (see `tab1` above).

Of particular importance is `app-routing.module.ts`. We'll deal with it in chapter 4 "Navigation" (starting on page 75).

assets

contains all media files that are delivered with an app.

environments

contains predefined or custom information for the build process.

theme

contains central theming and styling files. After initial creation of an app, this folder contains the file `variables.scss`. We will get to know these in more detail in chapter 8 "Theming, Styling, Customizing" (starting on page 331).

global.scss

imports all global Ionic style files.

index.html

is the start file of an app. Typically, metadata and references to external JavaScripts are put in the header of `index.html`. In the body tag you can find the `app-root` tag, the entry point for every Ionic app.

package.json

contains a lot of meta-data about a project. Mostly it will be used for managing dependencies of a project.

Others

All other folders and files that I have not listed here for the sake of clarity, we'll get to know in the further course of this book.

3.5 The side menu app for our book project

Now it's time to dive into our big Ionic adventure. We create our second app – the base for our entire book project. This new app will have a chic side menu, as many newer apps have one.

Go back to your Ionic projects main folder. Then write

```
$ ionic start bob-tours sidemenu --type=angular
```

After Ionic finished the creation process, we change into the project folder with

```
$ cd bob-tours
```

and start our new app in the browser with

```
$ ionic serve
```

And that's the first look at our new side menu app:

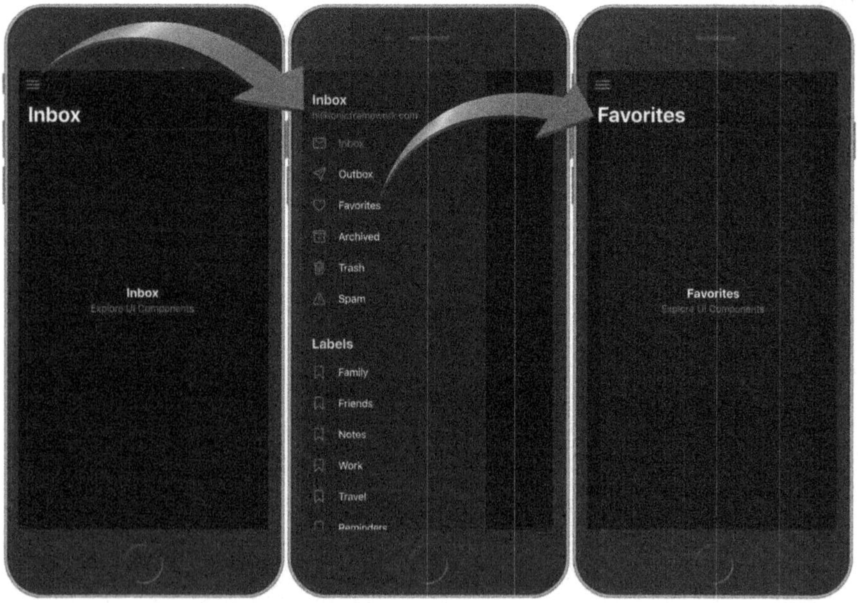

If you click on the menu button, the side menu is displayed and reveals to us that the app consists of a few pages, below it contains a few labels. This is now the basis of our "BoB Tours" app, whereby we will later replace the sample pages with our own.

For practice you can switch from the color scheme *dark* to *light* again.

Do you remember how to do that? If not, see page 67.

I also do this to save some ink for letterpress in the following ;-)

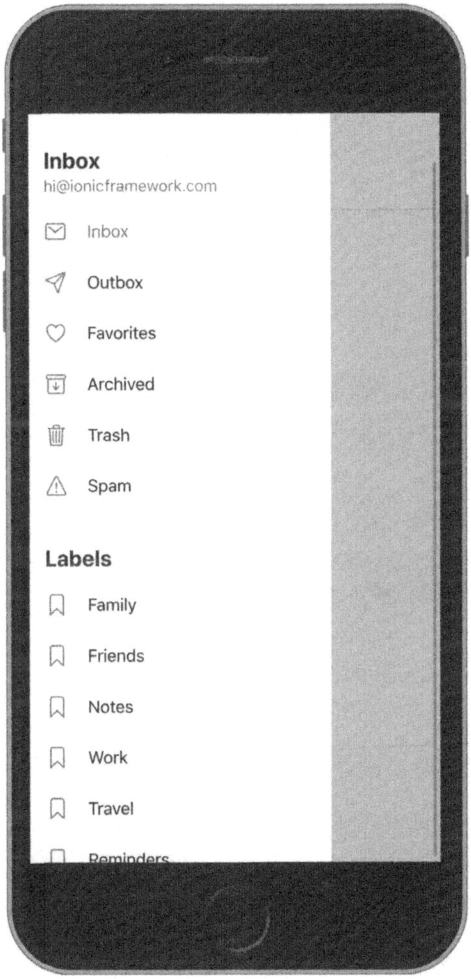

Summary

In this chapter you have programmed your first apps. Congratulations!

You now know `ionic start` and `ionic serve` and how to set up the Chrome DevTools to simulate an app-like look.

You also have an overview of the project structure of an Ionic app.

4 Navigation

4.1 Have a plan

If you're planning an app its a good idea to think about its page navigation early. You shouldn't code at the drop of a hat. So take a pencil and sketch your plan! For our app **BoB-Tours** I've drawn the following navigation draft (not with a pencil, but with Apple Keynote):

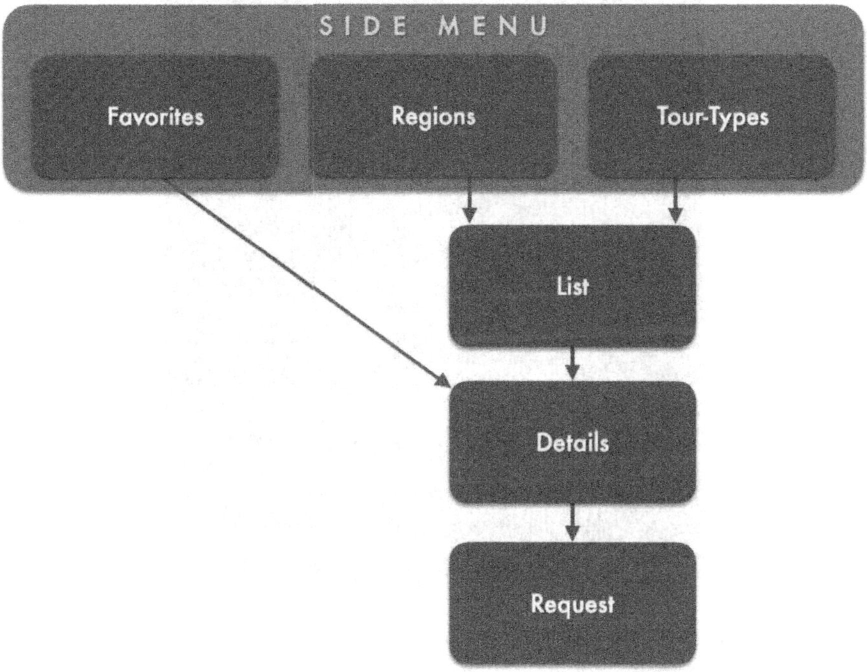

The pages in the horizontal (`Favorites`, `Regions`, `Tour-Types`) should form our menu pages. From there you get to the following pages `List`, `Details` and `Request`, where it goes from the `Favorites` directly to the `Details`.

Let's get down to business and first take a look at the folder structure of the current app. As we can see, there is a `folder` directory automatically generated by our sidemenu template containing a single app page.

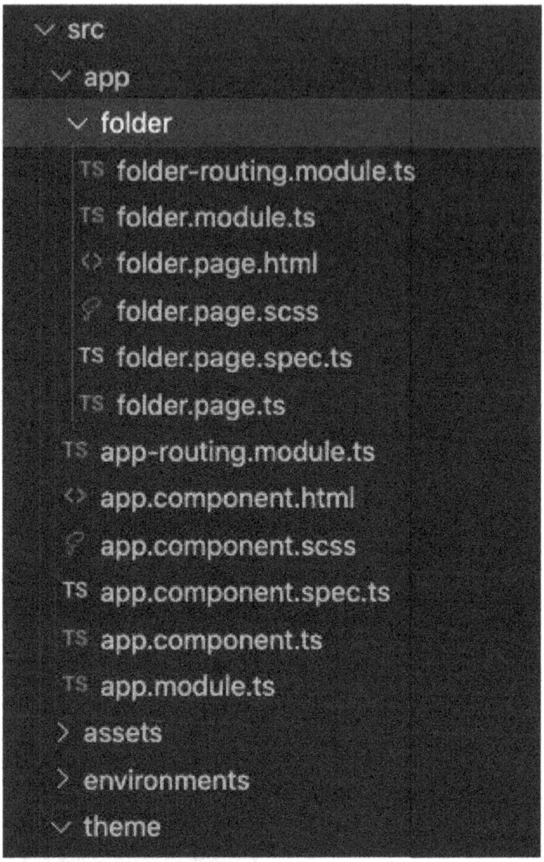

We could change it manually and already use it for our app. The missing pages would then have to be completed. Just stupid that one page always consists of several files (`x.routing.module.ts`, `x.module.ts`, `x.page.html`, `x.page.scss`, `x.page.specs.ts` and `x.page.ts`). That's where boring routine work comes to us to create all these pages, right?

No! Ionic thanks! In this task, the integrated code generator will help us.

4.2 Generate pages

Ionic's code generator

Ionic owns a code generator. We can call it with the command `generate` or simply short with `g`. Let's have a look at the documentation of this command. By typing

```
$ ionic generate -help
```

we get the following explanation:

```
This command uses the Angular CLI to generate features such as pages,
components, directives, services, etc.

      - For a full list of available types, use npx ng g --help
      - For a list of options for a types, use npx ng g <type> --help

    You can specify a path to nest your feature within any number of
subdirectories. For example, specify a name of
    "pages/New Page" to generate page files at src/app/pages/new-
page/.

    To test a generator before file modifications are made, use the
--dry-run option.

  Usage:
    $ ionic generate <type> <name>

  Inputs:

    type ........................... The type of feature (e.g. page,
component, directive, service)
    name ........................... The name/path of the feature
being generated

  Examples:

    $ ionic generate
    $ ionic generate page
    $ ionic generate page contact
    $ ionic generate component contact/form
    $ ionic generate component login-form --change-detection=OnPush
    $ ionic generate directive ripple --skip-import
    $ ionic generate service api/user
```

All right, `generate page` sounds very good! Let's try this:

```
$ ionic generate page pages/Favorites
```

The Ionic CLI generates a page named `Favorites`:

```
> ng generate page pages/Favorites
CREATE src/app/pages/favorites/favorites-routing.module.ts (359 bytes)
CREATE src/app/pages/favorites/favorites.module.ts (493 bytes)
CREATE src/app/pages/favorites/favorites.page.scss (0 bytes)
CREATE src/app/pages/favorites/favorites.page.html (128 bytes)
CREATE src/app/pages/favorites/favorites.page.spec.ts (668 bytes)
CREATE src/app/pages/favorites/favorites.page.ts (268 bytes)
UPDATE src/app/app-routing.module.ts (647 bytes)
[OK] Generated page!
```

In a new folder named `pages` we get a subfolder `favorites` with all required page files in it. We also get an updated `app-routing.module.ts`. In `app-routing.module.ts`, as described in "2.5 Routing and Lazy Loading" (starting on page 36), navigation between the pages of an app is organized. We will soon tune this module.

But now let's create the other pages with the help of `g` (short form for `generate`):

```
$ ionic g page pages/Regions
$ ionic g page pages/Tour-Types
$ ionic g page pages/List
$ ionic g page pages/Details
$ ionic g page pages/Request
```

Clean-up

The following cleanups have to be done:

1. Deleting the unnecessary `folder` directory
2. Deleting the unnecessary `folder` path
3. Changing the root path
4. Defining the menu pages
5. Modifying the menu UI

1. Deleting the unnecessary folder directory

We don't need the `folder` directory with its several (page) files that were generated by the `sidemenu` template directly in the `app` folder. So let's delete this directory and its content.

2. Deleting the unnecessary folder path

In `src/app/app-routing.module.ts` we also delete the following lines:

```
{
    path: 'folder/:id',
    loadChildren: () => import('./folder/folder.module')
      .then( m => m.FolderPageModule)
},
```

3. Changing the root path

Then we change the `redirectTo` value in the root path from `folder/Inbox` to `favorites`.

Now the complete code of your modified `src/app/app-routing.module.ts` should look like this:

```
import { NgModule } from '@angular/core';
import { PreloadAllModules, RouterModule, Routes }
         from '@angular/router';

const routes: Routes = [
  {
    path: '',
    redirectTo: 'favorites',
    pathMatch: 'full'
  },
  {
    path: 'favorites',
    loadChildren:
      () => import('./pages/favorites/favorites.module')
        .then(m => m.FavoritesPageModule)
  },
```

```
  {
    path: 'regions',
    loadChildren:
      () => import('./pages/regions/regions.module')
        .then(m => m.RegionsPageModule)
  },
  {
    path: 'tour-types',
    loadChildren:
      () => import('./pages/tour-types/tour-types.module')
        .then(m => m.TourTypesPageModule)
  },
  {
    path: 'list',
    loadChildren:
      () => import('./pages/list/list.module')
        .then(m => m.ListPageModule)
  },
  {
    path: 'details',
    loadChildren:
      () => import('./pages/details/details.module')
        .then(m => m.DetailsPageModule)
  },
  {
    path: 'request',
    loadChildren:
      () => import('./pages/request/request.module')
        .then(m => m.RequestPageModule)
  }
];

@NgModule({
  imports: [
    RouterModule.forRoot(routes,
    { preloadingStrategy: PreloadAllModules })
  ],
  exports: [RouterModule]
})
export class AppRoutingModule { }
```

4. Defining the menu pages

Now we replace the `appPages` array elements in `src/app/app.component.ts` with our own menu pages as follows (see the bold printed code):

```
import { Component } from '@angular/core';
import { Platform } from '@ionic/angular';
import { SplashScreen }
  from '@ionic-native/splash-screen/ngx';
import { StatusBar }
  from '@ionic-native/status-bar/ngx';
@Component({
  selector: 'app-root',
  templateUrl: 'app.component.html'
})
export class AppComponent {
  public appPages = [
    {
      title: 'Favorites',
      url: '/favorites',
      icon: 'star'
    },
    {
      title: 'Regions',
      url: '/regions',
      icon: 'images'
    },
    {
      title: 'Tour-Types',
      url: '/tour-types',
      icon: 'bus'
    }
  ];
  public labels = ['Family', 'Friends', 'Notes', 'Work',
                   'Travel', 'Reminders'];
  constructor(
    private platform: Platform,
    private splashScreen: SplashScreen,
    private statusBar: StatusBar
  ) {
    this.initializeApp();
  }
```

```
  initializeApp() {
    this.platform.ready().then(() => {
      this.statusBar.styleDefault();
      this.splashScreen.hide();
  });
  }
}
```

5. Modifying the menu UI

At last we delete the labels array in `src/app/app.component.ts` and a few UI elements in `src/app/app.component.html` (see the italic lines below):

```
<ion-app>
  <ion-split-pane contentId="main-content">
    <ion-menu contentId="main-content" type="overlay">
      <ion-content>
        <ion-list id="inbox-list">
          <ion-list-header>Inbox</ion-list-header>
          <ion-note>hi@ionicframework.com</ion-note>

          <ion-menu-toggle auto-hide="false"
            *ngFor="let p of appPages; let i = index">
            <ion-item (click)="selectedIndex = i"
                      routerDirection="root"
                      [routerLink]="[p.url]"
                      lines="none"
                      detail="false"
                      [class.selected]="selectedIndex == i">
              <ion-icon slot="start"
                        [ios]="p.icon + '-outline'"
                        [md]="p.icon + '-sharp'"></ion-icon>
              <ion-label>{{ p.title }}</ion-label>
            </ion-item>
          </ion-menu-toggle>
        </ion-list>

        <ion-list id="labels-list">
          <ion-list-header>Labels</ion-list-header>
```

```
        <ion-item *ngFor="let label of labels"
                  lines="none">
          <ion-icon slot="start"
                    ios="bookmark-outline"
                    md="bookmark-sharp"></ion-icon>
          <ion-label>{{ label }}</ion-label>
        </ion-item>
      </ion-list>
    </ion-content>
  </ion-menu>
  <ion-router-outlet id="main-content"></ion-router-outlet>
 </ion-split-pane>
</ion-app>
```

The side menu

Now we are almost ready with building our own side menu. Try

```
$ ionic serve
```

and our app shows the three side menu entries `Favorites`, `Regions` and `Tour-Types` and should look like this in the browser:

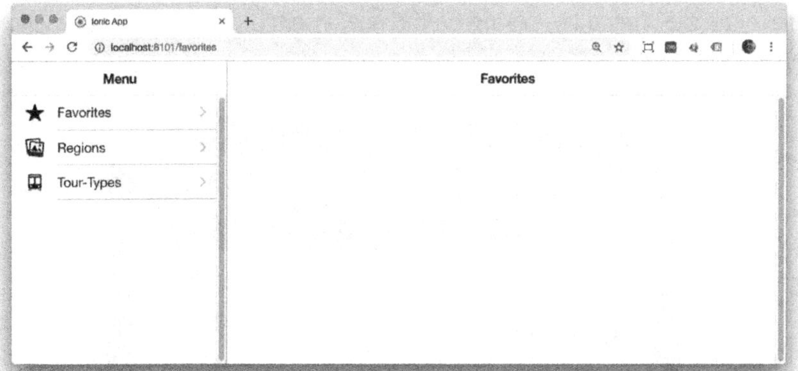

But wait – when you activate `Toggle device toolbar` in the `Developer Tools` to show our app in mobile style, you see that a button for achieving the side menu is missing.

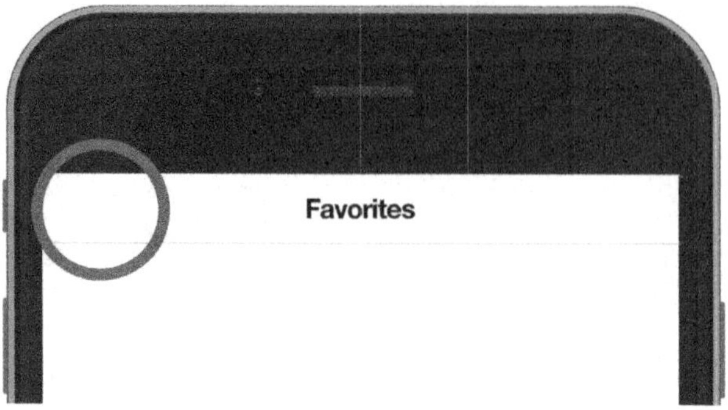

Let's fix this by adding the following (bold) lines to each of the headers of `favorites.page.html`, `regions.page.html` and `tour-types.page.html`:

```
<ion-header>
  <ion-toolbar>
    <ion-buttons slot="start">
      <ion-menu-button></ion-menu-button>
    </ion-buttons>
    <ion-title>Favorites</ion-title>
  </ion-toolbar>
</ion-header>
```

Now our app works as expected and you can switch to every main page and achieve the side menu by clicking on the now inserted „sandwich" icon (menu button) on every page.

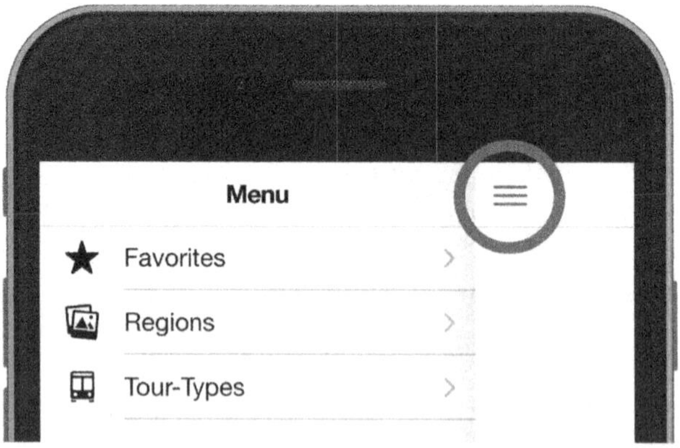

4.3 Routing

app-routing.module.ts

The concepts of Routing and Lazy Loading in Angular/Ionic are described in chapter 2 „Angular Essentials“ (see 2.5 Routing and Lazy Loading, starting on page 36).

As we have seen the root configuration for our router lives in the `src/app/app-routing.module.ts` file. For all our generated pages the CLI defined the corresponding routes automatically.

For example look at the route for the page `Details`:

```
{
    path: 'details',
    loadChildren:
      () => import('./pages/details/details.module')
        .then(m => m.DetailsPageModule)
}
```

It's a lazy loaded route that renders the `DetailsPageModule` where the outlet is defined in the HTML in the `app.component.html`:

```
<ion-router-outlet id="main-content"></ion-router-outlet>
```

When you navigate to the `/favorites` path in the browser, it will render the specific component in the HTML outlet.

A button or link is the most basic way to navigate to one of our defined routes. Let's say, we want to navigate from `Favorites` to `Details`. We can simply create a button in the `favorites.page.html` file like this one:

```
<ion-content class="ion-padding">
  <ion-button href="/details">Show details</ion-button>
</ion-content>
```

routerLink / routerDirection

A more advanced and my preferred way to switch to another page is using the `routerLink` attribute in combination with the `routerDirection` attribute:

```
<ion-content class="ion-padding">
  <ion-button routerLink="/details"
              routerDirection="forward">
    Show details
  </ion-button>
</ion-content>
```

In this way we get a smooth forward animation while switching between pages.

Adding back buttons

Of course, to come back from `Details` to `Favorites`, we should add a back button to the header of the `details.page.html file`:

```
<ion-header>
  <ion-toolbar>
      <ion-buttons slot="start">
        <ion-back-button></ion-back-button>
      </ion-buttons>
    <ion-title>Details</ion-title>
  </ion-toolbar>
</ion-header>
```

The Ionic back button navigates back in the app's history upon click. `<ion-back-button>` is smart enough to know *what to render* based on the mode and *when to show* based on the navigation stack. When there's no history, the attribute `defaultHref` can be used to define the url to navigate back to by default.

Let's complete our navigation stack by implementing a next route from `Details` to `Request`.

Again we add a button in the content area – now in `details.page.html`:

```
<ion-content class="ion-padding">
  <ion-button routerLink="/request"
              routerDirection="forward">
    Request a Tour
  </ion-button>
</ion-content>
```

And in the header of `request.page.html` we add another back button:

```
<ion-header>
  <ion-toolbar>
    <ion-buttons slot="start">
      <ion-back-button></ion-back-button>
    </ion-buttons>
    <ion-title>Request</ion-title>
  </ion-toolbar>
</ion-header>
```

Our app navigation so far:

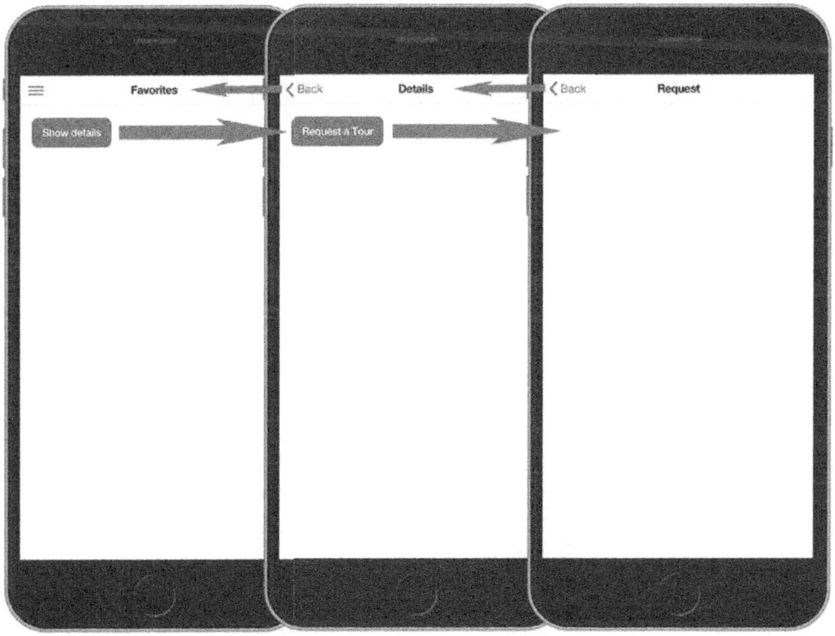

At least it would be perfect to be able to navigate directly back from `Request` to `Favorites`.

Let's do this by adding a button in the content area of `request.page.html`:

```
<ion-content class="ion-padding">
  <ion-button routerLink="/favorites"
              routerDirection="root">
    Back to Favorites
  </ion-button>
</ion-content>
```

So far, so nice! But what's an app without any data? And how will data be brought from one page to another? These questions will be answered in the next division of this chapter.

4.4 Extract Data from Routes with ActivatedRoute

Let's add some data to our app and see, how we can bring them from one page to another. For this purpose we:

1. Add a few tour objects
2. Create a selectable list of tours
3. Prepare the Details page to get a selected tour
4. Show a selected tour in the Details page title

1. Add a few tour objects

Let's create a little array of tour objects in `favorites.page.ts` just above the constructor of the component:

```
import { Component, OnInit } from '@angular/core';

@Component({
  selector: 'app-favorites',
  templateUrl: './favorites.page.html',
  styleUrls: ['./favorites.page.scss'],
})
export class FavoritesPage implements OnInit {

  tours = [
    { ID: 1, Title: 'City walk' },
    { ID: 2, Title: 'On the trails of Beethoven' },
    { ID: 3, Title: 'Villa Hammerschmidt' }
  ];

  constructor() { }

  ngOnInit() {
  }

}
```

2. Create a selectable list of tours

In `favorites.page.html` we remove the previously built button in the content area and add an `ion-list` instead to show our tours on the page:

```
<ion-content class="ion-padding">
  <ion-list>
    <ion-item *ngFor="let tour of tours"
              [routerLink]="['/details', tour]"
              routerDirection="forward">
      {{ tour.Title }}
    </ion-item>
  </ion-list>
</ion-content>
```

As explained in chapter 2 "Angular Essentials" (see "2.7 *ngFor", starting on page 40), `*ngFor` causes an array (`tours`) to loop through and an UI element (`ion-item`) to be rendered as many times as there are items (a `tour` element) in the array.

The `Title` property of every tour is then be displayed as text by Content Projection (see "2.6 Content Projection", on page 39).

Look at the line

`[routerLink]="['/details', tour]"`

more exactly!

Two parameters are passed to `routerLink`:

1. the path to the next page (`'/details'`) and

2. the `tour` object selected by the user

We shortly will receive this object on the details page.

3. Prepare the Details page to get a selected tour

In `details.page.ts` we add the following bold formatted code:

```
import { Component, OnInit } from '@angular/core';
import { ActivatedRoute } from '@angular/router';

@Component({
  selector: 'app-details',
  templateUrl: './details.page.html',
  styleUrls: ['./details.page.scss'],
})
export class DetailsPage implements OnInit {

  tour = null;

  constructor(private activatedRoute: ActivatedRoute) { }

  ngOnInit() {
    console.log(this.activatedRoute);
    this.tour = this.activatedRoute.snapshot.params;
  }

}
```

To get data from the calling (previous) page, we can use the `ActivatedRoute` from `@angular/router`. To use it we have to import it with

```
import { ActivatedRoute } from '@angular/router';
```

and to inject it into the constructor:

```
constructor(private activatedRoute: ActivatedRoute)
```

We declare a new tour variable and instantiate it with a `null` value:

```
tour = null;
```

This variable will hold the incoming selected tour object.

The exciting data transfer finally takes place in `ngOnInit`:

```
this.tour = this.activatedRoute.snapshot.params;
```

ActivatedRoute has a property `snapshot`, which in turn provides the tour object through its `params` property. This is exactly the tour object, that of the previous page over

```
[routerLink]="['/details', tour]"
```

was passed on.

The concepts of Routing and Lazy Loading in Angular/Ionic are described in chapter 2 „Angular Essentials“ (see 2.5 Routing and Lazy Loading, starting on page 36).

I invite you to check out the many other parameters of `ActivatedRoute` in the DevTools. For this I have inserted the line

```
console.log(this.activatedRoute);
```

4. Show a selected tour in the Details page title

Now we again can use Content Projection (see chapter 2 “Angular Essentials”, 2.6 Content Projection, on page 39) to show the `Title` property of a chosen tour in the header of `details.page.html`:

```
<ion-header>
  <ion-toolbar>
    <ion-buttons slot="start">
      <ion-back-button></ion-back-button>
    </ion-buttons>
    <ion-title>{{ tour.Title }}</ion-title>
  </ion-toolbar>
</ion-header>

<ion-content class="ion-padding">
  ...
</ion-content>
```

Here's our app in action:

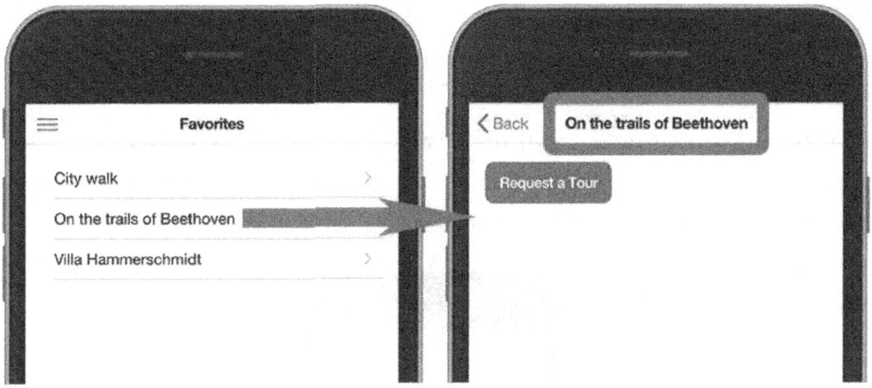

Attention! If we use `routerLink` with a data parameter, **we are relying on sending the data through the URL**. So, if we want to pass some object from one page to another, this isn't a suitable method to do that. You could send all of the data for your object through the URL by turning your object into a JSON string, but it's not an entirely practical solution in a lot of cases.

Usually, the best way to tackle this situation is to simply pass an `id` through the URL, and then use that `id` to grab the rest of the data through a provider/service. We will explore this in the next chapter (chapter 5 "Services & Storage", page 97).

But yet, as a first demonstration of using `routerLink`, we are satisfied with this simple solution.

Further informations you'll find in the official Ionic documentation:

- https://ionicframework.com/docs/api/router-outlet
- https://ionicframework.com/docs/api/back-button

4.5 Pro Tip - Install the Augury Chrome Plugin

Install the `Augury` plugin for Google Chrome to inspect and debug routing issues. It allows you to visualize the router tree, which is especially as your Ionic app starts adding multiple lazy-loaded pages and named outlets.

It's easy to use: After the installation activate the Google Chrome DevTools, switch to the new `Augury` entry and click on `RouteTree`. Now `Augury` shows you a visualization of the router tree and the nature of every route in our app:

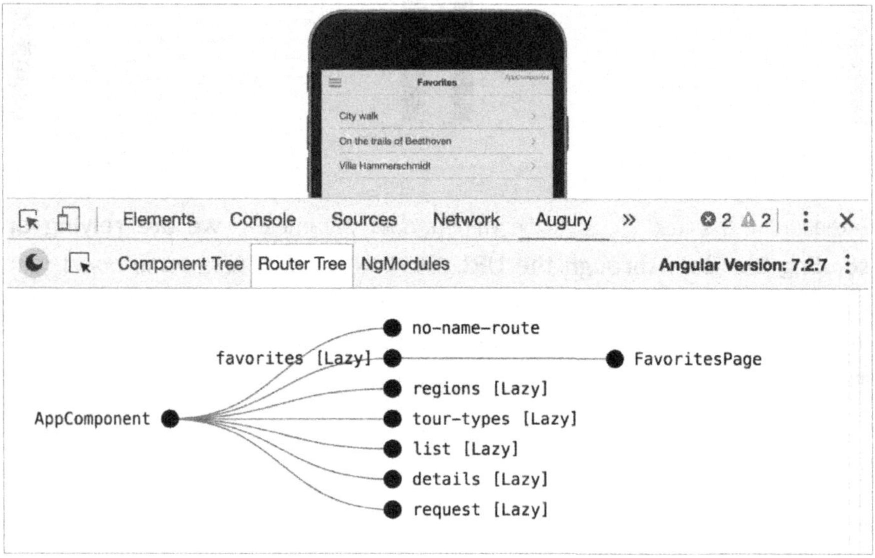

Summary

In this chapter you've used Ionic's code generator to create some pages.

You got to know the `app-routing.module.ts` file, which defines the routes to the pages of an app.

You now know how to use `ActivatedRoute` to transfer data from one app page to the next.

You've got a pro tip to use the Augury Chrome Plugin to visualize the router tree of an app.

5 Services & Storage

Nearly every app uses services to retrieve, update, save or delete data. Of course, our app won't do an exception here.

5.1 Database Backend with Google Firebase

Before we get started with our first data service, we prepare our backend. I use `Firebase`, a simply to use and free online database management system at Google. A complete Introduction to `Firebase` would run out of the scope of this book and there's plenty of tutorials and literature about this topic. Let's concentrate on functions that we need for our "BoB Tours" app. These functions will basically suffice to realize many other app ideas.

The setting up of your own Firebase takes place in four steps:

1. Create a Firebase account
2. Add a project in the Firebase console
3. Fill the database with data
4. Set rules for database access

1. Create a Firebase account

First you set up a free Firebase account via ► https://firebase.google.com/

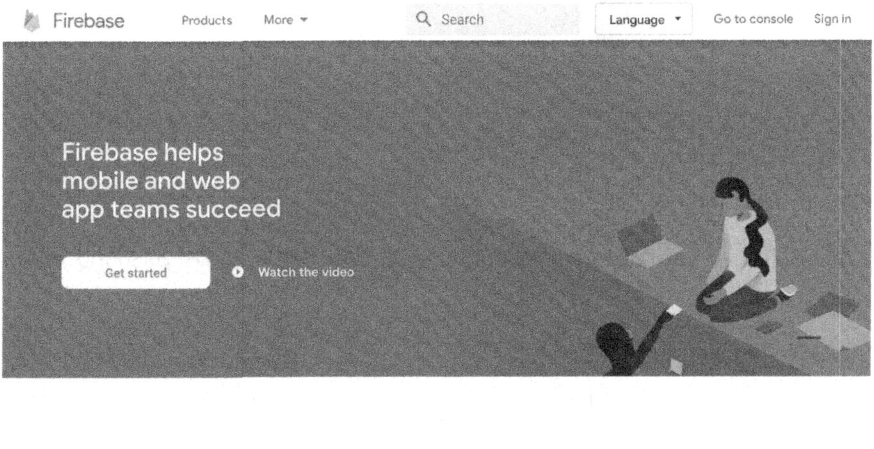

2. Add a project in the Firebase console

Once that's done, go to the Firebase console

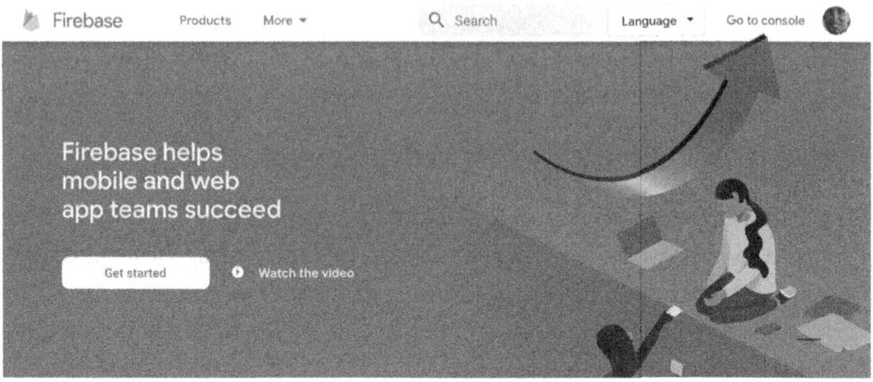

and add a new project.

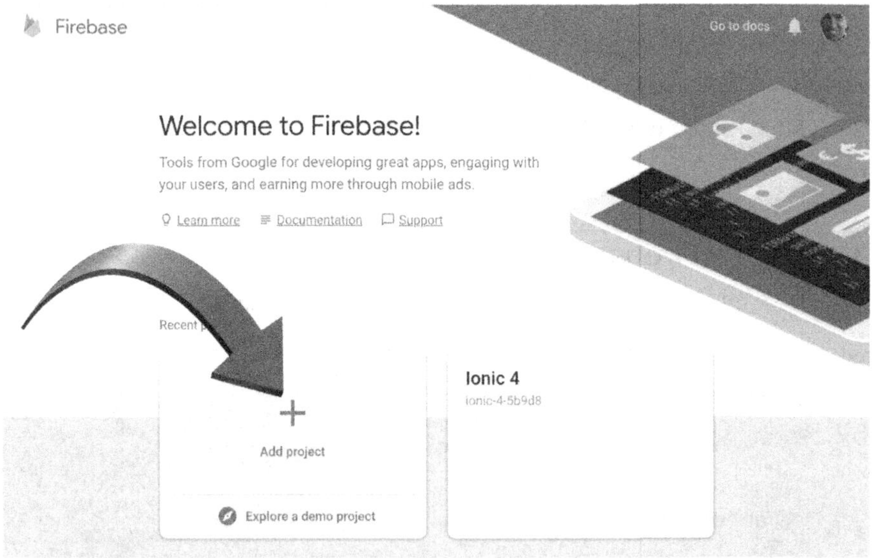

You do that via the **Add project** button. Give it the name "BoB-Tours-App".

3. Fill the database with data

In the sidebar (left) we click on **Database**. The entry `null` tells us that the database is empty.

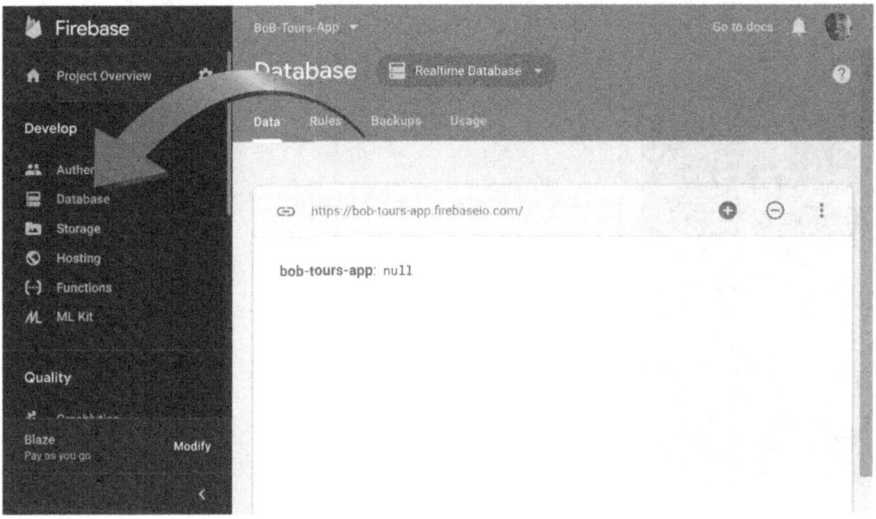

Click on the menu button (far right) and select the entry **Import JSON**.

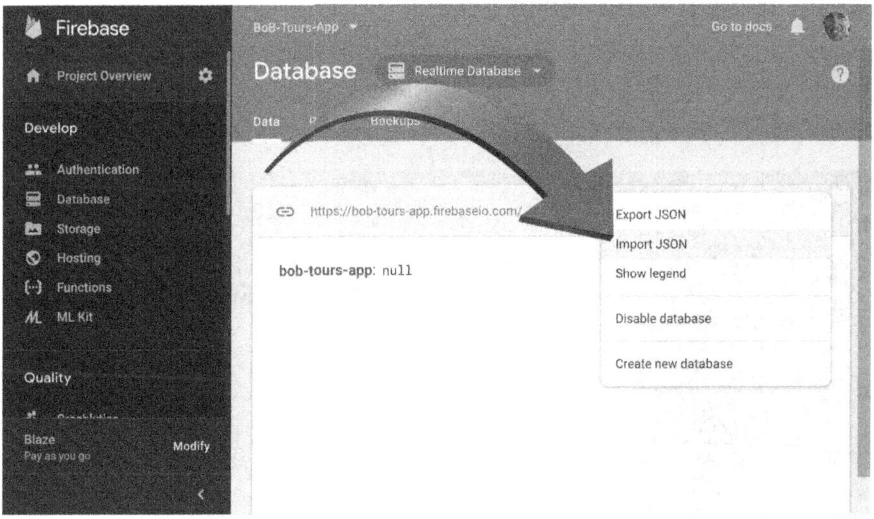

In the dialog box that opens, select the file `bob-tours-data.json` (from my book's website) and click on **Import**. We have now created an online database with the collections `Regions`, `Tours` and `Tourtypes`.

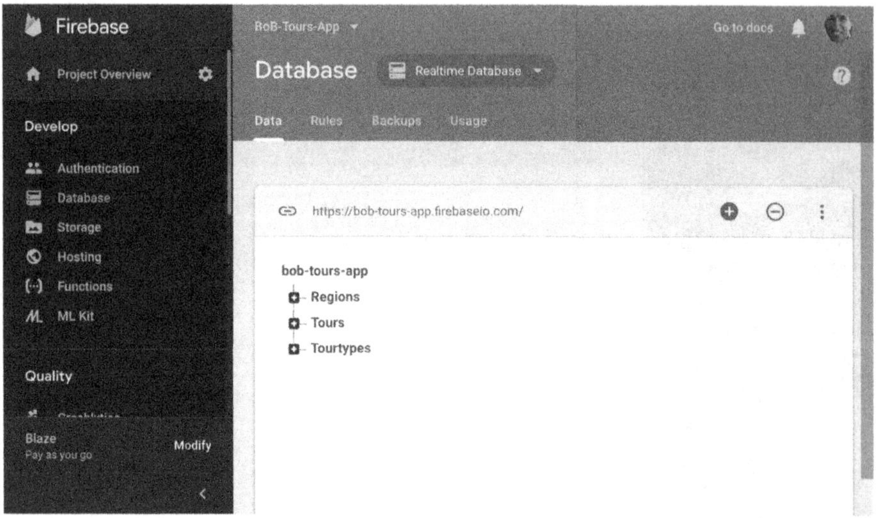

One last step is missing...

4. Set rules for database access

Finally, we need to adjust the permissions of the database to allow our app anonymous read access. We switch to the view **Rules**, change the rules for the key `read` to the value `true` and confirm the changes by clicking on **Publish**.

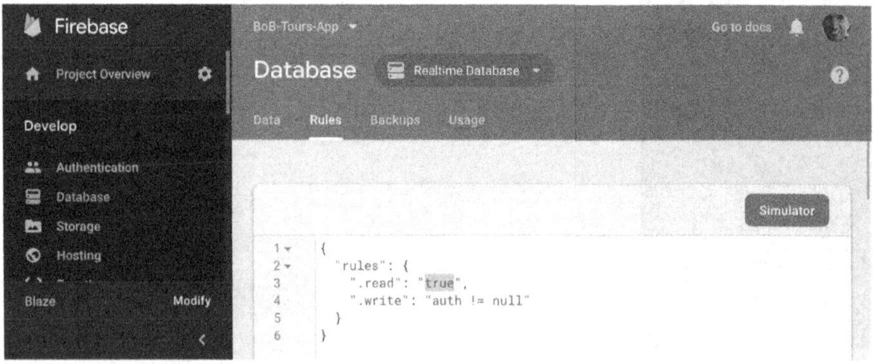

Our database backend is now ready to start, waiting to be used by our app.

5.2 An HTTPClient Service

To communicate with online databases, we create a `service` (Ionic 3 developers know it as `provider`). This service will undertake the task to provide our app over the HTTP protocol with data from a database backend.

Why write a service?

Our following task starts so simple that it is tempting to write the code inside the app page itself and skip creating a service.

However, our data access won't stay this simple. We'll later post-process the data, add error handling, and maybe some retry logic to cope with intermittent connectivity. Our page component quickly becomes cluttered and harder to understand, harder to test, and the data access logic can't be re-used or standardized.

That's why it is a best practice to separate presentation of data from data access by encapsulating data access in a separate service and delegating to that service in the component, even in simple cases like this one.

Create a service

In Terminal we write

```
$ ionic g service services/bob-tours
```

and let the Ionic CLI (more precisely Angular) do the work for us.

```
> ng generate service services/bob-tours
CREATE src/app/services/bob-tours.service.spec.ts (344 bytes)
CREATE src/app/services/bob-tours.service.ts (137 bytes)
[OK] Generated service!
```

After finishing the creation process we have a service or let's say, the shell of a service.

You find it in the `services` folder that we told the CLI to create and to place the service inside it. The folder contains two files:

- `bob-tours.service.spec.ts`
- `bob-tours.service.ts`

As noted earlier, a `spec` file is used for testing. You'll find out more about this in Chapter 11 "Debugging & Testing" (starting from page 447).

Now we are only interested in the file `bob-tours.service.ts`.

Let's have a look at it:

```
import { Injectable } from '@angular/core';

@Injectable({
  providedIn: 'root'
})
export class BobToursService {

  constructor() { }
}
```

Programming the data access

We see, our service is a simple class – but a class with the `@Injectable` decorator that allows us to inject this class and its functionality into every place of our app where this functionality is needed. The concept of `injection` is briefly described in chapter 2 "Angular Essentials" (see "2.4 Dependency Injection", on page 34).

We now add a little functionality (bold formatted code):

```
import { Injectable } from '@angular/core';
import { HttpClient } from '@angular/common/http';

@Injectable({
  providedIn: 'root'
})
export class BobToursService {

  baseUrl = 'https://bob-tours-app.firebaseio.com/';

  constructor(private http: HttpClient) { }

  getRegions() {
    let requestUrl = `${this.baseUrl}/Regions.json`;
    return this.http.get(requestUrl).toPromise();
  }
}
```

Explanations to the code:

We use the `HttpClient` from `@angular/common/http`. Therefore we need to import it with

```
import { HttpClient } from '@angular/common/http';
```

and inject it with

```
constructor(private http: HttpClient) { }
```

into the constructor of our service class.

Above the constructor, we declared a base url containing the root path to our database call:

```
baseUrl = 'https://bob-tours-app.firebaseio.com/';
```

We then created a function named `getRegions()`, where we defined our request url:

```
let requestUrl = `${this.baseUrl}/Regions.json`;
```

Pay attention to the special syntax with the character ` at the beginning and at the end of the whole string. In conjunction with the `$` sign and the curly braces, we can concatenate the variable `this.baseUrl` with the following string part to form a complete expression.

The function finally returns with

```
this.http.get(requestUrl).toPromise()
```

a Promise. Actually, `this.http.get()` is an Observable, but what we do with the attached `toPromise()` method we just convert it to a `Promise`.

I briefly described Promises and Observables in chapter 2 "Angular Essentials" (see "2.9 Promises" on page 44 and "2.10 Observables" on page 46).

Bring the service to the Regions page

To use our service in `regions.page.ts` we code the following:

```
import { Component, OnInit } from '@angular/core';
import { BobToursService }
         from 'src/app/services/bob-tours.service';
```

```
@Component({
  selector: 'app-regions',
  templateUrl: './regions.page.html',
  styleUrls: ['./regions.page.scss'],
})
export class RegionsPage implements OnInit {

  regions: any;

  constructor(private btService:BobToursService) { }

  ngOnInit() {
    this.btService.getRegions()
    .then(data => this.regions = data);
  }

}
```

The code in a nutshell:

We import our service with

```
import { BobToursService }
         from 'src/app/services/bob-tours.service';
```

and inject it into the constructor of the page:

```
constructor(private btService:BobToursService) { }
```

Above the constructor, we declare a `regions` object variable:

In the `ngOnInit()` method we call our new service with:

```
this.btService.getRegions()
    .then(data => this.regions = data);
```

Since our service call is a Promise, we can handle an asynchronously delivering of the data with a `then()` construct. The lambda expression in parentheses

```
data => this.regions = data
```

means "If data arrives, pass that data to `this.regions`" (our local page variable).

Bring the data to the UI

In `regions.page.html` we add a list in the content area of the page:

```
<ion-header>
  <ion-toolbar>
    <ion-buttons slot="start">
      <ion-menu-button></ion-menu-button>
    </ion-buttons>
    <ion-title>Regions</ion-title>
  </ion-toolbar>
</ion-header>

<ion-content class="ion-padding">
  <ion-list>
    <ion-item *ngFor="let region of regions">
      {{region.Name}}
    </ion-item>
  </ion-list>
</ion-content>
```

A typical `*ngFor` closure ensures that a separate list entry is created for each region read from the database. Using Content Projection, we output the name of each region.

No provider for HttpClient!

When we start our app with

```
$ ionic serve
```

we run into an error (look at the Chrome's `Developer Tools Console`):

```
core.js:6014 ERROR Error: Uncaught (in promise): NullInjectorError:
StaticInjectorError(AppModule)[HttpClient]:
  StaticInjectorError(Platform: core)[HttpClient]:
    NullInjectorError: No provider for HttpClient!
NullInjectorError: StaticInjectorError(AppModule)[HttpClient]:
  StaticInjectorError(Platform: core)[HttpClient]:
    NullInjectorError: No provider for HttpClient!
    at NullInjector.get (core.js:855)
    at resolveToken (core.js:17514)
    at tryResolveToken (core.js:17440)
    at StaticInjector.get (core.js:17266)
```

```
    at resolveToken (core.js:17514)
    at tryResolveToken (core.js:17440)
    at StaticInjector.get (core.js:17266)
    at resolveNgModuleDep (core.js:30393)
    at NgModuleRef_.get (core.js:31578)
    at injectInjectorOnly (core.js:734)
    at resolvePromise (zone-evergreen.js:797)
    at resolvePromise (zone-evergreen.js:754)
    at zone-evergreen.js:858
    at ZoneDelegate.invokeTask (zone-evergreen.js:391)
    at Object.onInvokeTask (core.js:39680)
    at ZoneDelegate.invokeTask (zone-evergreen.js:390)
    at Zone.runTask (zone-evergreen.js:168)
    at drainMicroTaskQueue (zone-evergreen.js:559)
    at ZoneTask.invokeTask [as invoke] (zone-evergreen.js:469)
    at invokeTask (zone-evergreen.js:1603)
```

Uups! What's wrong? Did we miss anything? Yes – and the key indication to that is found in those few words:

```
No provider for HttpClient!
```

What does that mean?

We use Angular's `HttpClient` module on a page, but our app doesn't know that. It's not enough to import and inject it in a page component. What we are supposed to do is to import its corresponding `HttpClientModule` on *app* level! I intentionally did let you make this mistake – believe me, I myself did make it often enough in my early Ionic days ;-) Hopefully from now on you remember what to do when this error occurs - I'll show it now to you:

Add the HttpClientModule to the app

Open `app.module.ts` and add the following bold formatted code:

```
import { NgModule } from '@angular/core';
import { BrowserModule } from '@angular/platform-browser';
import { RouteReuseStrategy } from '@angular/router';
import { IonicModule, IonicRouteStrategy }
         from '@ionic/angular';
import { SplashScreen }
         from '@ionic-native/splash-screen/ngx';
import { StatusBar } from '@ionic-native/status-bar/ngx';
```

```
import { AppComponent } from './app.component';
import { AppRoutingModule } from './app-routing.module';
import { HttpClientModule } from '@angular/common/http';

@NgModule({
  declarations: [AppComponent],
  entryComponents: [],
  imports: [
    BrowserModule,
    IonicModule.forRoot(),
    AppRoutingModule,
    HttpClientModule
  ],
  providers: [
    StatusBar,
    SplashScreen,
    { provide: RouteReuseStrategy, useClass: IonicRouteStrate-
gy }
  ],
  bootstrap: [AppComponent]
})
export class AppModule {}
```

By adding the `HttpClientModule` to our imports, we are making the functionality that is necessary to make HTTP requests available throughout the application and the precondition for using `HttpClient` as we did in `regions.page.ts`.

Finally: Successful data call

Now our code is complete and we again can start a next try with

```
$ ionic serve
```

and will be rewarded by a `Regions` page filled with data coming from a database!

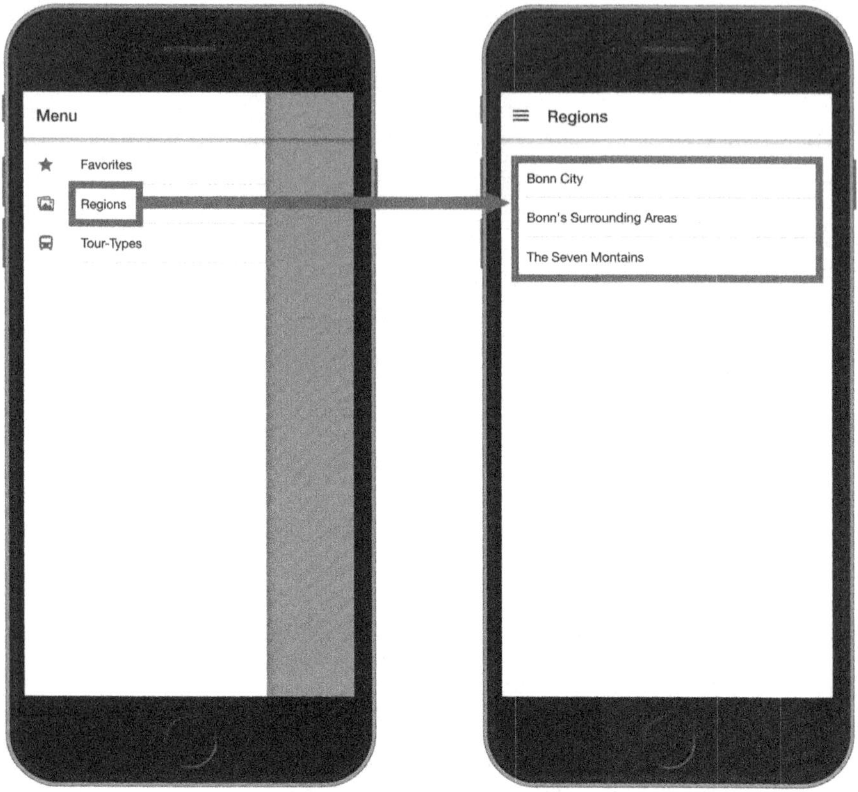

Perfect, isn't it? Not quite. We have one little flaw and that has to do with the event, *when* the database is asked for data. Let's check this.

In the `regions.page.ts` file we wrote:

```
ngOnInit() {
    this.btService.getRegions()
    .then(data => this.regions = data);
}
```

What this code exactly does is: *every* time, the `Regions` page is initialized in the `ngOnInit` hook (see "2.3 Lifecycle Hooks", starting on page 30), the database is asked for the data. We easily can verify this with a look into the `Developer Tools > Network`.

Switch between the side menu and the other pages in our app several times and you'll get a result like this:

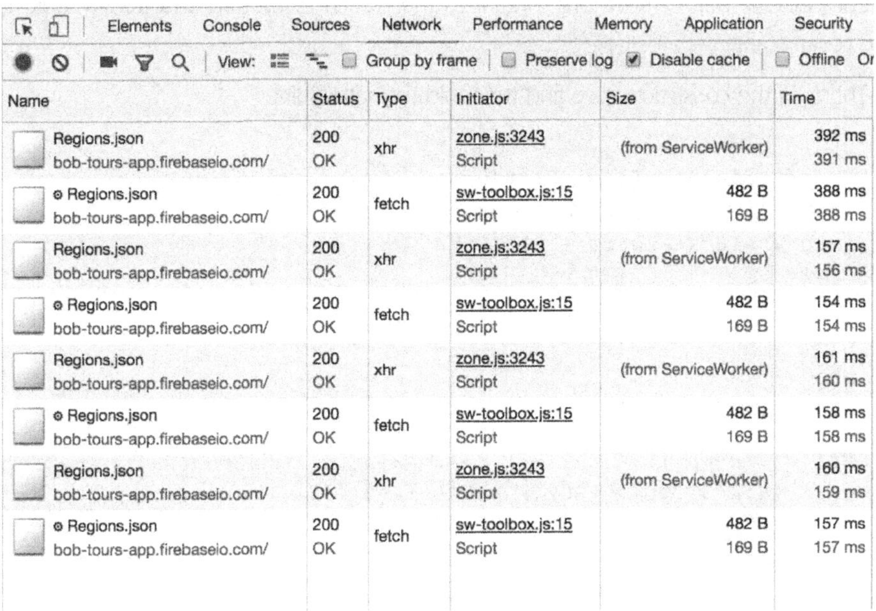

Name	Status	Type	Initiator	Size	Time
Regions.json bob-tours-app.firebaseio.com/	200 OK	xhr	zone.js:3243 Script	(from ServiceWorker)	392 ms 391 ms
Regions.json bob-tours-app.firebaseio.com/	200 OK	fetch	sw-toolbox.js:15 Script	482 B 169 B	388 ms 388 ms
Regions.json bob-tours-app.firebaseio.com/	200 OK	xhr	zone.js:3243 Script	(from ServiceWorker)	157 ms 156 ms
Regions.json bob-tours-app.firebaseio.com/	200 OK	fetch	sw-toolbox.js:15 Script	482 B 169 B	154 ms 154 ms
Regions.json bob-tours-app.firebaseio.com/	200 OK	xhr	zone.js:3243 Script	(from ServiceWorker)	161 ms 160 ms
Regions.json bob-tours-app.firebaseio.com/	200 OK	fetch	sw-toolbox.js:15 Script	482 B 169 B	158 ms 158 ms
Regions.json bob-tours-app.firebaseio.com/	200 OK	xhr	zone.js:3243 Script	(from ServiceWorker)	160 ms 159 ms
Regions.json bob-tours-app.firebaseio.com/	200 OK	fetch	sw-toolbox.js:15 Script	482 B 169 B	157 ms 157 ms

Granted, the retrieved data amount of 482 bytes is tiny and the retrieval times are quite fast. But unnecessary calls should nevertheless be avoided. Because on a smartphone, this can feel a bit slower than in our browser, especially if the user has a slow Internet connection!

There is simply no need for our app to retrieve the data from the database *each time* it views the page. So let's look at the question of whether there are other events where we could accommodate our HTTP call.

As described in chapter 2 "Angular Essentials" (see division "2.3 Lifecycle Hooks", starting on page 30), there are several hooks in a page component where code can be placed. But none of the hooks help us here, because with each of them the data would be reloaded when the page is viewed.

But what remains of the possibilities to load the data for `Regions` (and `TourTypes`) only *once* each time the app starts, even though the associated pages are reloaded each time?

The solution to our problem is to say goodbye to the hooks associated with page up and down and to think about a different approach.

Let's take a look at how Ionic organizes the launch of an app and take a look at `src/app/app.components.ts`.

There, in the constructor, we find the (bold formatted) line

```
constructor(
    private platform: Platform,
    private splashScreen: SplashScreen,
    private statusBar: StatusBar
  ) {
    this.initializeApp();
  }
```

This line calls the function

```
initializeApp() {
    this.platform.ready().then(() => {
      this.statusBar.styleDefault();
      this.splashScreen.hide();
    });
  }
```

How about if we *also* initialize our service here, i.e. load our `Regions` and `TourTypes`? Thus, the data retrieval would be done only *once* at app launch.

And that's exactly how we'll do it!

5.3 Place the service in the right place

Let's have a look at the start of our Ionic app in `app.components.ts`. Let's concentrate on the `initializeApp()` function at the end of the code:

```
import { Component } from '@angular/core';
import { Platform } from '@ionic/angular';
import { SplashScreen }
         from '@ionic-native/splash-screen/ngx';
import { StatusBar }
         from '@ionic-native/status-bar/ngx';

@Component({
  selector: 'app-root',
  templateUrl: 'app.component.html'
})
export class AppComponent {
  public appPages = [
    {
      title: 'Favorites',
      url: '/favorites',
      icon: 'star'
    },
    {
      title: 'Regions',
      url: '/regions',
      icon: 'images'
    },
    {
      title: 'Tour-Types',
      url: '/tour-types',
      icon: 'bus'
    }
  ];

  constructor(
    private platform: Platform,
    private splashScreen: SplashScreen,
    private statusBar: StatusBar
  ) {
    this.initializeApp();
  }
```

```
  initializeApp() {
    this.platform.ready().then(() => {
      this.statusBar.styleDefault();
      this.splashScreen.hide();
    });
  }

  ngOnInit() { }
}
```

We'll place our initialization of the data service right here, too. So the call for our data will be done exactly *once* at the app's start only.

Ok, let's build that. We have the following tasks:

1. Complement the service with an initialize function
2. Place the service initialization in the app component
3. Modify the Regions page

1. Complement the service with an initialize function

We begin with little additions in `bob-tours.service.ts`:

```
import { Injectable } from '@angular/core';
import { HttpClient } from '@angular/common/http';

@Injectable({
  providedIn: 'root'
})
export class BobToursService {

  public regions: any;

  baseUrl = 'https://bob-tours-app.firebaseio.com/';

  constructor(private http: HttpClient) { }

  initialize() {
    this.getRegions()
    .then(data => this.regions = data);
  }
```

```
  getRegions() {
    let requestUrl = `${this.baseUrl}/Regions.json`;
    return this.http.get(requestUrl).toPromise();
  }

}
```

First we declare a public property `regions` of type `any`.

Second we create an `initialize()` method, in which we call the service's own function `getRegions()` and transfer the data supplied from the database to the new public property `regions`.

2. Place the service initialization in the app component

Now we go back to `app.components.ts` and place our service initialization as follows:

```
import { Component } from '@angular/core';
import { Platform } from '@ionic/angular';
import { SplashScreen }
         from '@ionic-native/splash-screen/ngx';
import { StatusBar }
         from '@ionic-native/status-bar/ngx';
import { BobToursService }
         from './services/bob-tours.service';

@Component({
  selector: 'app-root',
  templateUrl: 'app.component.html'
})
export class AppComponent {
  public appPages = [
    {
      title: 'Favorites',
      url: '/favorites',
      icon: 'star'
    },
    {
      title: 'Regions',
      url: '/regions',
      icon: 'images'
```

```
    },
    {
      title: 'Tour-Types',
      url: '/tour-types',
      icon: 'bus'
    }
  ];

  constructor(
    private platform: Platform,
    private splashScreen: SplashScreen,
    private statusBar: StatusBar,
    private btService: BobToursService
  ) {
    this.initializeApp();
  }

  initializeApp() {
    this.platform.ready().then(() => {
      this.statusBar.styleDefault();
      this.splashScreen.hide();
      this.btService.initialize();
    });
  }
}
```

After importing `BobToursService` and injecting it into the constructor as `btService` we call its `initialize()` method within `initializeApp()`.

3. Modify the Regions page

In the `Regions` page we only change the code in the `ngOnInit` event:

```
import { Component, OnInit } from '@angular/core';
import { BobToursService }
         from 'src/app/services/bob-tours.service';

@Component({
  selector: 'app-regions',
  templateUrl: './regions.page.html',
  styleUrls: ['./regions.page.scss'],
})
```

```
export class RegionsPage implements OnInit {

  regions: any;

  constructor(private btService:BobToursService) { }

  ngOnInit() {
    this.regions = this.btService.regions;
  }
}
```

We delete the previous call for our service. Instead we set a reference to the `regions` variable of the service (bold formatted code above), where the data now comes from.

That's it. Start the app and check the `Developer Tools Network` protocol.

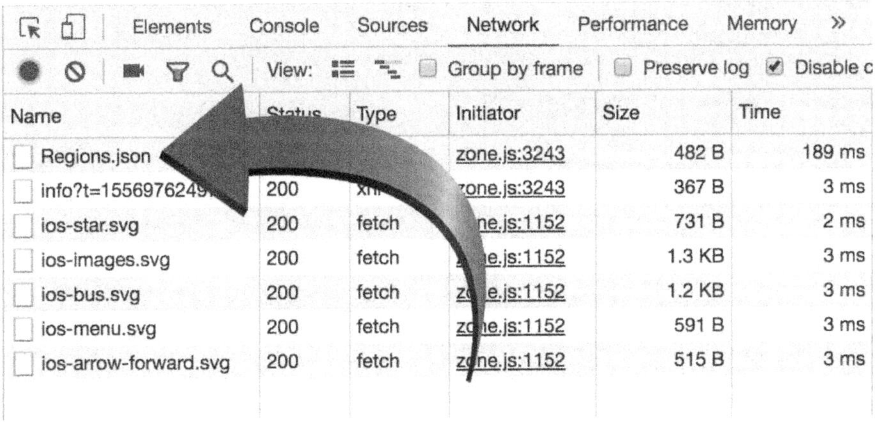

Our service is called only *once* at the app start - no matter how many times we switch between our pages.

5.4 Extend the service

After this successful refactoring we can implement the data call for the `TourTypes` data in the same way. Our tasks:

1. Get the TourTypes data from the database
2. Place the service in the Tour-Types page
3. Show the data on the Tour-Types page

1. Get the Tour-Types data from the database

In `bob-tours.service.ts` we add:

```
import { Injectable } from '@angular/core';
import { HttpClient } from '@angular/common/http';

@Injectable({
  providedIn: 'root'
})
export class BobToursService {

  public regions: any;
  public tourtypes: any;

  baseUrl = 'https://bob-tours-app.firebaseio.com/';

  constructor(private http: HttpClient) { }

  initialize() {

    this.getRegions()
    .then(data => this.regions = data);
    this.getTourtypes()
    .then(data => this.tourtypes = data);
  }

  getRegions() {
    let requestUrl = `${this.baseUrl}/Regions.json`;
    return this.http.get(requestUrl).toPromise();
  }
```

```
  getTourtypes() {
    let requestUrl = `${this.baseUrl}/Tourtypes.json`;
    return this.http.get(requestUrl).toPromise();
  }

}
```

We give our service another public property called `tourtypes`, also of type `any`.

```
public tourtypes: any;
```

We create a method `getTourtypes()`, which corresponds to the structure of the method `getRegions()`. The difference is in the data request URL targeted here on `Tourtypes.json`.

```
getTourtypes() {
    let requestUrl = `${this.baseUrl}/Tourtypes.json`;
    return this.http.get(requestUrl).toPromise();
}
```

The method is now also called within `initialize()` and passed the retrieved data to the public property `tourtypes`.

```
this.getTourtypes()
    .then(data => this.tourtypes = data);
```

2. Place the service in the Tour-Types page

To bring the data into the `Tour-Types` page in `tour-types.page.ts` we add:

```
import { Component, OnInit } from '@angular/core';
import { BobToursService }
         from 'src/app/services/bob-tours.service';

@Component({
  selector: 'app-tour-types',
  templateUrl: './tour-types.page.html',
  styleUrls: ['./tour-types.page.scss'],
})
export class TourTypesPage implements OnInit {

  tourtypes: any;
```

```
  constructor(private btService:BobToursService) { }

  ngOnInit() {
    this.tourtypes = this.btService.tourtypes;
  }

}
```

After importing `BobToursService` and injecting it into the constructor as `btService`, we assign the `tourtypes` provided by the service to the page property `this.tourtypes`.

3. Show the data on the Tour-Types page

To show the data on the page in `tour-types.page.html` we add:

```
<ion-header>
  <ion-toolbar>
    <ion-buttons slot="start">
      <ion-menu-button></ion-menu-button>
    </ion-buttons>
    <ion-title>Tour-Types</ion-title>
  </ion-toolbar>
</ion-header>

<ion-content class="ion-padding">
  <ion-list>
    <ion-item *ngFor="let tourtype of tourtypes">
      {{tourtype.Name}}
    </ion-item>
  </ion-list>
</ion-content>
```

Again: A typical `*ngFor` closure ensures that a separate list entry is created for each tour type read from the service. Using Content Projection, we output the name of each tour type.

Start the app and check the newly created page `Tour-Types`:

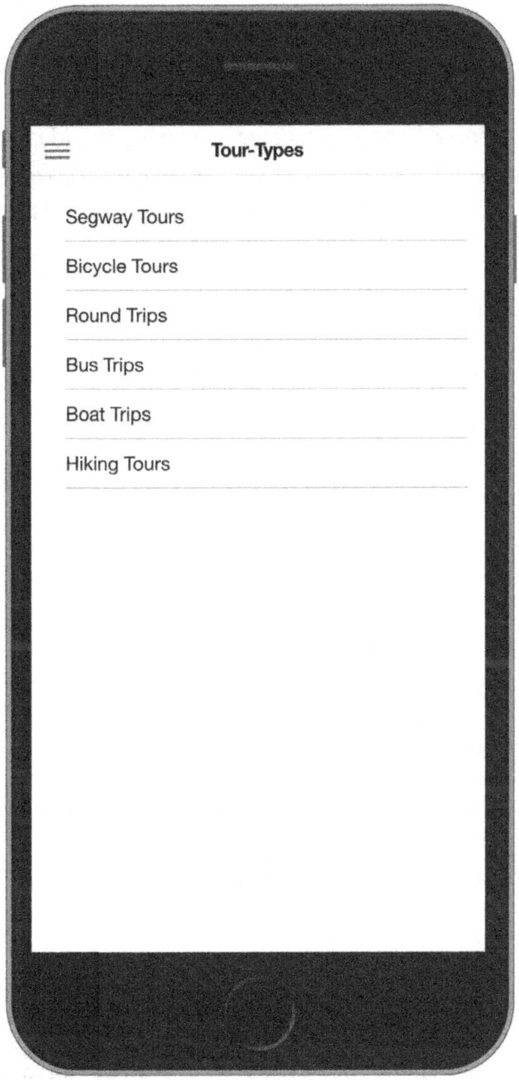

5.5 Sorting data with Lodash

Let's sort the `Tour-Types` in alphabetical order. We handle this in the service and extend it for this purpose with the **Lodash** library. Lodash is a very useful utility library for JavaScript and is already included in Ionic. I recommend to have a look at the documentation of Lodash whenever you have the idea to sort, group, re-order or manipulate arrays or collections. Lodash will provide you with smart solutions for these sorts of requirements. More informations about Lodash you can find here:

► https://lodash.com/

In `bob-tours.service.ts` we only add:

```
import { Injectable } from '@angular/core';
import { HttpClient } from '@angular/common/http';
import _ from 'lodash';

@Injectable({
  providedIn: 'root'
})
export class BobToursService {

  public regions: any;
  public tourtypes: any;

  baseUrl = 'https://bob-tours-app.firebaseio.com/';

  constructor(private http: HttpClient) { }

  initialize() {
    this.getRegions()
    .then(data => this.regions = data);
    this.getTourtypes()
    .then(data => this.tourtypes = _.sortBy(data, 'Name'));
  }

  getRegions() {
    let requestUrl = `${this.baseUrl}/Regions.json`;
    return this.http.get(requestUrl).toPromise();
  }
```

```
  getTourtypes() {
    let requestUrl = `${this.baseUrl}/Tourtypes.json`;
    return this.http.get(requestUrl).toPromise();
  }

}
```

We import the Lodash library with:

```
import _ from 'lodash';
```

We can sort the incoming data from our `getTourtypes()` method with:

```
_.sortBy(data, 'Name')
```

The first parameter is the data to be sorted. The second parameter is the property to sort by. And this is the result with sorted list items:

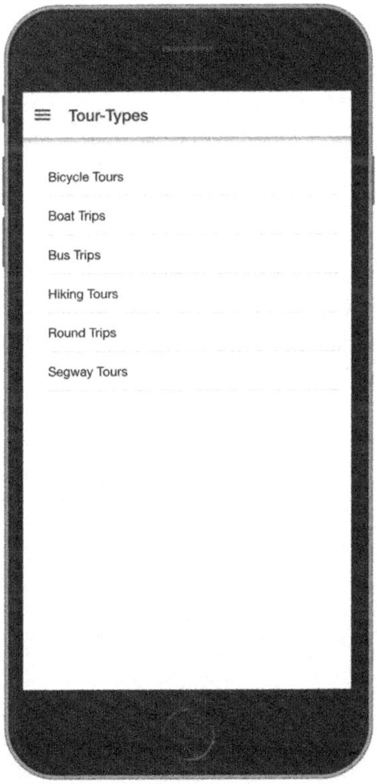

5.6 Filtering data

Complete the service

Last but not least we fetch the biggest data object from the database: the `Tours` data. To do so we extend the `bob-tours.service.ts` again:

```
import { Injectable } from '@angular/core';
import { HttpClient } from '@angular/common/http';
import _ from 'lodash';

@Injectable({
  providedIn: 'root'
})
export class BobToursService {

  public regions: any;
  public tourtypes: any;
  public tours: any;
  baseUrl = 'https://bob-tours-app.firebaseio.com/';

  constructor(private http: HttpClient) { }

  initialize() {
    this.getRegions()
    .then(data => this.regions = data);
    this.getTourtypes()
   .then(data => this.tourtypes = _.sortBy(data, 'Name'));
    this.getTours()
    .then(data => this.tours = _.sortBy(data, 'Title'));
  }

  getRegions() {
    let requestUrl = `${this.baseUrl}/Regions.json`;
    return this.http.get(requestUrl).toPromise();
  }

  getTourtypes() {
    let requestUrl = `${this.baseUrl}/Tourtypes.json`;
    return this.http.get(requestUrl).toPromise();
  }
```

```
  getTours() {
    let requestUrl = `${this.baseUrl}/Tours.json`;
    return this.http.get(requestUrl).toPromise();
  }
}
```

We give our service another public property called `tours`, also of type `any`.

```
public tours: any;
```

We create a method `getTours()`, which corresponds to the structure of the methods `getRegions()` and `getTourTypes()`. The difference is in the data request URL targeted here on `Tours.json`.

```
getTours() {
    let requestUrl = `${this.baseUrl}/Tours.json`;
    return this.http.get(requestUrl).toPromise();
}
```

The method is now also called within `initialize()` and passed the retrieved data to the public property `tours` and is sorted by the `Title` property.

```
this.getTours()
.then(data => this.tourtypes = _.sortBy(data, 'Title'));
```

Bring the service to the ListPage

To bring the `Tours` data into `list.page.ts` we write:

```
import { Component, OnInit } from '@angular/core';
import { BobToursService }
         from 'src/app/services/bob-tours.service';

@Component({
  selector: 'app-list',
  templateUrl: './list.page.html',
  styleUrls: ['./list.page.scss'],
})
export class ListPage implements OnInit {

  tours: any;
```

```
  constructor(private btService: BobToursService) { }

  ngOnInit() {
    this.tours = this.btService.tours;
  }
}
```

After importing `BobToursService` and injecting it into the constructor as `btService`, we assign the `tours` provided by the service to the page property `this.tours`.

Show the tours in the ListPage

In `list.page.html` we add:

```
<ion-header>
  <ion-toolbar>
    <ion-buttons slot="start">
      <ion-back-button></ion-back-button>
    </ion-buttons>
    <ion-title>List</ion-title>
  </ion-toolbar>
</ion-header>

<ion-content class="ion-padding">
  <ion-list>
    <ion-item *ngFor="let tour of tours">
      {{tour.Title}}
    </ion-item>
  </ion-list>
</ion-content>
```

To show a back button on the page we add in the header's toolbar:

```
<ion-buttons slot="start">
  <ion-back-button></ion-back-button>
</ion-buttons>
```

And to show all tours on the page we create the usual list structure with `*ngFor`:

```
<ion-list>
  <ion-item *ngFor="let tour of tours">
    {{tour.Title}}
  </ion-item>
</ion-list>
```

Filtering

The following things are left to do:

1. Navigate from the `Regions` or `Tour-Types` page to the `List` page
2. Filter the tours on the `List` page depending on the previous selection

1. Navigate from RegionsPage to ListPage

Let's begin with the navigation from `Regions` to `List`. In `regions.page.html` we add:

```
<ion-header>
  <ion-toolbar>
    <ion-buttons slot="start">
      <ion-menu-button></ion-menu-button>
    </ion-buttons>
    <ion-title>Regions</ion-title>
  </ion-toolbar>
</ion-header>

<ion-content class="ion-padding">
  <ion-list>
    <ion-item *ngFor="let region of regions"
              [routerLink]="['/list']"
              routerDirection="forward">
      {{region.Name}}
    </ion-item>
  </ion-list>
</ion-content>
```

You remember `routerLink` and `routerDirection`? If not, skip a few pages backwards to chapter 4 "Navigation" (see 4.3 Routing, page 85).

When we now start the app and click on one of the items of the `Regions` page, we always get the *complete* list of tours. Great – but what's missing is a *filtering* function to show tours from the selected region only.

What can be the *criteria* for filtering the tour data? To answer this question we should inspect the `Regions` and a `Tour` object in our database:

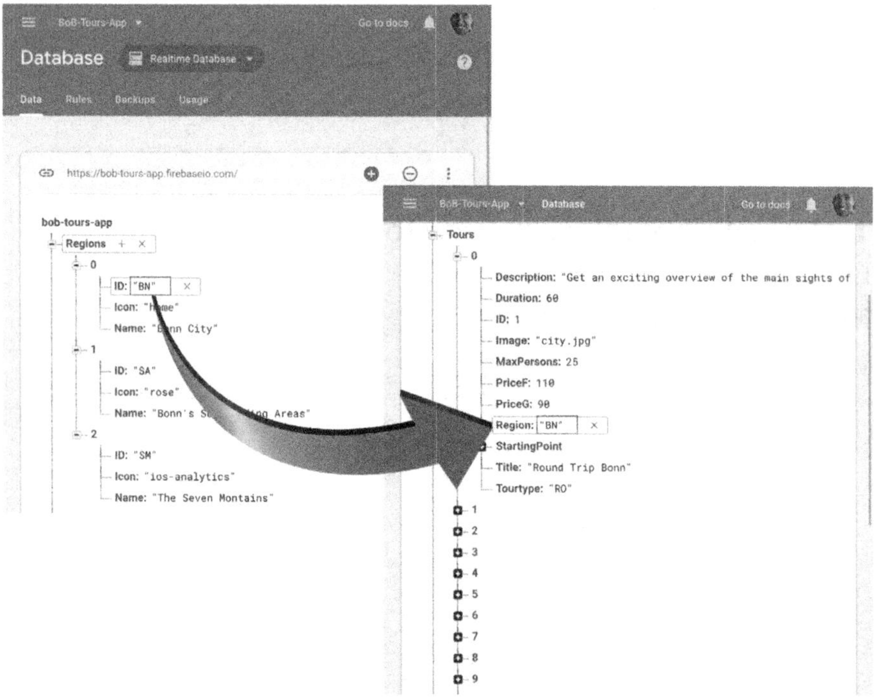

As you can see, each region has an `ID` property and each tour has a `Region` property that matches one of the region IDs. So we can filter that!

Let's expand `regions.page.html`:

```
<ion-header>
  <ion-toolbar>
    <ion-buttons slot="start">
      <ion-menu-button></ion-menu-button>
    </ion-buttons>
```

```
    <ion-title>Regions</ion-title>
  </ion-toolbar>
</ion-header>

<ion-content class="ion-padding">
  <ion-list>
    <ion-item *ngFor="let region of regions"
              [routerLink]="['/list',
                { Category: 'Region',
                  Criteria: region.ID,
                  Name: region.Name
                }
              ]"
              routerDirection="forward">
      {{region.Name}}
    </ion-item>
  </ion-list>
</ion-content>
```

What we did: We gave `[routerLink]` a *second* parameter. This consists of an object with the three properties `Category`, `Criteria` and `Name`.

2. Filter the tours on ListPage

Now we are able to use `Category` and `Criteria` for filtering (later we will see what `Name` is needed for). We can write this in `list.page.ts`:

```
import { Component, OnInit } from '@angular/core';
import { BobToursService }
         from 'src/app/services/bob-tours.service';
import { ActivatedRoute } from '@angular/router';
import _ from 'lodash';

@Component({
  selector: 'app-list',
  templateUrl: './list.page.html',
  styleUrls: ['./list.page.scss'],
})
export class ListPage implements OnInit {

  tours: any;
  selection: any;
```

```
  constructor(private btService:BobToursService,
              private activatedRoute: ActivatedRoute) { }

  ngOnInit() {
    this.selection = this.activatedRoute.snapshot.params;
    let category = this.selection.Category;
    let criteria = this.selection.Criteria;
    this.tours = _.filter(
      this.btService.tours,
      [ category, criteria ]
    );
  }

}
```

We import `ActivatedRoute`, because we need it to get the incoming data from the previous page (see “2.5 Routing and Lazy Loading”, starting on page 36) with

```
import { ActivatedRoute } from '@angular/router';
```

and inject it into the constructor with

```
private activatedRoute: ActivatedRoute
```

We declare a variable called `selection` and in `ngOnInit()` we assign it the incoming data:

```
this.selection = this.activatedRoute.snapshot.params;
```

`this.activatedRoute.snapshot.params` and after its assignment the variable `selection` contains the object we put in the second parameter, you remember?

From this we extract the `category` and the `criteria`:

```
let category = this.selection.Category;
let criteria = this.selection.ID;
```

Finally we use the filter function from Lodash (of course we had to import it) to filter all tours by the category `'Region'` and a selected criteria, for example `'BN'`.

```
this.tours = _.filter(this.btService.tours,
                      [ category, criteria ]);
```

What about the `Name` property? Because we put the `Name` property of a selected region as third parameter to the `routerLink` params object, we can use it for projecting the title into `list.page.html` as follows:

```
<ion-header>
  <ion-toolbar>
    <ion-buttons slot="start">
      <ion-back-button></ion-back-button>
    </ion-buttons>
    <ion-title>{{selection.Name}}</ion-title>
  </ion-toolbar>
</ion-header>
<ion-content class="ion-padding">
  <ion-list>
    <ion-item *ngFor="let tour of tours">
      {{tour.Title}}
    </ion-item>
  </ion-list>
</ion-content>
```

Look at our app with tours filtered by `Region`:

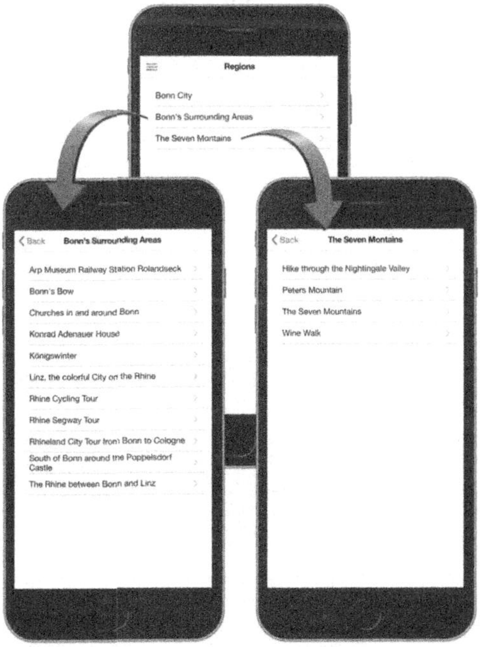

Navigate from TourTypesPage to ListPage

In the same manner we finally apply the navigation and filter logic to the TourTypesPage.

Because we have well parameterized the filtering in our service, it already works when we make the following addition in `tour-types.pages.html`:

```
<ion-header>
  <ion-toolbar>
    <ion-buttons slot="start">
      <ion-menu-button></ion-menu-button>
    </ion-buttons>
    <ion-title>Tour-Types</ion-title>
  </ion-toolbar>
</ion-header>

<ion-content class="ion-padding">
  <ion-list>
    <ion-item *ngFor="let tourtype of tourtypes"
              [routerLink]="['/list',
                { Category: 'Tourtype',
                   Criteria: tourtype.ID,
                   Name: tourtype.Name
                }
              ]"
              routerDirection="forward">
      {{tourtype.Name}}
    </ion-item>
  </ion-list>
</ion-content>
```

Our app now can filter tours by `Tour-Types`:

5.7 Using a route parameter

We should also integrate the `Details` page into our navigation.

If you look back at our navigation concept in chapter 4 “Navigation” (4.1 Have a plan, page 75), you see, that the `Details` page is reached from the `List` page – and later on, of course – by the `Favorites` page, too. From the `Details` page you can navigate to the `Request` page (we always built this route).

Let me show you a slightly different usage of `routerLink`. In order to ensure that this alternative works, we we'll solve the following tasks:

1. Modify the route path

2. Place a route parameter in [routerLink]

3. Get the route parameter

1. Modify the route path

Let's modify the path entry of our route to the `DetailsPageModule` in `app-routing.module.ts`:

```
...

{
    path: 'details/:id',
    loadChildren:
      () => import('./pages/details/details.module')
      .then(m => m.DetailsPageModule)
}

...
```

With appending `:id` to the path we place a route parameter in the path. For example, to see the tour details page for tour with ID 5, we must use the following URL:

`http://localhost:8100/details/5`

2. Place a route parameter in [routerLink]

Let's open the `list.page.html` and add the following (bold formatted) code:

```
<ion-header>
  <ion-toolbar>
    <ion-buttons slot="start">
      <ion-back-button></ion-back-button>
    </ion-buttons>
    <ion-title>{{selection.Name}}</ion-title>
  </ion-toolbar>
</ion-header>

<ion-content class="ion-padding">
  <ion-list>
    <ion-item *ngFor="let tour of tours"
              [routerLink]="'/details/' + tour.ID"
              routerDirection="forward">
      {{tour.Title}}
    </ion-item>
  </ion-list>
</ion-content>
```

What does that mean?

As a single parameter we add the `tour.ID` to `'/details/'`. That's the expected route parameter we defined in `app-routing.module.ts`.

3. Get the route parameter

What we now can do in `details.page.ts` to get the `id` and to determine the belonging tour object, is the following:

```
import { Component, OnInit } from '@angular/core';
import { ActivatedRoute } from '@angular/router';
import { BobToursService }
         from 'src/app/services/bob-tours.service';
import _ from 'lodash';

@Component({
  selector: 'app-details',
```

```
  templateUrl: './details.page.html',
  styleUrls: ['./details.page.scss'],
})
export class DetailsPage implements OnInit {

  tour = null;

  constructor(private activatedRoute: ActivatedRoute,
              public btService: BobToursService) { }

  ngOnInit() {
    let id = this.activatedRoute.snapshot.paramMap.get('id');
    this.tour = _.find(this.btService.tours, ['ID',
                                             parseInt(id)]);
  }

}
```

We import our service

```
import { BobToursService }
        from 'src/app/services/bob-tours.service';
```

and inject it into the constructor

```
public btService: BobToursService
```

In `ngOnInit` we grab the `id` route parameter with the following line of code:

```
let id = this.activatedRoute.snapshot.paramMap.get('id');
```

Because again we imported our favorite library Lodash

```
import _ from 'lodash';
```

we now can use it to find the tour with the given id:

```
this.tour = _.find(this.btService.tours, ['ID',
                                          parseInt(id)]);
```

Note: The `id` parameter is supplied as a *string*. However, the IDs of our tour objects read from the database are available as *integers*. Therefore we have to use `parseInt(id)` to convert the given `id` string to an integer so that a tour can be found.

Navigation completed

Let's start our app. We can now call the `Regions` of the side menu, for example, select a region and by clicking on one of the listed tours to view their details. Well, really much indicated - aside from the title and the Request button - nothing is here (which we will of course change later).

Hint: The Navigation from `FavoritesPage` to `DetailsPage` is broken now – but we'll fix this in a minute.

5.8 Local Storage

Nearly every app lets the user store his personal preferences. We want to provide such a functionality, too. It's appropriate to let the user save tours as favorites and collect them on a `Favorites` page.

A very simple way to locally store a small amount of data in an app, is the so called `Local Storage`.

Create a favorites service

Let's create a service that manages the user's favorites:

```
$ ionic g service services/favorites
```

In the freshly generated `favorites.service.ts` we code:

```
import { Injectable } from '@angular/core';

@Injectable({
  providedIn: 'root'
})
export class FavoritesService {

  public favIDs: Array<number>;
  public favTours: Array<any>;

  constructor() { }

  initialize(tours) {
    this.favTours = [];
    this.favIDs = JSON.parse(window.localStorage
                             .getItem('FavoritesIDs'));
    if (this.favIDs == null) {
      this.favIDs = [];
    } else  {
      tours.forEach(tour => {
        if (this.favIDs.indexOf(tour.ID) != -1) {
          this.favTours.push(tour);
        }
      });
```

```
    }
  }

  add(tour) {
    this.favIDs.push(tour.ID);
    this.favTours.push(tour);
    window.localStorage.setItem('FavoritesIDs',
                                JSON.stringify(this.favIDs));
  }

  remove(tour) {
    let removeIndex:number = this.favIDs.indexOf(tour.ID);
    if (removeIndex != -1) {
      this.favIDs.splice(removeIndex, 1);
      this.favTours.splice(removeIndex, 1);
      window.localStorage.setItem('FavoritesIDs',
                                JSON.stringify(this.favIDs));
    }
  }

}
```

Our provider has two properties, `favIDs` and `favTours`, and the methods `initialize`, `add` and `remove`. Their functionality in more detail:

initialize(tours)

In `initialize(tours)` we get all tours (from BobToursService, as we can see later). With

```
this.favTours = [];
```

we create an empty array. We will use it immediately.

The next line of code reads the key `'FavoritesIDs'` from `windows.localStorage` using its `getItem` method. To transform the result string into an array, we need `JSON.parse`:

```
this.favIDs = JSON.parse(window.localStorage
                         .getItem('FavoritesIDs'));
```

If there are no entries in the Local Storage yet

```
if (this.favIDs == null) {
```

we create an empty array of `favIDs`:

```
this.favIDs = [];
```

Otherwise

```
} else  {
```

we go through all the tours and search for the right tours based on the `IDs` read from the local storage

```
tours.forEach(tour => {
        if (this.favIDs.indexOf(tour.ID) != -1) {
```

and add the found tours to the `favTours` array:

```
this.favTours.push(tour);
```

add(tours)

In `add(tours)` we react to the fact that the user has clicked the "Add to Favorites" button (as we can see later).

```
this.favIDs.push(tour.ID);
this.favTours.push(tour);
window.localStorage.setItem('FavoritesIDs',
                            JSON.stringify(this.favIDs));
```

We add the `tour.ID` to the `favIDs` array and add the whole tour object to the `favTours` array. Finally we save the stringified `favIDs` array to the Local Storage using its `setItem` method. `setItem` expects the key (`'FavoritesIDs'`) and the value (`this.favDIs`).

remove(tour)

In `remove(tours)` we react to the fact that the user has clicked the "Remove from Favorites" button (as we can see later).

With

```
let removeIndex:number = this.favIDs.indexOf(tour.ID);
```

we get the index (array position) of the tour that is to be removed.

If there is an index

```
if (removeIndex != -1) {
```

we remove the array elements with the `splice` method

```
this.favIDs.splice(removeIndex, 1);
this.favTours.splice(removeIndex, 1);
```

Finally we save the stringified `favIDs` array to the Local Storage using its `setItem` method.

```
window.localStorage.setItem('FavoritesIDs',
                            JSON.stringify(this.favIDs));
```

Integrate the service in our app

How can we integrate the `FavoritesService`? It's obvious, that for the initialization we need access to the tours to pick the favorite tours out of them. And the place, where we get the tours directly, is our `BobToursService`. So, why not to place a service within a service? That makes sense in this context (to be honest: in a real life app I would try to avoid such dependencies in principle; but let's keep the code simple here).

We add some new code to `bob-tours.service.ts`:

```
import { Injectable } from '@angular/core';
import { HttpClient } from '@angular/common/http';
import { FavoritesService } from './favorites.service';
import _ from 'lodash';

@Injectable({
  providedIn: 'root'
})
export class BobToursService {

  public regions: any;
  public tourtypes: any;
  public tours: any;

  baseUrl = 'https://bob-tours-app.firebaseio.com/';
```

```
  constructor(private http: HttpClient,
              public favService: FavoritesService) { }

  initialize() {
    this.getRegions().then(data => this.regions = data);
    this.getTourtypes().then(data => this.tourtypes
                                    = _.sortBy(data, 'Name'));
     this.getTours().then(data => {
      this.tours = _.sortBy(data, 'Title');
      this.favService.initialize(this.tours);
    });
  }

  getRegions() {
    let requestUrl = `${this.baseUrl}/Regions.json`;
    return this.http.get(requestUrl).toPromise();
  }

  getTourtypes() {
    let requestUrl = `${this.baseUrl}/Tourtypes.json`;
    return this.http.get(requestUrl).toPromise();
  }

  getTours() {
    let requestUrl = `${this.baseUrl}/Tours.json`;
    return this.http.get(requestUrl).toPromise();
  }

}
```

You are almost an Ionic veteran and realize what we have done here: The new FavoritesService was imported, injected into the constructor and called in the `initialize` method of the BobToursService via its own `initialize` method, where all tours are handed over and are now also available in FavoritesService.

Show the favorites on the FavoritesPage

Now we can display the favorite tour titles on the `Favorites` page. Of course, that's only possible, when we import and inject the `FavoritesService` into `favorites.page.ts`, too:

```
import { Component, OnInit } from '@angular/core';
import { FavoritesService }
         from 'src/app/services/favorites.service';
@Component({
  selector: 'app-favorites',
  templateUrl: './favorites.page.html',
  styleUrls: ['./favorites.page.scss'],
})
export class FavoritesPage implements OnInit {

  /* tours = [
    { ID: 1, Title: 'City walk' },
    { ID: 2, Title: 'On the trails of Beethoven' },
    { ID: 3, Title: 'Villa Hammerschmidt' }
  ]; */

  constructor(public favService: FavoritesService) { }

  ngOnInit() { }

}
```

You see that I commented out the mock array `tours` – you can delete it, because in a few seconds we use the *real* favorites tours.

In `favorites.page.html` we change:

```
<ion-header>
  <ion-toolbar>
    <ion-buttons slot="start">
      <ion-menu-button></ion-menu-button>
    </ion-buttons>
    <ion-title>Favorites</ion-title>
  </ion-toolbar>
</ion-header>

<ion-content class="ion-padding">
  <ion-list>
    <ion-item *ngFor="let tour of favService.favTours"
              [routerLink]="'/details/' + tour.ID"
              routerDirection="forward">
      {{ tour.Title }}
```

```
    </ion-item>
    <ion-item *ngIf="favService.favTours?.length==0">
      You didn't choose any favorites yet!
    </ion-item>
  </ion-list>
</ion-content>
```

The `*ngFor` loop iterates through `favService.favTours` now. This property (array) will hold all user-defined favorites later. In `[routerLink]` we again use the now known `tour.ID` route parameter to specify the tour to be displayed on DetailsPage.

An interesting detail is the second `ion-item`:

```
<ion-item *ngIf="favService.favTours?.length==0">
  You didn't choose any favorites yet!
</ion-item>
```

The `*ngIf` directive says: Show me only, if there's no element in the `favService.favTours` array. This is the case if the user hasn't yet selected a favorite. And that's exactly what we show him as a hint.

Use the favorites service at DetailsPage

Let's use the `FavoritesService` at the `Details` page for:

- adding a tour as a favorite
- removing a tour as a favorite
- showing different buttons, depending on wether a tour is a favorite or not

To implement this, we add the following in `details.page.ts`:

```
import { Component, OnInit } from '@angular/core';
import { ActivatedRoute } from '@angular/router';
import { BobToursService }
         from 'src/app/services/bob-tours.service';
import { FavoritesService }
         from 'src/app/services/favorites.service';
import _ from 'lodash';

@Component({
  selector: 'app-details',
  templateUrl: './details.page.html',
```

```
  styleUrls: ['./details.page.scss'],
})
export class DetailsPage implements OnInit {

  tour = null;
  isFavorite: boolean;

  constructor(private activatedRoute: ActivatedRoute,
              public btService: BobToursService,
              public favService: FavoritesService) { }

  ngOnInit() {
    let id = this.activatedRoute.snapshot.paramMap.get('id');
    this.tour =
      _.find(this.btService.tours, ['ID', parseInt(id)]);
    this.isFavorite =
      this.favService.favIDs.indexOf(parseInt(id)) != -1;
  }

}
```

We import the `FavoritesService` and inject it as `favService` into the constructor.

We also declare a boolean variable `isFavorite`. We set its value at every `ngOnInit` call. Therefore we try to find the `id` of the given tour in the `this.favService.favIDs` array using `indexOf` . If `id` isn't found, the result is `-1`. The tour is then not a (already saved) favorite and `isFavorite` becomes `false`. If the `id` is found, the tour is a favorite and `isFavorite` becomes `true`.

We'll use this `isFavorite` flag now in `details.page.html`:

```
<ion-header>
  <ion-toolbar>
    <ion-buttons slot="start">
      <ion-back-button></ion-back-button>
    </ion-buttons>
    <ion-title>{{ tour.Title }}</ion-title>
  </ion-toolbar>
</ion-header>

<ion-content class="ion-padding">
  <ion-button routerLink="/request"
```

```
                routerDirection="forward">
        Request a Tour
    </ion-button>
</ion-content>

<ion-footer class="ion-padding">
    <ion-button (click)="favService.add(tour);
                        isFavorite=true;"
                *ngIf="!isFavorite"
                expand="block">
                Add to Favorites
    </ion-button>
    <ion-button (click)="favService.remove(tour);
                        isFavorite=false;"
                *ngIf="isFavorite"
                expand="block">
                Remove from Favorites
    </ion-button>
</ion-footer>
```

In a footer component we have two buttons, whose visibility is now controlled by the `isFavorite` flag. If the displayed tour isn't yet a favorite, the "Add to Favorites" button will be displayed. If a tour is already a favorite, the "Remove from Favorites" button appears.

The `click` event of the "Add to Favorites" button triggers the `add` method of the FavoritesService. It also sets `isFavorite` to `true` to control the visibility logic of the buttons.

The `click` event of the "Remove from Favorites" button triggers the `remove` method of the FavoritesService. It also sets `isFavorite` to `false` to control the visibility logic of the buttons, too.

Our favorites management is complete and we can see it all in the running app:

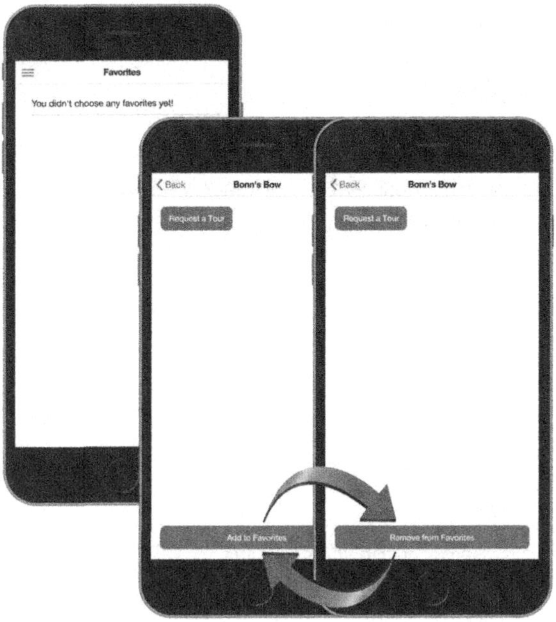

In Chrome's DevTools, you can view the contents of Local Storage in the `Application` panel:

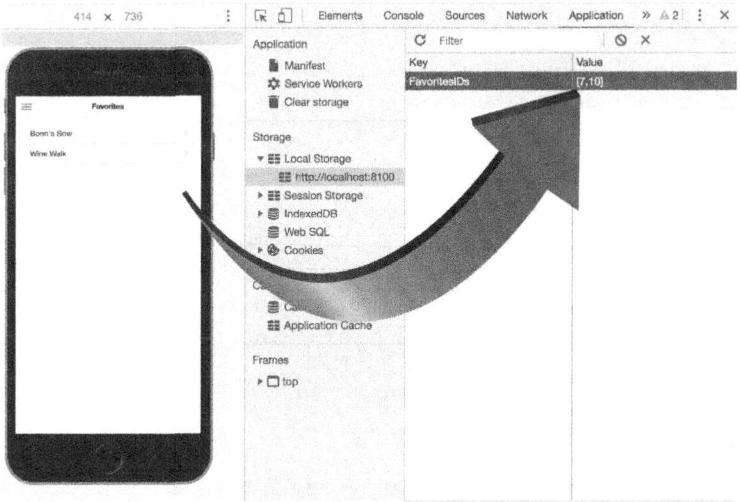

5.9 Ionic Storage

Ionic Storage is an easy way to store key/value pairs and JSON objects. `Storage` uses a variety of storage engines underneath, picking the best one available depending on the platform.

When running in a native app context, Storage will prioritize using `SQLite` (if it's installed), as it's one of the most stable and widely used file-based databases, and avoids some of the pitfalls of things like `LocalStorage` and `IndexedDB`, such as the OS deciding to clear out such data in low disk-space situations.

When running in the web or as a Progressive Web App, `Storage` will attempt to use `IndexedDB`, `WebSQL`, and `LocalStorage`, in that order.

Usage

First, install the package:

```
$ npm install --save @ionic/storage
```

Next, add it to the imports list in your `src/app/app.module.ts`:

```
import { NgModule } from '@angular/core';
import { BrowserModule } from '@angular/platform-browser';
import { RouteReuseStrategy } from '@angular/router';

import { IonicModule, IonicRouteStrategy }
         from '@ionic/angular';
import { SplashScreen }
         from '@ionic-native/splash-screen/ngx';
import { StatusBar } from '@ionic-native/status-bar/ngx';

import { AppComponent } from './app.component';
import { AppRoutingModule } from './app-routing.module';
import { HttpClientModule } from '@angular/common/http';
import { IonicStorageModule } from '@ionic/storage';

@NgModule({
  declarations: [AppComponent],
  entryComponents: [],
  imports: [
```

```
    BrowserModule,
    IonicModule.forRoot(),
    AppRoutingModule,
    HttpClientModule,
    IonicStorageModule.forRoot()
  ],
  providers: [
    StatusBar,
    SplashScreen,
    { provide: RouteReuseStrategy, useClass: IonicRouteStrate-
gy }
  ],
  bootstrap: [AppComponent]
})
export class AppModule {}
```

Refactoring the favorites service

Instead of `LocalStorage` we want to use `Ionic Storage` now. So let's modify our `favorites.service.ts` as follows:

```
import { Injectable } from '@angular/core';
import { Storage } from '@ionic/storage';

@Injectable({
  providedIn: 'root'
})
export class FavoritesService {

  public favIDs: Array<number>;
  public favTours: Array<any>;

  constructor(private storage: Storage) { }

  initialize(tours) {
    this.favTours = [];
    // this.favIDs =
       JSON.parse(window.localStorage.getItem('FavoritesIDs'));
    this.storage.ready().then(() => {
      this.storage.get('FavoritesIDs').then(ids => {
        this.favIDs = ids;
```

```
        if (this.favIDs == null) {
          this.favIDs = [];
        } else  {
          tours.forEach(tour => {
            if (this.favIDs.indexOf(tour.ID) != -1) {
              this.favTours.push(tour);
            }
          });
        }
      });
    });
  }

  add(tour) {
    this.favIDs.push(tour.ID);
    this.favTours.push(tour);
    // window.localStorage.setItem('FavoritesIDs',
    // JSON.stringify(this.favIDs));
    this.storage.set('FavoritesIDs', this.favIDs);
  }

  remove(tour) {
    let removeIndex:number = this.favIDs.indexOf(tour.ID);
    if (removeIndex != -1) {
      this.favIDs.splice(removeIndex, 1);
      this.favTours.splice(removeIndex, 1);
      // window.localStorage.setItem('FavoritesIDs',
      // JSON.stringify(this.favIDs));
      this.storage.set('FavoritesIDs', this.favIDs);
    }
  }

}
```

You see, the implementation of Ionic Storage is straightforward.

We import Storage

```
import { Storage } from '@ionic/storage';
```

and inject it into the constructor

```
constructor(private storage: Storage) { }
```

In the initialize function we check, if the storage is ready

```
this.storage.ready().then(() => {
```

and then read its content with

```
this.storage.get('FavoritesIDs').then(ids => {
  this.favIDs = ids;
```

In the `add` and `remove` methods we write the entire `favIDs` array each into the storage. That's it!

Here too, in Chrome's DevTools, you can view the contents of Ionic Storage in the `Application` panel:

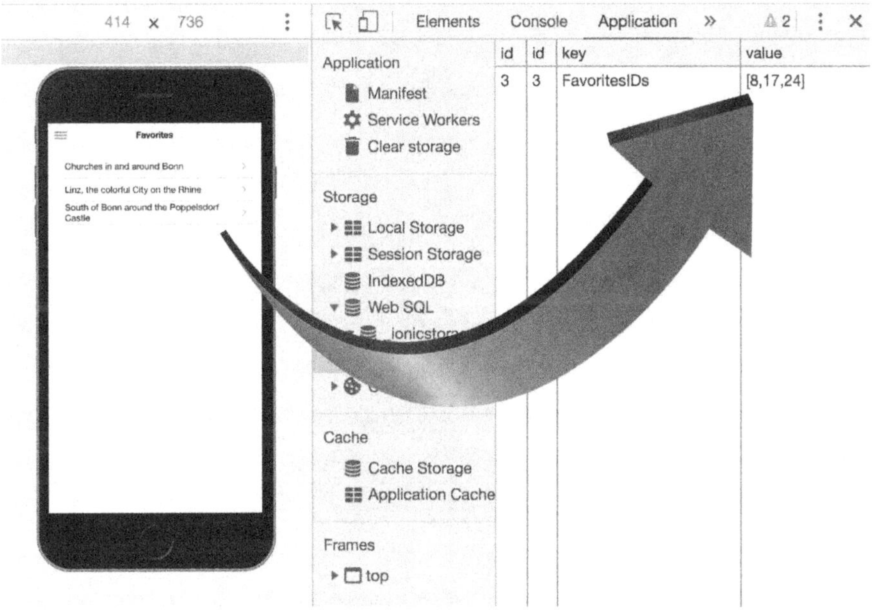

Summary

In this chapter, you got to know Google Firebase. You have read data from a database with the aid of `HttpClient`.

You sorted and filtered data using the Lodash library to make it appealing in the app.

You got to know route parameters as a supplement to the Angular routing concept.

Finally, with Local Storage and Ionic Storage, you've used a variety of ways to store user-specific data.

6 UI Components

6.1 Introduction

Ionic apps are made of high-level building blocks called Components, which allow you to quickly construct the UI for your app. Ionic comes stock with a number of components, including cards, lists, and tabs.

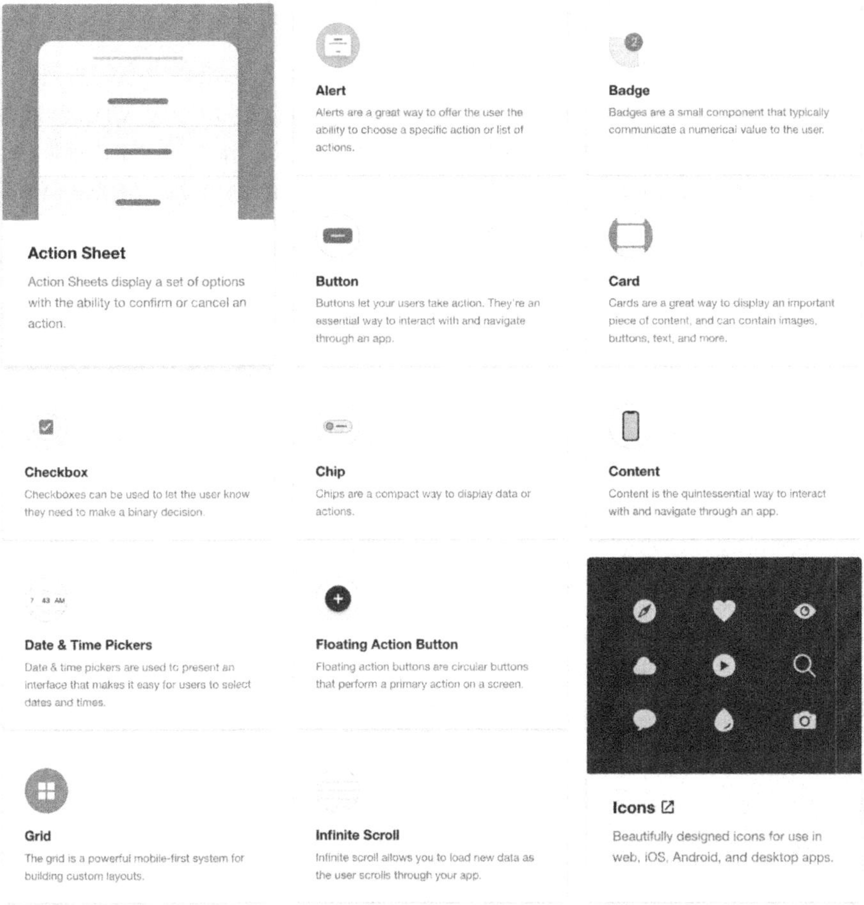

Each Ionic component consists of one or more custom elements. Each custom element, in turn, may expose properties, methods, events, and CSS custom properties.

The components are simply to use, modify and extend in many ways. I recommend to read the very, very good documentation on:

- https://ionicframework.com/docs/components

For a deeper insight you should dive into the API docs here:

- https://ionicframework.com/docs/api

With the wide variety of components my first intention was to only write about a hand-picked selection of them. But it's such a fun to use them, that I decided to talk about *every* component! You can't only explore them all in this chapter - you'll bring them also into our app and let them groove ;-)

6.2 Action Sheet

An Action Sheet is a dialog that displays a set of options. It appears on top of the app's content and must be manually dismissed by the user before they can resume interaction with the app. To emphasize the modal character of an action sheet the background of the app will automatically be darkened while the sheet is open.

Sometimes Action Sheets are used as an alternative for menus, but respect, that the Ionic documentation points out, not to use them for *navigation*.

There are multiple ways to dismiss the Action Sheet, including tapping the backdrop or hitting the escape key on desktop.

An Action Sheet for the DetailsPage

Instead of all the buttons we want to have only one `Options` button for providing the different (future) actions.

We redesign the `details.page.html`. For reasons of better traceability, I have commented out the previous code (see italic formatted lines of code). You are welcome to delete it.

```
<ion-header>
  <ion-toolbar>
    <ion-buttons slot="start">
      <ion-back-button></ion-back-button>
    </ion-buttons>
    <ion-title>{{ tour.Title }}</ion-title>
  </ion-toolbar>
</ion-header>

<ion-content class="ion-padding">
  <!-- <ion-button routerLink="/request"
              routerDirection="forward">
    Request a Tour
  </ion-button> -->
</ion-content>
```

```
<ion-footer class="ion-padding">
  <ion-button expand="block" (click)="presentActionSheet()">
    Options
  </ion-button>
  <!-- <ion-button (click)="favService.add(tour);
isFavorite=true;"
              *ngIf="!isFavorite"
              expand="block">
              Add to Favorites
  </ion-button>
  <ion-button (click)="favService.remove(tour);
isFavorite=false;"
              *ngIf="isFavorite"
              expand="block">
              Remove from Favorites
  </ion-button> -->
</ion-footer>
```

As you can see, we place the "Options" button in the footer division of our page. This is the usual place for an Action Sheet. The

```
expand="block"
```

attribute specifies the button as an inline full-width block with rounded corners.

With

```
(click)="presentActionSheet()"
```

we define a click event and bind it to a `presentActionSheet()` method, which we will encode immediately afterwards.

In `details.page.ts` we add:

```
import { Component, OnInit } from '@angular/core';
import { ActivatedRoute } from '@angular/router';
import { BobToursService }
         from 'src/app/services/bob-tours.service';
import { FavoritesService }
         from 'src/app/services/favorites.service';
import { ActionSheetController } from '@ionic/angular';
import _ from 'lodash';

@Component({
```

```
  selector: 'app-details',
  templateUrl: './details.page.html',
  styleUrls: ['./details.page.scss'],
})
export class DetailsPage implements OnInit {

  tour = null;
  isFavorite: boolean;

  constructor(private activatedRoute: ActivatedRoute,
              public btService: BobToursService,
              public favService: FavoritesService,
              private actionSheetCtrl: ActionSheetController)
{ }

  ngOnInit() {
    let id = this.activatedRoute.snapshot.paramMap.get('id');
    this.tour =
      _.find(this.btService.tours, ['ID', parseInt(id)]);
    this.isFavorite =
      this.favService.favIDs.indexOf(parseInt(id)) != -1;
  }

  async presentActionSheet() {
    const actionSheet = await this.actionSheetCtrl.create({
      header: 'Tour',
      buttons: [
        {
          text: 'Request',
          handler: () => {
          // We implement this later with a Modal Controller.
            window.location.href = "/request";
          }
        },
        {
          text: (this.isFavorite) ? 'Remove from Favorites'
                                  : 'Add to Favorites',
          role: (this.isFavorite) ? 'destructive' : '',
          handler: () => {
            if (this.isFavorite) {
              this.favService.remove(this.tour);
              this.isFavorite = false;
```

```
            } else {
              this.favService.add(this.tour);
              this.isFavorite = true;
            }
          }
        },
        {
          text: 'Cancel',
          role: 'cancel'
        }
      ]
    });
    await actionSheet.present();
  }

}
```

To create an Action Sheet, we need a so-called `ActionSheetController`. We import this with

`import { ActionSheetController } from '@ionic/angular';`

and inject it into the constructor:

`private actionSheetCtrl: ActionSheetController`

Now we write our `presentActionSheet()` method.

The special thing about this method is that it contains asynchronous calls and therefore we have to mark the method as `async`:

`async presentActionSheet() {`

If you are not yet familiar with the subject of asynchrony, please read the section "2.11 Async / Await" (starting on page 51) in chapter 2 "Angular Essentials".

Our first asynchronous call is

`const actionSheet = await this.actionSheetCtrl.create({`

In this line of code, we define a constant called `actionSheet`. It receives our Action Sheet as soon as it's created (asynchronously) using the `this.actionSheetCtrl.create(...)` method.

This method expects an object as its parameter. Like every JSON object, the object expression is enclosed in curly braces. Don't forget them.

Within the object we define a header

```
header: 'Tour',
```

and an array of three buttons, where each button is an object again. Let's start with the first button:

```
{
  text: 'Request',
  handler: () => {
    // We implement this later with a Modal Controller.
    window.location.href = "/request";
  }
}
```

This button gets the label `'Request'` as well as an event handler, to which we pass the path to the next page with a simple `href` instruction. We'll rebuild this part later. But for now it works that way.

Our second button:

```
{
  text: (this.isFavorite) ? 'Remove from Favorites'
                          : 'Add to Favorites',
  role: (this.isFavorite) ? 'destructive' : '',
  handler: () => {
    if (this.isFavorite) {
      this.favService.remove(this.tour);
      this.isFavorite = false;
    } else {
      this.favService.add(this.tour);
      this.isFavorite = true;
    }
  }
}
```

Via its property `text` this button gets the label `'Remove from Favorites'` or `'Add to Favorites'`, depending on the value of `this.isFavorite`. You remember this Boolean variable? If not, please read page 143.

The `role` property sets a special look - depending on the target platform. Again, depending on `isFavorite`, we can ensure that, for example, in the iOS world, the button turns red when it receives the label `'Remove from Favorites'`. This makes it clear to the user that a click on the button performs a destructive action. On the other hand, labeled `'Add to Favorites'` and without a role property the button will have the default look for the platform.

The handler property calls `this.favService.remove(this.tour)` or `this.favService.add(this.tour)`, again – depending on the value of `this.isFavorite`.

Our third button:

```
{
  text: 'Cancel',
  role: 'cancel'
}
```

Via its property `text` this button gets the label `'Cancel'`. The `role` gets the value `'cancel'` what means, that this button will always load as the bottom button, no matter where they are in the array and additionally, if the action sheet is dismissed by tapping the backdrop, then it will fire the handler from the button with the cancel role. And since we have not defined a handler for this button, the action sheet will also be closed when you click this button.

Finally we need to present the Action Sheet with

```
await actionSheet.present();
```

This is an asynchronous call, too.

Let's see our Action Sheet in action:

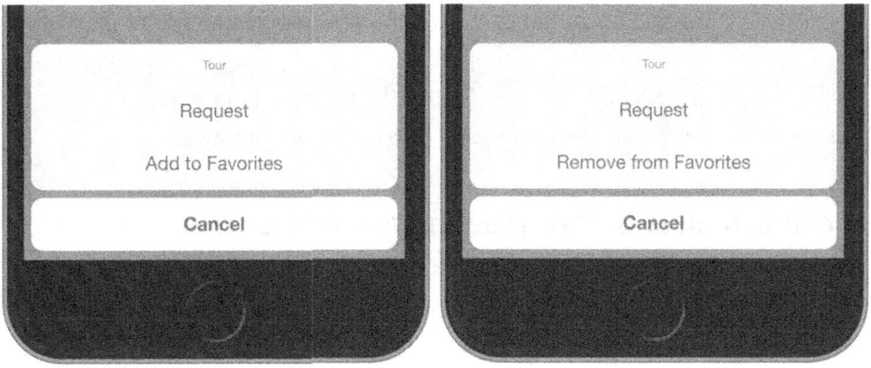

More informations about Action Sheets you'll find here:

- https://ionicframework.com/docs/api/action-sheet
- https://ionicframework.com/docs/api/action-sheet-controller

6.3 Alert

An Alert is a dialog that presents users with information or collects information from the user using inputs. An Alert appears on top of the app's content, and must be manually dismissed by the user before they can resume interaction with the app. It can also optionally have a header, subHeader and message.

A confirm alert before deleting a favorite

Let's ask the user before deleting a favorite. We enhance the `details.page.ts`:

```
import { Component, OnInit } from '@angular/core';
import { ActivatedRoute } from '@angular/router';
import { BobToursService }
         from 'src/app/services/bob-tours.service';
import { FavoritesService }
         from 'src/app/services/favorites.service';
import { ActionSheetController, AlertController }
         from '@ionic/angular';
import _ from 'lodash';

@Component({
  selector: 'app-details',
  templateUrl: './details.page.html',
  styleUrls: ['./details.page.scss'],
})
export class DetailsPage implements OnInit {

  tour = null;
  isFavorite: boolean;

  constructor(private activatedRoute: ActivatedRoute,
              public btService: BobToursService,
              public favService: FavoritesService,
              private actionSheetCtrl: ActionSheetController,
              private alertCtrl: AlertController) { }

  ngOnInit() {
    let id =
      this.activatedRoute.snapshot.paramMap.get('id');
    this.tour =
```

```
    _.find(this.btService.tours, ['ID', parseInt(id)]);
  this.isFavorite =
       this.favService.favIDs.indexOf(parseInt(id)) != -1;
}

async presentActionSheet() {
  const actionSheet = await this.actionSheetCtrl.create({
    header: 'Tour',
    buttons: [
      {
        text: 'Request',
        handler: () => {
        // We implement this later with a Modal Controller.
        }
      },
      {
        text: (this.isFavorite) ? 'Remove from Favorites'
                                : 'Add to Favorites',
        role: (this.isFavorite) ? 'destructive' : '',
        handler: () => {
          if (this.isFavorite) {
            this.presentAlert();
            //this.favService.remove(this.tour);
            //this.isFavorite = false;
          } else {
            this.favService.add(this.tour);
            this.isFavorite = true;
          }
        }
      },
      {
        text: 'Cancel',
        role: 'cancel'
      }
    ]
  });
  await actionSheet.present();
}

async presentAlert() {
  const alert = await this.alertCtrl.create({
    header: 'Remove Favorite?',
```

```
      message: 'Do you really want to remove this Favorite?',
      buttons: [
        {
          text: 'No'
        },
        {
          text: 'Yes',
          handler: () => {
            this.favService.remove(this.tour);
            this.isFavorite = false;
          }
        }
    ]
    });
    await alert.present();
  }

}
```

An Alert is similar to an Action Sheet. We need an `AlertController`, which we import with

```
import { ActionSheetController, AlertController }
         from '@ionic/angular';
```

and inject into the constructor:

```
private alertCtrl: AlertController
```

Now we write our `presentAlert()` method.

The special thing about this method is – as with `presentActionSheet()` before – that it contains asynchronous calls and therefore we have to mark the method as `async`:

```
async presentAlert() {
```

If you are not yet familiar with the subject of asynchrony, please read the section "2.11 Async / Await" (starting on page 51) in chapter 2 "Angular Essentials".

Our first asynchronous call is

```
const alert = await this.alertCtrl.create({
```

In this line of code, we define a constant called `alert`. It receives our Alert control as soon as it's created (asynchronously) using the `this.alertCtrl.create(...)` method.

This method expects an object as its parameter. Like every JSON object., the object expression is enclosed in curly braces. Don't forget them.

Within the object we define a header

```
header: 'Remove Favorite?',
```

a message

```
message: 'Do you really want to remove this Favorite?'
```

and an array of two buttons, where each button is an object again. Let's start with the first button:

```
{
  text: 'No'
}
```

This is a simple `'No'` button. Without a handler it closes the Alert by clicking on it.

Our second button:

```
{
  text: 'Yes',
  handler: () => {
    this.favService.remove(this.tour);
    this.isFavorite = false;
  }
}
```

It's labeled with `'Yes'` and owns a handler. This handler contains the code that were previously placed in `presentActionSheet()` (see commented lines).

We (asynchronously) present our Alert with

```
await alert.present();
```

Finally we call `presentAlert()` out of the Action Sheet with

```
this.presentAlert();
```

Let's see our Alert in action:

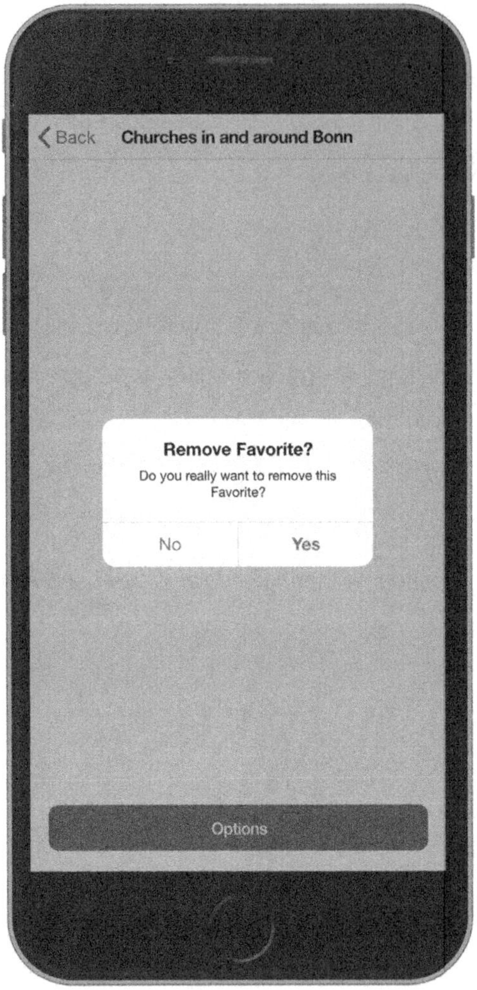

More informations about the Alert you can find here:

- https://ionicframework.com/docs/api/alert
- https://ionicframework.com/docs/api/alert-controller

6.4 Badge

Badges are inline block elements that usually appear near another element. Typically they contain a number or other characters. They can be used as a notification that there are additional items associated with an element and indicate how many items there are.

Count the tours

In our app we can use Badges to show the numbers of each different kind of tours on the `Regions` and `Tour-Types` pages.

RegionsPage

Let's start with `regions.page.ts`:

```
import { Component, OnInit } from '@angular/core';
import { BobToursService }
         from 'src/app/services/bob-tours.service';
import _ from 'lodash';

@Component({
  selector: 'app-regions',
  templateUrl: './regions.page.html',
  styleUrls: ['./regions.page.scss'],
})
export class RegionsPage implements OnInit {

  regions: any;

  constructor(private btService:BobToursService) { }

  ngOnInit() {
    this.regions = this.btService.regions;
    this.regions.forEach(region => {
      const tours =
        _.filter(this.btService.tours, ['Region', region.ID]);
      region['Count'] = tours.length;
    });
  }
}
```

We use Lodash again. So we need to import it with

```
import _ from 'lodash';
```

In `ngOnInit` we count. That means we start with a `forEach` loop across all regions:

```
this.regions.forEach(region => {
```

In each run we determine the number of tours to a particular `region.ID` by using the Lodash `filter` method:

```
const tours =
  _.filter(this.btService.tours, ['Region', region.ID]);
```

The result of the filtered (counted) tours is saved in a variable `tours`. So in each run we can easily grab the `length` property of `tours` and assign it on the fly to each `region` as new `Count` property:

```
region['Count'] = tours.length;
```

In `regions.page.html` we add:

```
<ion-header>
  <ion-toolbar>
    <ion-buttons slot="start">
      <ion-menu-button></ion-menu-button>
    </ion-buttons>
    <ion-title>Regions</ion-title>
  </ion-toolbar>
</ion-header>

<ion-content class="ion-padding">
  <ion-list>
    <ion-item *ngFor="let region of regions"
              [routerLink]="['/list', {
                Category: 'Region',
                ID: region.ID,
                Name: region.Name
              } ]"
              routerDirection="forward">
      {{region.Name}}
      <ion-badge slot="end">{{region.Count}}</ion-badge>
    </ion-item>
  </ion-list>
</ion-content>
```

We use the `ion-badge` tag in conjunction with the `slot="end"` directive for a right-justified alignment.

Our app with Badges will look like that:

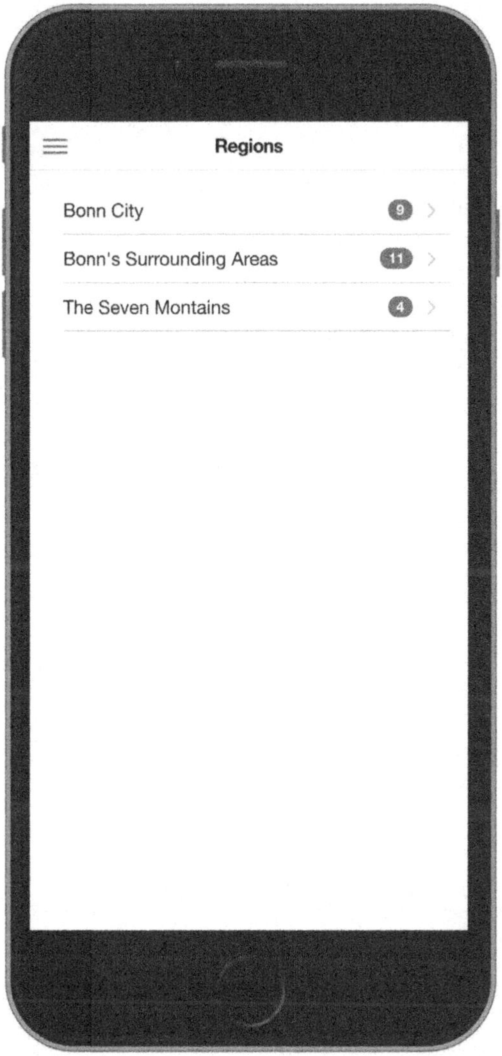

TourTypesPage

In the same manner we extend the `Tour-Types` page.

Let's start with `tour-types.page.ts`:

```
import { Component, OnInit } from '@angular/core';
import { BobToursService }
        from 'src/app/services/bob-tours.service';
import _ from 'lodash';

@Component({
  selector: 'app-tour-types',
  templateUrl: './tour-types.page.html',
  styleUrls: ['./tour-types.page.scss'],
})
export class TourTypesPage implements OnInit {

  tourtypes: any;

  constructor(private btService:BobToursService) { }

  ngOnInit() {
    this.tourtypes = this.btService.tourtypes;
    this.tourtypes.forEach(tourtype => {
      const tours = _.filter(this.btService.tours,
                             ['Tourtype', tourtype.ID]);
      tourtype['Count'] = tours.length;
    });
  }

}
```

We use Lodash here again. So we need to import it with

```
import _ from 'lodash';
```

In `ngOnInit` we count. That means we start with a `forEach` loop across all tour-types:

```
this.tourtypes.forEach(tourtype => {
```

In each run we determine the number of tours to a particular `tourtype.ID` by using the Lodash `filter` method:

```
const tours =
  _.filter(this.btService.tours, ['Tourtype', tourtype.ID]);
```

The result of the filtered (counted) tours is saved in a variable `tours`. So in each run we can easily grab the `length` property of `tours` and assign it on the fly to each `tourtype` as new `Count` property:

```
tourtype['Count'] = tours.length;
```

And in `tour-types.page.html` we add:

```
<ion-header>
  <ion-toolbar>
    <ion-buttons slot="start">
      <ion-menu-button></ion-menu-button>
    </ion-buttons>
    <ion-title>Tour-Types</ion-title>
  </ion-toolbar>
</ion-header>

<ion-content class="ion-padding">
  <ion-list>
    <ion-item *ngFor="let tourtype of tourtypes"
              [routerLink]="['/list', {
                Category: 'Tourtype',
                ID: tourtype.ID,
                Name: tourtype.Name
              } ]"
              routerDirection="forward">
      {{tourtype.Name}}
      <ion-badge slot="end">{{tourtype.Count}}</ion-badge>
    </ion-item>
  </ion-list>
</ion-content>
```

We use the `ion-badge` tag again in conjunction with the `slot="end"` directive for a right-justified alignment of each Badge component.

The result will look like that:

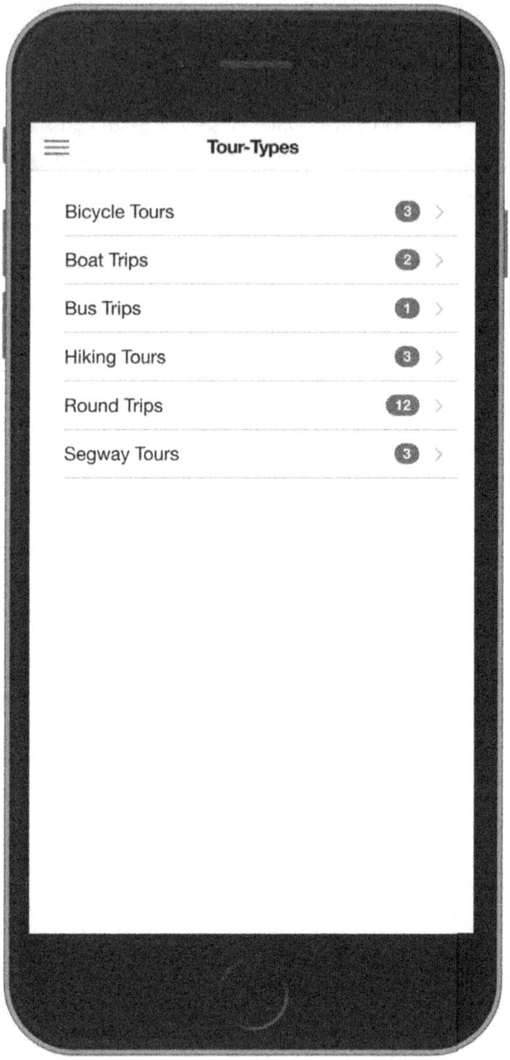

More informations about Badges you'll find here:

► https://ionicframework.com/docs/api/badge

6.5 Button

Buttons are essential elements for user interaction and navigation in an app. It should always be clear, which action is triggered by a button. Buttons can have a label and/or an icon. Their appearance can be influenced by many attributes.

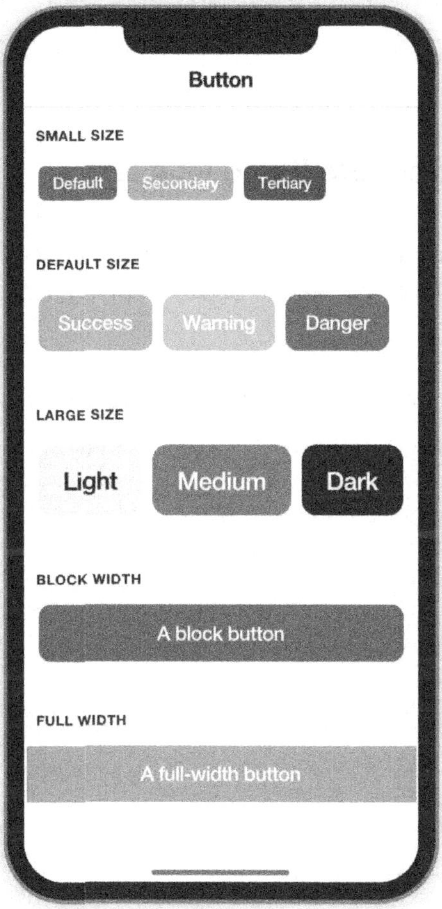

In our app we already use Buttons on nearly every page, so I think it's not necessary to deliver another example for its usage here.

If you're interested in more details about Buttons, read here:

► https://ionicframework.com/docs/api/button

6.6 Card

Cards are perfect components to organize informations in a structured manner. For a mobile user experience Cards are furthermore an easy way to present texts and images pretty well on different display sizes. A Card can be a single component, but is often made up of some header, title, subtitle and content.

In our app we can use a Card to show detailed tour informations on the `DetailsPage`.

Preparation: translate IDs to long terms

A little preparation work is to manage: the translation of the `Regions` and `TourTypes` IDs, e.g. "SM" and "RT" to their according long terms, "The Seven Mountains" and "Round Trips". We want to display them as additional informations.

In `details.page.ts` we write the code to handle this task:

```
import { Component, OnInit } from '@angular/core';
import { ActivatedRoute } from '@angular/router';
import { BobToursService }
         from 'src/app/services/bob-tours.service';
import { FavoritesService }
         from 'src/app/services/favorites.service';
import { ActionSheetController, AlertController }
         from '@ionic/angular';
import _ from 'lodash';

@Component({
  selector: 'app-details',
  templateUrl: './details.page.html',
  styleUrls: ['./details.page.scss'],
})
export class DetailsPage implements OnInit {

  tour = null;
  isFavorite: boolean;
  region: string;
  tourtype: string;
```

```
  constructor(private activatedRoute: ActivatedRoute,
              public btService: BobToursService,
              public favService: FavoritesService,
              private actionSheetCtrl: ActionSheetController,
              private alertCtrl: AlertController) { }

  ngOnInit() {

    let id = this.activatedRoute.snapshot.paramMap.get('id');

    this.tour = _.find(
      this.btService.tours,
      ['ID', parseInt(id)]
    );

    this.isFavorite =
         this.favService.favIDs.indexOf(parseInt(id)) != -1;

    this.region = _.find(
      this.btService.regions,
      { 'ID': this.tour.Region }
    ).Name;

    this.tourtype = _.find(
      this.btService.tourtypes,
      { 'ID': this.tour.Tourtype }
    ).Name;
  }

  async presentActionSheet() {
    ...
  }

  async presentAlert() {
    ...
  }

}
```

First we define two string variables: `region` and `tourtype`. These variables will get the long texts that we want to display:

```
region: string;
tourtype: string;
```

Let's use a Lodash `find` function to find the matching region:

```
this.region = _.find(
  this.btService.regions,
  { 'ID': this.tour.Region }
)
```

We only need the value of the property `Name` from the found `Region` object.

```
.Name;
```

In the result this value is assigned to `this.region`. This is our long term that we'll display.

In the same manner we find the long term for the `TourType` of a tour and assign it to `this.tourtype`.

Show details within a card

Finally let's design our Card on `details.page.html`:

```
<ion-header>
  <ion-toolbar>
    <ion-buttons slot="start">
      <ion-back-button></ion-back-button>
    </ion-buttons>
    <ion-title>Tour Details</ion-title>
  </ion-toolbar>
</ion-header>

<ion-content class="ion-padding">
  <ion-card>
    <ion-card-header>
      <ion-card-subtitle>
        {{tourtype}} / {{region}}
      </ion-card-subtitle>
      <ion-card-title>
        {{tour.Title}}
      </ion-card-title>
    </ion-card-header>
    <ion-card-content>
```

```
      {{tour.Description}}
    </ion-card-content>
  </ion-card>
</ion-content>

<ion-footer class="ion-padding">
  <ion-button expand="block" (click)="presentActionSheet()">
    Options
  </ion-button>
</ion-footer>
```

First, we change the title of our page simply in `Tour Details`.

In the content area, we now define an `ion-card` with two areas:

- `ion-card-header`
- `ion-card-content`

The `ion-card-header` itself contains two elements:

- `ion-card-subtitle`
- `ion-card-title`

Let's have a look at `ion-card-subtitle`:

```
<ion-card-subtitle>
  {{tourtype}}/{{region}}
</ion-card-subtitle>
```

Within this subtitle we display the previously determined long terms of `tourtype` and `region` with typical content projection (see "2.6 Content Projection" on page 39).

And into the `ion-card-title`

```
<ion-card-title>
  {{tour.Title}}
</ion-card-title>
```

we project the tour title (was previously in the header's `ion-title` tag).

Finally the ion-card-content contains the whole tour description:

```
<ion-card-content>
  {{tour.Description}}
</ion-card-content>
```

Let's see our newly designed DetailsPage with a Card:

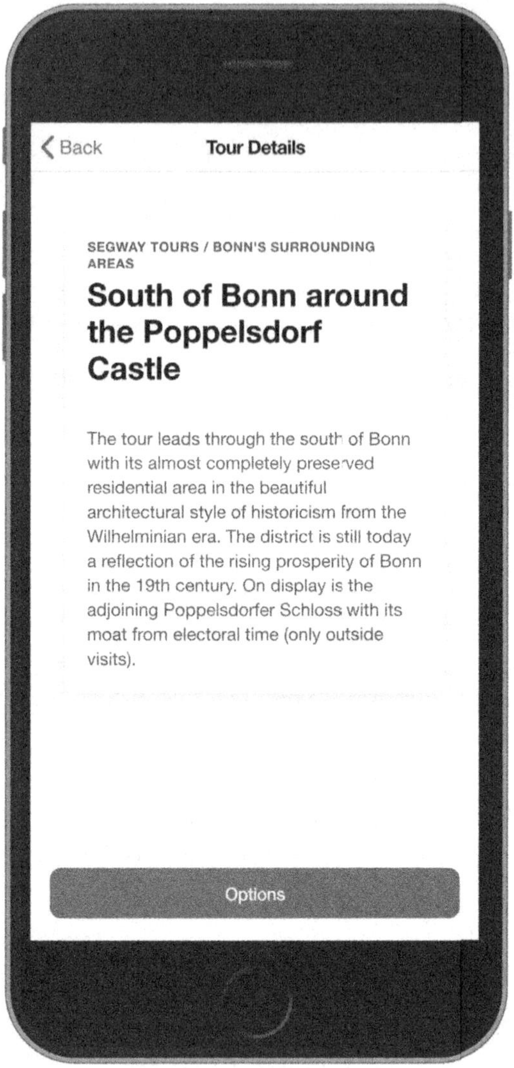

More about Cards you can find here:

- https://ionicframework.com/docs/api/card

6.7 Checkbox

Checkboxes allow the selection of multiple options from a set of options. They appear as checked (ticked) when activated. Clicking on a Checkbox will toggle the `checked` property. By setting the `checked` property they can also be checked programmatically.

Create user settings

We use a Checkbox to give the user (later) a choice to receive messages or not.

First, we write a little code into `app.components.ts`:

```
import { Component } from '@angular/core';
import { Platform } from '@ionic/angular';
import { SplashScreen } from '@ionic-native/splash-
screen/ngx';
import { StatusBar } from '@ionic-native/status-bar/ngx';
import { BobToursService } from './services/bob-
tours.service';


@Component({
  selector: 'app-root',
  templateUrl: 'app.component.html'
})
export class AppComponent {
  public appPages = [
    {
      title: 'Favorites',
      url: '/favorites',
      icon: 'star'
    },
    {
      title: 'Regions',
      url: '/regions',
      icon: 'images'
    },
    {
      title: 'Tour-Types',
      url: '/tour-types',
      icon: 'bus'
```

```
    }
  ];

  settings: any = {};

  constructor(
    private platform: Platform,
    private splashScreen: SplashScreen,
    private statusBar: StatusBar,
    public btService: BobToursService
  ) {
    this.initializeApp();
  }

  initializeApp() {
    this.platform.ready().then(() => {
      this.statusBar.styleDefault();
      this.splashScreen.hide();
      this.btService.initialize();
    });
  }

  // User has changed his/her settings.
  updateSettings() {
    console.log(this.settings.notifications);
  }

}
```

We declare a variable `settings` of type any and instantiate it as empty object. This variable will hold all user settings which we will gradually build into our app.

The method `updateSettings()` initially only outputs the value of `this.settings.notifications` in the console. We'll expand it later.

In `app.component.html` we add:

```
<ion-app>
  <ion-split-pane contentId="main-content">
    <ion-menu contentId="main-content" type="overlay">
```

```
    <ion-content>
      <ion-list id="inbox-list">
        <ion-menu-toggle auto-hide="false"
          *ngFor="let p of appPages; let i = index">
          <ion-item routerDirection="root"
                    [routerLink]="[p.url]" lines="none"
                    detail="false">
            <ion-icon slot="start"
                      [ios]="p.icon + '-outline'"
                      [md]="p.icon + '-sharp'"></ion-icon>
            <ion-label>{{ p.title }}</ion-label>
          </ion-item>
        </ion-menu-toggle>
      </ion-list>
    </ion-content>

    <ion-footer>
      <ion-list>
        <ion-list-header>Settings</ion-list-header>
        <ion-item>
          <ion-label>Allow messages</ion-label>
          <ion-checkbox [(ngModel)]="settings.notifications"
                        (ionChange)="updateSettings()">
          </ion-checkbox>
        </ion-item>
      </ion-list>
    </ion-footer>

  </ion-menu>
  <ion-router-outlet id="main-content"></ion-router-outlet>
</ion-split-pane>
</ion-app>
```

In the new footer area we define a list with a header entry and initially one single item. Within the item we have two elements: a label `'Allow messages'` and a Checkbox component.

Let's have a closer look at the Checkbox. The line of code

```
[(ngModel)]="settings.notifications"
```

means: Bind the content (value) of the Checkbox to the pages' `settings.notifications`. The outer brackets represent the binding from *source-to-view* and the inner parentheses from *view-to-source*. It's Angular's syntax for two-way data binding. We'll see it in action later.

The other line of code

```
(ionChange)="updateSettings()"
```

means: If the user changes the value of the Checkbox, call the `updateSettings()` method on our page.

Finally we have to do a last thing. We have to import `FormsModule` into the `app.module.ts`. If we don't do that we run into an error, because without this module we wouldn't be able to use `[(ngModel)]` for data binding.

Note: In every *page* component this module is already imported.

So let's do it:

```
import { NgModule } from '@angular/core';
import { BrowserModule } from '@angular/platform-browser';
import { RouteReuseStrategy } from '@angular/router';

import { IonicModule, IonicRouteStrategy }
  from '@ionic/angular';
import { SplashScreen }
  from '@ionic-native/splash-screen/ngx';
import { StatusBar } from '@ionic-native/status-bar/ngx';

import { AppComponent } from './app.component';
import { AppRoutingModule } from './app-routing.module';
import { HttpClientModule } from '@angular/common/http';
import { IonicStorageModule } from '@ionic/storage';

import { FormsModule } from '@angular/forms';

@NgModule({
  declarations: [AppComponent],
  entryComponents: [],
  imports: [
    BrowserModule,
    IonicModule.forRoot(),
```

```
    AppRoutingModule,
    HttpClientModule,
    IonicStorageModule.forRoot(),
    FormsModule
  ],
  providers: [
    StatusBar,
    SplashScreen,
    { provide: RouteReuseStrategy, useClass: IonicRouteStrate-
gy }
  ],
  bootstrap: [AppComponent]
})
export class AppModule {}
```

Now let's start our app and see the Checkbox (and console) in action:

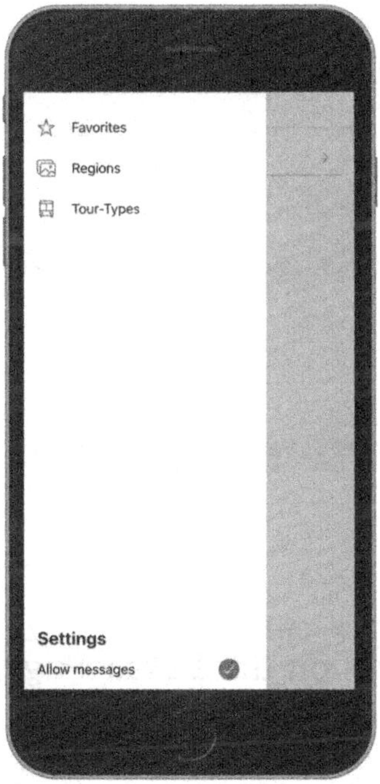

More about Checkboxes you can find here:

- https://ionicframework.com/docs/api/checkbox

6.8 Chip

Chips represent complex entities in small blocks, such as a contact. A Chip can contain several different elements such as avatars, text, and icons.

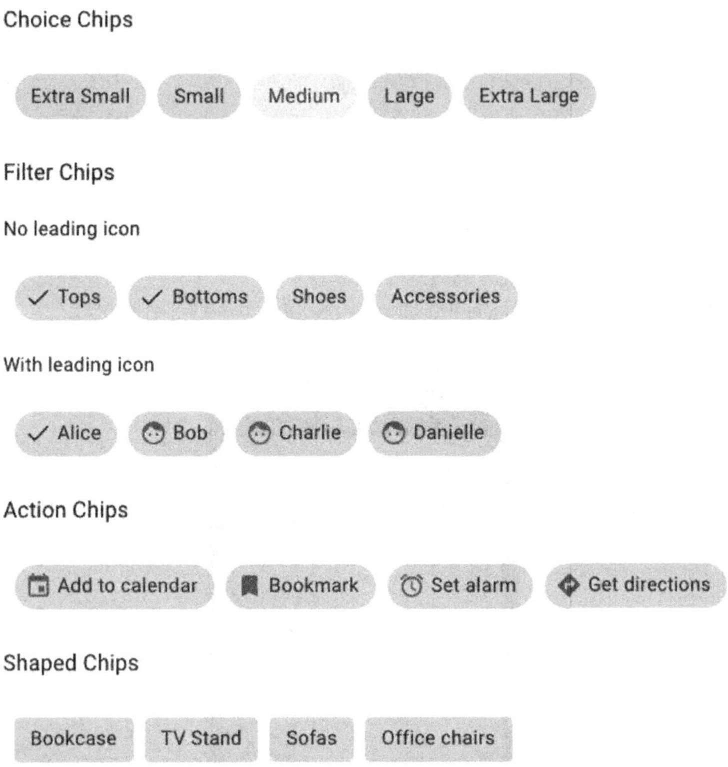

Detailed information on the DetailsPage

Let's add a few information Chips on the `details.page.html`:

```
<ion-header>
  <ion-toolbar>
    <ion-buttons slot="start">
      <ion-back-button></ion-back-button>
    </ion-buttons>
```

```
    <ion-title>Tour Details</ion-title>
  </ion-toolbar>
</ion-header>

<ion-content class="ion-padding">
  <ion-card>
    <ion-card-header>
      <ion-card-subtitle>{{tourtype}} / {{region}}</ion-card-sub-
title>
      <ion-card-title>{{tour.Title}}</ion-card-title>
    </ion-card-header>
    <ion-card-content>
      {{tour.Description}}
      <hr />
      <ion-chip>
        <ion-icon name="stopwatch"></ion-icon>
        <ion-label>{{tour.Duration}} min</ion-label>
      </ion-chip>
      <ion-chip>
        <ion-label>up to {{tour.MaxPersons}}</ion-label>
        <ion-icon name="people"></ion-icon>
      </ion-chip>
      <ion-chip>
        <ion-icon name="language"></ion-icon>
        <ion-label>{{tour.PriceG}} &euro; (German)</ion-label>
      </ion-chip>
      <ion-chip>
        <ion-icon name="globe"></ion-icon>
        <ion-label>
          {{tour.PriceF}} &euro; (Other language)
        </ion-label>
      </ion-chip>
    </ion-card-content>
  </ion-card>
</ion-content>

<ion-footer class="ion-padding">
  <ion-button expand="block" (click)="presentActionSheet()">
    Options
  </ion-button>
</ion-footer>
```

As you can see, I always combine an icon with a label in the Chips. The result looks like this:

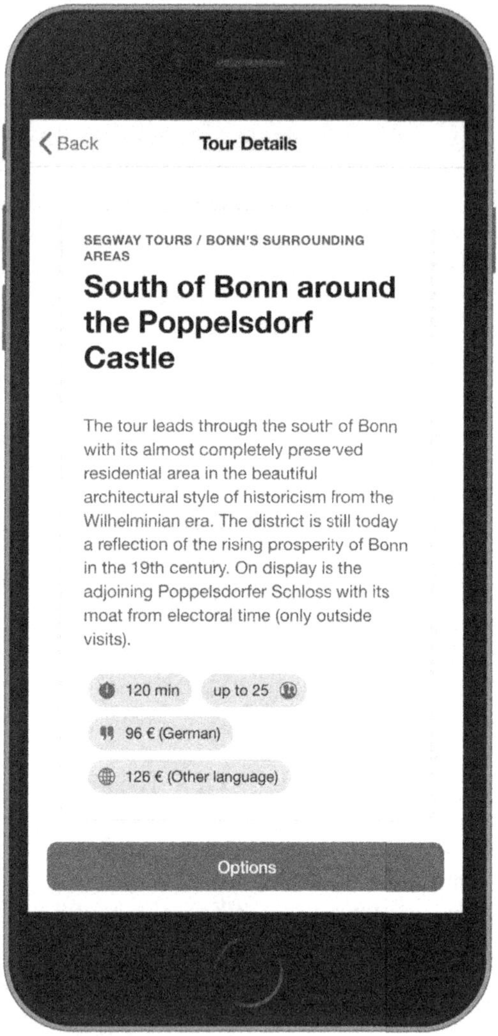

More about Chips you can find here:

► https://ionicframework.com/docs/api/chip

6.9 Date & Time Pickers

Datetimes present a picker interface from the bottom of a page, making it easy for users to select dates and times. The picker displays scrollable columns that can be used to individually select years, months, days, hours and minute values. Datetimes are similar to the native `input` elements of type `datetime-local`, however, Ionic's Datetime component makes it easy to display the date and time in a preferred format, and manage the datetime values.

A tour request with date and time

We want to use two Picker components, one for date and one for time, to let the user request a tour for his/her desired schedule and time.

We begin in `request.page.ts`:

```
import { Component, OnInit } from '@angular/core';

@Component({
  selector: 'app-request',
  templateUrl: './request.page.html',
  styleUrls: ['./request.page.scss'],
})
export class RequestPage implements OnInit {

  constructor() { }

  request: any = {};
  day_after_tomorrow: string;
  two_years_later: string;

  ngOnInit() {

    // start date - at the earliest the day after tomorrow
    let today = new Date();
    let day_after_tomorrow
      = new Date(today.getTime() + 1000*60*60*24*2);
    this.day_after_tomorrow
      = day_after_tomorrow.toISOString().slice(0, 10);
```

```
// end date - at the latest in two years
    let two_years_later
      = new Date(day_after_tomorrow.getTime()
        + 1000*60*60*24*365*2);
    this.two_years_later = two_years_later.toISOString()
                                             .slice(0, 10);

  }

  // user clicked 'Send request'
  send() {
    console.log('Requested tour for',
                this.request.Date,
                this.request.Time);
  }

}
```

We declare three variables: `request` of type `any` (instantiated as empty object), and the strings `day_after_tomorrow` and `two_years_later`:

```
request: any = {};
day_after_tomorrow: string;
two_years_later: string;
```

In `ngOnInit()`, the start and end dates for our Datetime component are calculated. Here, we assume the following consideration: A tour request should be possible from the point of view of our imaginary tourism company at the earliest for the day after tomorrow and a maximum of two years in advance.

Example: If the user asks for a tour on January 1st 2020, our calculation should determine January 3rd 2020 (issued as "2020-01-03") as the earliest and January 3rd 2022 (issued as "2022-01-03") as latest inquiry date.

The starting value is today's date:

```
let today = new Date();
```

The day after tomorrow (start date) we calculate with:

```
let day_after_tomorrow
  = new Date(today.getTime() + 1000*60*60*24*2);
```

We're using the `getTime()` function and add a multiplication with milliseconds, seconds, minutes, hours, and two days.

Since the Datetime component expects calendar data in ISO 8601 format, we format it with `toISOString()` and assign it to the string variable `this.day_after_tomorrow`. We're not interested in the time, so we use `slice(0,10)` to shorten the string to the first 10 digits:

```
this.day_after_tomorrow
  = day_after_tomorrow.toISOString().slice(0, 10);
```

In the same manner we calculate a date (end date) two years later and use the previously calculated `day_after_tomorrow`:

```
let two_years_later
  = new Date(day_after_tomorrow.getTime()
    + 1000*60*60*24*365*2);
```

Again, we convert the whole thing into an ISO string and assign the (shortened) result to the string variable `this.two_years_later`:

```
this.two_years_later = two_years_later.toISOString()
                                      .slice(0, 10);
```

Now we design the UI in `request.page.html`:

```
<ion-header>
  <ion-toolbar>
      <ion-buttons slot="start">
          <ion-back-button></ion-back-button>
        </ion-buttons>
    <ion-title>Request</ion-title>
  </ion-toolbar>
</ion-header>

<ion-content class="ion-padding">
  <ion-list>

   <!-- Date -->
   <ion-item>
    <ion-label>Date</ion-label>
    <ion-datetime [(ngModel)]="request.Date"
                  min="{{day_after_tomorrow}}"
                  max="{{two_years_later}}"
```

```
                 display-format="DDD, MMMM DD YYYY"
                 picker-format="MMMM DD YYYY"
                 placeholder=
                   "Please choose your desired date!">
    </ion-datetime>
   </ion-item>

   <!-- Time -->
   <ion-item>
    <ion-label>Time</ion-label>
    <ion-datetime [(ngModel)]="request.Time"
                 hourValues="9,10,11,12,13,14,15,16,17"
                 minuteValues="0,15,30,45"
                 display-format="hh:mm A"
                 picker-format="h mm"
                 placeholder=
                   "Please choose your desired time!">
    </ion-datetime>
   </ion-item>
  </ion-list>
</ion-content>

<ion-footer class="ion-padding">
    <ion-button expand="block"
               routerLink="/favorites"
               routerDirection="root">
      Back to Favorites
    </ion-button>
    <ion-button expand="block" (click)="send()">
      Send request
    </ion-button>
</ion-footer>
```

Within the content area we define a list with two list items. Each list item contains a label and a datetime component, one for the *date* and one for the *time*.

Let's have a look at the first line of code of the datetime component for the date:

```
<ion-datetime [(ngModel)]="request.Date"
```

This line of code binds the selected date value of the component via `[(ngModel)]` (Angular's two-way data binding) to the property `Date` of our page's `request` object. With

```
min="{{day_after_tomorrow}}"
```

we assign the calculated start date to the component. With

```
max="{{two_years_later}}"
```

we assign the calculated end date to the component. With

```
display-format="DDD, MMMM DD YYYY"
```

we determine how the date should be formatted and displayed after leaving the input interface, whereas

```
picker-format="MMMM DD YYYY"
```

determines which columns should be shown in the interface, the order of the columns, and which format to use within each column.

A list with all valid formatting expressions you can find in the link below.

With

```
placeholder="Please choose your desired date!"
```

we determine the text to display when there's no date selected yet.

Now let's have a look at the Datetime component for the time:

```
<ion-datetime [(ngModel)]="request.Time"
```

binds the selected time value of the component via `[(ngModel)]` to the property `Time` of our page's `request` object. With

```
hourValues="9,10,11,12,13,14,15,16,17"
```

we control exactly which hours to display, the `hourValues` input can take a number, an array of numbers, or a string of comma separated numbers.

With

```
MinuteValues="0,15,30,45"
```

we control exactly which minutes to display, the `minuteValues` input can take a number, an array of numbers, or a string of comma separated numbers.

Here the user can only select every 15 minutes. With

```
display-format="hh:mm A"
```

we determine how the time should be formatted and displayed after leaving the input interface, whereas

```
picker-format="h mm"
```

determines which columns should be shown in the interface, the order of the columns, and which format to use within each column.

A list with all valid formatting expressions you can find in the link below.

With

```
placeholder="Please choose your desired time!"
```

we determine the text to display when there's no time selected yet.

Here is our Datetime component in action:

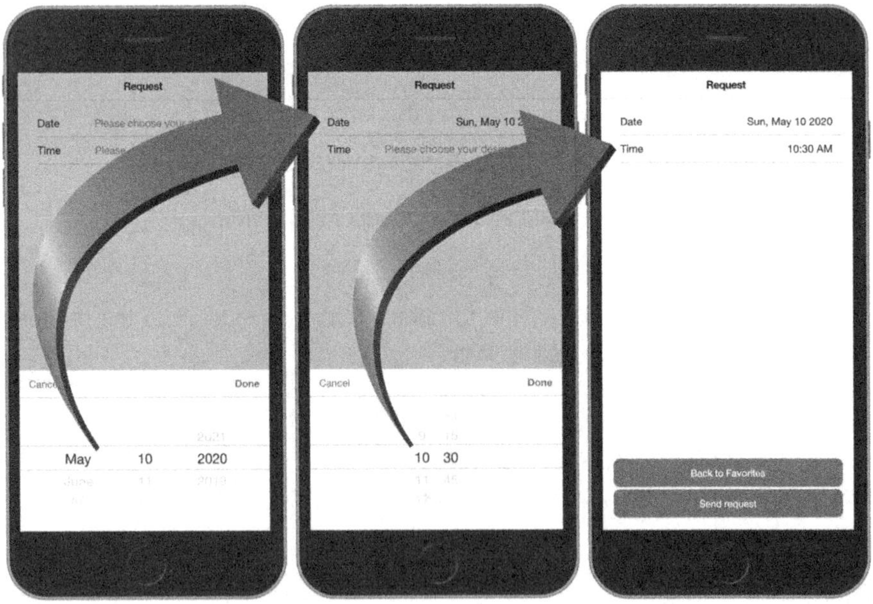

More about Date and Time Pickers as well as about an universal Picker component you can find here:

- https://ionicframework.com/docs/api/datetime
- https://ionicframework.com/docs/api/picker

If you need time-consuming date functions, I can recommend the JavaScript library *moment.js*:

- https://momentjs.com/

6.10 Floating Action Button

Floating Action Buttons (FABs) represent the primary action in an application. By default, they have a circular shape. When pressed, the button may open more related actions. As the name suggests, FABs generally float over the content in a fixed position. This isn't achieved exclusively by using an `<ion-fab-button>FAB</ion-fab-button>`. They need to be wrapped with an `<ion-fab>` component in order to be fixed over the content.

If the FAB button isn't wrapped with `<ion-fab>`, it will scroll with the content. FAB buttons have a default size, a mini size and can accept different colors.

Social media buttons

With a FAB we can easily create a group of social media buttons under the hood of a single "share" button.

First, let's start in `details.page.ts`:

```
import { Component, OnInit } from '@angular/core';
import { ActivatedRoute } from '@angular/router';
import { BobToursService }
         from 'src/app/services/bob-tours.service';
import { FavoritesService }
         from 'src/app/services/favorites.service';
import { ActionSheetController, AlertController }
         from '@ionic/angular';
import _ from 'lodash';

@Component({
  selector: 'app-details',
  templateUrl: './details.page.html',
  styleUrls: ['./details.page.scss'],
})
export class DetailsPage implements OnInit {

  tour = null;
  isFavorite: boolean;

  region: string;
```

```
  tourtype: string;

  showSocial: boolean;

  constructor(private activatedRoute: ActivatedRoute,
              public btService: BobToursService,
              public favService: FavoritesService,
              private actionSheetCtrl: ActionSheetController,
              private alertCtrl: AlertController) { }

  ngOnInit() {
    ...
  }

  async presentActionSheet() {
    ...
  }

  async presentAlert() {
    ...
  }

  // user clicked share button
  toggleSocial() {
    this.showSocial = !this.showSocial;
  }

  // user clicked one of the social app buttons
  openSocial(app) {
    console.log('User wants to share this tour via '
             + app + '!');
  }

}
```

We declare a boolean variable `showSocial` which we switch in the method `toggle-Social()` between `true` and `false`. We'll see what it's good for.

Another method `openSocial()` is initially only for the output of a text in the console to show what social app has been chosen.

Next, in `details.page.html` we add:

```
<ion-header>
  <ion-toolbar>
    <ion-buttons slot="start">
      <ion-back-button></ion-back-button>
    </ion-buttons>
    <ion-title>Tour Details</ion-title>
  </ion-toolbar>
</ion-header>

<ion-content class="ion-padding">
  ...
</ion-content>

<ion-footer class="ion-padding" style="height: 80px;">
  <ion-button (click)="presentActionSheet()"
             *ngIf="!showSocial">
    Options
  </ion-button>
  <!-- A (FAB) share button -->
  <ion-fab vertical="bottom" horizontal="end" slot="fixed"
          (click)="toggleSocial()">
      <ion-fab-button>
        <ion-icon name="share-social"></ion-icon>
      </ion-fab-button>
      <ion-fab-list side="start">
        <ion-fab-button (click)="openSocial('facebook')">
            <ion-icon name="logo-facebook"></ion-icon>
        </ion-fab-button>
        <ion-fab-button (click)="openSocial('instagram')">
          <ion-icon name="logo-instagram"></ion-icon>
        </ion-fab-button>
        <ion-fab-button (click)="openSocial('twitter')">
          <ion-icon name="logo-twitter"></ion-icon>
        </ion-fab-button>
        <ion-fab-button (click)="openSocial('whatsapp')">
          <ion-icon name="logo-whatsapp"></ion-icon>
        </ion-fab-button>
      </ion-fab-list>
  </ion-fab>
</ion-footer>
```

In the footer area of the page we do a little styling:

```
style="height: 80px;"
```

Our “Options” button for calling the ActionSheet (see “6.2 Action Sheet” on page 153) is now controlled by

```
*ngIf="!showSocial"
```

That means: If the value of `showSocial` is `false`, show the “Options” button, otherwise hide it. As you will soon see, our FAB button needs space to spread out. It gets this space by hiding the ”Options” buttons in the manner just described.

With

```
<ion-fab vertical="bottom" horizontal="end" slot="fixed"
        (click)="toggleSocial()">
```

we place a FAB button on the right end in the footer area. We add a click handler to call to our `toggleSocial()` method that controls the `toogleSocial` variable.

Within `ion-fab` as container we define some `ion-fab-button` elements with icons and click handlers to call our `openSocial()` method and pass different app names. Have a look at the console output in the Chrome DevTools to get them.

The FAB button in action - collapsed and expanded:

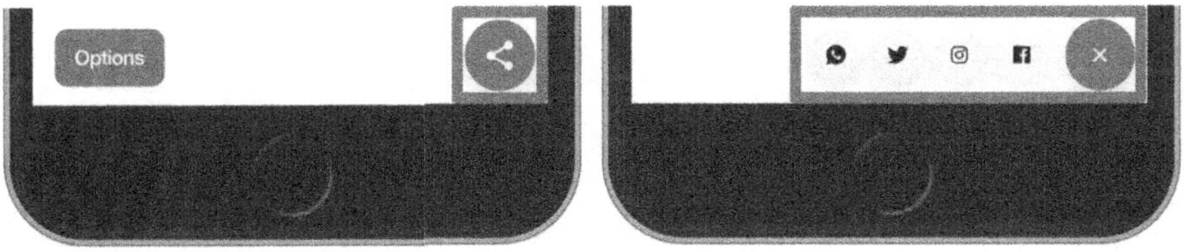

More about FABs you can find here:

- https://ionicframework.com/docs/api/fab
- https://ionicframework.com/docs/api/fab-list

6.11 Grid

Ionic's Grid system is a powerful mobile-first system for building custom layouts and based on the Flexible Box Layout Module (short: Flexbox). Flexbox was designed as a one-dimensional layout model, and as a method that could offer space distribution between items in an interface and powerful alignment capabilities. When I describe Flexbox as being one dimensional I'm describing the fact that Flexbox deals with layout in one dimension at a time – either as a *row* or as a *column*. This can be contrasted with the two-dimensional model of CSS Grid Layout, which controls columns and rows together.

Grid is composed of three units – a grid, row(s) and column(s). Columns will expand to fill the row, and will resize to fit additional columns. It is based on a 12 column layout with different breakpoints based on the screen size. The number of columns can be customized using CSS.

Optimize the DetailsPage layout

In our app we can optimize the content layout of the `DetailsPage` with a Grid component. Let's open `details.page.html` and rearrange our Chips in a responsive Grid:

```
<ion-header>
  ...
</ion-header>

<ion-content class="ion-padding">
  <ion-card>
    <ion-card-header>
      <ion-card-subtitle>{{tourtype}} / {{region}}</ion-card-
subtitle>
      <ion-card-title>{{tour.Title}}</ion-card-title>
    </ion-card-header>
    <ion-card-content>
      {{tour.Description}}
      <hr />
      <ion-grid no-padding>
        <ion-row style="margin-left: -12px;">
          <ion-col size-xs="12" size-md="auto">
            <ion-chip>
```

```
        <ion-icon name="stopwatch"></ion-icon>
        <ion-label>{{tour.Duration}} min</ion-label>
      </ion-chip>
    </ion-col>
    <ion-col size-xs="12" size-md="auto">
      <ion-chip>
        <ion-label>up to {{tour.MaxPersons}}</ion-label>
        <ion-icon name="people"></ion-icon>
      </ion-chip>
    </ion-col>
    <ion-col size-xs="12" size-md="auto">
      <ion-chip>
        <ion-icon name="language"></ion-icon>
        <ion-label>
          {{tour.PriceG}} &euro; (German)
        </ion-label>
      </ion-chip>
    </ion-col>
    <ion-col size-xs="12" size-md="auto">
      <ion-chip>
        <ion-icon name="globe"></ion-icon>
        <ion-label>
          {{tour.PriceF}} &euro; (Other language)
        </ion-label>
      </ion-chip>
    </ion-col>
  </ion-row>
 </ion-grid>
</ion-card-content>
</ion-card>
</ion-content>

<ion-footer padding style="height: 80px;">
  ...
</ion-footer>
```

We define a Grid with one row and four columns. Its task is, depending on the available display width, to arrange the chips either in one or more rows or, if it is particularly narrow, among themselves.

How do we achieve this?

Take a closer look at the attributes of a single column:

```
<ion-col size-xs="12" size-md="auto">
```

The first attribute `size-xs="12"` specifies that with extra small (`xs`) display size, one column will get the full width of 12 units.

The second attribute `size-md="auto"` specifies that with middle (`md`) display size, one column will get an automatic width.

The default breakpoints are for `xs` a `min-width` of `0px` and for `md` a `min-width` of `768px`. In other words: If the display has a width up to 767px, each chip gets a full 12-unit-wide column, so each Chip stands in its own "row" (visually speaking, not technical). If the display has a width greater than 767px, each column gets an automatic width, i.e. each becomes as wide as the respective embedded Chip needs as space.

You'll find the information for these and all other breakpoints in the Ionic documentation (3rd link below).

Now, let's see our optimized DetailsPage in action:

The left picture shows our app on an iPhone screen. In portrait mode my iPhone 6 has a width of 414px, so the `xs` directive makes sure that each Chip is displayed in a full width column (with 12 units).

The right picture shows our app on an iPad screen. In portrait mode it has a width of 768px – exact the width of the `md` breakpoint, so it arranges all Chips in one single row, because every column uses auto-width and everything together fits in a single row.

More about responsive Grids you can find here:

- https://ionicframework.com/docs/api/grid
- https://ionicframework.com/docs/layout/grid
- https://ionicframework.com/docs/layout/css-utilities#ionic-breakpoints

6.12 Icons

Pictures say more than a thousand words. We see a symbol and immediately understand what is meant. That's why there is no app that wants to be operated intuitively, comes over to icons.

Ionic has more than 1.100 (!) Icons that can be addressed via a `name` attribute. Ionic calls them *Ionicons* (an acronym for *Ionic icons*, of course).

The Ionicons are available in three versions: `Outline`, `Filled`, `Sharp`. You can choose a version by its `name`, for example:

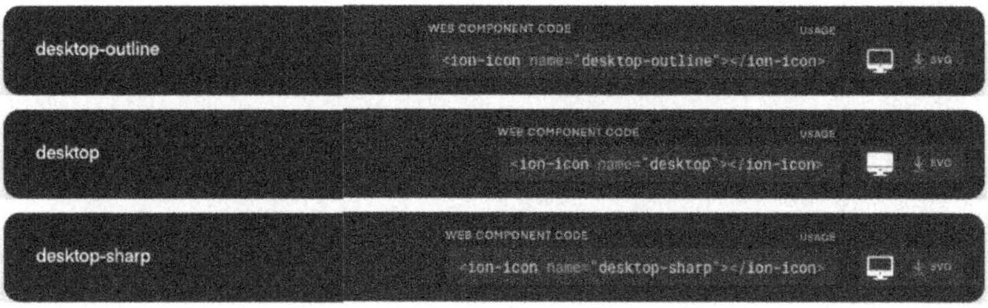

Icons for RegionsPage

We want to enrich the list views for `Regions` and `Tour-Types` with icons. Let's start with the `Regions` list. "Quite by accident", I already prepared something in the data objects: Each object has the property `Icon`. This contains - who would have thought this - the name of an Ionicon, like `"home"`:

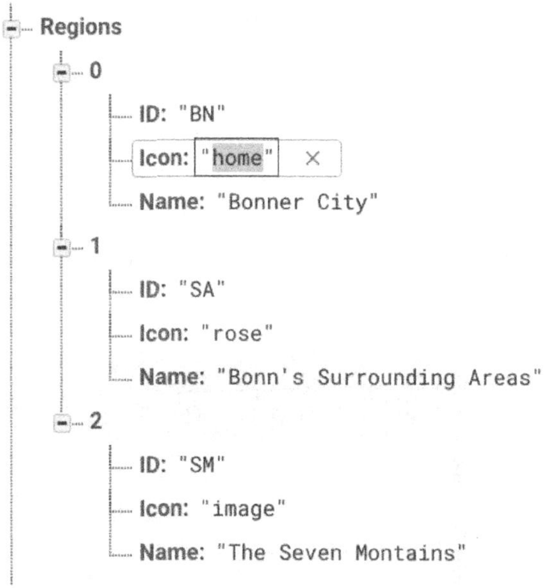

With this data, it's easy to add icons to our list in `regions.page.html`:

```
<ion-header>
  <ion-toolbar>
    <ion-buttons slot="start">
      <ion-menu-button></ion-menu-button>
    </ion-buttons>
    <ion-title>Regions</ion-title>
  </ion-toolbar>
</ion-header>

<ion-content class="ion-padding">
  <ion-list>
    <ion-item *ngFor="let region of regions"
              [routerLink]="['/list',
                             { Category: 'Region',
                               ID: region.ID,
                               Name: region.Name } ]"
              routerDirection="forward">
      <ion-icon name="{{region.Icon}}"
                slot="start"></ion-icon>
      {{region.Name}}
      <ion-badge slot="end">{{region.Count}}</ion-badge>
    </ion-item>
  </ion-list>
</ion-content>
```

The use of the Ionicon component is very simple: Using the `Name` property, we pass the name from the respective region object via Code Projection. Via the `slot` attribute we determine that the icon should be displayed at the `start` (beginning) of a list entry. And that's the optical result:

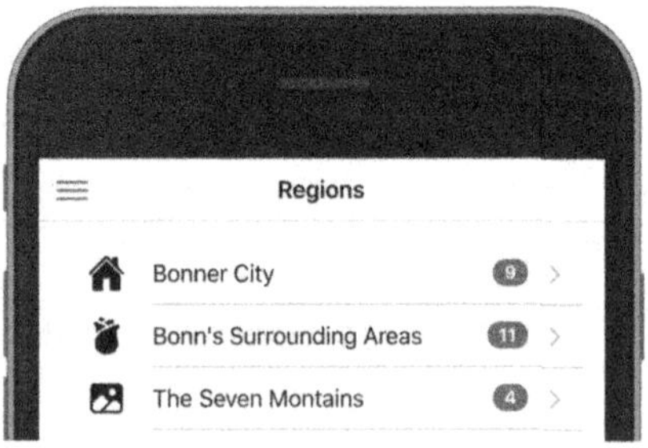

Icons for TourTypesPage

Also for the tour types I've stored icon information in the database:

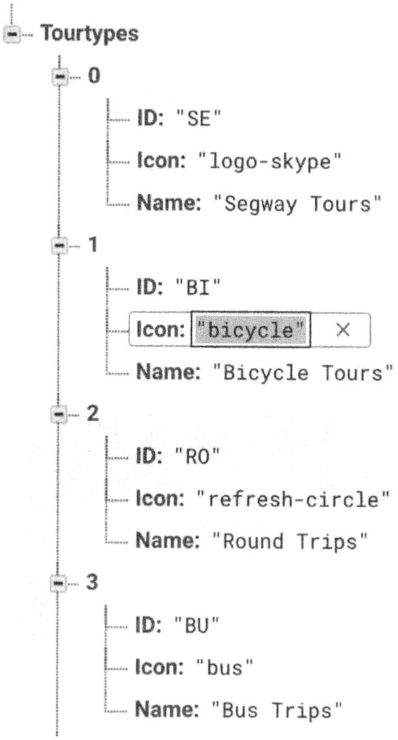

Let's spend `tour-types.page.html` a few icons in the same manner:

```
<ion-header>
  <ion-toolbar>
    <ion-buttons slot="start">
      <ion-menu-button></ion-menu-button>
    </ion-buttons>
    <ion-title>Tour-Types</ion-title>
  </ion-toolbar>
</ion-header>

<ion-content class="ion-padding">
  <ion-list>
```

```
    <ion-item *ngFor="let tourtype of tourtypes"
              [routerLink]="['/list',
                             { Category: 'Tourtype',
                               ID: tourtype.ID,
                               Name: tourtype.Name } ]"
              routerDirection="forward">
      <ion-icon name="{{tourtype.Icon}}"
                slot="start"></ion-icon>
      {{tourtype.Name}}
      <ion-badge slot="end">{{tourtype.Count}}</ion-badge>
    </ion-item>
  </ion-list>
</ion-content>
```

And here the TourTypesPage with Ionicons:

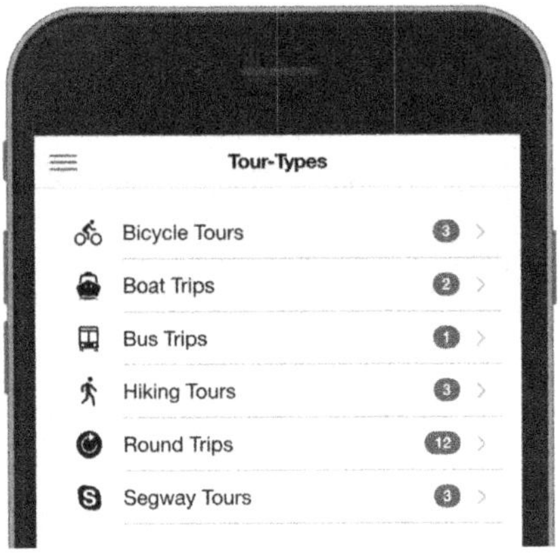

So much for now to icons. In chapter 7, "Theming, Styling, Customizing" (starting on page 331), we'll tune our icons a little bit more.

All Ionicons you can find here:

► https://ionicons.com/

6.13 Images

What would an app be without pictures or photos? I'm sure you've been waiting for this topic, right?

Of course, Ionic makes it easy to get pictures into our app. For this we can use the standard HTML tag `img` or the new Ionic component `ion-img`. The `ion-img` component is a tag that will lazily load an image when ever the tag is in the viewport. This is extremely useful when generating a large list as images are only loaded when they're visible.

DetailsPage with nice pictures

In our app, it makes sense to include a picture of each tour on the `Details` page.

So, let's complete the `details.page.html`:

```
<ion-header>
  ...
</ion-header>

<ion-content class="ion-padding">
  <ion-card>
    <ion-card-header>
      <ion-card-subtitle>
        {{tourtype}} / {{region}}
      </ion-card-subtitle>
      <ion-card-title>{{tour.Title}}</ion-card-title>
    </ion-card-header>
    <ion-card-content>
      <ion-img src="https://ionic.andreas-dormann.de/img/big/
               {{tour.Image}}"></ion-img>
      <hr />
      {{tour.Description}}
      <hr />
      <ion-grid no-padding>
        ...
      </ion-grid>
    </ion-card-content>
  </ion-card>
</ion-content>
```

```
<ion-footer padding style="height: 80px;">
  ...
</ion-footer>
```

The `ion-img` component has a `src` attribute to which we pass the path to our online image. The name of the respective image file is obtained from the loaded database data via Code Projection.

Our DetailsPage with pictures:

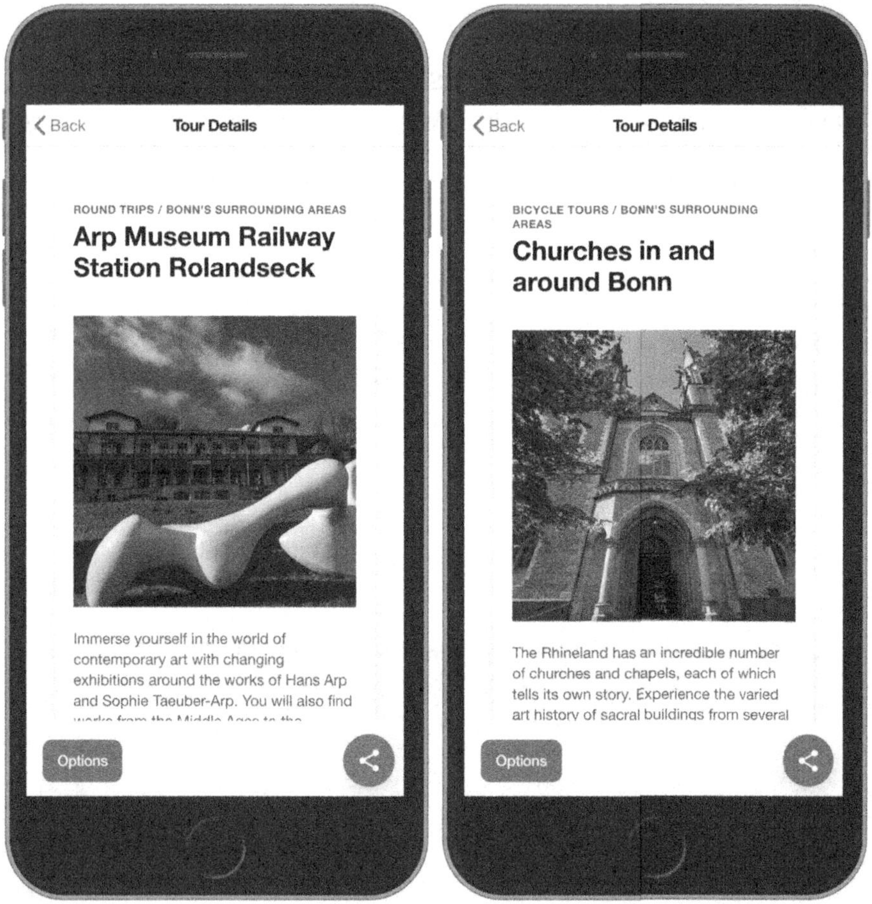

Hint: Since Ionic 4.2 it is possible to use `ion-img` combined with the `ionError` event. The `ionError` event is emitted when an image fails to load. This can be useful to load default images in case the specified image isn't found.

In the HTML file you can write:

```
<ion-img src="/assets/goodcop.jpg"
         (ionError)="loadDefault($event)"></ion-img>
<ion-img src="/assets/badcop.jpg"
         (ionError)="loadDefault($event)"></ion-img>
```

And in the corresponding ts file you can code:

```
loadDefault(event) {
    event.target.src = '/assets/img/default.png';
}
```

More about Images and related topics you can find here:

- https://ionicframework.com/docs/api/avatar
- https://ionicframework.com/docs/api/img
- https://ionicframework.com/docs/api/thumbnail

6.14 Input

Input components are important for collecting and managing user input. They should follow platform-specific guidelines and be intuitive to use. Ionic provides all the necessary ingredients for this.

The Input component in Ionic is a wrapper to the HTML input element with custom styling and additional functionality. It accepts most of the same properties as the HTML input, but works great on desktop devices and integrates with the keyboard on mobile devices.

It is meant for text `type` inputs only, such as `"text"`, `"password"`, `"email"`, `"number"`, `"search"`, `"tel"`, and `"url"`. It supports all standard text input events including keyup, keydown, keypress, and more.

Complete our request form

Let's add a few input components to `request.page.html`:

```
<ion-header>
  <ion-toolbar>
      <ion-buttons slot="start">
          <ion-back-button></ion-back-button>
        </ion-buttons>
    <ion-title>Request</ion-title>
  </ion-toolbar>
</ion-header>

<ion-content class="ion-padding">
  <ion-list>
   <!-- Date -->
   <ion-item>
    <ion-label>Date</ion-label>
    <ion-datetime [(ngModel)]="request.Date"
                  min="{{day_after_tomorrow}}"
                  max="{{two_years_later}}"
                  display-format="DDD, MMMM DD YYYY"
                  picker-format="MMMM DD YYYY"
                  placeholder="Choose your desired date!">
    </ion-datetime>
   </ion-item>
```

```
    <!-- Time -->
    <ion-item>
     <ion-label>Time (15 min steps)</ion-label>
     <ion-datetime [(ngModel)]="request.Time"
                   hourValues="9,10,11,12,13,14,15,16,17"
                   minuteValues="0,15,30,45"
                   display-format="hh:mm A"
                   picker-format="h mm"
                   placeholder="Choose your desired time!">
     </ion-datetime>
    <ion-item>
    <!-- First name -->
    <ion-item>
      <ion-label>First name</ion-label>
      <ion-input type="text" [(ngModel)]="request.FirstName">
      </ion-input>
    </ion-item>
    <!-- Last name -->
    <ion-item>
      <ion-label>Last name</ion-label>
      <ion-input type="text" [(ngModel)]="request.LastName">
      </ion-input>
    </ion-item>
    <!-- Email -->
    <ion-item>
      <ion-label>Email</ion-label>
      <ion-input type="email" [(ngModel)]="request.Email">
      </ion-input>
    </ion-item>
  </ion-list>
</ion-content>

<ion-footer class="ion-padding">
    <ion-button expand="block"
                routerLink="/favorites"
                routerDirection="root">
      Back to Favorites
    </ion-button>
    <ion-button expand="block" (click)="send()">
      Send request
    </ion-button>
</ion-footer>
```

In each `ion-item` tag we combine a label with an Input component. Nothing fancy.

Have a look at the Email Input. There we use `type="email"`. That means on a mobile device a different virtual keyboard is shown.

Again, we bind the user data via `[(ngModel)]` directives to our request object: `FirstName`, `LastName` and `Email`.

These bound data can be used in `request.page.ts` as follows:

```
import { Component, OnInit } from '@angular/core';

...

export class RequestPage implements OnInit {

  constructor() { }

  ...

  ngOnInit() {
    ...
  }

  // user clicked 'Send request'
  send() {

    console.log('Requested tour for',
                this.request.Date,
                this.request.Time);

    console.log('by', this.request.FirstName,
                      this.request.LastName,
                      this.request.Email);
  }
}
```

That's it for the moment.

In the context of user inputs it's always a good idea to think a little about form validation. We discuss that topic in an own chapter (see 7 "Form validation" on page 307).

Our updated RequestPage with First name, Last name and Email Inputs:

More about Input – and its relative: TextArea – you can find here:

- https://ionicframework.com/docs/api/input
- https://ionicframework.com/docs/api/textarea

6.15 List

Lists are used to replace information in a line. They represent a central design component in many apps - as in our app.

Lists are made up of multiple rows of items which can contain text, buttons, toggles, icons, thumbnails, and much more. Lists generally contain items with similar data content, such as images and text.

Lists support several interactions including swiping items to reveal options, dragging to reorder items within the list, and deleting items.

Make the list pretty

We can make the purely textual listing of tour titles more appealing by adding thumbnails, i.e. small photos. We can also add another info such as the duration of a tour to the List. The whole thing is easy to implement in Ionic again.

Let's extend the list of `list.page.html`:

```
<ion-header>
  <ion-toolbar>
    <ion-buttons slot="start">
      <ion-back-button></ion-back-button>
    </ion-buttons>
    <ion-title>{{selection.Name}}</ion-title>
  </ion-toolbar>
</ion-header>

<ion-content class="ion-padding">
  <ion-list>
    <ion-item *ngFor="let tour of tours"
              [routerLink]="'/details/' + tour.ID"
              routerDirection="forward">
      <ion-thumbnail slot="start">
        <img src="https://ionic.andreas-dormann.de/img/small/
                {{tour.Image}}">
      </ion-thumbnail>
      <ion-label>
        <h2 class="ion-text-wrap">{{tour.Title}}</h2>
        <p>Duration: {{tour.Duration}} min</p>
      </ion-label>
```

```
    </ion-item>
  </ion-list>
</ion-content>
```

With the code lines

```
<ion-thumbnail slot="start">
...
</ion-thumbnail>
```

we added an `ion-thumbnail` tag at the start slot of each list item. To show a picture within a thumbnail we need to embed an image:

```
<img src="https://ionic.andreas-dormann.de/img/small/
                {{tour.Image}}">
```

As source we use an absolute file path to the (online) picture in combination with the code injected variable `tour.Image`. It's the name of the image, for example `'Bonn.jpg'`, that comes from the tour data from our database.

Next, we extend an `ion-label` tag

```
<ion-label>
  <h2 class="ion-text-wrap">{{tour.Title}}</h2>
  <p>Duration: {{tour.Duration}} min</p>
</ion-label>
```

with a level 2 heading `h2` to display the `tour.Title` and a paragraph `p` to show the `tour.Duration`. Since the titles can sometimes be a bit longer, we also give the `h2` tag the class `"ion-text-wrap"`. So the text can be wrapped.

Here's the newly designed ListPage:

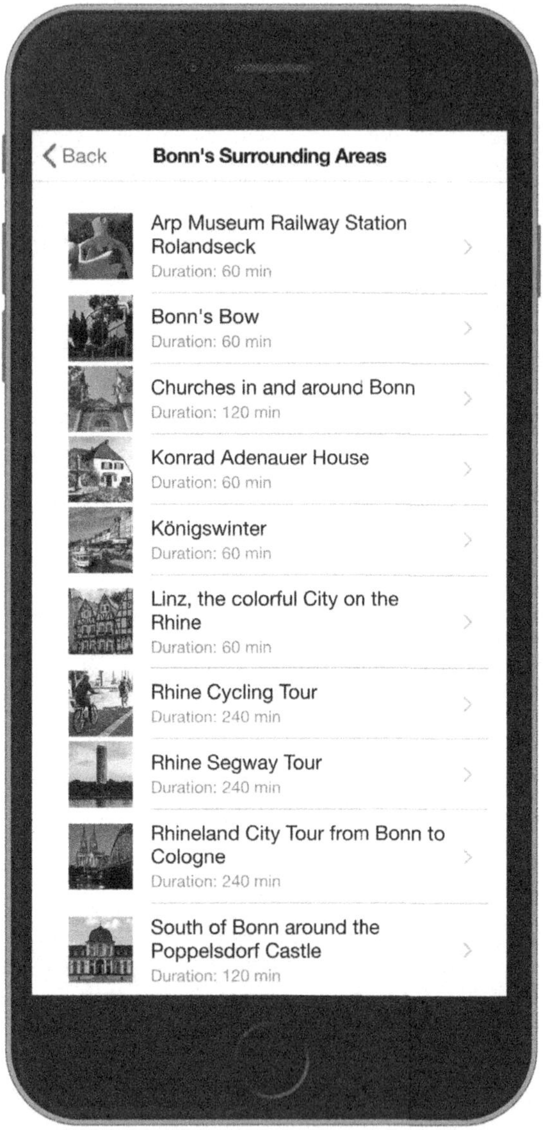

More structure in the request page

To give our request page a better structure inside its content area, we also extend the `request.page.html`:

```
<ion-header>
  ...
</ion-header>

<ion-content class="ion-padding">
  <ion-list>

    <!-- Schedule group -->
    <ion-item-group>
      <ion-item-divider>
          <ion-label>Desired schedule</ion-label>
      </ion-item-divider>
      <!-- Date -->
      <ion-item>
        <ion-label>Date</ion-label>
        <ion-datetime [(ngModel)]="request.Date"
                      min="{{day_after_tomorrow}}"
                      max="{{two_years_later}}"
                      display-format="DDD, MMMM DD YYYY"
                      picker-format="MMMM DD YYYY"
                      placeholder="Choose your desired date!">
        </ion-datetime>
      </ion-item>
      <!-- Time -->
      <ion-item>
        <ion-label>Time (15 min steps)</ion-label>
        <ion-datetime [(ngModel)]="request.Time"
                      hourValues="9,10,11,12,13,14,15,16,17"
                      minuteValues="0,15,30,45"
                      display-format="hh:mm A"
                      picker-format="h mm"
                      placeholder="Choose your desired time!">
        </ion-datetime>
      </ion-item>
    </ion-item-group>
```

```
<!-- Contact information group -->
    <ion-item-group>
      <ion-item-divider>
          <ion-label>Your contact information</ion-label>
      </ion-item-divider>
      <!-- First name -->
      <ion-item>
        <ion-label>First name</ion-label>
        <ion-input type="text" [(ngModel)]="request.FirstName">
        </ion-input>
      </ion-item>
      <!-- Last name -->
      <ion-item>
        <ion-label>Last name</ion-label>
        <ion-input type="text"
                   [(ngModel)]="request.LastName">
        </ion-input>
      </ion-item>
      <!-- Email -->
      <ion-item>
        <ion-label>Email</ion-label>
        <ion-input type="email" [(ngModel)]="request.Email">
        </ion-input>
      </ion-item>
    </ion-item-group>

  </ion-list>
</ion-content>

<ion-footer class="ion-padding">
    ...
</ion-footer>
```

With the addition of `ion-item-group` components in combination with `ion-item-divider` and `ion-label`, we are able to visually better structure the form areas.

As an alternative for the `ion-item-divider` tag you can try `ion-list-header`.

Here's our RequestPage with more structure (left: iOS style, right: Android style):

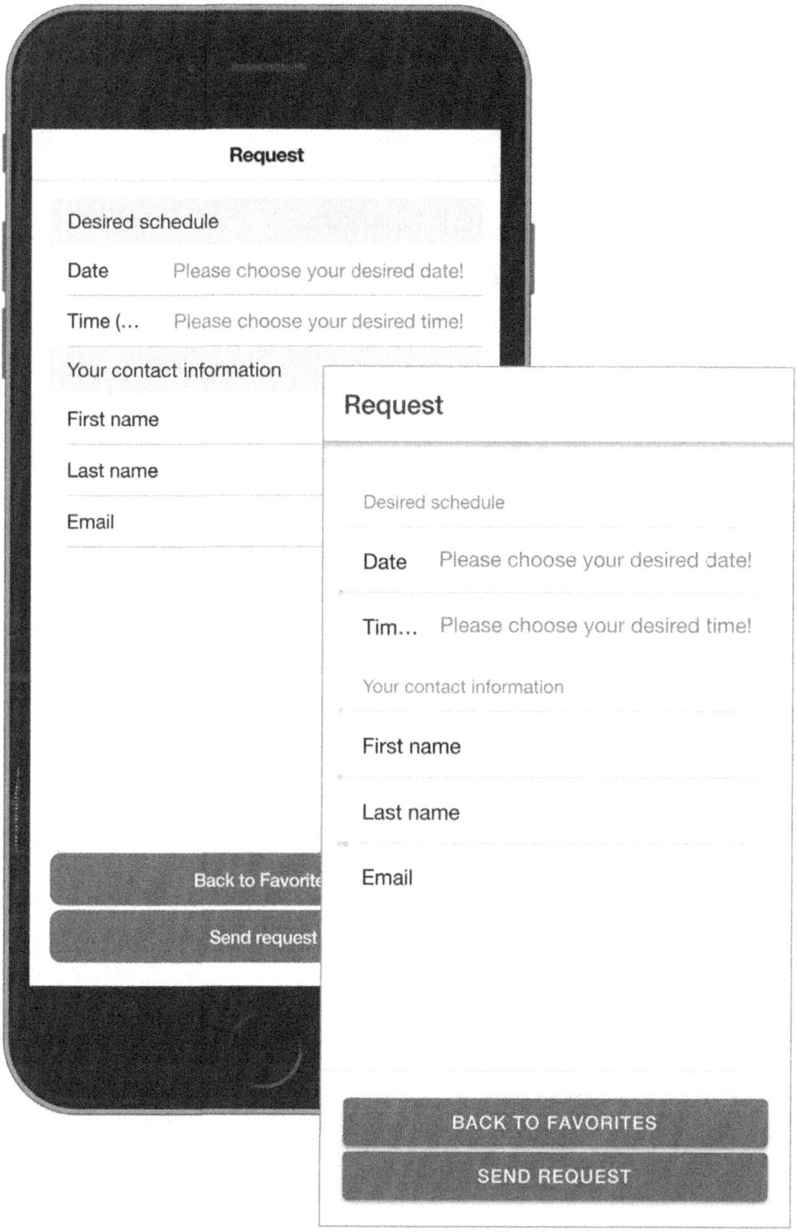

You can find more about Lists and related topics here:

- https://ionicframework.com/docs/api/list
- https://ionicframework.com/docs/api/avatar
- https://ionicframework.com/docs/api/item-divider
- https://ionicframework.com/docs/api/item-group
- https://ionicframework.com/docs/api/label
- https://ionicframework.com/docs/api/list-header
- https://ionicframework.com/docs/api/thumbnail

6.16 Menu

The Menu component is a navigation drawer that slides in from the side of the current view. By default, it slides in from the left, but the side can be overridden. The Menu will be displayed differently based on the mode, however the display type can be changed to any of the available Menu types. The Menu element should be a sibling to the root content element. There can be any number of Menus attached to the content. These can be controlled from the templates, or programmatically using the MenuController.

We had good luck to use the `side menu` template to start our app, because the whole structure for using a Menu is already built in. But this is the right place to have a closer look at our app's UI architecture.

Let's inspect `app.component.html` and see how `ion-menu` and the related `ion-menu-toggle` are used:

```
<ion-app>

  <ion-split-pane contentId="main-content">

    <ion-menu contentId="main-content" type="overlay">

      <ion-content>
        <ion-list id="inbox-list">
          <ion-menu-toggle auto-hide="false"
            *ngFor="let p of appPages; let i = index">
            <ion-item routerDirection="root"
                      [routerLink]="[p.url]"
                      lines="none" detail="false">
              <ion-icon slot="start"
                        [ios]="p.icon + '-outline'"
                        [md]="p.icon + '-sharp'"></ion-icon>
              <ion-label>{{ p.title }}</ion-label>
            </ion-item>
          </ion-menu-toggle>
        </ion-list>
      </ion-content>

      <ion-footer>
        <ion-list>
```

```
          <ion-list-header>Settings</ion-list-header>
          <ion-item>
            <ion-label>Allow messages</ion-label>
            <ion-checkbox [(ngModel)]="settings.notifications"
                          (ionChange)="updateSettings()">
            </ion-checkbox>
          </ion-item>
        </ion-list>
      </ion-footer>

    </ion-menu>

    <ion-router-outlet id="main-content"></ion-router-outlet>

  </ion-split-pane>

</ion-app>
```

Our `ion-menu` tag encloses

- a content area
- a footer area

Thus, the structure of a Menu corresponds to the structure of a page (we could add a header area, too).

The `ion-menu-toggle` tag can be used to toggle a Menu open or closed.

We use it here with an `*ngFor` loop through all entries in the `appPages` array.

By default, it's only visible when the selected Menu is active. A Menu is active when it can be opened/closed. If the Menu is disabled or it's being presented as a Split-Pane (as in our case), the Menu is marked as non-active and `ion-menu-toggle` hides itself. In our case it's desired to keep `ion-menu-toggle` always visible, so the `autoHide` property is set to `false`.

Our current menu:

There are a few related topics to Menu. You can find them here:

- https://ionicframework.com/docs/api/menu
- https://ionicframework.com/docs/api/menu-button
- https://ionicframework.com/docs/api/menu-controller
- https://ionicframework.com/docs/api/menu-toggle
- https://ionicframework.com/docs/api/split-pane

6.17 Modal

Modals are used as temporary slide ins, often for something like logins or a choice of options, or when filtering items in a list, as well as many other use cases. A Modal is a dialog that appears on top of the app's content, and must be dismissed by the app before interaction can resume. Modals can be created using a Modal Controller. They can be customized by passing modal options in the Modal controller's create method.

The request form as modal

We'll realize the request as modal in four steps:

1. We import RequestPage in `details.module.ts`.
2. We modify `details.page.ts` to call the request modally.
3. We add the selected tour title and a cancel button to `request.page.html`.
4. We grab the tour and spend a cancel function to `request.page.ts`.

1. Import RequestPage into the DetailsPage module

Let's begin with importing the RequestPage component into `details.module.ts`:

```
import { NgModule } from '@angular/core';
import { CommonModule } from '@angular/common';
import { FormsModule } from '@angular/forms';
import { IonicModule } from '@ionic/angular';

import { DetailsPageRoutingModule } from './details-routing.-
module';
import { DetailsPage } from './details.page';

import { RequestPage } from './../request/request.page';

@NgModule({
  imports: [
    CommonModule,
    FormsModule,
    IonicModule,
    DetailsPageRoutingModule
```

```
  ],
  declarations: [DetailsPage, RequestPage],
  entryComponents: [RequestPage]
})
export class DetailsPageModule { }
```

When lazy loading a Modal (our RequestPage), it's important to note that the Modal won't be loaded when it's opened, but rather when the module that imports the Modal's module (our DetailsPage) is loaded. So it's necessary to import our RequestPage into the module of the DetailsPage, namely `details.module.ts`.

In addition to the usual import line

```
import { RequestPage } from './../request/request.page';
```

we need also to make an entry in the `declarations`

```
declarations: [DetailsPage, RequestPage]
```

as well as an entry in the `entryComponents`:

```
entryComponents: [RequestPage]
```

2. Calling the request as modal

We now modify `details.page.ts` to call the request modally:

```
import { Component, OnInit } from '@angular/core';
import { ActivatedRoute } from '@angular/router';
import { BobToursService }
         from 'src/app/services/bob-tours.service';
import { FavoritesService }
         from 'src/app/services/favorites.service';
import { ActionSheetController, AlertController,
         ModalController }
         from '@ionic/angular';
import { RequestPage } from './../request/request.page';
import _ from 'lodash';
@Component({
  selector: 'app-details',
  templateUrl: './details.page.html',
  styleUrls: ['./details.page.scss'],
```

```
})
export class DetailsPage implements OnInit {

  tour = null;
  isFavorite: boolean;

  region: string;
  tourtype: string;

  showSocial: boolean;

  constructor(private activatedRoute: ActivatedRoute,
              public btService: BobToursService,
              public favService: FavoritesService,
              private actionSheetCtrl: ActionSheetController,
              private alertCtrl: AlertController,
              private modalCtrl: ModalController) { }

  ngOnInit() {
    ...
  }

  // Action Sheet
  async presentActionSheet() {
    const actionSheet = await this.actionSheetCtrl.create({
      header: 'Tour',
      buttons: [
        {
          text: 'Request',
          handler: () => {
            this.presentModal();
            // window.location.href = "/request";
          }
        },
        {
          text: (this.isFavorite) ? 'Remove from Favorites'
                                  : 'Add to Favorites',
          role: (this.isFavorite) ? 'destructive' : '',
          handler: () => {
            if (this.isFavorite) {
              this.presentAlert();
              //this.favService.remove(this.tour);
```

```
            //this.isFavorite = false;
          } else {
            this.favService.add(this.tour);
            this.isFavorite = true;
          }
        }
      },
      {
        text: 'Cancel',
        role: 'cancel'
      }
    ]
  });
  await actionSheet.present();
}

async presentAlert() {
  ...
}

toggleSocial() {
  ...
}

openSocial(app) {
  ...
}

// user clicked 'request' button
async presentModal() {
  const modal = await this.modalCtrl.create({
    component: RequestPage,
    componentProps: this.tour
  });
  modal.present();
}

}
```

To be able to show a component as Modal we need a ModalController. So we import it with

```
import { ..., ..., ModalController }
```

and inject it as variable `modalCtrl` into the constructor with

```
private modalCtrl: ModalController
```

We also should not forget to import our RequestPage with

```
import { RequestPage } from './../request/request.page';
```

We will see immediately what this import is necessary for.

Now comes the exciting part: We replace the simple call

```
window.location.href = "/request";
```

now through

```
this.presentModal();
```

We write the `presentModal()` method as `async`:

```
async presentModal() {
```

because we want to generate our Modal asynchronously:

```
const modal = await this.modalCtrl.create({
```

The create method expects (as with ActionSheetController or AlertController) an object in which we must set at least one property `component`.

```
component: RequestPage
```

Here we assign the RequestPage to be called.

We also set the property `componentProps`

```
componentProps: this.tour
```

and thus pass the current tour object to the Modal.

3. Extend the request page

Let's now add a few information about the selected tour and a cancel button to `request.page.html`:

```
<ion-header>
  <ion-toolbar>
    <!-- <ion-buttons slot="start">
```

```
      <ion-back-button></ion-back-button>
    </ion-buttons> -->
    <ion-title>Request</ion-title>
    <ion-buttons slot="end">
      <ion-button (click)="cancel()">Cancel</ion-button>
    </ion-buttons>
  </ion-toolbar>
</ion-header>

<ion-content class="ion-padding">
  <ion-list>

    <!-- Tour info group -->
    <ion-item-group>
      <ion-item-divider>
        <ion-label>Tour</ion-label>
      </ion-item-divider>
      <ion-item>
        <ion-thumbnail slot="start">
          <img src="https://ionic.andreas-dormann.de/
                    img/small/{{tour.Image}}">
        </ion-thumbnail>
        <ion-label>
          <h2 text-wrap>{{tour.Title}}</h2>
          <p>Duration: {{tour.Duration}} min</p>
        </ion-label>
      </ion-item>
    </ion-item-group>

    <!-- Schedule group -->
    <ion-item-group>
      <ion-item-divider>
          <ion-label>Desired schedule</ion-label>
      </ion-item-divider>
      <!-- Date -->
      <ion-item>
        <ion-label>Date</ion-label>
        <ion-datetime [(ngModel)]="request.Date"
                      min="{{day_after_tomorrow}}"
                      max="{{two_years_later}}"
                      display-format="DDD, MMMM DD YYYY"
                      picker-format="MMMM DD YYYY"
```

```
                  placeholder="Choose your desired date!">
      </ion-datetime>
    </ion-item>
    <!-- Time -->
    <ion-item>
      <ion-label>Time (15 min steps)</ion-label>
      <ion-datetime [(ngModel)]="request.Time"
                  hourValues="9,10,11,12,13,14,15,16,17"
                  minuteValues="0,15,30,45"
                  display-format="hh:mm A"
                  picker-format="h mm"
                  placeholder="Choose your desired time!">
      </ion-datetime>
    </ion-item>
  </ion-item-group>

  <!-- Contact information group -->
  <ion-item-group>
    <ion-item-divider>
        <ion-label>Your contact information</ion-label>
    </ion-item-divider>
    <!-- First name -->
    <ion-item>
      <ion-label>First name</ion-label>
      <ion-input type="text" [(ngModel)]="request.FirstName">
      </ion-input>
    </ion-item>
    <!-- Last name -->
    <ion-item>
      <ion-label>Last name</ion-label>
      <ion-input type="text"
                 [(ngModel)]="request.LastName">
      </ion-input>
    </ion-item>
    <!-- Email -->
    <ion-item>
      <ion-label>Email</ion-label>
      <ion-input type="email" [(ngModel)]="request.Email">
      </ion-input>
    </ion-item>
  </ion-item-group>
```

```
  </ion-list>
</ion-content>

<ion-footer class="ion-padding"> ... </ion-footer>
```

We remove the previous `ion-back-button`. Instead, with

```
<ion-buttons slot="end">
  <ion-button (click)="cancel()">Cancel</ion-button>
</ion-buttons>
```

we place a `Cancel` button in the upper right corner and assign a `cancel()` method in the `click` handler, which we will write shortly.

Then we add an `ion-item-group` component with a `ion-item-divider` and an `ion-label` to place a title on top of the group:

```
<ion-item-divider>
  <ion-label>Tour</ion-label>
</ion-item-divider>
```

Within an `ion-item` we place a thumbnail with an image

```
<ion-thumbnail slot="start">
  <img src="http://ionic.andreas-dormann.de/img/small/
            {{tour.Image}}">
</ion-thumbnail>
```

and a label with a header and a paragraph to show the title and the duration of a tour:

```
<ion-label>
  <h2 text-wrap>{{tour.Title}}</h2>
  <p>Duration: {{tour.Duration}} min</p>
</ion-label>
```

4. Get the tour and let the modal dismiss itself

Finally we grab the tour information and supplement a cancel function to `request.page.ts`:

```
import { Component, OnInit } from '@angular/core';
import { ModalController, NavParams } from '@ionic/angular';

@Component({
  selector: 'app-request',
  templateUrl: './request.page.html',
  styleUrls: ['./request.page.scss'],
})
export class RequestPage implements OnInit {

  tour: any = {};
  request: any = {};
  day_after_tomorrow: string;
  two_years_later: string;

  constructor(
    private modalCtrl: ModalController,
    private navParams: NavParams
  ) {
    this.tour = navParams.data;
  }

  ngOnInit() {
   ...
  }

  send() {
    ...
  }

  // user clicked 'Cancel'
  cancel() {
    this.modalCtrl.dismiss();
  }

}
```

In order to be able to receive the tour data that we have submitted via the `componentProps` property of the ModalController in `details.page.ts`, we need `NavParams`. We import this with

```
import { ..., NavParams } from '@ionic/angular';
```

and inject it into the constructor as variable `navParams`.

```
constructor(navParams: NavParams)
```

So with

```
this.tour = navParams.data;
```

we can assign the data to the previously declared and set tour object.

At the end: You also have to be able to close the modal somehow.

For this we need the `ModalController` class that we import with

```
import { ModalController, ... } from '@ionic/angular';
```

and inject it into the constructor as variable `modalCtrl`.

Finally, we can write our `close()` method

```
cancel() {
  this.modalCtrl.dismiss();
}
```

and close our Modal with its `dismiss` method.

That's it.

Let's look at the RequestPage as Modal (best in iPad format):

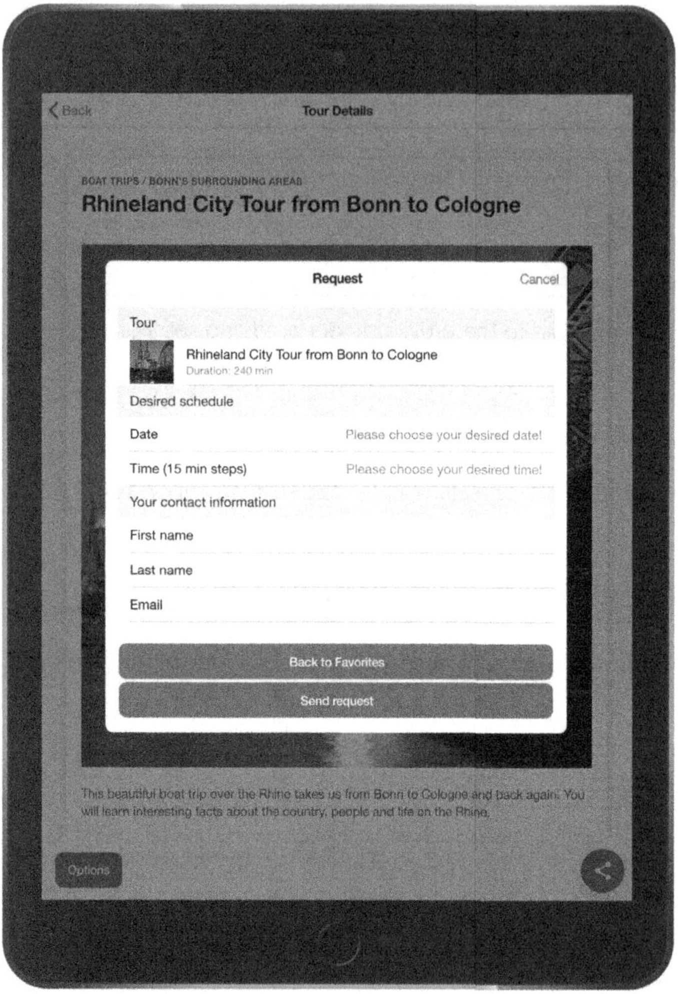

More information about Modals you can find here:

- https://ionicframework.com/docs/api/modal
- https://ionicframework.com/docs/api/modal-controller
- https://ionicframework.com/docs/api/backdrop

6.18 Popover

A Popover is a dialog that appears on top of the current page. It can be used for anything, but generally it is used for overflow actions that don't fit in the navigation bar. To present a Popover, call the `present` method on a Popover instance. In order to position the Popover relative to the element clicked, a click event needs to be passed into the options of the the present method. If the event isn't passed, the Popover will be positioned in the center of the viewport.

A popover with information about this app

Let's use a Popover to show some information about our app. We will do the following tasks:

1. Create an `AboutComponent` (to show as Popover).
2. Import the component to `app.module.ts`.
3. Write an `about()` function in `app.component.ts`.
4. Place some HTML in `app.component.html` to call the `about()` function.

Ok, let's start.

1. Create an AboutComponent

You've never created a component before? Of course, you did! Because you created pages - and pages are components. Creating an ordinary component is very similar to creating a page. We use the Ionic CLI for this task:

```
$ ionic g component components/about
```

In the new `src/app/components/about.component.html` we write:

```
<div class="ion-text-center ion-padding">
  <h3>BoB Tours App</h3>
  <small>Created with love by</small>
  <p>Andreas Dormann</p>
  <small>&copy; 2020</small>
</div>
```

Of course you can use *your* name. After all, it's *your* app ;-)

2. Import the component to our app module

Open `app.module.ts` and add the following (bold formatted) code:

```
import { NgModule } from '@angular/core';
import { BrowserModule } from '@angular/platform-browser';
import { RouteReuseStrategy } from '@angular/router';

import { IonicModule, IonicRouteStrategy }
         from '@ionic/angular';
import { SplashScreen }
         from '@ionic-native/splash-screen/ngx';
import { StatusBar } from '@ionic-native/status-bar/ngx';

import { AppComponent } from './app.component';
import { AppRoutingModule } from './app-routing.module';
import { HttpClientModule } from '@angular/common/http';
import { IonicStorageModule } from '@ionic/storage';

import { FormsModule } from '@angular/forms';

import { AboutComponent }
         from './components/about/about.component';

@NgModule({
  declarations: [AppComponent, AboutComponent],
  entryComponents: [AboutComponent],
  imports: [
    BrowserModule,
    IonicModule.forRoot(),
    AppRoutingModule,
    HttpClientModule,
    IonicStorageModule.forRoot(),
    FormsModule
  ],
  providers: [
    StatusBar,
    SplashScreen,
    { provide: RouteReuseStrategy, useClass: IonicRouteStrate-
gy }
  ],
  bootstrap: [AppComponent]
})
```

```
export class AppModule {}
```

In addition to the usual import line

```
import { AboutComponent }
         from './components/about/about.component';
```

we need also to make an entry in the `declarations`

```
declarations: [AppComponent, AboutComponent]
```

as well as an entry in the `entryComponents`:

```
entryComponents: [AboutComponent],
```

3. Write an about() function

In `app.component.ts` add the following (bold formatted) code:

```
import { Component } from '@angular/core';
import { Platform, PopoverController } from '@ionic/angular';
import { SplashScreen }
         from '@ionic-native/splash-screen/ngx';
import { StatusBar } from '@ionic-native/status-bar/ngx';
import { BobToursService }
         from './services/bob-tours.service';
import { AboutComponent }
         from './components/about/about.component';

@Component({
  selector: 'app-root',
  templateUrl: 'app.component.html'
})
export class AppComponent {

  public appPages = [
    ...
  ];

  settings: any = {};

  constructor(
```

```
    private platform: Platform,
    private splashScreen: SplashScreen,
    private statusBar: StatusBar,
    public btService: BobToursService,
    private popoverCtrl: PopoverController
  ) {
    this.initializeApp();
  }

  initializeApp() {
    ...
  }

  // User has changed his/her settings
  updateSettings() {
    ...
  }

  // User clicked on 'About this app'
  async about() {
    const popover = await this.popoverCtrl.create({
      component: AboutComponent,
      translucent: true
    });
    await popover.present();
  }

}
```

We import a PopoverController with

```
import { ..., PopoverController } from '@ionic/angular';
```

and inject it as variable `popoverCtrl` into the constructor:

```
constructor(... private popoverCtrl: PopoverController)
```

We only have to write a single line to import `AboutComponent`.

```
import { AboutComponent }
  from './components/about/about.component';
```

It's not necessary to inject `AboutComponent` into the constructor.

Then we write our `about()` method and declare it as `async`,

```
async about() {
```

because we want to use two asynchronous methods.

First we create the popover with

```
const popover = await this.popoverCtrl.create({
```

The create method expects an object with at least a property `component`, where we assign our AboutComponent:

```
component: AboutComponent
```

With another property translucent

```
translucent: true
```

we influence the the appearance of the component. It's not hard to guess how.

After creating the Popover we show it by calling

```
await popover.present();
```

We don't need a close method. A simple tap outside the Popover will close it automatically.

4. Place some HTML to call the popover

Finally we place some HTML in `app.component.html` to extend the side menu with an item "About this app":

```
<ion-app>

  <ion-split-pane>

    <ion-menu>

      <ion-header>
        <ion-toolbar>
          <ion-title>Menu</ion-title>
        </ion-toolbar>
      </ion-header>
```

```
      <ion-content>
        <ion-list>
          <ion-menu-toggle *ngFor="let p of appPages"
                           auto-hide="false">
            <ion-item [routerDirection]="'root'"
                      [routerLink]="[p.url]">
              <ion-icon slot="start"
                        [name]="p.icon"></ion-icon>
              <ion-label>
                {{p.title}}
              </ion-label>
            </ion-item>
          </ion-menu-toggle>
          <ion-item (click)="about()">
            <ion-icon slot="start" name="information-circle">
            </ion-icon>
            <ion-label>About this app</ion-label>
          </ion-item>
        </ion-list>
      </ion-content>

      <ion-footer>
        ...
      </ion-footer>

    </ion-menu>

    <ion-router-outlet main></ion-router-outlet>

  </ion-split-pane>

</ion-app>
```

In the content area, directly below the closing `</ion-menu-toggle>` tag, we add a new list item with embedded icon and label. A click handler references to the `about()` method we created before.

That's it.

Our side menu with "About this app" Popover:

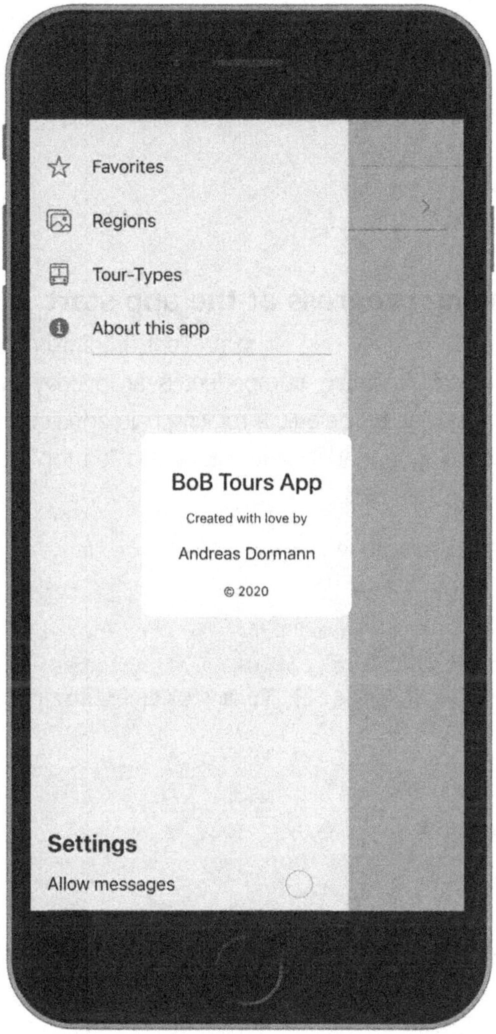

More informations about Popover you can find here:

- https://ionicframework.com/docs/api/popover
- https://ionicframework.com/docs/api/popover-controller

6.19 Progress Indicators

Compared to the previous versions Ionic has significantly expanded its offer of Progress Indicators. At the start are now:

- ion-loading / ion-loading-controller
- ion-progress-bar
- ion-skeleton-text
- ion-spinner

Show the loading progress at the app start

We want to use a `LoadingController` to prevent users from starting actions until all tour data is loaded. A loading component is an overlay that is shown while indicating a loading activity. By default, a rotating halo appears. This can be hidden or modified. The Loading Indicator will be displayed "on top" above all other elements.

This functionality is best placed in `bob-tours.service.ts`:

```
import { Injectable } from '@angular/core';
import { HttpClient } from '@angular/common/http';
import { FavoritesService } from './favorites.service';
import { LoadingController } from '@ionic/angular';
import _ from 'lodash';

@Injectable({
  providedIn: 'root'
})
export class BobToursService {

  public regions: any;
  public tourtypes: any;
  public tours: any;

  baseUrl = 'https://bob-tours-app.firebaseio.com/';

  constructor(private http: HttpClient,
              public favService: FavoritesService,
              private loadingCtrl: LoadingController) { }

  async initialize() {
```

```
    const loading = await this.loadingCtrl.create({
      message: 'Loading tour data...',
      spinner: 'crescent'
    });
    await loading.present();
    await this.getRegions()
          .then(data => this.regions = data);
    await this.getTourtypes().
          then(data => this.tourtypes =
               _.sortBy(data, 'Name'));
    await this.getTours()
          .then(data => {
                this.tours = _.sortBy(data, 'Title');
                this.favService.initialize(this.tours);
          });
    await loading.dismiss();
  }

  getRegions() {
    let requestUrl = `${this.baseUrl}/Regions.json`;
    return this.http.get(requestUrl).toPromise();
  }

  getTourtypes() {
    let requestUrl = `${this.baseUrl}/Tourtypes.json`;
    return this.http.get(requestUrl).toPromise();
  }

  getTours() {
    let requestUrl = `${this.baseUrl}/Tours.json`;
    return this.http.get(requestUrl).toPromise();
  }

}
```

We import the LoadingController with

```
import { LoadingController } from '@ionic/angular';
```

and inject it as variable `loadingCtrl` into the constructor:

```
constructor(... private loadingCtrl: LoadingController)
```

Now we make an asynchronous `initialize` from our originally synchronous method by prefixing it with `async`.

```
async initialize() {
```

That's crucial. Because our LoadingController should be displayed *before* the start of the service calls and only be hidden *after* finishing the last call. This is definitely an *asynchronous* workflow, isn't it?

With

```
const loading = await this.loadingCtrl.create({
```

we create a LoadingController. And as you already know from the many other controllers, its create method expects an object as a parameter. Its property `message` gets textual information about what's happening:

```
message: 'Loading tour data...',
```

With the property `spinner` we define the appearance of the loading animation:

```
spinner: 'crescent'
```

There are a few more spinner animations: "bubbles" | "circles" | "crescent" | "dots" | "lines" | "lines-small" | null | undefined

If a value isn't passed to `spinner` the Loading Indicator will use the spinner specified by the platform.

Now we show the LoadingController with

```
await loading.present();
```

All subsequent service calls are made asynchronous (prefixed with `async` again), i.e.. we wait until each call ends before we start the next one:

```
await this.getRegions().then(...);
await this.getTourtypes().then(...);
await this.getTours().then(...);
```

Finally, we hide the LoadingController with

```
await loading.dismiss();
```

A word about this workflow: In real life, we would parallelize service calls to save the user's time. In our case, the calls are so brief that we would not have much pleasure in seeing our LoadingController. That's why we – exceptionally – call one service after another here.

Our new LoadingController in action:

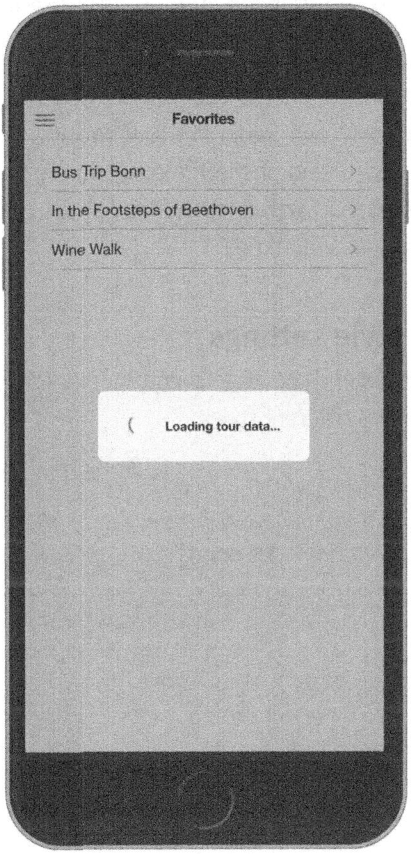

More informations about Progress Indicators you can find here:

- https://ionicframework.com/docs/api/loading
- https://ionicframework.com/docs/api/loading-controller
- https://ionicframework.com/docs/api/progress-bar
- https://ionicframework.com/docs/api/skeleton-text
- https://ionicframework.com/docs/api/spinner

6.20 Radio

Like the Checkbox a Radio is an input component representing a boolean value. Radios are generally used as a set of related options inside of a group, but they can also be used alone. Pressing on a Radio will check it. They can also be checked programmatically by setting the `checked` property.

An `ion-radio-group` can be used to group a set of radios. When Radios are inside of a Radio Group, only one Radio in the group will be checked at any time. Pressing a Radio will check it and uncheck the previously selected Radio, if there is one. If a Radio isn't in a group with another Radio, then both Radios will have the ability to be checked at the same time.

Two Radios for style settings

In our app, we want to extend the page menu by two Radios, with which you can choose (later) between two different styles.

To do this, we first prepare `app.component.ts` to hold the Radio data:

```
import { Component } from '@angular/core';
import { Platform, PopoverController } from '@ionic/angular';
import { SplashScreen }
         from '@ionic-native/splash-screen/ngx';
import { StatusBar } from '@ionic-native/status-bar/ngx';
import { BobToursService }
         from './services/bob-tours.service';
import { AboutComponent }
         from './components/about/about.component';
import { Storage } from '@ionic/storage';

@Component({
  selector: 'app-root',
  templateUrl: 'app.component.html'
})
export class AppComponent {
  public appPages = [
    ...
  ];

  settings: any = {};
```

```
constructor(
  private platform: Platform,
  private splashScreen: SplashScreen,
  private statusBar: StatusBar,
  public btService: BobToursService,
  private popoverCtrl: PopoverController,
  private storage: Storage
) {
  this.initializeApp();
}

initializeApp() {
  this.platform.ready().then(() => {
    this.statusBar.styleDefault();
    this.splashScreen.hide();
    this.btService.initialize();
    this.loadSettings();
  });
}

// Load settings
loadSettings() {
  this.storage.ready().then(() => {
    this.storage.get('settings').then(settings => {
      if (settings == null) {
        this.settings.style = 'summer-style';
      } else {
        this.settings = settings;
      }
    });
  });
}

// User has changed his/her settings
updateSettings() {
  this.storage.set('settings', this.settings);
  console.log(this.settings);
}

// User clicked on 'About this app'
async about() {
  const popover = await this.popoverCtrl.create({
```

```
      component: AboutComponent,
      translucent: true
    });
    await popover.present();
  }

}
```

After importing `Storage` with

```
import { Storage } from '@ionic/storage';
```

we inject it as variable `storage` into the constructor:

```
private storage: Storage
```

In `initializeApp()` we add a call to a new function `loadSettings()`.

In this new function we write

```
this.storage.ready().then(() => {
```

to wait for the storage engine to be ready to start. With

```
this.storage.get('settings').then(settings => {
```

we get the storage content of the `settings` key. At the very first start of the app the content will be `null`, so with

```
if (settings == null) {
  this.settings.style = 'summer-style';
}
```

we set a default value. If we get content we assign it to our `settings` property:

```
else {
  this.settings = settings;
}
```

In the `updateSettings` function we save the current settings with

```
this.storage.set('settings', this.settings);
```

and show their content in the console with

```
console.log(this.settings);
```

We'll now add a `radio group` and two `ion-radio` items in `app.component.html`:

```
<ion-app>

  <ion-split-pane>

    <ion-menu>

      <ion-header>
        <ion-toolbar>
          <ion-title>Menu</ion-title>
        </ion-toolbar>
      </ion-header>

      <ion-content>
       ...
      </ion-content>

      <ion-footer>
        <ion-list>

          <ion-list-header>Settings</ion-list-header>

          <ion-radio-group [(ngModel)]="settings.style"
                           (ionChange)="updateSettings()">

            <ion-item>
              <ion-label>Azure-Style</ion-label>
              <ion-radio value="azure-style"></ion-radio>
            </ion-item>

            <ion-item>
              <ion-label>Summer-Style</ion-label>
              <ion-radio value="summer-style"></ion-radio>
            </ion-item>

          </ion-radio-group>

          <ion-item>
            <ion-label>Allow messages</ion-label>
            <ion-checkbox
              [(ngModel)]="settings.notifications"
```

```
            (ionChange)="updateSettings()">
          </ion-checkbox>
        </ion-item>

      </ion-list>
    </ion-footer>

  </ion-menu>

  <ion-router-outlet main></ion-router-outlet>

</ion-split-pane>

</ion-app>
```

With the attribute `ion-radio-group` our list becomes a component, within which there can only ever be *one* selected Radio element. With the instruction

```
[(ngModel)]="settings.style"
```

we tie the Radio Group to the new `style` property of our `settings` object. This receives the respective value of the selected Radios, either `"azure-style"` or `"summer-style"`. Now to the instruction

```
(ionChange)="updateSettings()"
```

If the user clicks on one of the Radios, `updateSettings()` executed, where it stores the whole `settings` object in the storage. Thus, our app now has permanently storable user settings, which are again available at the next start of the app via `loadSettings()`.

Here is our app with the extended side menu and Radios:

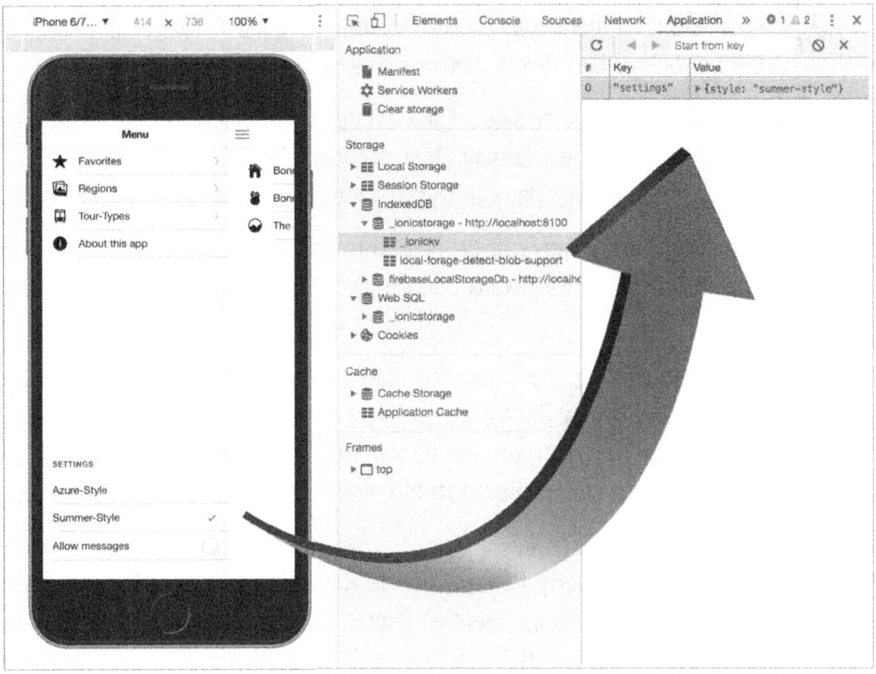

You can also use the `Chrome Developer Tools > Application > Storage` to take a look at the storage and view the saved user settings.

More informations about Radios and Radio Groups you can find here:

- https://ionicframework.com/docs/api/radio
- https://ionicframework.com/docs/api/radio-group

6.21 Range

A Range is an input element that allows the user to enter a range of values. A Range consists of one or two sliders that move along a bar.

Labels can be placed on either side of the Range by adding the `range-left` or `range-right` property to the element. The element doesn't have to be an `ion-label`, it can be added to any element to place it to the left or right of the Range.

Minimum and maximum values can be passed to the Range through the `min` and `max` properties, respectively. By default, the Range sets the `min` to `0` and the `max` to `100`.

The `step` property specifies the value granularity of the Range's value. It can be useful to set the `step` when the value isn't in increments of `1`. Setting the `step` property will show tick marks on the Range for each step. The `snaps` property can be set to automatically move the knob to the nearest tick mark based on the step property value.

Setting the `dualKnobs` property to `true` on the Range component will enable two knobs on the Range. If the Range has two knobs, the value will be an object containing two properties: `lower` and `upper`.

Find the price – a range filter for our tours

We'll build a Range element in our side menu to give the user the possibility to filter the offered tours by price. We will use all the options described above.

Let's start with a filter function in `bob-tours.service.ts`:

```
import { Injectable } from '@angular/core';
import { HttpClient } from '@angular/common/http';
import { FavoritesService } from './favorites.service';
import { LoadingController } from '@ionic/angular';
import _ from 'lodash';

@Injectable({
  providedIn: 'root'
})
export class BobToursService {

  public regions: any;
```

```
  public tourtypes: any;
  public tours: any;
  public all_tours: any;

  baseUrl = 'https://bob-tours-app.firebaseio.com/';

  constructor(private http: HttpClient,
              public favService: FavoritesService,
              private loadingCtrl: LoadingController) { }

  async initialize() {
    const loading = await this.loadingCtrl.create({
      message: 'Loading tour data...',
      spinner: 'crescent'
    });
    await loading.present();
    await this.getRegions().then(data => this.regions = data);
    await this.getTourtypes()
          .then(data => this.tourtypes
                    = _.sortBy(data, 'Name'));
    await this.getTours().then(data => {
      this.tours = _.sortBy(data, 'Title');
      this.all_tours = _.sortBy(data, 'Title');
      this.favService.initialize(this.all_tours);
    });
    await loading.dismiss();
  }

  // Reads regions as json formatted data from Google Fire-
base.
  getRegions() {
    let requestUrl = `${this.baseUrl}/Regions.json`;
    return this.http.get(requestUrl).toPromise();
  }

  // Reads tour types as json formatted data from Google
Firebase.
  getTourtypes() {
    let requestUrl = `${this.baseUrl}/Tourtypes.json`;
    return this.http.get(requestUrl).toPromise();
  }
```

```
// Reads tours as json formatted data from Google Firebase.
getTours() {
  let requestUrl = `${this.baseUrl}/Tours.json`;
  return this.http.get(requestUrl).toPromise();
}

// Filtering tours by Price.
filterTours(price):number {
  this.tours = _.filter(this.all_tours, function(tour) {
    return tour.PriceG >= price.lower
        && tour.PriceG <= price.upper;
  });
  return this.tours.length;
}
```

First, we declare the new variable `all_tours`. In `initialize()` with

```
this.all_tours = _.sortBy(data, 'Title');
```

we put there all tour data from the database sorted by `Title`. Now follows the filter function `filterTours(price)`, which receives as a parameter a price, more precisely, a price range with the properties `lower` (lowest price range) and `upper` (highest price range).

In an Lodash filter function, we now check each tour for whether its price is within this price range. As a result we get back an array with all suitable tours in `this.tours`. In other words, from the total amount of tours in `this.all_tours`, we'll filter out the priced tours and give them to `this.tours`. The function itself delivers over

```
return this.tours.length;
```

the number of filtered tours as numerical value.

Now we integrate the new filter function in our side menu code. Therefore we complete `app.component.ts`:

```
import { Component } from '@angular/core';
import { Platform, PopoverController } from '@ionic/angular';
import { SplashScreen } from '@ionic-native/splash-
screen/ngx';
import { StatusBar } from '@ionic-native/status-bar/ngx';
```

```
import { BobToursService } from './services/bob-
tours.service';
import { AboutComponent }
         from './components/about/about.component';
import { Storage } from '@ionic/storage';

@Component({
  selector: 'app-root',
  templateUrl: 'app.component.html'
})
export class AppComponent {
  public appPages = [
    ...
  ];

  settings: any = {};
  price:    any = { lower: 80, upper: 400};
  hits:     number = 24;

  constructor(
    private platform: Platform,
    private splashScreen: SplashScreen,
    private statusBar: StatusBar,
    public btService: BobToursService,
    private popoverCtrl: PopoverController,
    private storage: Storage
  ) {
    this.initializeApp();
  }

  initializeApp() {
    this.platform.ready().then(() => {
      this.statusBar.styleDefault();
      this.splashScreen.hide();
      this.btService.initialize();
      this.loadSettings();
    });
  }

  // Loading settings
  loadSettings() {
   ...
```

```
  }

  // User has changed his/her settings
  updateSettings() {
    ...
  }

  // User clicked on 'About this app'
  async about() {
    ...
  }

  // User has changed price range.
  filterByPrice() {
    this.hits = this.btService.filterTours(this.price);
  }

}
```

First, we declare the two new variables `price` and `hits`. To `price` we assign an object with the properties `lower` and `upper` and the values 80 and 400. Both variables will soon be bound to the UI.

In `filterByPrice()` we call the previously defined `filterTours` method and pass the price range object to it.

At the end we add the price range filter to our UI and add the following HTML lines to `app.component.html`:

```
<ion-app>

  <ion-split-pane>

    <ion-menu>

      <ion-header>
        <ion-toolbar>
          <ion-title>Menu</ion-title>
        </ion-toolbar>
      </ion-header>

      <ion-content>
```

```
  ...
</ion-content>

<ion-footer>
  <ion-list>

    <ion-radio-group [(ngModel)]="settings.style"
                     (ionChange)="updateSettings()">

      <ion-list-header>
        Price from {{price.lower}} to {{price.upper}} EUR
       ({{hits}} hits)
        <ion-badge slot="end">{{hits}}</ion-badge>
      </ion-list-header>

      <ion-item>
        <ion-range min="80" max="400" step="20"
                   pin="true" snaps="true"
                   dualKnobs="true"
                   [(ngModel)]="price"
                   (ionChange)="filterByPrice()">
          <ion-label slot="start">80</ion-label>
          <ion-label slot="end">400</ion-label>
        </ion-range>
      </ion-item>

      <ion-list-header>Settings</ion-list-header>

      <ion-item>
        <ion-label>Azure-Style</ion-label>
        <ion-radio value="azure-style"></ion-radio>
      </ion-item>

      <ion-item>
        <ion-label>Summer-Style</ion-label>
        <ion-radio value="summer-style"></ion-radio>
      </ion-item>

      <ion-item>
        <ion-label>Allow messages</ion-label>
        <ion-checkbox [(ngModel)]="settings.notifications"
                      (ionChange)="updateSettings()">
```

```
                </ion-checkbox>
              </ion-item>

            </ion-radio-group>

          </ion-list>
        </ion-footer>

      </ion-menu>

      <ion-router-outlet main></ion-router-outlet>

    </ion-split-pane>

  </ion-app>
```

With the code

```
<ion-list-header>
  Price from {{price.lower}} to {{price.upper}} EUR ({{hits}} hits)
  <ion-badge slot="end">{{hits}}</ion-badge>
</ion-list-header>
```

we create a list heading, which is the current price range as well as the number of hits of the filtering in brackets.

Within an `ion-item tag` we define the Range element.

With

```
min="80" max="400"
```

we set the lower and upper value range. With

```
step="20"
```

a value grid is specified for the sliders.

```
pin="true
```

ensures that the current value is displayed when a slider is pressed and with

```
snaps="true"
```

the knob snaps to tick marks evenly spaced based on the step property value.

```
dualKnobs="true"
```

indicates two sliding buttons. Default is just a slider (`dualKnobs = "false"`).

```
[(ngModel)]="price"
```

binds the Range element to the `price` variable. With

```
(ionChange)="filterByPrice()"
```

we respond to any change that the user makes via the sliders. We've just written the function.

Finally, the two lines take care

```
<ion-label slot="start">80</ion-label>
<ion-label slot="end">400</ion-label>
```

for the label of the Range element.

Optimizations

We should make a small optimization. Since it can now happen that a column has no more tours to offer due to a "strict" filtering, i.e. displays its Badge value `0`, we should spare the user that he clicks here in the void. In such a case we will deactivate the relevant list entry.

Here is the supplement in `regions.page.html`:

```
<ion-header>
  <ion-toolbar>
    <ion-buttons slot="start">
      <ion-menu-button></ion-menu-button>
    </ion-buttons>
    <ion-title>Regions</ion-title>
  </ion-toolbar>
</ion-header>

<ion-content class="ion-padding">
  <ion-list>
    <ion-item *ngFor="let region of regions"
              [routerLink]="['/list', {
                Category: 'Region',
                ID: region.ID,
                Name: region.Name
```

```
            } ]"
            routerDirection="forward"
            [disabled]="region.Count==0">
      <ion-icon name="{{region.Icon}}" slot="start">
      </ion-icon>
      {{region.Name}}
      <ion-badge slot="end">{{region.Count}}</ion-badge>
    </ion-item>
  </ion-list>
</ion-content>
```

And here's the additional HTML / angular directive in `tour-types.page.html`:

```
<ion-header>
  <ion-toolbar>
    <ion-buttons slot="start">
      <ion-menu-button></ion-menu-button>
    </ion-buttons>
    <ion-title>Tour-Types</ion-title>
  </ion-toolbar>
</ion-header>

<ion-content class="ion-padding">
  <ion-list>
    <ion-item *ngFor="let tourtype of tourtypes"
            [routerLink]="['/list', {
               Category: 'Tourtype',
               ID: tourtype.ID,
               Name: tourtype.Name
            }]"
            routerDirection="forward"
            [disabled]="tourtype.Count==0">
      <ion-icon name="{{tourtype.Icon}}" slot="start">
      </ion-icon>
      {{tourtype.Name}}
      <ion-badge slot="end">{{tourtype.Count}}</ion-badge>
    </ion-item>
  </ion-list>
</ion-content>
```

Our app has a little flaw – maybe you have already noticed it: The Badge numbers that indicate the number of available tours, update only when we switch from "Tour-Types" to "Regions" or vice versa in the side menu. But an update should take place immediately as soon as the price range is changed. We'll fix that in Chapter 8 "Theming, Styling, Customizing" (see "UI-Design for Tablets (Split Pane Layout)" on page 382).

Here is our Range element in action:

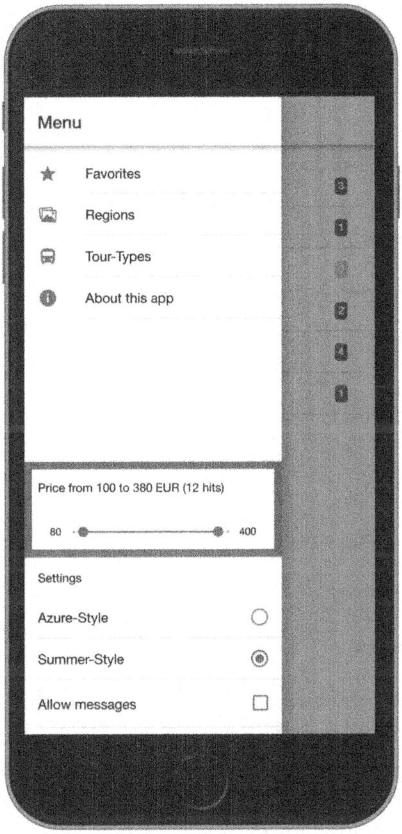

More informations about the Range component you can find here:

► https://ionicframework.com/docs/api/range

6.22 Reorder

Lists that can be freely ordered by the user are a standard functionality that an app should master. Fortunately, Ionic supports us in this, so that the implementation isn't a big deal.

It's Ionic's Reorder component that allows an item to be dragged to change its order. It must be used within an `ion-reorder-group` to provide a visual drag and drop interface.

`ion-reorder` is the anchor users will use to drag and drop items inside the `ion-reorder-group`.

Ordering our favorites

In our app, the favorites list should be able to be put in a sequence by the user that corresponds to his own ideas.

To do this, we first add some code to `favorites.service.ts`:

```
import { Injectable } from '@angular/core';
import { Storage } from '@ionic/storage';

@Injectable({
  providedIn: 'root'
})
export class FavoritesService {

  public favIDs: Array<number>;
  public favTours: Array<any>;

  constructor(private storage: Storage) { }

  initialize(tours) {
    this.favTours = [];
    this.storage.ready().then(() => {
      this.storage.get('FavoritesIDs').then(ids => {
        this.favIDs = ids;
        if (this.favIDs == null) {
          this.favIDs = [];
        } else {
          this.favIDs.forEach(favID => {
```

```
          let tour = tours.filter(t => t.ID == favID)[0];
          this.favTours.push(tour);
        });
        // tours.forEach(tour => {
        //   if (this.favIDs.indexOf(tour.ID) != -1) {
        //     this.favTours.push(tour);
        //   }
        // });
      }
    });
  });
}

add(tour) {
  this.favIDs.push(tour.ID);
  this.favTours.push(tour);
  this.storage.set('FavoritesIDs', this.favIDs);
}

remove(tour) {
  let removeIndex:number = this.favIDs.indexOf(tour.ID);
  if (removeIndex != -1) {
    this.favIDs.splice(removeIndex, 1);
    this.favTours.splice(removeIndex, 1);
    this.storage.set('FavoritesIDs', this.favIDs);
  }
}

reorder(ev) {
  ev.detail.complete(this.favTours);
  this.favIDs = this.favTours.map(tour => tour.ID);
  this.storage.set('FavoritesIDs', this.favIDs);
}

}
```

We replace our previous `forEach` loop with a loop through all `favIDs`:

```
this.favIDs.forEach(favID => {
  let tour = tours.filter(t => t.ID == favID)[0];
  this.favTours.push(tour);
});
```

This ensures that the favorites are now displayed in the saved sequence.

Then we add a reorder function, where we get an event object (called `ev` here). Where this event object comes from, we will see soon. Anyway - with

```
ev.detail.complete(this.favTours);
```

we can access the new order of tours and assign them to `favTours`.

To adjust the order of `favIDs` accordingly, we use a map function on `favTours`:

```
this.favIDs = this.favTours.map(tour => tour.ID);
```

With

```
this.storage.set('FavoritesIDs', this.favIDs);
```

we store the new `favIDs` order in our storage.

Finally we change the UI in `favorites.page.html`:

```
<ion-header>
  <ion-toolbar>
    <ion-buttons slot="start">
      <ion-menu-button></ion-menu-button>
    </ion-buttons>
    <ion-title>Favorites</ion-title>
  </ion-toolbar>
</ion-header>

<ion-content class="ion-padding">

  <ion-list>

    <ion-reorder-group
      (ionItemReorder)="favService.reorder($event)"
      disabled="false">
      <ion-item *ngFor="let tour of favService.favTours"
                [routerLink]="'/details/' + tour.ID"
                routerDirection="forward">
        <ion-reorder slot="start">
          <ion-icon name="swap-vertical-outline"></ion-icon>
        </ion-reorder>
        <ion-label>{{ tour?.Title }}</ion-label>
      </ion-item>
```

```
    </ion-reorder-group>
    <ion-item *ngIf="favService.favTours?.length==0">
      You didn't choose any favorites yet!
     </ion-item>

  </ion-list>
</ion-content>

<ion-footer class="ion-padding"
            *ngIf="favService.favTours?.length>1">
  <small>
    You can reorder your favorites by drag-drop an item using
    the <ion-icon name="swap-vertical-outline"></ion-icon>
icon!
  </small>
</ion-footer>
```

We create an `ion-reorder-group`, which gives us an `ionItemReorder` event. Just this event we used earlier in the reorder function:

```
(ionItemReorder)="favService.reorder($event)"
```

The `detail` property of the `ionItemReorder` event includes all of the relevant information about the reorder operation, including the `from` and `to` indexes. In the context of reordering, an item moves `from` an index `to` a new index. We use `detail's complete` method to get the completely new order of `favTours`.

The reorder gesture is disabled by default, so we have to enable it to drag and drop items:

```
disabled="false"
```

To visualize that the list entries can be sorted, with

```
<ion-reorder slot="start">
  <ion-icon name="swap-vertical-outline"></ion-icon>
</ion-reorder>
```

we add an `ion-reorder` tag at the beginning of each line and give it a `swap` icon.

Last but not least, our FavoritesPage gets a footer that only becomes visible if the user has added more than one favorite:

```
<ion-footer ... *ngIf="favService.favTours?.length>1">
```

Inside the footer, we give a hint that the list entries can be reordered:

```
<small>
  You can reorder your favorites by drag-drop an item using
  the <ion-icon name="swap-vertical-outline"></ion-icon> icon!
</small>
```

Our FavoritesPage with List entries that can be reordered:

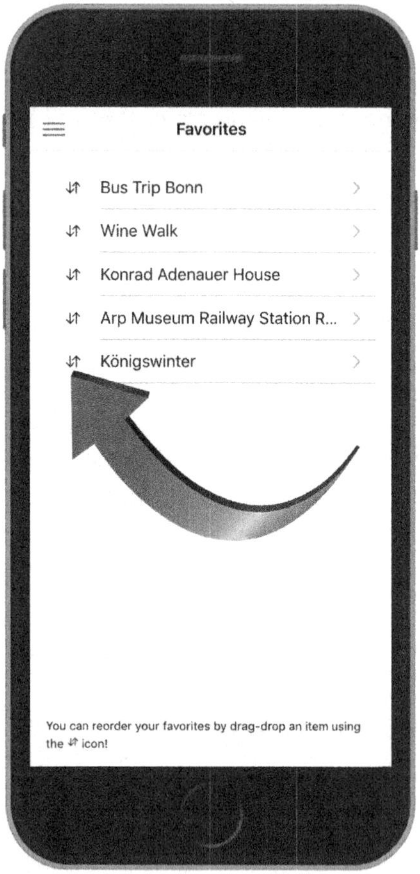

More informations about Reorder you can find here:

- ▶ https://ionicframework.com/docs/api/reorder
- ▶ https://ionicframework.com/docs/api/reorder-group

6.23 Searchbar

A Searchbar is always a great help when it comes to browsing larger databases. The Searchbar in Ionic offers us a finished component that should be used instead of an input to search lists. A clear button is displayed upon entering input in the search bar's text field. Clicking on the clear button will erase the text field and the input will remain focused. A cancel button can be enabled which will clear the input and lose the focus upon click.

Search for tours

In our app, we want to integrate a Searchbar in the tour list, if necessary to shorten a longer hit list by entering a search term and get to the destination faster.

Let's start in `list.page.html`:

```
<ion-header>
  <ion-toolbar>
    <ion-buttons slot="start">
      <ion-back-button></ion-back-button>
    </ion-buttons>
    <ion-title>{{selection.Name}}</ion-title>
  </ion-toolbar>
</ion-header>

<ion-content class="ion-padding">
  <ion-searchbar (ionChange)="search($event)"
                 placeholder="Search"
                 clearIcon>
  </ion-searchbar>
  <ion-list>
    <ion-item *ngFor="let tour of tours"
              [routerLink]="'/details/' + tour.ID"
              routerDirection="forward">
      <ion-thumbnail slot="start">
        <img src="http://ionic.andreas-dormann.de/img/small/
                  {{tour.Image}}">
      </ion-thumbnail>
      <ion-label>
        <h2 text-wrap>{{tour.Title}}</h2>
        <p>Duration: {{tour.Duration}} min</p>
```

```
      </ion-label>
    </ion-item>
  </ion-list>
</ion-content>
```

As you can see, installing a Searchbar is a breeze. If the user inserts something in the Searchbar, an `ionChange` event will be triggered. For this event, we assign the `search()` function to be written immediately, giving it the `$event` object of `ion-Change`:

```
(ionChange)="search($event)"
```

With

```
placeholder="Search"
```

we show a placeholder text as long as the user hasn't yet entered their own search text.

```
clearIcon
```

sets the clear icon (defaults to `"close-circle"` for `ios` and `"close"` for `md`).

And now we write our search function in `list.page.ts`:

```
import { Component, OnInit } from '@angular/core';
import { BobToursService }
         from 'src/app/services/bob-tours.service';
import { ActivatedRoute } from '@angular/router';
import _ from 'lodash';

@Component({
  selector: 'app-list',
  templateUrl: './list.page.html',
  styleUrls: ['./list.page.scss'],
})
export class ListPage implements OnInit {

  tours: any;
  selection: any;

  constructor(private btService:BobToursService,
              private activatedRoute: ActivatedRoute) { }
```

```
  ngOnInit() {
    this.selection = this.activatedRoute.snapshot.params;
    let category = this.selection.Category;
    let criteria = this.selection.Criteria;
    this.tours = _.filter(this.btService.tours,
                          [category, criteria]);
  }

  // User typed a search term into the Searchbar
  search(ev) {

    let searchText = ev.detail.value;

    // 1st filter by category & criteria
    this.tours = _.filter(this.btService.tours,
                          [this.selection.Category,
                           this.selection.Criteria]);

    // 2nd filter by searchText (if not empty)
    if (searchText != '') {
      this.tours = this.tours.filter((tour) => {
        return (tour.Title.toLowerCase()
                .indexOf(searchText.toLowerCase()) > -1);
      });
    }
  }

}
```

The search text entered by the user is in `ev.detail.value`, so with

```
let searchText = ev.detail.value;
```

we can assign it to a variable `searchText`.

With

```
this.tours = _.filter(this.btService.tours,
                      [this.selection.Category,
                      this.selection.Criteria]);
```

we first filter for category and criteria and assign the result to `this.tours` (as we already do in `ngOnInit`).

If `searchText` contains a search expression, with

```
this.tours = this.tours.filter((tour) => {
  return (tour.Title.toLowerCase()
          .indexOf(searchText.toLowerCase()) > -1);
  });
}
```

we continue to filter `this.tours` and only search out the tours where the search text appears in the title of a tour. Usually you compare the lowercase strings with `toLowerCase()`. So it doesn't matter which upper or lower case the user uses.

Our ListPage with new Searchbar in action:

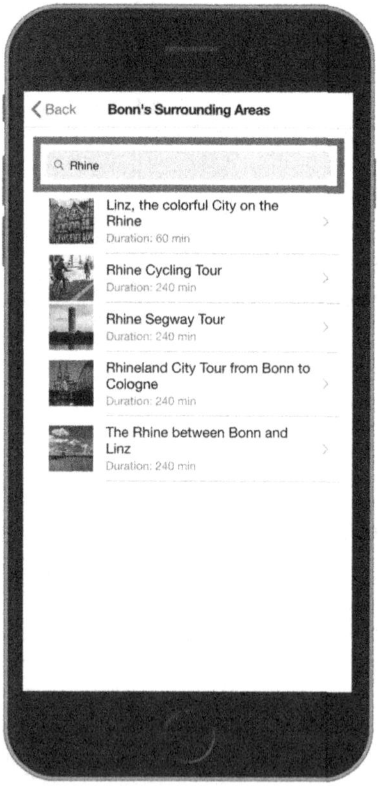

More informations about Searchbar you can find here:

► https://ionicframework.com/docs/api/searchbar

6.24 Segment

Segments display a group of related buttons, sometimes known as segmented controls, in a horizontal row. They can be displayed inside of a toolbar or the main content.

Their functionality is similar to tabs, where selecting one will deselect all others. Segments are useful for toggling between different views inside of the content. Tabs should be used instead of a Segment when clicking on a control should navigate between pages.

Toggling between different views

If you've read this book carefully, it's no secret that our app will finally be equipped with some cool map features. To be able to toggle between their different views, we'll use a segment on the map page: What map page, you may ask? You're right, we don't have a map page so far. So there's something to prepare.

A quick overview of what we are doing now:

1. We create a `MapPage`.
2. We add the MapPage to `details.module.ts`.
3. We expand the ActionSheet in the `DetailsPage` with a 'Map/Route' option.
4. We add a Segment component with three buttons to `MapPage`.

1. Create a map page

So, let's start and create a map page with the Ionic CLI:

```
$ ionic g page pages/Map
```

Let's have a look at `app-routing.module.ts`:

```
import { NgModule } from '@angular/core';
import { PreloadAllModules, RouterModule, Routes } from '@angular/router';

const routes: Routes = [
  {
    path: '',
```

```
    redirectTo: 'favorites',
    pathMatch: 'full'
  },
  {
    path: 'favorites',
    loadChildren:
      () => import('./pages/favorites/favorites.module')
            .then(m => m.FavoritesPageModule)
  },
  {
    path: 'regions',
    loadChildren:
      () => import('./pages/regions/regions.module')
            .then(m => m.RegionsPageModule)
  },
  {
    path: 'tour-types',
    loadChildren:
      () => import('./pages/tour-types/tour-types.module')
            .then(m => m.TourTypesPageModule)
  },
  {
    path: 'list',
    loadChildren:
      () => import('./pages/list/list.module')
            .then(m => m.ListPageModule)
  },
  {
    path: 'details/:id',
    loadChildren:
      () => import('./pages/details/details.module')
            .then(m => m.DetailsPageModule)
  },
  {
    path: 'request',
    loadChildren:
      () => import('./pages/request/request.module')
            .then(m => m.RequestPageModule)
  },
```

```
  {
    path: 'map',
    loadChildren:
      () => import('./pages/map/map.module')
            .then( m => m.MapPageModule)
  }
];

@NgModule({
  imports: [
    RouterModule.forRoot(routes, { preloadingStrategy:
PreloadAllModules })
  ],
  exports: [RouterModule]
})
export class AppRoutingModule { }
```

As we can see, there's a new entry for a `'map'` path, automatically built by the `gen-erate (g)` command. There's nothing more to do here for us.

2. Add the MapPage to the DetailsPage Module

In order to be able to call the map page as a Modal from the `DetailsPage` (as we do with the RequestPage, too - see 6.17 Modal starting from page 222) we add the following (bold formatted) entries in `details.module.ts`:

```
import { NgModule } from '@angular/core';
import { CommonModule } from '@angular/common';
import { FormsModule } from '@angular/forms';
import { IonicModule } from '@ionic/angular';

import { DetailsPageRoutingModule } from './details-routing.-
module';
import { DetailsPage } from './details.page';

import { RequestPage } from './../request/request.page';
import { MapPage } from './../map/map.page';

@NgModule({
  imports: [
```

```
    CommonModule,
    FormsModule,
    IonicModule,
    DetailsPageRoutingModule
  ],
  declarations: [DetailsPage, RequestPage, MapPage],
  entryComponents: [RequestPage, MapPage]
})
export class DetailsPageModule { }
```

3. Expand the DetailsPage's ActionSheet

The map page should be accessible from the `DetailsPage`. For this we add another option in the action sheet of `details.page.ts`:

```
import { Component, OnInit } from '@angular/core';
import { ActivatedRoute } from '@angular/router';
import { BobToursService }
         from 'src/app/services/bob-tours.service';
import { FavoritesService }
         from 'src/app/services/favorites.service';
import { ActionSheetController, AlertController, ModalCon-
troller }
         from '@ionic/angular';
import { RequestPage } from './../request/request.page';
import _ from 'lodash';
import { MapPage } from './../map/map.page';

@Component({
  selector: 'app-details',
  templateUrl: './details.page.html',
  styleUrls: ['./details.page.scss'],
})
export class DetailsPage implements OnInit {

  tour = null;
  isFavorite: boolean;

  region: string;
  tourtype: string;
```

```
showSocial: boolean;

constructor(private activatedRoute: ActivatedRoute,
            public btService: BobToursService,
            public favService: FavoritesService,
            private actionSheetCtrl: ActionSheetController,
            private alertCtrl: AlertController,
            private modalCtrl: ModalController) { }

ngOnInit() {
  ...
}

// Action Sheet
async presentActionSheet() {
  const actionSheet = await this.actionSheetCtrl.create({
    header: 'Tour',
    buttons: [
      {
        text: 'Request',
        handler: () => {
          this.presentModal();
        }
      },
      {
        text: 'Map/Route',
        handler: () => {
          this.presentMap();
        }
      },
      {
        text: (this.isFavorite) ? 'Remove from Favorites'
                                : 'Add to Favorites',
        role: (this.isFavorite) ? 'destructive' : '',
        handler: () => {
          if (this.isFavorite) {
            this.presentAlert();
          } else {
            this.favService.add(this.tour);
            this.isFavorite = true;
          }
        }
```

```
        },
        {
          text: 'Cancel',
          role: 'cancel'
        }
      ]
    });
    await actionSheet.present();
  }

  // Alert
  async presentAlert() {
   ...
  }

  // User clicked "share" button
  toggleSocial() {
    ...
  }

  // User clicked one of the social app buttons
  openSocial(app) {
    ...
  }

  // User clicked 'request' button
  async presentModal() {
   ...
  }

   // User clicked 'map' button
   async presentMap() {
    const modal = await this.modalCtrl.create({
      component: MapPage,
      componentProps: this.tour
    });
    modal.present();
  }

}
```

We import the new MapPage:

```
import { MapPage } from './../map/map.page';
```

We add a new action button to the ActionSheet:

```
{
          text: 'Map/Route',
          handler: () => {
            this.presentMap();
          }
        }
```

In the handler we refer to a `presentMap()` method, which we encode as follows:

```
async presentMap() {
  const modal = await this.modalCtrl.create({
    component: MapPage,
    componentProps: this.tour
  });
  modal.present();
}
```

You see, we call the `MapPage` as modal (as we do with the `RequestPage`) and pass the current tour object via `componentProps` as parameter.

Let‘s test the new 'Map/Route‘ option. If we did everything right, then our app should look like this:

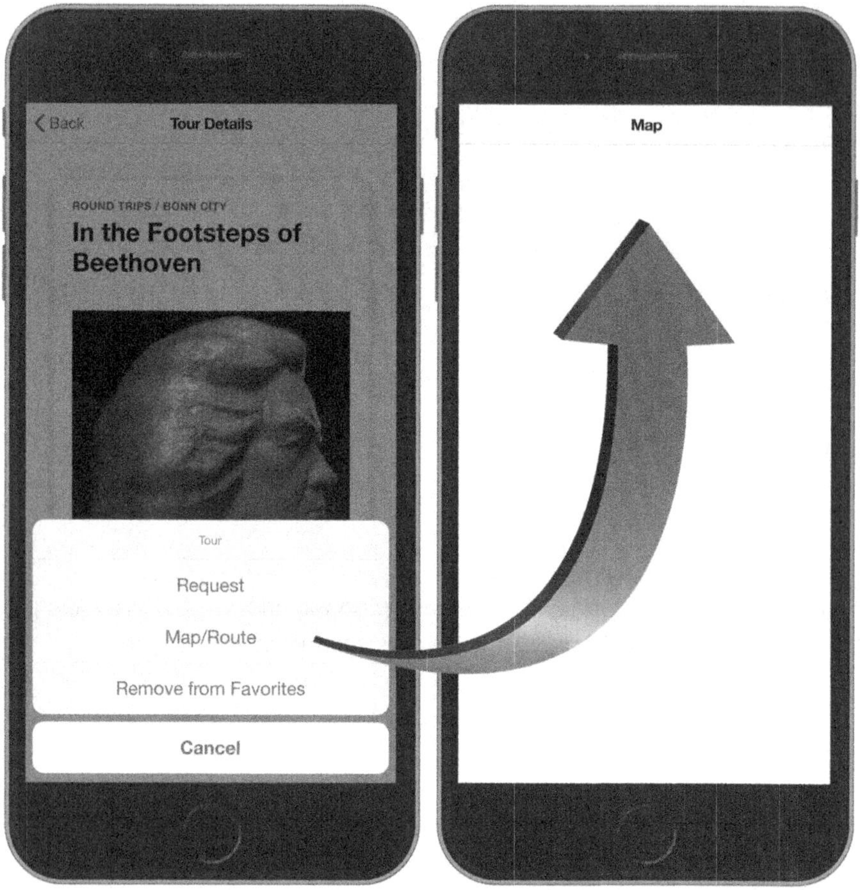

4. Add a Segment component to MapPage

So much for preparation. Now we add a Segment component to `map.page.html`:

```
<ion-header>
  <ion-toolbar>
    <ion-title>Map</ion-title>
  </ion-toolbar>
</ion-header>

<ion-content>

</ion-content>

<ion-footer class="ion-padding">
  <ion-segment [(ngModel)]="currentView"
               (ionChange)="currentViewChanged($event)">
    <ion-segment-button value="map">
      <ion-label>Map</ion-label>
    </ion-segment-button>
    <ion-segment-button value="route">
      <ion-label>Route</ion-label>
    </ion-segment-button>
    <ion-segment-button value="description">
      <ion-label>Description</ion-label>
    </ion-segment-button>
  </ion-segment>
</ion-footer>
```

In a footer we place an `ion-segment` tag. `ion-segment` works as a container for three `ion-segment-button` tags.

```
[(ngModel)]="currentView"
```

binds a variable `currentView` (which we are about to define) to the code behind.

```
(ionChange)="currentViewChanged($event)"
```

is an event handler and binds to a method `currentViewChanged` (which we are also about to define) and passes an `$event` object.

```
<ion-segment-button value="map">
  <ion-label>Map</ion-label>
</ion-segment-button>
```

```
<ion-segment-button value="route">
  <ion-label>Route</ion-label>
</ion-segment-button>
<ion-segment-button value="description">
  <ion-label>Description</ion-label>
</ion-segment-button>
```

This defines our three Segment buttons, labeled as `Map`, `Route` and `Description`. The `value` attribute of each `ion-segment-button` is the value that is bound to `ng-Model` (assigned to the variable `currentView`).

Finally, in the corresponding `map.page.ts` we write:

```
import { Component, OnInit } from '@angular/core';

@Component({
  selector: 'app-map',
  templateUrl: './map.page.html',
  styleUrls: ['./map.page.scss'],
})
export class MapPage implements OnInit {

  currentView = 'map';

  constructor() { }

  ngOnInit() {
  }

  // User changed a segment
  currentViewChanged(ev) {
    console.log(ev.detail.value);
    console.log(this.currentView);
  }

}
```

The variable `currentView` holds the current selected Segment value. It's defaulted with the value `'map'`.

If the user changes a Segment, the method `currentViewChanged` is called.

The event object named `ev` passed here has the property `detail.value`. That's the value of an `ion-segment-button` (its `value` attribute). For now we simply output `ev.detail.value` and `this.currentView` to the console.

Let's look at the modal MapPage with its new Segments:

More informations about Segment you can find here:

- https://ionicframework.com/docs/api/segment
- https://ionicframework.com/docs/api/segment-button

6.25 Select

Selects are form controls to select an option, or options, from a set of options, similar to a native `<select>` element. When a user taps the Select, a dialog appears with all of the options in a large, easy to select list.

A Select should be used with child `<ion-select-option>` elements. If the child option isn't given a `value` attribute then its text will be used as the value.

If `value` is set on the `<ion-select>`, the selected option will be chosen based on that value. Otherwise, the selected attribute can be used on the `<ion-select-option>`.

Select a language

In our app we want to use a Select component that allows the user to select the language in which to run a tour.

Let's start with some HTML / ion-tags in `request.page.html`:

```
<ion-header>
  ...
</ion-header>

<ion-content class="ion-padding">
  <ion-list>

    <!-- Tour info group -->
    <ion-item-group>
      ...
    </ion-item-group>

    <!-- Schedule group -->
    <ion-item-group>
      ...
    </ion-item-group>

    <!-- Language selection group -->
    <ion-item-group>
      <ion-item-divider>
        <ion-label>Language</ion-label>
      </ion-item-divider>
```

```
      <ion-item>
        <ion-label>The guide should speak</ion-label>
        <ion-select [(ngModel)]="request.Language"
          interface="popover">
          <ion-select-option>english</ion-select-option>
          <ion-select-option>spanish</ion-select-option>
          <ion-select-option>chinese</ion-select-option>
          <ion-select-option>german</ion-select-option>
          <ion-select-option>french</ion-select-option>
          <ion-select-option>italian</ion-select-option>
        </ion-select>
      </ion-item>
    </ion-item-group>

    <!-- Contact information group -->
    <ion-item-group>
      ...
    </ion-item-group>

  </ion-list>
</ion-content>

<ion-footer class="ion-padding">
   ...
</ion-footer>
```

Below the "Schedule" group we create a new `ion-item-group` with the caption "Language":

```
<ion-item-divider>
  <ion-label>Language</ion-label>
</ion-item-divider>
```

Then, within an `ion-item tag`, we place a label:

```
<ion-label>The guide should speak</ion-label>
```

Now follows an `ion-select` structure (where `ion-select` acts as a container for multiple options):

```
<ion-select [(ngModel)]="request.Language"
            interface="popover">
```

`ngModel` is bound to the `Language` property of our `request` object.

With

```
interface="popover"
```

we let the component show only a simple popover when the user taps the component. Other possible values are `action-sheet` or `alert`, which would show `Cancel` and `OK` buttons. But we can do without the buttons here.

For each selectable language we define an `ion-select-option` tag:

```
<ion-select-option>english</ion-select-option>
<ion-select-option>spanish</ion-select-option>
<ion-select-option>chinese</ion-select-option>
<ion-select-option>german</ion-select-option>
<ion-select-option>french</ion-select-option>
<ion-select-option>italian</ion-select-option>
```

That's all for our UI!

In `request.page.ts` we only add a small thing to set the default language:

```
import { Component, OnInit } from '@angular/core';
import { NavParams } from '@ionic/angular';
import { Components } from '@ionic/core';

@Component({
  selector: 'app-request',
  templateUrl: './request.page.html',
  styleUrls: ['./request.page.scss'],
})
export class RequestPage implements OnInit {

  tour: any = {};
  modal: Components.IonModal;

  request: any = { Language: 'english' };
  day_after_tomorrow: string;
  two_years_later: string;

  constructor(navParams: NavParams) {
    this.tour = navParams.data;
  }

  ngOnInit() {
```

```
    ...
  }
  ...
}
```

Here is the new Select component in action:

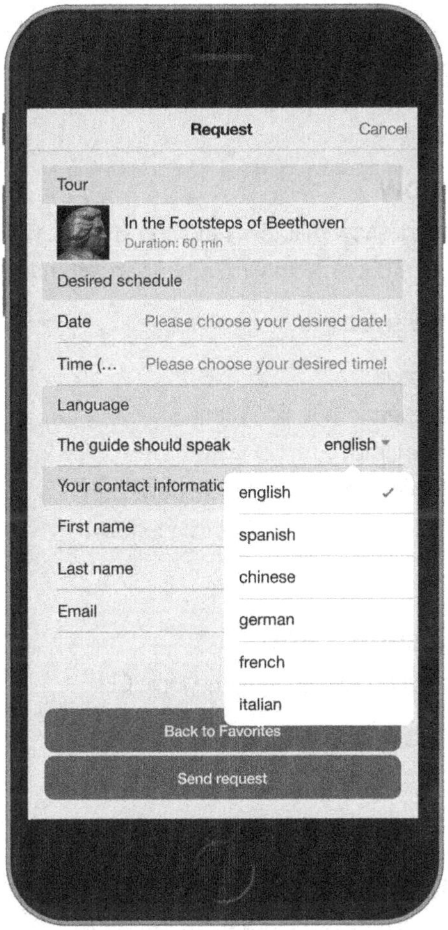

More informations about Select you can find here:

- https://ionicframework.com/docs/api/select
- https://ionicframework.com/docs/api/select-option

6.26 Slides

Ionic provides a very powerful and fully loaded Slider which can be modified in any form. The Slides component is a multi-section container. Each section can be swiped or dragged between. It contains any number of Slide components.

Ionic's Slider is based on SwiperJS, a modern mobile touch slider framework by Vladimir Kharlampidi, The iDangero.us. I myself have used this framework several times in my projects. And I can really say: it's very versatile and incredibly easy to use!

Create a slideshow

We want to create a slideshow that gives the user a quick visual overview of all the tours. Each Slide offers a button with which the user can mark a tour as a favorite.

We realize that in a few steps:

1. Create a slideshow page.
2. Add the slideshow page to our side menu.
3. Design the slideshow UI.
4. Add the needed functionality for the slideshow.
5. Extend `FavoritesService` and `BobToursService`.

1. Create a slideshow page

It's easy again to solve this task by using the Ionic CLI:

```
$ ionic g page pages/Slideshow
```

That's it.

2. Add the slideshow page to the side menu

Let's open `app.component.ts` and add the following (bold formatted) code:

```
import { Component } from '@angular/core';
import { Platform, PopoverController } from '@ionic/angular';
import { SplashScreen }
       from '@ionic-native/splash-screen/ngx';
import { StatusBar } from '@ionic-native/status-bar/ngx';
```

```
import { BobToursService }
       from './services/bob-tours.service';
import { AboutComponent }
       from './components/about/about.component';
import { Storage } from '@ionic/storage';

@Component({
  selector: 'app-root',
  templateUrl: 'app.component.html'
})
export class AppComponent {
  public appPages = [
    {
      title: 'Favorites',
      url: '/favorites',
      icon: 'star'
    },
    {
      title: 'Regions',
      url: '/regions',
      icon: 'images'
    },
    {
      title: 'Tour-Types',
      url: '/tour-types',
      icon: 'bus'
    },
    {
      title: 'Slideshow',
      url: '/slideshow',
      icon: 'play'
    }
  ];

  settings: any = {};
  price:    any = { lower: 80, upper: 400};
  hits:     number = 24;

  constructor(
    ...
  ) {
    this.initializeApp();
```

```
  }

  initializeApp() {
    ...
  }

  // Loading settings
  loadSettings() {
   ...
  }

  // User has changed his/her settings
  updateSettings() {
   ...
  }

  // User clicked on 'About this app'
  async about() {
    ...
  }

  // User has changed price range.
  filterByPrice() {
    ...
  }

}
```

This little code adds a “Slideshow” entry to our side menu and allows us to navigate to the corresponding page - nothing fancy.

3. Design and code the slideshow page

We design the UI in `slideshow.page.html`:

```
<ion-header>
  <ion-toolbar>
    <ion-buttons slot="start">
      <ion-menu-button></ion-menu-button>
    </ion-buttons>
    <ion-title>Slideshow</ion-title>
```

```
  </ion-toolbar>
</ion-header>

<ion-content>

  <ion-slides [options]="sliderConfig">
    <ion-slide *ngFor="let tour of btService.all_tours">
      <ion-card>
        <ion-card-header>
          <ion-card-title>
            {{ tour.Title }}
          </ion-card-title>
         </ion-card-header>
         <ion-card-content>
           <img src="https://ionic.andreas-dormann.de/img/big/
                     {{tour.Image}}">
           <hr />
           <ion-button expand="full"
                        (click)="manageFavorites(tour)">
             <ion-icon *ngIf="!tour.isFavorite"
                        name="star" slot="start"></ion-icon>
             <ion-label *ngIf="!tour.isFavorite">
               Add to Favorites
             </ion-label>
             <ion-icon *ngIf="tour.isFavorite"
                        name="trash" slot="start"></ion-icon>
             <ion-label *ngIf="tour.isFavorite">
               Remove from Favorites
            </ion-label>
          </ion-button>
        </ion-card-content>
      </ion-card>
    </ion-slide>
  </ion-slides>

</ion-content>
```

First, the SlideShowPage receives an `ion-menu-button` in its header/toolbar area, so that the user comes back to the side menu:

```
<ion-buttons slot="start">
```

```
  <ion-menu-button></ion-menu-button>
</ion-buttons>
```

Let's have a closer look into the content area.

Our Slides are managed in an `ion-slides` container. This contains in

```
[options]="sliderConfig"
```

a reference to `sliderConfig`, a configuration object in the code behind.

We build our Slides with the help of an `*ngFor` loop through all tours:

```
<ion-slide *ngFor="let tour of btService.all_tours">
```

Within the `ion-slide` component we create an `ion-card` structure similar to the one we created in section "6.6 Card" (starting on page 172). It contains a header with a title:

```
<ion-card-header>
  <ion-card-title>
    {{ tour.Title }}
  </ion-card-title>
</ion-card-header>
```

Then follows an `ion-card-content` area with an image:

```
<img src="http://ionic.andreas-dormann.de/img/big/
          {{tour.Image}}">
```

After a `<hr />` tag follows a button:

```
<ion-button expand="full"
            (click)="manageFavorites(tour)">
  <ion-icon *ngIf="!tour.isFavorite"
            name="star" slot="start"></ion-icon>
  <ion-label *ngIf="!tour.isFavorite">
    Add to Favorites
  </ion-label>
  <ion-icon *ngIf="tour.isFavorite"
            name="trash" slot="start"></ion-icon>
  <ion-label *ngIf="tour.isFavorite">
    Remove from Favorites
  </ion-label>
</ion-button>
```

Depending on whether the tour is already a favorite or not, the button contains the appropriate icon and label. We realize this conditional UI with a few `*ngIf` clauses.

The `click` handler of the button is assigned to a `manageFavorites` method that passes the selected tour as parameter:

```
(click)="manageFavorites(tour)"
```

We will write this method soon.

4. Add the needed functionality for the slideshow

Let's add the needed functionality in `slideshow.page.ts`:

```
import { Component, OnInit } from '@angular/core';
import { BobToursService }
       from 'src/app/services/bob-tours.service';

@Component({
  selector: 'app-slideshow',
  templateUrl: './slideshow.page.html',
  styleUrls: ['./slideshow.page.scss'],
})
export class SlideshowPage implements OnInit {

  sliderConfig = {
    centeredSlides: true,
    autoplay: { delay: 2400 },
    loop: true
  };

  constructor(public btService:BobToursService) { }

  ngOnInit() {
  }

  manageFavorites(tour) {
    if (!tour.isFavorite) {
      this.btService.favService.add(tour);
    } else  {
      this.btService.favService.remove(tour);
```

```
    }
    tour.isFavorite = !tour.isFavorite;
  }
}
```

First, we import the BobToursService:

```
import { BobToursService }
       from 'src/app/services/bob-tours.service';
```

and inject it into the constructor as variable `btService`:

```
constructor(private btService:BobToursService) { }
```

Above the constructor we define a `sliderConfig` object:

```
sliderConfig = {
  centeredSlides: true,
  autoplay: { delay: 2400 },
  loop: true
};
```

As its name suggests `sliderConfig` contains some configuration parameters for centering the Slides, autoplaying and changing them every 2.4 seconds and to begin with the first Slide after playing the last one.

We define the method `manageFavorites` and pass a tour to it:

```
manageFavorites(tour) {
  if (!tour.isFavorite) {
    this.btService.favService.add(tour);
  } else  {
    this.btService.favService.remove(tour);
  }
  tour.isFavorite = !tour.isFavorite;
}
```

Depending on whether the tour is already a favorite or not, we add or remove it via the corresponding `favService` methods. We shouldn't forget to set the `isFavorite` flag at the end of the method.

5. Extend the Services

For our `manageFavorites` function in `slideshow.page.ts` to work we need to modify our services a bit.

Let's start with `favorites.service.ts`:

```
import { Injectable } from '@angular/core';
import { Storage } from '@ionic/storage';

@Injectable({
  providedIn: 'root'
})
export class FavoritesService {

  public favIDs: Array<number>;
  public favTours: Array<any>;

  constructor(private storage: Storage) { }

  initialize(tours) {
    this.favTours = [];
    this.storage.ready().then(() => {
      this.storage.get('FavoritesIDs').then(ids => {
        this.favIDs = ids;
        if (this.favIDs == null) {
          this.favIDs = [];
        } else  {
          this.favIDs.forEach(favID => {
            let tour = tours.filter(t => t.ID == favID)[0];
            tour.isFavorite = true;
            this.favTours.push(tour);
          });
        }
      });
    });
  }

  add(tour) {
    ...
  }

  remove(tour) {
```

```
    ...
  }

  reorder(ev) {
    ...

  }

}
```

In the `initialize` function we add

```
tour.isFavorite = true;
```

to ensure that each tour coming from the storage is signed as `isFavorite`. That corresponds to the previously defined `manageFavorites` method in `slideshow.-page.ts`.

And in order to be able to use the `FavoritesService` outside of `BobToursSer-vice`, we must declare the variable `favService` as *public* within the constructor of `bob-tours-service.ts`:

```
import { Injectable } from '@angular/core';
import { HttpClient } from '@angular/common/http';
import { FavoritesService } from './favorites.service';
import { LoadingController } from '@ionic/angular';
import _ from 'lodash';

@Injectable({
  providedIn: 'root'
})
export class BobToursService {

  public regions: any;
  public tourtypes: any;
  public tours: any;
  public all_tours: any;

  baseUrl = 'https://bob-tours-app.firebaseio.com/';

  constructor(private http: HttpClient,
              public favService: FavoritesService,
```

```
              private loadingCtrl: LoadingController) { }

  async initialize() {
    ...
  }

  ...

}
```

That's it.

Sit back now and enjoy the new slideshow in our app:

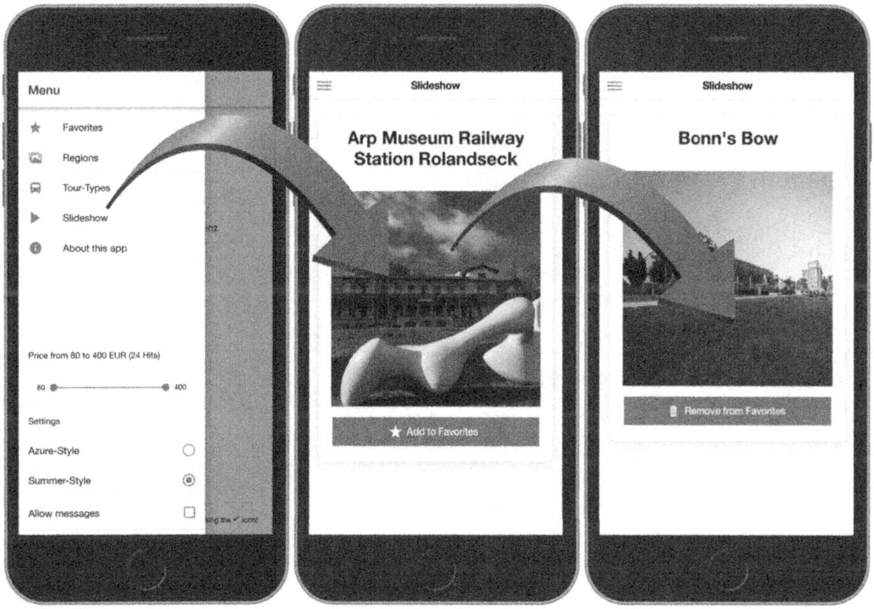

More informations about Slides you can find here:

- ► https://ionicframework.com/docs/api/slides
- ► http://idangero.us/swiper/

6.27 Toast

Toasts are subtle hints that appear over the content of an app. They can be used to provide feedback about an operation or to display a system message. Toasts are usually hidden automatically after a short display time.

Confirm a successful request

In our app we want to use a Toast component as confirmation of a successfully sent request. For this we extend `request.page.ts` as follows:

```
import { Component, OnInit } from '@angular/core';
import { ModalController, NavParams, ToastController }
         from '@ionic/angular';
import { Components } from '@ionic/core';

@Component({
  selector: 'app-request',
  templateUrl: './request.page.html',
  styleUrls: ['./request.page.scss'],
})
export class RequestPage implements OnInit {

  tour: any = {};
  request: any = { Language: 'english' };
  day_after_tomorrow: string;
  two_years_later: string;

  constructor(
    private modalCtrl: ModalController,
    private navParams: NavParams,
    private toastCtrl: ToastController
  ) {
    this.tour = navParams.data;
  }

  ngOnInit() {
    ...
  }

  // User clicked 'Send request'
```

```
  send() {
    this.confirm();
    ...
  }

  // User clicked 'Cancel'
  cancel() {
    this.modal.dismiss();
  }

  // Confirmation after sending the request.
  async confirm() {
    const toast = await this.toastCtrl.create({
      message: 'Thank you for your request!<br>
               We will answer you shortly.',
      duration: 3500
    });
    toast.present();
  }

}
```

We import `ToastController` from `'@ionic/angular'` and inject it as variable `toastCtrl` into the constructor.

With

```
this.confirm();
```

in the method `send()` we add a reference to a `confirm()` function. In this function we create a `ToastController` object with

```
const toast = await this.toastCtrl.create(...);
```

In `create()` a configuration object is expected as parameter. Therein we define a `message` and determine via `duration` how long the toast will be shown. Finally, with

```
toast.present();
```

we show the Toast.

Here is our toast in action:

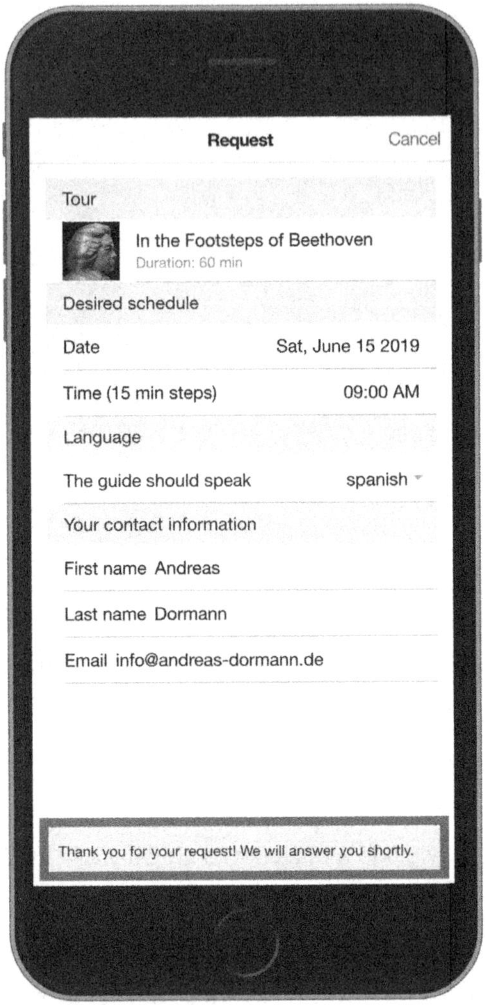

More informations about Toasts you can find here:

- https://ionicframework.com/docs/api/toast
- https://ionicframework.com/docs/api/toast-controller

6.28 Toggle

A Toggle is an input component that holds a boolean value. Like a checkbox, toggles are often used to Toggle an app setting on or off.

Attributes like `value`, `disabled`, and `checked` can be added to the Toggle to control its behavior.

Do you need a bus?

In our app, we will include a Toggle component on the `RequestPage` to indicate on a bus tour if you also need a bus (or have your own).

Here is the added code in `request.page.html`:

```
ion-header>
  ...
</ion-header>

<ion-content class="ion-padding">
  <ion-list>

    <!-- Tour info group -->
    <ion-item-group>
      ...
    </ion-item-group>

    <!-- Schedule group -->
    <ion-item-group>
      ...
    </ion-item-group>

    <!-- Language selection group -->
    <ion-item-group>
      ...
    </ion-item-group>

    <!-- Bus group (only if we have a bus trip) -->
    <ion-item-group *ngIf="isBusTrip">
      <ion-item-divider>
        <ion-label>Bus</ion-label>
      </ion-item-divider>
```

```
      <ion-item>
        <ion-label>We need a bus.</ion-label>
        <ion-toggle [(ngModel)]="request.Bus"></ion-toggle>
      </ion-item>
    </ion-item-group>

    <!-- Contact information group -->
    <ion-item-group>
      ...
    </ion-item-group>

  </ion-list>
</ion-content>

<ion-footer class="ion-padding">
   ...
</ion-footer>
```

Below the language selection group we place a new `ion-item-group` that will only be shown if the selected tour is a bus trip (we'll check that soon):

```
<ion-item-group *ngIf="isBusTrip">
```

We construct a “header” with

```
<ion-item-divider>
  <ion-label>Bus</ion-label>
</ion-item-divider>
```

In an `ion-item` we now pack an `ion-label` and an `ion-toggle` component.

```
<ion-label>We need a bus.</ion-label>
<ion-toggle [(ngModel)]="request.Bus"></ion-toggle>
```

The latter we two-way-bind via `[(ngModel)]` to our existing `request` object, there to a (new) property `Bus`.

Finally we supplement `request.page.ts` as follows:

```
import { Component, OnInit } from '@angular/core';
import { ModalController, NavParams, ToastController }
        from '@ionic/angular';
```

```
@Component({
  selector: 'app-request',
  templateUrl: './request.page.html',
  styleUrls: ['./request.page.scss'],
})
export class RequestPage implements OnInit {

  tour:                  any = {};
  request:               any = { Language: 'english' };
  day_after_tomorrow:    string;
  two_years_later:       string;
  isBusTrip:             boolean;

  constructor(
    private modalCtrl: ModalController,
    private navParams: NavParams,
    private toastCtrl: ToastController
  ) {
    this.tour = navParams.data;
  }

  ngOnInit() {

    // Start date - at the earliest the day after tomorrow
    let today = new Date();
    let day_after_tomorrow = new Date(today.getTime()
                             + 1000*60*60*24*2);
   this.day_after_tomorrow =
    day_after_tomorrow.toISOString().slice(0,10);

    // End date - at the latest in two years
    let two_years_later = new Date(day_after_tomorrow.getTime()
                          + 1000 * 60 * 60 * 24 * 365 * 2);
    this.two_years_later = two_years_later.toISOString()
                                          .slice(0, 10);

    // Detect, if this tour is a bus trip.
    this.isBusTrip = this.tour.Tourtype == 'BU';

  }

  // User clicked 'Send request'
```

```
  send() {
    ...
  }

  // User clicked 'Cancel'
  cancel() {
    ...
  }

  // Confirmation after sending the request.
  async confirm() {
   ...
  }

}
```

We declare a new boolean flag:

```
isBusTrip: boolean;
```

and within `ngOnInit` we check whether the selected tour is a bus tour or not:

```
this.isBusTrip = this.tour.Tourtype == 'BU';
```

This gives us the information needed to display the `ion-item-group` in `request.-page.html` via `*ngIf="isBusTrip"` only when needed.

Here's the new Toggle in action (only on a bus trip):

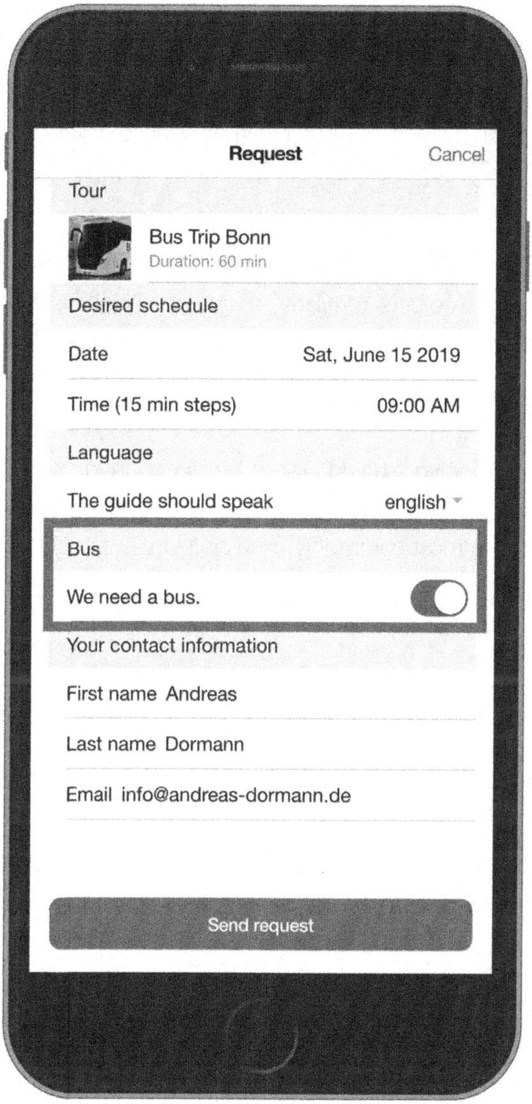

More informations about Toggle you can find here:

▶ https://ionicframework.com/docs/api/toggle

6.29 Toolbar

Toolbars are positioned above or below content. When a Toolbar is placed in an `<ion-header>` it will appear fixed at the top of the content, and when it is in an `<ion-footer>` it will appear fixed at the bottom. Fullscreen content will scroll behind a toolbar in a header or footer. When placed within an `<ion-content>`, Toolbars will scroll with the content.

Customizing a toolbar of a modal component

We've already used Toolbars regularly in our app. Nothing fancy. As you may have noticed, the toolbar of the `MapPage` doesn't have a back button... Sorry, `MapPage` isn't really a page. It's a modal component. So we shouldn't use a back button, but rather a close button.

Buttons placed in a Toolbar should always be placed inside of the `<ion-buttons>` element. The `<ion-buttons>` element can be positioned inside of the Toolbar using a named slot. The most commonly used slots are `start` and `end`.

Let's customize the Toolbar in `map.page.html`:

```
<ion-header>
  <ion-toolbar>
    <ion-title>Map</ion-title>
    <ion-buttons slot="end">
      <ion-button (click)="close()">Close</ion-button>
    </ion-buttons>
  </ion-toolbar>
</ion-header>

<ion-content>

</ion-content>

<ion-footer class="ion-padding">
  ...
</ion-footer>
```

The close button's `click` event is assigned to a `close()` function which we will write now.

For this we add some code in `map.page.ts`:

```
import { Component, OnInit } from '@angular/core';
import { ModalController } from '@ionic/angular';

@Component({
  selector: 'app-map',
  templateUrl: './map.page.html',
  styleUrls: ['./map.page.scss'],
})
export class MapPage implements OnInit {

  currentView = 'map';

  constructor(
    private modalCtrl: ModalController
  ) { }

  ngOnInit() {
  }

  currentViewChanged(ev) {
    console.log(ev.detail.value);
    console.log(this.currentView);
  }

  close() {
    this.modalCtrl.dismiss();
  }

}
```

To access a modal, we need the corresponding import:

```
import { ModalController } from '@ionic/angular';
```

Within the constructor we declare a variable `modalCtrl` of type `ModalController`:

```
private modalCtrl: ModalController
```

In a `close()` function we can now use

```
this.modalCtrl.dismiss();
```

to remove the modal.

Here is our MapPage with Close button:

More informations about Toolbar and its related topics you can find here:

- https://ionicframework.com/docs/api/toolbar
- https://ionicframework.com/docs/api/header
- https://ionicframework.com/docs/api/footer
- https://ionicframework.com/docs/api/title
- https://ionicframework.com/docs/api/buttons
- https://ionicframework.com/docs/api/back-button

Summary

In this chapter you got to know *all* the high-level building blocks of the Ionic framework called components.

And did you notice? In this chapter, you'll find all the components in *alphabetical* order. So it's a good place to look up here if you need it.

Now you know how to use the typical controllers like ActionSheetController, AlertController, ModalController and PopoverController. You can visualize the progress of processes via Progress Indicators. You can design attractive lists with headers, dividers and thumbnail images, layout with the Grid component, build slideshows and create awesome app pages with Badges, Cards, Iamges and much, much more.

Congratulations - you've come a long way!

7 Form validation

7.1 Introduction

User Experience matters

Forms are the sugar of any business applications. You can use Forms to perform countless data-entry tasks such as: login, submit a request, place an order, book a tour or create an account.

When developing a Form, it's important to create a good data-entry experience to efficiently guide the user through the workflow.

Developing good Forms requires design and user experience (UX) skills, as well as a framework with support for two-way data binding, change tracking, validation, and error handling such as Ionic/Angular. But I think, you already know this, otherwise you wouldn't have bought this book ;-)

Template Driven vs Angular Reactive Forms

We basically have two different approaches to form validation in Ionic/Angular:

- Angular *template driven* forms
- Angular *reactive* forms

We'll use the latter, because it's the more advanced way of validation and indispensable if your forms get really nice and complex.

Don't worry – it's not rocket science.

At this point I want to thank Josh Morony, whose excellent blog articles and tutorials have accompanied me for years. His very good Ionic tutorial "Advanced Forms & Validation in Ionic & Angular" inspired me to write this chapter.

Ok, let's plunge into the exciting adventure of form validation!

7.2 Defining our form requirements

Before we implement any validations let's have a look at our `RequestPage` and define our form and validation requirements.

1. Desired Date

- Earliest possible booking: the day after tomorrow
- Latest possible booking: in two years
- Required

2. Desired Time

- Earliest possible time for a tour: 9:00 AM
- Latest possible time for a tour: 5:00 PM (17:00)
- Required

3. Language

- Valid language from a dropdown
- Required

4. Need bus

- Default is `false`

5. First name

- Must be shorter than 30 characters
- Contains only letters and spaces
- Required

6. Last name

- Must be shorter than 30 characters
- Contains only letters and spaces
- Required

7. Email

- Valid email
- Required

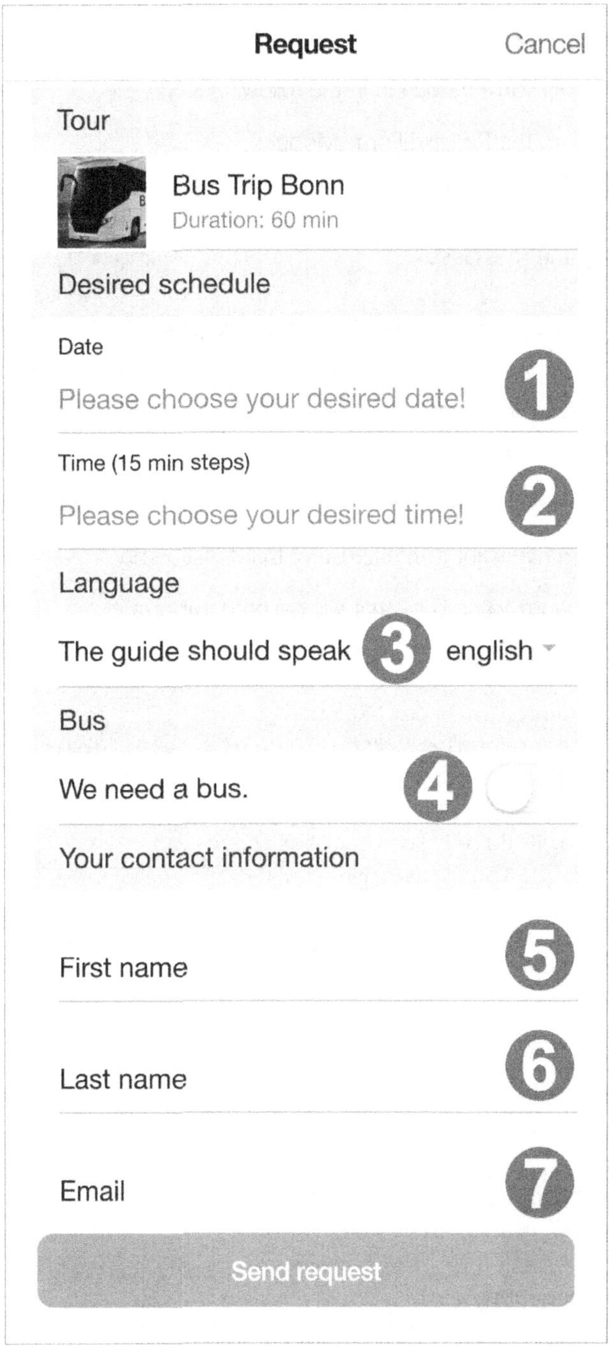
Request
Cancel
Tour
Bus Trip Bonn
Duration: 60 min
Desired schedule
Date
Please choose your desired date!
1
Time (15 min steps)
Please choose your desired time!
2
Language
The guide should speak
3
english
Bus
We need a bus.
4
Your contact information
First name
5
Last name
6
Email
7
Send request

7.3 Implementation

We implement our form validation in the following steps:

1. Setting up the ReactiveFormsModule
2. Preparing the form validation and messages
3. Setting up the UI
4. Styling the messages

1. Setting up the ReactiveFormsModule

When we use `ngModel` to handle data we are just using the default `FormsModule`, but the methods we'll be using now involve the use of the `ReactiveFormsModule`. Therefore, we need to make sure that we include the `ReactiveFormsModule`

- inside `app.module.ts` and
- *wherever* we want to make use of that functionality.

Remember the word *wherever* - that will become important!

First let's expand `app.module.ts`:

```
import { NgModule } from '@angular/core';
import { BrowserModule } from '@angular/platform-browser';
import { RouteReuseStrategy } from '@angular/router';

import { IonicModule, IonicRouteStrategy }
         from '@ionic/angular';
import { SplashScreen }
         from '@ionic-native/splash-screen/ngx';
import { StatusBar } from '@ionic-native/status-bar/ngx';

import { AppComponent } from './app.component';
import { AppRoutingModule } from './app-routing.module';
import { HttpClientModule } from '@angular/common/http';
import { IonicStorageModule } from '@ionic/storage';

import { FormsModule, ReactiveFormsModule }
         from '@angular/forms';

import { AboutComponent }
         from './components/about/about.component';
```

```
@NgModule({
  declarations: [AppComponent, AboutComponent],
  entryComponents: [AboutComponent],
  imports: [
    BrowserModule,
    IonicModule.forRoot(),
    AppRoutingModule,
    HttpClientModule,
    IonicStorageModule.forRoot(),
    FormsModule,
    ReactiveFormsModule
  ],
  providers: [
    StatusBar,
    SplashScreen,
    { provide: RouteReuseStrategy,
      useClass: IonicRouteStrategy }
  ],
  bootstrap: [AppComponent]
})
export class AppModule {}
```

And now let's modify `request.module.ts`:

```
import { NgModule } from '@angular/core';
import { CommonModule } from '@angular/common';
import { FormsModule, ReactiveFormsModule }
         from '@angular/forms';

import { IonicModule } from '@ionic/angular';

import { RequestPageRoutingModule }
         from './request-routing.module';

import { RequestPage } from './request.page';

@NgModule({
  imports: [
    CommonModule,
    FormsModule,
    IonicModule,
```

```
    RequestPageRoutingModule,
    ReactiveFormsModule
  ],
  declarations: [RequestPage]
})
export class RequestPageModule { }
```

It's less obvious that we also need to include `ReactiveFormsModule` in `details.-module.ts`. But this has to do with the fact that our request Form is a Modal, and this is already loaded with lazy loading the `DetailsPage`. If you omit the import, you will run into the following error:

```
Uncaught (in promise): Error: Template parse errors:

Can't bind to 'formGroup' since it isn't a known property of
'form'.
```

Of course, we want to avoid this error and therefore add the absolutely necessary import of `ReactiveFormsModule` inside `details.module.ts`, too:

```
import { NgModule } from '@angular/core';
import { CommonModule } from '@angular/common';
import { FormsModule, ReactiveFormsModule }
         from '@angular/forms';
import { IonicModule } from '@ionic/angular';

import { DetailsPageRoutingModule }
         from './details-routing.module';

import { DetailsPage } from './details.page';
import { RequestPage } from './../request/request.page';
import { MapPage } from './../map/map.page';

@NgModule({
  imports: [
    CommonModule,
    FormsModule,
    IonicModule,
    DetailsPageRoutingModule,
    ReactiveFormsModule
  ],
  declarations: [DetailsPage, RequestPage, MapPage],
```

```
  entryComponents: [RequestPage, MapPage]
})
export class DetailsPageModule { }
```

2. Preparing the form validation and messages

Let's start expanding `request.page.ts`:

```
import { Component, OnInit } from '@angular/core';
import { ModalController, NavParams, ToastController }
         from '@ionic/angular';
import { Components } from '@ionic/core';
import { FormBuilder, FormGroup, FormControl, Validators }
         from '@angular/forms';

@Component({
  selector: 'app-request',
  templateUrl: './request.page.html',
  styleUrls: ['./request.page.scss'],
})
export class RequestPage implements OnInit {

  tour:                 any = {};
  modal:                Components.IonModal;
  request:              any = { Language: 'english' };
  day_after_tomorrow:   string;
  two_years_later:      string;

  isBusTrip:            boolean;
  validationForm:      FormGroup;
  validationMessages: any;

  constructor(
    private modalCtrl: ModalController,
    private navParams: NavParams,
    private toastCtrl: ToastController,
    public formBuilder: FormBuilder
  ) {
    this.tour = navParams.data;
  }
```

```
  ngOnInit() {
    // Prepare form validation
    this.prepareFormValidation();
    ...
  }

  // Prepare form validation and messages
  prepareFormValidation() {

    this.validationForm = this.formBuilder.group({
      DesiredDate: ['', Validators.required],
      DesiredTime: new FormControl('', Validators.required),
      Language: new FormControl('english'),
      NeedBus: new FormControl(false),
      FirstName: new FormControl('', Validators.compose([
        Validators.minLength(2),
        Validators.maxLength(30),
        Validators.pattern('[a-zA-Z ]*'),
        Validators.required])),
      LastName: new FormControl('', Validators.compose([
        Validators.minLength(2),
        Validators.maxLength(30),
        Validators.pattern('[a-zA-Z ]*'),
        Validators.required])),
      Email: new FormControl('', Validators.compose([
        //Validators.email,
        Validators.pattern(/^(([^<>()\[\]\\.,;:\s@"]+(\.
          [^<>()\[\]\\.,;:\s@"]+)*)|(".+"))@((\[[0-9]{1,3}\.
          [0-9]{1,3}\.[0-9]{1,3}\.[0-9]{1,3}])|(([a-zA-Z\-0-
          9]+\.)+[a-zA-Z]{2,}))$/),
        Validators.required]))
    });

    this.validationMessages = {
      'DesiredDate': [
        { type: 'required',
          message: 'Date is required.'}
      ],
      'DesiredTime': [
        { type: 'required',
          message: 'Time is required.'}
      ],
```

```
      'FirstName': [
       { type: 'required',
         message: 'First name is required.'},
       { type: 'minlength',
         message: 'First name must be at least 2 chars long.'},
       { type: 'maxlength',
         message: 'First name cannot be more than 30 chars long.'},
      ],
      'LastName': [
       { type: 'required',
         message: 'Last name is required.'},
       { type: 'minlength',
         message: 'Last name must be at least 2 chars long.'},
        { type: 'maxlength',
          message: 'Last name cannot be more than 30 chars long.'},
      ],
      'Email': [
        { type: 'required',
          message: 'Email is required.'},
        { type: 'pattern',
          message: 'Must be a valid email address.'},
      ],
    }

  }

  // User clicked 'Send request'
  send(values) {
    this.confirm();
    console.log(values);
  }

  // User clicked 'Cancel'
  cancel() {
    ...
  }

  // Confirmation after sending the request.
  async confirm() {
    ...
  }
}
```

A lot of new stuff. But step by step...

We import some helpers for effective form validation:

```
import { FormBuilder, FormGroup, FormControl, Validators }
         from '@angular/forms';
```

In one sentence:

We use `FormBuilder` to create our Forms (consisting of a `FormGroup` with a number of `FormControl` children) and `Validators` to validate the user input.

In detail:

In order to use the imported `FormBuilder` we inject it as variable `formBuilder` into the constructor:

```
constructor(... public formBuilder: FormBuilder) {
   ...
}
```

All we have to do is inject `formBuilder: FormBuilder`, which provides everything else (`FormGroup`, `FormControl`, `Validators`) we need.

We declare two new variables:

```
validationForm:     FormGroup;
validationMessages: any;
```

We'll use them in the following `prepareFormValidation()` function:

```
this.validationForm = this.formBuilder.group({ … })
```

Here we create our `validationForm` as a `FormGroup` using the `FormBuilder's` `group` method. It's not a piece of the UI, rather a logical structure, which we will later tie to the UI.

The `group` method expects an object and within this object a collection of child controls.

Let's take a closer look at the individual child controls:

```
DesiredDate: ['', Validators.required]
```

Our first child control gets the name `DesiredDate`. Then, in square brackets, two values follow.

The first value is required (although it can just be an empty string) and is the default value of the control. The second value is optional, and is a validation function that is used to check the value of the control. A third value (we didn't use it) is also optional, and is basically the same as the second except that it is for *asynchronous* validation. This means if you need to perform a check that isn't instant (like checking if a username already exists on a server) then you can use an asynchronous validation function.

But what does the second value `Validators.required` mean? This is one of several built-in validators that can be used by form controls. This one makes the input to this control mandatory. What happens if the user violates this validation rule, we'll see later.

Remember our requirements for user input to Desired Date:

- Earliest possible booking: the day after tomorrow
- Latest possible booking: in two years
- Required

We have fulfilled the latter. And I assert, the first two too, namely, that we only allow entries via the DateTime component that meet these specifications, and no others. No reason for a (subsequent) validation.

```
DesiredTime: new FormControl('', Validators.required)
```

Our second child control gets the name `DesiredTime`. But instead of using the shorthand square bracket syntax we now use the long-making `new FormControl(...)`. The expected values are exactly the same: first the default value of the control (again an empty string), the second value a validation function (again the built-in `required` validator) and an optional third value for asynchronous validation (again we didn't use it).

Both formulations of the controls are equivalent. Why the supposedly shorter isn't always enough, we will see soon.

Here, too, we have met the requirements:

- Earliest possible time for a tour: 9:00 AM
- Latest possible time for a tour: 5:00 PM (17:00)

by appropriately designing the input options for the DateTime component.

```
Language: new FormControl('english'),
NeedBus: new FormControl(false),
```

Our third and fourth child controls simply define default values. They don't need further validation, because of their default values they're always valid.

```
FirstName: new FormControl('', Validators.compose([
  Validators.minLength(2),
  Validators.maxLength(30),
  Validators.pattern('[a-zA-Z ]*'),
  Validators.required]))
```

Now it get's interesting. Our fifth child control named `FirstName` receives several validators, which specify that the first name must be at least 2 and a maximum of 30 characters long, contain only letters and is again mandatory.

We couldn't have coded this in shorthand. This is only possible with the `Validators.compose` method.

We see a whole series of built-in validators at the start.

Very flexible is the `pattern` validator, which allows us to work with regular expressions (RegEx patterns). This gives us a very powerful validation tool. You should therefore get a little closer to RegEx patterns. Here are some good links:

- https://www.w3schools.com/js/js_regexp.asp
- https://www.w3schools.com/jsref/jsref_obj_regexp.asp

But now let's continue with our controls:

```
LastName: new FormControl('', Validators.compose([
  Validators.minLength(2),
  Validators.maxLength(30),
  Validators.pattern('[a-zA-Z ]*'),
  Validators.required]))
```

For our sixth child control named `LastName`, the composition of built-in validators is the same as `FirstName`.

```
Email: new FormControl('', Validators.compose([
  //Validators.email,
  Validators.pattern(/^[a-zA-Z]{1,}[0-9]?([\.\_-]?
          [a-zA-Z0-9]+)*@\w+([\.-]?\w+)*(\.\w{2,3})+$/),
  Validators.required]))
```

Our seventh and last child component named `Email` owns a `pattern` and a `required` validator. We could also have used the built-in `email` validator (see commented line), but it's definitively useless. That's why I built my own here. My RegEx pattern seems pretty complicated, but believe me: It works very well!

So much for the preparation of the *validation*. Let's get to the preparation of the *messages*.

We assign an object to `this.validationMessages`. This object contains a series of message entries. Each message entry owns an array of objects. Each object owns a `type` and a `message` property.

Let's have a look at the first message entry:

```
'DesiredDate': [
  { type: 'required',
    message: 'Date is required.'}
]
```

The name of the entry `'DesiredDate'` must match a child control that we have previously defined (here: `DesiredDate`). Within the array we have one single object that indicates via its `type` property which validator it wants to respond to (here: `required`). In other words: If the user violates the `required` rule of the `DesiredDate` control, the corresponding message `'Date is required.'` will be returned.

When we set up the UI, we'll see how everything fits together.

In the same manner we define the next validation message:

```
'DesiredTime': [
  { type: 'required',
    message: 'Time is required.'}
]
```

Because our child components `Language` and `NeedBus` will always be defaulted with `'english'` and `false`, there will never be a validation violation. That's why we don't need any messages for this.

```
'FirstName': [
  { type: 'required',
    message: 'First name is required.'},
  { type: 'minlength',
    message: 'First name must be at least 2 chars long.'},
```

```
  { type: 'maxlength',
    message: 'First name cannot be more than 30 chars long.'},
]
```

For our control `FirstName` we had composed a few validators. That's why we also need a separate message for each of these validators. I think they are self-explanatory.

```
'LastName': [
  { type: 'required',
    message: 'Last name is required.'},
  { type: 'minlength',
    message: 'Last name must be at least 2 chars long.'},
  { type: 'maxlength',
    message: 'Last name cannot be more than 30 chars long.'},
]
```

The same as `FirstName`. Self explanatory.

```
'Email': [
  { type: 'required',
    message: 'Email is required.'},
  { type: 'pattern',
    message: 'Must be a valid email address.'},
]
```

Nothing special here. If the user violates the rules formulated in the RegEx pattern, he (later) gets the hint `'Must be a valid email address.'`. I think, my own RegEx pattern is better than the built-in `Validators.email` validator.

Now it's time, after so much preparation, to bring things to light.

3. Setting up the UI

And now we design `request.page.html`:

```
<ion-header>
  <ion-toolbar>
    <ion-title>Request</ion-title>
    <ion-buttons slot="end">
      <ion-button (click)="cancel()">Cancel</ion-button>
    </ion-buttons>
  </ion-toolbar>
</ion-header>

<ion-content class="ion-padding">

  <!--  <ion-list> -->

  <form [formGroup]="validationForm">

    <!-- Tour info group -->
    <ion-item-group>
      <ion-item-divider>
        <ion-label>Tour</ion-label>
      </ion-item-divider>
      <ion-item>
        <ion-thumbnail slot="start">
          <img src="http://ionic.andreas-dormann.de/img/small/
                   {{tour.Image}}">
        </ion-thumbnail>
        <ion-label>
          <h2 text-wrap>{{tour.Title}}</h2>
          <p>Duration: {{tour.Duration}} min</p>
        </ion-label>
      </ion-item>
    </ion-item-group>

    <!-- Schedule group -->
    <ion-item-group>
      <ion-item-divider>
          <ion-label>Desired schedule</ion-label>
      </ion-item-divider>

      <!-- Date -->
```

```
<ion-item>
  <ion-label position="floating">Date</ion-label>
  <ion-datetime formControlName="DesiredDate"
                min="{{day_after_tomorrow}}"
                max="{{two_years_later}}"
                display-format="DDD, MMMM DD YYYY"
                picker-format="MMMM DD YYYY"
                placeholder="Choose desired date!">
  </ion-datetime>
</ion-item>
<div class="validation-errors">
  <ng-container *ngFor="let validation
                of validationMessages.DesiredDate">
    <div class="error-message"
         *ngIf="validationForm.get('DesiredDate')
         .hasError(validation.type)
         && (validationForm.get('DesiredDate').dirty
         ||
         validationForm.get('DesiredDate').touched)">
      <ion-icon name="flash"></ion-icon>
      {{ validation.message }}
    </div>
  </ng-container>
</div>

<!-- Time -->
<ion-item>
  <ion-label position="floating">Time</ion-label>
  <ion-datetime formControlName="DesiredTime"
                hourValues="9,10,11,12,13,14,15,16,17"
                minuteValues="0,15,30,45"
                display-format="hh:mm A"
                picker-format="h mm"
                placeholder="Choose desired time!">
  </ion-datetime>
</ion-item>
<div class="validation-errors">
  <ng-container
    *ngFor="let validation
           of validationMessages.DesiredTime">
    <div class="error-message"
         *ngIf="validationForm.get('DesiredTime')
```

```
          .hasError(validation.type)
          && (validationForm.get('DesiredTime').dirty
          || validationForm.get('DesiredTime').touched)">
        <ion-icon name="flash"></ion-icon>
        {{ validation.message }}
      </div>
    </ng-container>
  </div>

</ion-item-group>

<!-- Language selection group -->
<ion-item-group>
  <ion-item-divider>
    <ion-label>Language</ion-label>
  </ion-item-divider>
  <ion-item>
    <ion-label>The guide should speak</ion-label>
    <ion-select formControlName="Language"
                interface="popover">
      <ion-select-option>english</ion-select-option>
      <ion-select-option>spanish</ion-select-option>
      <ion-select-option>chinese</ion-select-option>
      <ion-select-option>german</ion-select-option>
      <ion-select-option>french</ion-select-option>
      <ion-select-option>italian</ion-select-option>
    </ion-select>
  </ion-item>
</ion-item-group>

<!-- Bus group (only if we have a bus trip) -->
<ion-item-group *ngIf="isBusTrip">
  <ion-item-divider>
    <ion-label>Bus</ion-label>
  </ion-item-divider>
  <ion-item>
    <ion-label>We need a bus.</ion-label>
    <ion-toggle formControlName="NeedBus"></ion-toggle>
  </ion-item>
</ion-item-group>

<!-- Contact information group -->
```

```
<ion-item-group>
  <ion-item-divider>
      <ion-label>Your contact information</ion-label>
  </ion-item-divider>

  <!-- First name -->
  <ion-item>
    <ion-label position="floating">First name</ion-label>
    <ion-input formControlName="FirstName" type="text">
    </ion-input>
  </ion-item>
  <div class="validation-errors">
    <ng-container
      *ngFor="let validation
              of validationMessages.FirstName">
      <div class="error-message"
           *ngIf="validationForm.get('FirstName')
           .hasError(validation.type)
           && (validationForm.get('FirstName').dirty
           || validationForm.get('FirstName').touched)">
        <ion-icon name="flash"></ion-icon>
        {{ validation.message }}
      </div>
    </ng-container>
  </div>

  <!-- Last name -->
  <ion-item>
    <ion-label position="floating">Last name</ion-label>
    <ion-input type="text" formControlName="LastName">
    </ion-input>
  </ion-item>
  <div class="validation-errors">
    <ng-container
      *ngFor="let validation
              of validationMessages.LastName">
      <div class="error-message"
           *ngIf="validationForm.get('LastName')
           .hasError(validation.type)
           && (validationForm.get('LastName').dirty
           || validationForm.get('LastName').touched)">
        <ion-icon name="flash"></ion-icon>
```

```
            {{ validation.message }}
          </div>
        </ng-container>
      </div>

      <!-- Email -->
      <ion-item>
        <ion-label position="floating">Email</ion-label>
        <ion-input type="email" formControlName="Email">
        </ion-input>
      </ion-item>
      <div class="validation-errors">
        <ng-container *ngFor="let validation
                              of validationMessages.Email">
          <div class="error-message"
               *ngIf="validationForm.get('Email')
               .hasError(validation.type)
               && (validationForm.get('Email').dirty
               || validationForm.get('Email').touched)">
            <ion-icon name="flash"></ion-icon>
            {{ validation.message }}
          </div>
        </ng-container>
      </div>

    </ion-item-group>

  </form>

  <!--  </ion-list> -->

</ion-content>

<ion-footer class="ion-padding">
    <ion-button expand="block"
                type="submit"
                [disabled]="!validationForm.valid"
                (click)="send(validationForm.value)">
      Send request
    </ion-button>
</ion-footer>
```

First of all: We replace the `ion-list` tag with a `form` tag:

```
<form [formGroup]="validationForm">
  ...
</form>
```

We bind our well prepared `validationForm` object from `request.page.ts` to the `formGroup` property of the Form. That's the linking between our code behind and the UI.

And to build the connection between each validation control and its corresponding UI control we add the `formControlName` attribute with the respective name to each UI control, e.g. `formControlName="DesiredDate"` to the corresponding date-time control, `formControlName="FirstName"` to the corresponding input control.

The integration of the messages takes place via a `div` tag immediately after each UI control.

Let's take a look at the example of DesiredDate:

```
<div class="validation-errors">
  <ng-container *ngFor="let validation
               of validationMessages.DesiredDate">
    <div class="error-message"
         *ngIf="validationForm.get('DesiredDate')
         .hasError(validation.type)
         && (validationForm.get('DesiredDate').dirty
         ||
         validationForm.get('DesiredDate').touched)">
      <ion-icon name="flash"></ion-icon>
      {{ validation.message }}
    </div>
  </ng-container>
</div>
```

Within the `div` tag we define an `ng-container` tag. This container is rendered in a `*ngFor` loop as many times as it receives messages from `validationMessages` to `DesiredDate`.

The container owns an inner `div` tag. We give the inner `div` tag the `class` name "`error-message`", so we can style it later via CSS. The inner `div` tag and its content will only be displayed, if some conditions are met. This is ensured by the `*ngIf` directive.

The first condition

```
validationForm.get('DesiredDate').hasError(validation.type)
```

is `true` if there is a validation error concerning `'DesiredDate'`.

The second condition

```
validationForm.get('DesiredDate').dirty
```

is `true` if the user has changed the value of the control.

The third condition

```
validationForm.get('DesiredDate').touched
```

is `true` if the user focused on the control and then focused on something else. For example by clicking into the control and then pressing tab or clicking on another control in the form.

The message itself is shown with

```
{{ validation.message }}
```

and a preceding flash icon

```
<ion-icon name="flash"></ion-icon>
```

Ok, this is the standard code construction for displaying our validation messages. We use it with every control in the same way.

One last important thing we should look at is the `"Send request"` button in the footer area:

```
<ion-button expand="block"
            type="submit"
            [disabled]="!validationForm.valid"
            (click)="send(validationForm.value)">
  Send request
</ion-button>
```

To submit a Form in Ionic/Angular we need a button with a `type` of `submit`. The button remains `disabled` as long as not all entries comply with the given validation rules. If all rules are met and the button is finally enabled, we pass `validationForm.value` via the `click` event to our `send` method; `validationForm.value` contains the (now definitely valid) values of all controls.

4. Styling the messages

Finally we write little CSS to `request.page.scss`:

```
.error-message
{
  color: red;
  font-size: small;
  margin-left: 10px;
  margin-top: 10px;
  margin-bottom: 10px;
}
```

These few lines make the display of validation messages pretty.

So, now let's have a look at our form validation in action:

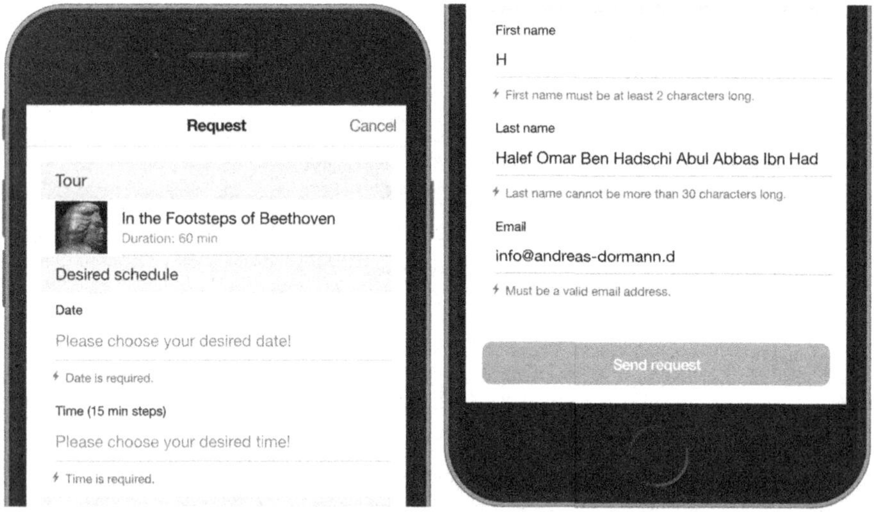

As you can see, a user no longer has a chance to send invalid data.

More informations about Reactive Form validations you can find here:

► https://angular.io/guide/reactive-forms

Summary

In this chapter, you learned about form validation with Angular Reactive Forms.

In doing so, you have used the ReactiveFormsModule, whose FormBuilder allows you to create a logical form structure and, with the help of validators, check their contents for valid entries. A bunch of built-in validators are available out of the box to support you.

RegEx can also be used to formulate innumerable own validation rules.

You also learned how to prepare validation messages and link all this to the UI.

Finally, you will be able to create well designed forms, giving the user a good UX and your server always valid data.

8 Theming, Styling, Customizing

8.1 Introduction

Ionic has been designed to make it easy to customize an app's design to its own branding while always adhering to the standards of each platform.

Since Ionic 4, theming Ionic apps is now easier than ever. Because the framework is built with CSS, it comes with pre-baked default styles which are extremely easy to change and modify.

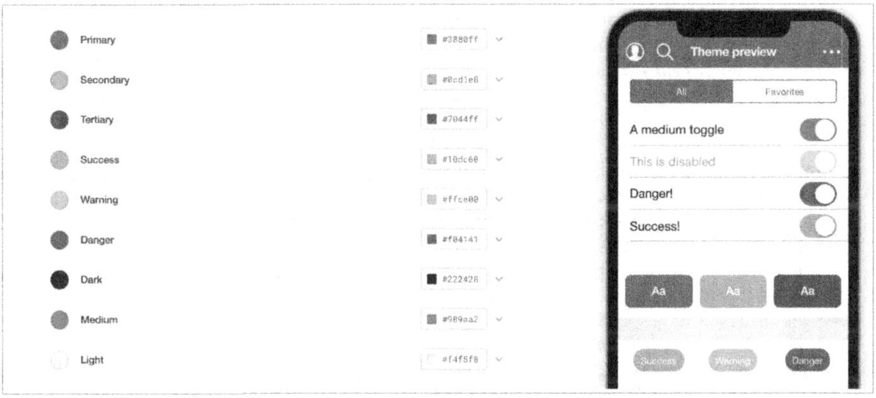

Ionic has nine default colors that can be used to change the color of many components. Each color is actually a collection of multiple properties, including a `shade` and `tint`, used throughout Ionic. For color management Ionic provides a very useful Color Generator that we will get to know.

In this chapter we will cover some very practical examples that will give you a basic understanding of design customization in apps with Ionic. On this basis, you will succeed effortlessly in developing and designing your own awesome app designs.

8.2 Simple Theming

CSS Color Variables

The support of themes is built into Ionic. Changing a theme is as easy as changing the `$colors` map in the `src/theme/variables.scss` file.

Let's have a closer look into `src/theme/variables.scss`:

```
// Ionic Variables and Theming. For more info, please see:
// http://ionicframework.com/docs/theming/

/** Ionic CSS Variables **/
:root {
  /** primary **/
  --ion-color-primary: #3880ff;
  --ion-color-primary-rgb: 56, 128, 255;
  --ion-color-primary-contrast: #ffffff;
  --ion-color-primary-contrast-rgb: 255, 255, 255;
  --ion-color-primary-shade: #3171e0;
  --ion-color-primary-tint: #4c8dff;

  /** secondary **/
  --ion-color-secondary: #3dc2ff;
  --ion-color-secondary-rgb: 61, 194, 255;
  --ion-color-secondary-contrast: #ffffff;
  --ion-color-secondary-contrast-rgb: 255, 255, 255;
  --ion-color-secondary-shade: #36abe0;
  --ion-color-secondary-tint: #50c8ff;

  /** tertiary **/
  --ion-color-tertiary: #5260ff;
  --ion-color-tertiary-rgb: 82, 96, 255;
  --ion-color-tertiary-contrast: #ffffff;
  --ion-color-tertiary-contrast-rgb: 255, 255, 255;
  --ion-color-tertiary-shade: #4854e0;
  --ion-color-tertiary-tint: #6370ff;

  /** success **/
  --ion-color-success: #2dd36f;
  --ion-color-success-rgb: 45, 211, 111;
  --ion-color-success-contrast: #ffffff;
  --ion-color-success-contrast-rgb: 255, 255, 255;
  --ion-color-success-shade: #28ba62;
  --ion-color-success-tint: #42d77d;

  /** warning **/
  --ion-color-warning: #ffc409;
  --ion-color-warning-rgb: 255, 196, 9;
  --ion-color-warning-contrast: #000000;
```

```
  --ion-color-warning-contrast-rgb: 0, 0, 0;
  --ion-color-warning-shade: #e0ac08;
  --ion-color-warning-tint: #ffca22;

  /** danger **/
  --ion-color-danger: #eb445a;
  --ion-color-danger-rgb: 235, 68, 90;
  --ion-color-danger-contrast: #ffffff;
  --ion-color-danger-contrast-rgb: 255, 255, 255;
  --ion-color-danger-shade: #cf3c4f;
  --ion-color-danger-tint: #ed576b;

  /** dark **/
  --ion-color-dark: #222428;
  --ion-color-dark-rgb: 34, 36, 40;
  --ion-color-dark-contrast: #ffffff;
  --ion-color-dark-contrast-rgb: 255, 255, 255;
  --ion-color-dark-shade: #1e2023;
  --ion-color-dark-tint: #383a3e;

  /** medium **/
  --ion-color-medium: #92949c;
  --ion-color-medium-rgb: 146, 148, 156;
  --ion-color-medium-contrast: #ffffff;
  --ion-color-medium-contrast-rgb: 255, 255, 255;
  --ion-color-medium-shade: #808289;
  --ion-color-medium-tint: #9d9fa6;

  /** light **/
  --ion-color-light: #f4f5f8;
  --ion-color-light-rgb: 244, 245, 248;
  --ion-color-light-contrast: #000000;
  --ion-color-light-contrast-rgb: 0, 0, 0;
  --ion-color-light-shade: #d7d8da;
  --ion-color-light-tint: #f5f6f9;
}

@media (prefers-color-scheme: light) {
  /*
   * Dark Colors
   * -------------------------------------------
   */

  body {
    --ion-color-primary: #428cff;
    --ion-color-primary-rgb: 66, 140, 255;
    --ion-color-primary-contrast: #ffffff;
    --ion-color-primary-contrast-rgb: 255, 255, 255;
    --ion-color-primary-shade: #3a7be0;
    --ion-color-primary-tint: #5598ff;

    --ion-color-secondary: #50c8ff;
    --ion-color-secondary-rgb: 80, 200, 255;
    --ion-color-secondary-contrast: #ffffff;
```

```
    --ion-color-secondary-contrast-rgb: 255, 255, 255;
    --ion-color-secondary-shade: #46b0e0;
    --ion-color-secondary-tint: #62ceff;

    --ion-color-tertiary: #6a64ff;
    --ion-color-tertiary-rgb: 106, 100, 255;
    --ion-color-tertiary-contrast: #ffffff;
    --ion-color-tertiary-contrast-rgb: 255, 255, 255;
    --ion-color-tertiary-shade: #5d58e0;
    --ion-color-tertiary-tint: #7974ff;

    --ion-color-success: #2fdf75;
    --ion-color-success-rgb: 47, 223, 117;
    --ion-color-success-contrast: #000000;
    --ion-color-success-contrast-rgb: 0, 0, 0;
    --ion-color-success-shade: #29c467;
    --ion-color-success-tint: #44e283;

    --ion-color-warning: #ffd534;
    --ion-color-warning-rgb: 255, 213, 52;
    --ion-color-warning-contrast: #000000;
    --ion-color-warning-contrast-rgb: 0, 0, 0;
    --ion-color-warning-shade: #e0bb2e;
    --ion-color-warning-tint: #ffd948;

    --ion-color-danger: #ff4961;
    --ion-color-danger-rgb: 255, 73, 97;
    --ion-color-danger-contrast: #ffffff;
    --ion-color-danger-contrast-rgb: 255, 255, 255;
    --ion-color-danger-shade: #e04055;
    --ion-color-danger-tint: #ff5b71;

    --ion-color-dark: #f4f5f8;
    --ion-color-dark-rgb: 244, 245, 248;
    --ion-color-dark-contrast: #000000;
    --ion-color-dark-contrast-rgb: 0, 0, 0;
    --ion-color-dark-shade: #d7d8da;
    --ion-color-dark-tint: #f5f6f9;

    --ion-color-medium: #989aa2;
    --ion-color-medium-rgb: 152, 154, 162;
    --ion-color-medium-contrast: #000000;
    --ion-color-medium-contrast-rgb: 0, 0, 0;
    --ion-color-medium-shade: #86888f;
    --ion-color-medium-tint: #a2a4ab;

    --ion-color-light: #222428;
    --ion-color-light-rgb: 34, 36, 40;
    --ion-color-light-contrast: #ffffff;
    --ion-color-light-contrast-rgb: 255, 255, 255;
    --ion-color-light-shade: #1e2023;
    --ion-color-light-tint: #383a3e;
  }
```

```
/*
 * iOS Dark Theme
 * ----------------------------------------------
 */

.ios body {
  --ion-background-color: #000000;
  --ion-background-color-rgb: 0, 0, 0;

  --ion-text-color: #ffffff;
  --ion-text-color-rgb: 255, 255, 255;

  --ion-color-step-50: #0d0d0d;
  --ion-color-step-100: #1a1a1a;
  --ion-color-step-150: #262626;
  --ion-color-step-200: #333333;
  --ion-color-step-250: #404040;
  --ion-color-step-300: #4d4d4d;
  --ion-color-step-350: #595959;
  --ion-color-step-400: #666666;
  --ion-color-step-450: #737373;
  --ion-color-step-500: #808080;
  --ion-color-step-550: #8c8c8c;
  --ion-color-step-600: #999999;
  --ion-color-step-650: #a6a6a6;
  --ion-color-step-700: #b3b3b3;
  --ion-color-step-750: #bfbfbf;
  --ion-color-step-800: #cccccc;
  --ion-color-step-850: #d9d9d9;
  --ion-color-step-900: #e6e6e6;
  --ion-color-step-950: #f2f2f2;

  --ion-toolbar-background: #0d0d0d;

  --ion-item-background: #1c1c1c;
  --ion-item-background-activated: #313131;
}

/*
 * Material Design Dark Theme
 * ----------------------------------------------
 */

.md body {
  --ion-background-color: #121212;
  --ion-background-color-rgb: 18, 18, 18;

  --ion-text-color: #ffffff;
  --ion-text-color-rgb: 255, 255, 255;

  --ion-border-color: #222222;

  --ion-color-step-50: #1e1e1e;
  --ion-color-step-100: #2a2a2a;
```

```
    --ion-color-step-150: #363636;
    --ion-color-step-200: #414141;
    --ion-color-step-250: #4d4d4d;
    --ion-color-step-300: #595959;
    --ion-color-step-350: #656565;
    --ion-color-step-400: #717171;
    --ion-color-step-450: #7d7d7d;
    --ion-color-step-500: #898989;
    --ion-color-step-550: #949494;
    --ion-color-step-600: #a0a0a0;
    --ion-color-step-650: #acacac;
    --ion-color-step-700: #b8b8b8;
    --ion-color-step-750: #c4c4c4;
    --ion-color-step-800: #d0d0d0;
    --ion-color-step-850: #dbdbdb;
    --ion-color-step-900: #e7e7e7;
    --ion-color-step-950: #f3f3f3;

    --ion-item-background: #1a1b1e;
  }

  ion-title.title-large {
    --color: white;
  }
}
```

The central meaning of "primary"

These are a lot of named color variables. Particular importance is attached to the first variable `primary` (`--ion-color-primary`). `primary` must be present because it is used by almost all Ionic components!

The simplest way to do a global theming is to change that particular `primary` color variables. Let's say, the corporate identity color of our imaginary company "BoB Tours" is `#ffae00`.

Let's try it now and set the following new colors value for `primary`:

```
/** Ionic CSS Variables **/
:root {
  /** primary **/
  --ion-color-primary: #ffae00;
  --ion-color-primary-rgb: 255,174,0;
  --ion-color-primary-contrast: #ffffff;
  --ion-color-primary-contrast-rgb: 255,255,255;
  --ion-color-primary-shade: #e09900;
  --ion-color-primary-tint: #ffb61a;
```

```
  /** secondary **/
  ...

}
```

You see, we defined `--ion-color-primary` with the color value `#ffae00`, the "BoB Tours" CI color. The color represents a warm yellow-orange.

Color Generator

But we also provided `--ion-color-primary-shade` and `-ion-color-primary-tint` with alternative values. Did I just think it up? No. In order to find suitable shade and tint colors for a basic color I used Ionic's so-called C*olor Generator*. You can find it here:

- https://ionicframework.com/docs/theming/color-generator

For a basic color, the Color Generator determines appropriate `shade` and `tint` colors. The whole thing is then conveniently issued as CSS code. You only need to copy it and paste/replace it into your `variables.scss`. That's how I did it.

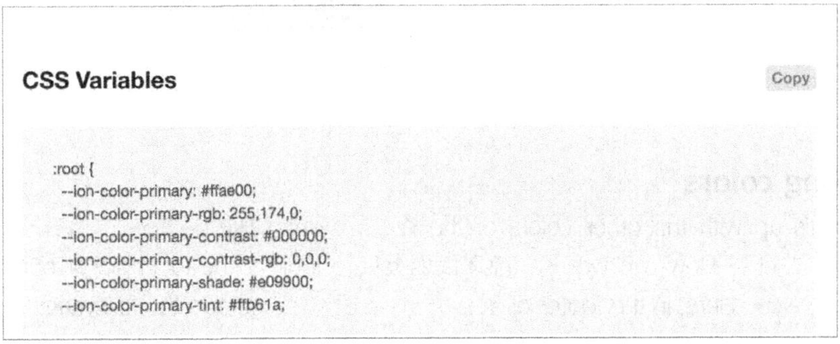

But look carefully: I have manually changed two values, namely:

```
--ion-color-primary-contrast: #ffffff;
--ion-color-primary-contrast-rgb: 255,255,255;
```

These are the color values for *white*; the Color Manager had suggested *black* (`#000000` and `0, 0, 0`) here. I didn't like that.

Now let's have a look at our slightly colored app:

Using colors

What's up with the other colors of the `$colors` map like `secondary`, `tertiary`, `danger` etc.? How can we use this? Let's take a look at the example of our `DetailsPage`. Here, in the footer of `details.page.html`, we add the following:

```
<ion-header>
  ...
</ion-header>
<ion-content class="ion-padding">
  ...
</ion-content>

<ion-footer padding style="height: 80px;">
  <ion-button *ngIf="!showSocial"
(click)="presentActionSheet()">
    Options
  </ion-button>
  <!-- A (FAB) share button -->
  <ion-fab vertical="bottom" horizontal="end" slot="fixed"
           (click)="toggleSocial()">
      <ion-fab-button>
        <ion-icon name="md-share"></ion-icon>
      </ion-fab-button>
      <ion-fab-list side="start">
        <ion-fab-button (click)="openSocial('facebook')"
                        color="tertiary">
            <ion-icon name="logo-facebook"></ion-icon>
        </ion-fab-button>
        <ion-fab-button (click)="openSocial('instagram')"
                        color="danger">
          <ion-icon name="logo-instagram"></ion-icon>
        </ion-fab-button>
        <ion-fab-button (click)="openSocial('twitter')"
                        color="secondary">
          <ion-icon name="logo-twitter"></ion-icon>
        </ion-fab-button>
        <ion-fab-button (click)="openSocial('whatsapp')"
                        color="success">
          <ion-icon name="logo-whatsapp"></ion-icon>
        </ion-fab-button>
      </ion-fab-list>
  </ion-fab>
</ion-footer>
```

To use one of the colors of the `$colors` map from `variables.scss` we just assign one of the variables to the attribute color.

Here is the result:

More informations about theming basics you can find here:

► https://ionicframework.com/docs/theming/basics

8.3 Local and global (S)CSS files

Global stylesheets

While Ionic Framework component styles are self-contained, there are several global stylesheets that should be included in order to use all of Ionic's features. Some of the stylesheets are required in order for an Ionic Framework app to look and behave properly, and others include optional utilities to quickly style your app.

The following CSS file must be included in order for Ionic Framework to work properly:

core.css (required)

This file is the only stylesheet that is *required* in order for Ionic components to work properly. It includes app specific styles, and allows the color property to work across components. If this file isn't included the colors won't show up and some elements may not appear properly.

The following CSS files are *recommended* to be included in an Ionic Framework app. If they are not included, some elements may have undesired styles. If Ionic Framework components are being used outside of an app, these files may not be necessary:

structure.css (recommended)

Applies styles to `<html>` and defaults `box-sizing` to border-box. It ensures scrolling behaves like native in mobile devices.

typography.css (recommended)

Typography changes the font-family of the entire document and modifies the font styles for heading elements. It also applies positioning styles to some native text elements.

normalize.css (recommended)

Makes browsers render all elements more consistently and in line with modern standards. It is based on Normalize.css.

display.css (recommended)

Adds utility classes to hide any element based on the breakpoint, see "8.4 CSS Utilities", starting on page 350, for usage information.

The following set of CSS files are *optional* and can safely be commented out or removed if the application isn't using any of the features:

padding.css (optional)
Adds utility classes to modify the padding or margin on any element, see "8.4 CSS Utilities", starting on page 350, for usage information.

float-elements.css (optional)
Adds utility classes to float an element based on the breakpoint and side, see "8.4 CSS Utilities", starting on page 350, for usage information.

text-alignment.css (optional)
Adds utility classes to align the text of an element or adjust the white space based on the breakpoint, see "8.4 CSS Utilities", starting on page 350, for usage information.

text-transformation.css (optional)
Adds utility classes to transform the text of an element to uppercase, lowercase or capitalize based on the breakpoint, see "8.4 CSS Utilities", starting on page 350, for usage information.

flex-utils.css (optional)
Adds utility classes to align flex containers and items, see "8.4 CSS Utilities", starting on page 350, for usage information.

Color the toolbar of a single page

What to do if you want to color the toolbar of a single page in `primary` color? Well, the easiest way would be to just write the following `color` attribute – for example – in `favorites.page.html`:

```
<ion-header>
  <ion-toolbar color="primary">
    <ion-buttons slot="start">
      <ion-menu-button></ion-menu-button>
    </ion-buttons>
    <ion-title>Favorites</ion-title>
  </ion-toolbar>
</ion-header>
```

```
<ion-content class="ion-padding">
  ...
</ion-content>

<ion-footer padding *ngIf="favService.favTours?.length>0">
  ...
</ion-footer>
```

Somewhat more advanced and flexible would be to add a style class to `favorites.page.html`:

```
<ion-header>
  <ion-toolbar class="myToolbarStyle">
    <ion-buttons slot="start">
      <ion-menu-button></ion-menu-button>
    </ion-buttons>
    <ion-title>Favorites</ion-title>
  </ion-toolbar>
</ion-header>

<ion-content class="ion-padding">
  ...
</ion-content>

<ion-footer padding *ngIf="favService.favTours?.length>0">
  ...
</ion-footer>
```

You must then write this style class with a style statement in the file `favorites.page.scss`:

```
.myToolbarStyle {
    --background:  var(--ion-color-primary);
}
```

Because we made a style `class` assignment in the FavoritesPage at `ion-toolbar`, we can colorize the background in the SCSS file with the primary color. If you are familiar with CSS, it seems to you somehow familiar, but somehow alien, right?

Well, Ionic uses so-called *CSS Custom Properties (CSS Variables)* and they are written by preceded `--`.

And where do you find these variables? Of course in the excellent documentation of Ionic:

- https://ionicframework.com/docs/theming/css-variables

The Ionic documentation itself links to one more resource, where the people of mozilla.org explain the basics to CSS Variables:

- https://developer.mozilla.org/en-US/docs/Web/CSS/Using_CSS_custom_properties

If you've read in there a little, you'll find your way quickly. Besides, we'll of course do some more theming and styling in this book.

Now let's see what our newly styled toolbar looks like:

Color the toolbar globally

The global file `src/app/variables.scss` is the global SCSS file in an Ionic app. We already got to know it (see “Simple Theming“, starting on page 332). It is used to define all styles that affect the entire app globally.

We could place the definition of the `myToolbarStyle` class at the very end of `variables.scss`:

```
// Ionic Variables and Theming. For more info, please see:
// http://ionicframework.com/docs/theming/

/** Ionic CSS Variables **/
:root {
  ...
}

.myToolbarStyle {
  --background:  var(--ion-color-primary);
}
```

We would then have to complete this class in *all* `page.html` files of our app, as we did in `favorites.page.html` earlier. But that has to be easier, right?

And yes, that *is* easier!

In `variables.scss` we place the following line after the open curly bracket of `:root`:

```
// Ionic Variables and Theming. For more info, please see:
// http://ionicframework.com/docs/theming/

/** Ionic CSS Variables **/
:root {

  /** global theming **/
  --ion-toolbar-background: var(--ion-color-primary);

  ...
}
```

This directive changes the background of the toolbars *on all pages* of our app:

However, we have produced a small flaw: At first glance the color of the side menu button, the font colors of the back buttons and the cancel button on the request and map page look like they have disappeared. In fact their color is now identical to the background color of the headers.

We correct this in `variables.scss` with a further style statements:

```
/** Ionic CSS Variables **/
:root {

  /** global theming **/
  --ion-toolbar-background: var(--ion-color-primary);

 .button {
    color: var(--ion-color-primary-contrast);
  }

  ...
}
```

This sets the font color of all buttons, including the "disappeared" ones, to `--ion-color-primary-contrast`. We remember: We manually set this variable to `#ffffff` (white) (see “8.2 Simple Theming”, section “Color Generator” on page 337). We can use `.button` as a class identifier, because Ionic automatically provides all the above components with the style class `"button"`.

And we make a final improvement by assigning the variable `--ion-color-primary-contrast` also to the (font) color of the toolbars:

```
/** Ionic CSS Variables **/
:root {
  ...

  /** global theming **/
  --ion-toolbar-background: var(--ion-color-primary);
  --ion-toolbar-color: var(--ion-color-primary-contrast);

  .button {
    color: var(--ion-color-primary-contrast);
  }
}
```

Here are the toolbars of our app with visible menu, back and cancel buttons.

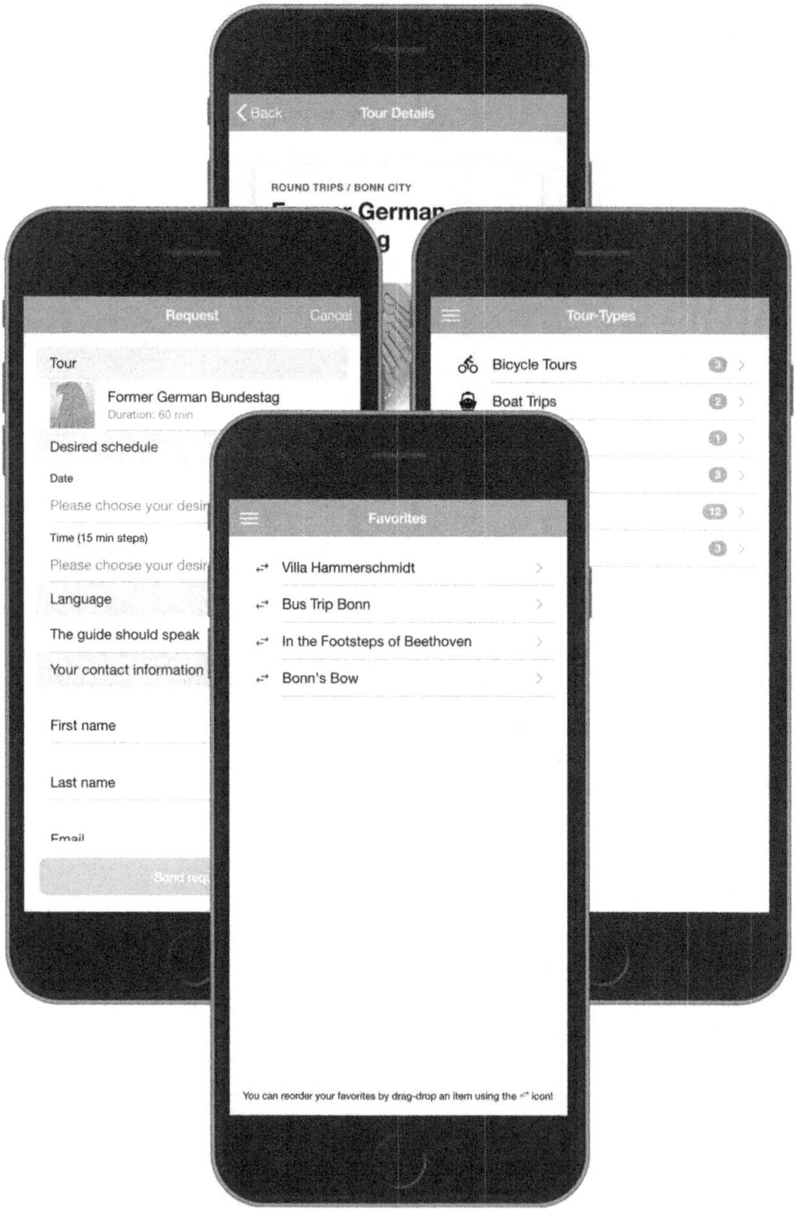

And the font color is matching, too:

You can see how we can give a custom look to our app with just a few changes.

That's it for the moment. I hope that you have now got a first feel for theming in Ionic.

More informations about using CSS Variables you can find here:

- https://ionicframework.com/docs/theming/css-variables
- https://angularfirebase.com/lessons/css-variables-in-ionic-4/

8.4 CSS Utilities

Ionic Framework provides a set of CSS utility classes that can be used on any element in order to modify the text, element placement or adjust the padding and margin.

Text modification

In `favorites.page.html` let's optimize the display of the reorder hint in the footer:

```
<ion-header>
  ...
</ion-header>

<ion-content class="ion-padding">
  ...
</ion-content>

<ion-footer padding *ngIf="favService.favTours?.length>0">
  <div class="ion-text-center ion-text-uppercase">
    <small style="color: var(--ion-color-primary);">
      You can reorder your favorites by drag-drop an item
      using the <ion-icon name="swap"></ion-icon> icon!
    </small>
  </div>
</ion-footer>
```

`ion-text-center` is an example for a text *alignment* utility class. The inline contents are centered. Other text alignment classes are for example `ion-text-start` or `ion-text-end`.

`ion-text-uppercase` is an example for a text *transformation*. It forces all characters to be converted to uppercase. Other text transformation classes are `ion-text-lowercase` and `ion-text-capitalize`.

With a `style` attribute, any CSS statement (and variable) can be integrated into an HTML element. So here we color the text in the primary color.

This is the hint modified by CSS utility classes and embedded styling:

Another example for text modification is `text-wrap`. We use it in `list.page.html` to wrap longer tour titles into two or more lines:

```
<ion-header>
  ...
</ion-header>

<ion-content class="ion-padding">
  ...
  <ion-list>
    <ion-item *ngFor="let tour of tours"
              [routerLink]="'/details/' + tour.ID"
              routerDirection="forward">
      ...
      <ion-label>
        <h2  class="ion-text-wrap">{{tour.Title}}</h2>
        <p>Duration: {{tour.Duration}} min</p>
      </ion-label>
    </ion-item>
  </ion-list>
</ion-content>
```

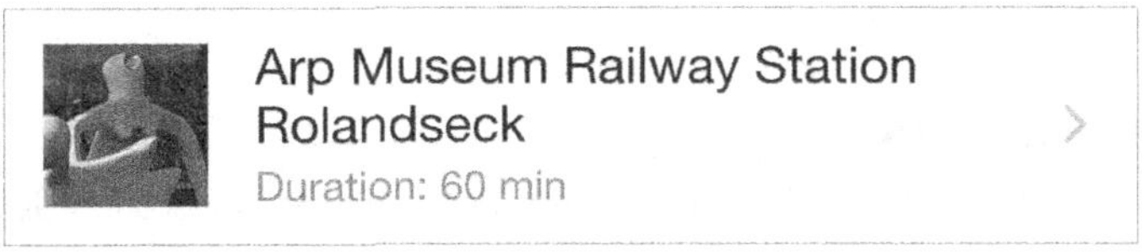

Element Placement

The placement of elements can be done in several ways, namely with:

- Float Elements, e.g. `ion-float-left`, `ion-float-right`
- Responsive Float Classes, e.g. `ion-float-{left}`, `ion-float-{right}`

Element Display

The display CSS property `ion-hide` determines if an element should be visible or not. The element will still be in the DOM, but not rendered, if it is hidden. There are also additional classes to modify the visibility based on the screen size (Responsive Display Attributes). Instead of just `ion-hide` for all screen sizes, use `ion-hide-{breakpoint}-{dir}` to only use the class on specific screen sizes, where `{breakpoint}` is one of the breakpoint names listed in **Ionic Breakpoints** (see below), and `{dir}` is whether the element should be hidden on all screen sizes above (`up`) or below (`down`) the specified breakpoint.

Content Space

The space between elements can be controlled by different parameters:

- Padding (default amount is 16px), e.g. `ion-padding` or `ion-padding-top`
- Margin (default is 16px), e.g. `ion-margin` or `ion-margin-top`

The padding area is the space between the content of the element and its border. The margin area extends the border area with an empty area used to separate the element from its neighbors.

Flex Properties

In Flex Properties we distinguish between:

- Flex Container properties, e.g. `ion-justify-content-center`, `ion-align-items-end`
- Flex Item Properties, e.g. `ion-align-self-center`

Ionic Breakpoints

Ionic uses breakpoints in media queries in order to style an application differently based on the screen size. The following breakpoint names are used in the utility classes listed above, where the class will apply when the width is met.

Breakpoint Name	Width
`xs`	`0`
`sm`	`576px`
`md`	`768px`
`lg`	`992px`
`xl`	`1200px`

We've already worked with breakpoints related to the Grid component (see "6.11 Grid", starting on page 196).

More informations about CSS utilities and related topics you can find here:

- https://ionicframework.com/docs/layout/css-utilities
- https://ionicframework.com/docs/layout/css-utilities#ionic-breakpoints

8.5 Advanced Theming

Colors

In the section "8.2 Simple Theming" (starting on page 332) we have already talked a bit about colors. Therefore I limit myself here to some additions.

You can define your **own color** by creating a class like this:

```
.ion-color-favorite {
  --ion-color-base: #69bb7b;
  --ion-color-base-rgb: 105,187,123;
  --ion-color-contrast: #ffffff;
  --ion-color-contrast-rgb: 255,255,255;
  --ion-color-shade: #5ca56c;
  --ion-color-tint: #78c288;
}
```

It's important to note that adding the class above doesn't automatically create the Ionic CSS variables for use in an application's stylesheets. This means that the variations beginning with `--ion-color-favorite` don't exist by adding the `.ion-color-favorite` class. These should be declared separately for use in an application, preferably in the `:root` section of `variables.scss`:

```
:root {
  --ion-color-favorite: #69bb7b;
  --ion-color-favorite-rgb: 105,187,123;
  --ion-color-favorite-contrast: #ffffff;
  --ion-color-favorite-contrast-rgb: 255,255,255;
  --ion-color-favorite-shade: #5ca56c;
  --ion-color-favorite-tint: #78c288;
}
```

Now the favorite color can be used in CSS like below to set the `background` and `color` on a `div`:

```
div {
  background: var(--ion-color-favorite);
  color: var(--ion-color-favorite-contrast);
}
```

The **application colors** are used in multiple places in Ionic. These are useful for easily creating themes that match a brand. You can address them via the following CSS variables:

Name	Description
`--ion-background-color`	Background color of entire app
`--ion-background-color-rgb`	Background color of entire app, rgb format
`--ion-text-color`	Text color of entire app
`--ion-text-color-rgb`	Text color of entire app, rgb format
`--ion-backdrop-color`	Color of the Backdrop component
`--ion-overlay-background-color`	Background color of the overlays
`--ion-border-color`	Border color
`--ion-box-shadow-color`	Box shadow color
`--ion-tab-bar-background`	Background of the Tab bar
`--ion-tab-bar-background-focused`	Background of the focused Tab bar
`--ion-tab-bar-border-color`	Border color of the Tab bar
`--ion-tab-bar-color`	Color of the Tab bar
`--ion-tab-bar-color-activated`	Color of the activated Tab
`--ion-toolbar-background`	Background of the Toolbar
`--ion-toolbar-border-color`	Border color of the Toolbar
`--ion-toolbar-color`	Color of the components in the Toolbar
`--ion-toolbar-color-activated`	Color of activated comps in the Toolbar
`--ion-toolbar-color-unchecked`	Color of unchecked comps in the Toolbar
`--ion-toolbar-color-checked`	Color of checked comps in the Toolbar
`--ion-item-background`	Background of the Item
`--ion-item-background-activated`	Background of the activated Item
`--ion-item-border-color`	Border color of the Item
`--ion-item-color`	Color of the components in the Item
`--ion-placeholder-color`	Color of the placeholder in inputs

While the previously mentioned variables are useful for changing the colors of an application, often times there is a need for variables used in multiple components. The following **global variables** are shared across components to change global padding settings and more:

Application Variables

Name	Description
`--ion-font-family`	Font family of the app
`--ion-statusbar-padding`	Statusbar padding top of the app
`--ion-safe-area-top`	Adjust the safe area inset top of the app
`--ion-safe-area-right`	Adjust the safe area inset right of the app
`--ion-safe-area-bottom`	Adjust the safe area inset bottom of the app
`--ion-safe-area-left`	Adjust the safe area inset left of the app
`--ion-margin`	Adjust the margin of the Margin attributes
`--ion-padding`	Adjust the padding of the Padding attributes

Grid Variables

Name	Description
`--ion-grid-columns`	Number of columns in the grid
`--ion-grid-padding-xs`	Padding of the grid for xs breakpoints
`--ion-grid-padding-sm`	Padding of the grid for sm breakpoints
`--ion-grid-padding-md`	Padding of the grid for md breakpoints
`--ion-grid-padding-lg`	Padding of the grid for lg breakpoints
`--ion-grid-padding-xl`	Padding of the grid for xl breakpoints
`--ion-grid-column-padding-xs`	Padding of grid columns for xs breakpoints
`--ion-grid-column-padding-sm`	Padding of grid columns for sm breakpoints
`--ion-grid-column-padding-md`	Padding of grid columns for md breakpoints
`--ion-grid-column-padding-lg`	Padding of grid columns for lg breakpoints
`--ion-grid-column-padding-xl`	Padding of grid columns for xl breakpoints

More informations about advanced theming you can find here:

- ▶ https://ionicframework.com/docs/theming/advanced

8.6 Fonts

Fonts can give an app an individual note. For large companies, they are usually even an integral part of branding. Whether desired individuality or compelling corporate design - in the use of other than the standard fonts, one or the other has to be considered in Ionic apps.

An individual app font

For our intention to integrate an individual font into our app, we should do the following steps:

1. Download the desired font files.
2. Create a `src/assets/font` folder and putting the fonts into it.
3. Write some font directives into `variables.scss`.
4. Little formatting of the UI.

1. Download the desired font files

I've chosen the free font `Orkney` from `fontlibrary.org` for our app.

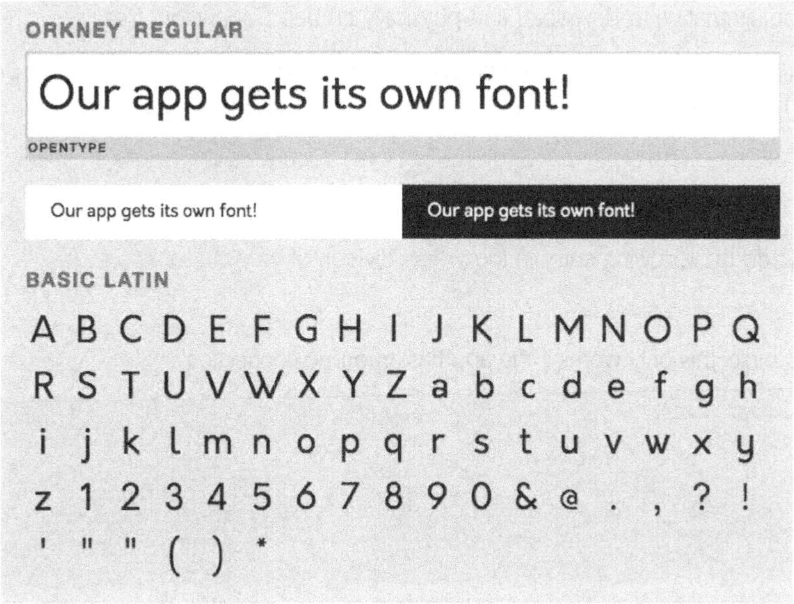

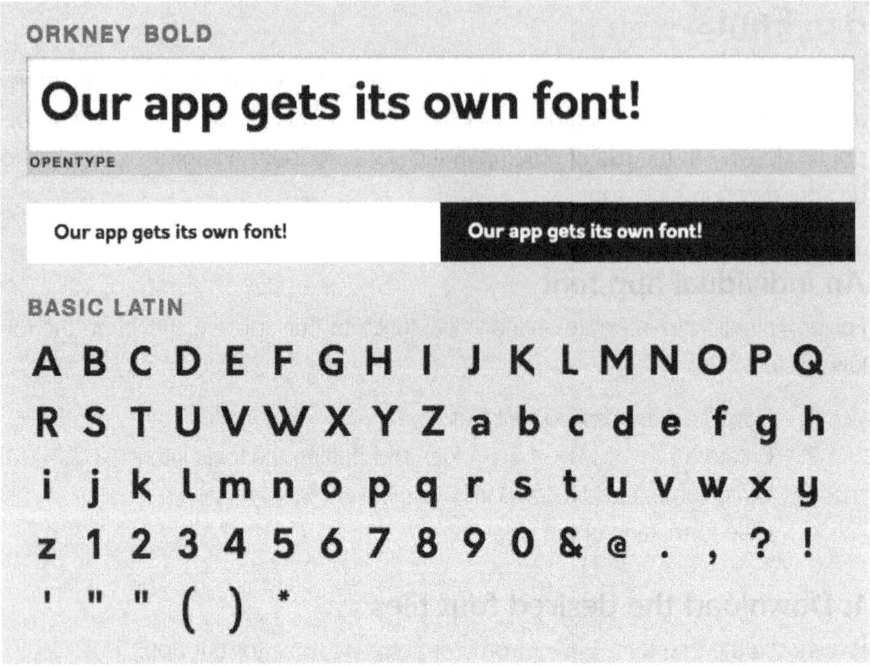

As an alternative to download and physically embed Google font files:

You can fetch the font-face definition from the web and copy a link reference to the header of `index.html` e.g.:

```
<link href="https://fonts.googleapis.com/css?
family=Odibee+Sans&display=swap" rel="stylesheet">
```

and add the following entry in the `:root` division of `variables.scss`:

```
--ion-font-family: "Odibee Sans";
```

Of course, this only works if the app has an online connection.

2. Create a src/assets/font folder for the fonts

We create an `assets/font` folder and copy the font files into it. For our app, the files `OrkneyRegular.ttf` and `OrkneyBold.ttf` are sufficient.

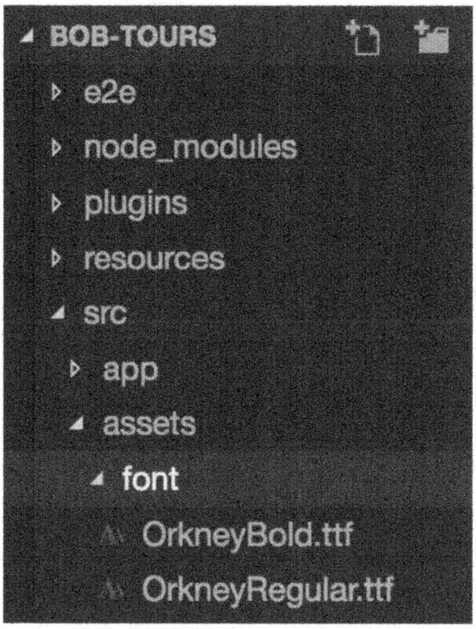

3. Write some font directives into variables.scss.

To integrate the fonts in our app, at the end in `variables.scss` we add:

```
/** Ionic CSS Variables **/
:root {
   ...
  @font-face {
    font-family: 'Orkney';
    font-style: normal;
    src: url('../assets/font/OrkneyRegular.ttf');
  }

  @font-face {
    font-family: 'Orkney';
    font-style: bold;
    src: url('../assets/font/OrkneyBold.ttf');
  }

  --ion-font-family: 'Orkney';
}
```

Here the declaration of the used fonts takes place. Every font-style (`normal`, `bold`) has to be declared individually. For example, if you want to use italicized text in your app, you should also declare an `italic` font style (and of course copy the corresponding font file into `assets/font`).

With the final line

```
--ion-font-family: 'Orkney';
```

we declare `Orkney` as default font for our app.

4. Little formatting of the UI

Each text is now displayed with the `normal` font `Orkney Regular`. In order to also use the `bold` font somewhere in our app, we add the following to `details.-page.html`:

```
<ion-header>
  ...
</ion-header>

<ion-content class="ion-padding">
  <ion-card>
    <ion-card-header>
      <ion-card-subtitle>
        {{tourtype}} / {{region}}
      </ion-card-subtitle>
      <ion-card-title style="font-weight:bold;">
       {{tour.Title}}
      </ion-card-title>
    </ion-card-header>
    <ion-card-content>
      ...
    </ion-card-content>
  </ion-card>
</ion-content>

<ion-footer padding style="height: 80px;">
  ...
</ion-footer>
```

Here our app with the new `Orkney` font:

8.7 Scalable Vector Graphics (SVG)

Scalable Vector Graphics (SVG) are ideal for use in hybrid and web apps. They have a small file size, are arbitrarily scalable without ever becoming pixelated and have a lot to offer.

Create a logo

In our app, we want to integrate an SVG graphic. The graphic contains the company logo of our imaginary tourism company BoB Tours and will grace the head of our "About this app" popover in the future.

We go through the following steps:

1. Download and introspecting the SVG.
2. Create a `src/assets/img` folder and putting the SVG into it.
3. Integrate the SVG.

1. Download and introspecting the SVG

You can download the SVG logo file from:

- http://ionic.andreas-dormann.de/img/bob-tours-logo.svg

Let's open the SVG file and have a look at its content:

```
<?xml version="1.0" encoding="utf-8"?>
<!-- Generator: Adobe Illustrator 21.0.2, SVG Export Plug-In .
SVG Version: 6.00 Build 0)  -->
<svg version="1.1" id="Logo"
xmlns="http://www.w3.org/2000/svg"
xmlns:xlink="http://www.w3.org/1999/xlink" x="0px" y="0px"
 viewBox="0 0 700 160" style="enable-background:new 0 0 700
160;" xml:space="preserve">
<style type="text/css">
.st0{fill:#FFFFFF;stroke:#000000;stroke-width:8.8818;stroke-
miterlimit:10;}
.st1{fill:#FEF100;}
.st2{fill:#FEAD00;}
.st3{fill:#FEFEFE;}
```

```
</style>
<path id="border_1_" class="st0" d="M685.2,155H14.8c-5.4,0-
9.8-5.2-9.8-11.5v-127C5,10.2,9.5,5,14.8,5h670.4

c5.4,0,9.8,5.2,9.8,11.5v126.9C695,149.8,690.5,155,685.2,155z"/
>
<g id="text">
<path id="s" d="M638,134.2c-6.1,0-11.6-1.4-16.8-4.2c-5.4-3-
9.5-7.1-12.1-12.3c-2-4-3-8.8-3-14.2c0-1.2,0.4-2.2,1.3-3
c0.8-0.8,1.9-1.3,3-
1.3h11.8c2,0,3.4,0.9,4.2,2.8c0.5,1.1,0.9,2.9,1.1,5.4c0.2,2,1.3
,3.5,3.1,4.5c2.1,1,5.4,1.6,9.8,1.6
c8.4,0,12.6-2.9,12.6-8.7c0-3.5-3.3-7.6-10-12.2l-21.4-14.7c-
8.3-5.7-12.5-13.4-12.5-22.9c0-6.4,1.9-12.1,5.8-17.2
c5.2-6.9,13.4-10.3,24.8-
10.3c8.1,0,14.6,1.4,19.7,4.2c6.4,3.6,9.7,9.3,9.7,17v5.4c0,1.2-
0.4,2.2-1.3,3c-0.8,0.8-1.9,1.3-3,1.3
h-10.5c-2.9,0-4.3-2.2-4.3-6.6c0-2.1-0.9-3.7-2.8-4.9c-1.7-1-
3.8-1.5-6.2-1.5h-3.2c-2.8,0-5,0.7-6.8,2.2c-1.9,1.6-2.8,3.7-
2.8,6.3
c0,2.8,1.7,5.5,5.2,8.2c3.3,2.5,7.9,5.8,13.7,9.7c6.7,4.5,11.4,7
.7,13.9,9.5c4.6,3.4,7.8,6.8,9.5,10.2s2.6,8,2.6,13.8
c0,8.8-3.8,16-11.4,21.6C654.8,131.7,646.9,134.2,638,134.2z"/>
   ...
</g>
<g id="sun">
<path id="light-rays" class="st1" d="M154.6,39.5c2.9-2,5.6-
4.1,8.5-6.2c1.6-1.2,3.1-2.3,4.7-3.5c0.8-0.6,1.5-1.1,2.3-
1.6 ..."/>
<path id="inner-circle" class="st2" d="M175.8,78.7c-0.1,7.5-
1.9,14.9-6.2,21.1c-4.1,6-10,10.9-16.8,13.5
c-6.8,2.6-14.6,3.1-21.7,1.4c-7.5-1.7-14.1-6-19.1-11.8c-9.7-
11.3-11.5-28.5-3.9-41.4c3.7-6.3,9.5-11.7,16.1-14.8
c6.6-3.1,14.2-4,21.3-
3c14.9,2.3,27.4,14.7,29.8,29.6C175.6,75,175.8,76.9,175.8,78.7z
M129.1,50.5 M135.8,48.4 M128.6,51
 M161.8,101.8L161.8,101.8L161.8,101.8L161.8,101.8z"/>
<path id="high-light" class="st3" d="M127.8,51.3c1-0.8,2.4-
1.2,3.6-1.6c1.5-0.5,3.1-1,4.6-1.2c3.2-0.6,6.5-0.6,9.8-0.2
c5.7,0.8,11.2,3.4,15.6,7.2c7.9,7,11.7,18,10.1,28.4c-0.5,3.3-
1.5,6.6-3.1,9.5c-0.8,1.6-1.8,3.1-2.8,4.5c-0.5,0.6-1,1.2-
1.5,1.8
```

```
c-0.3,0.3-1,1.4-1.5,1.4c0.1,0,1.5-2.1,1.6-2.3c0.8-1.2,1.5-
2.4,2.2-3.6c1.3-2.5,2.2-5.2,2.7-8c1-4.9,0.6-9.9-0.9-14.7
c-3.1-9.9-11.1-17.4-20.9-20.6c-3.1-1-6.4-1.6-9.7-1.7c-1.7,0-
3.3,0-5,0.2c-0.9,0.1-1.8,0.2-2.7,0.4
C129.2,51,128.5,51.3,127.8,51.3L127.8,51.3z"/>
</g>
</svg>
```

As an XML document, an SVG is constructed in a tree structure from various elements and attributes assigned to these elements. An SVG file usually starts with the XML declaration in the header area:

```
<?xml version="1.0" encoding="utf-8"?>
```

Following this header, as with all XML documents, is the root element; for SVG documents this has the name `svg`:

```
<svg version="1.1"
     id="Logo"
     xmlns="http://www.w3.org/2000/svg"
     xmlns:xlink="http://www.w3.org/1999/xlink"
     x="0px" y="0px"
     viewBox="0 0 700 160">
```

The `svg` root element usually contains a `version` info and an `id`. In order to uniquely associate the element and its content with the SVG namespace and give it a defined meaning that has to do with the SVG recommendations, the namespace is noted at the root element with the XML attribute structure `xmlns`. The attribute `viewBox` can be used to specify which area of the drawing plane should be displayed in the display area.

Style statements determine what specific elements should look like. Here, for example, a white fill and a black rounded border are defined in class `.st0`.

```
<style type="text/css">
  .st0{fill:#FFFFFF;
       stroke:#000000;
       stroke-width:8.8818;
       stroke-miterlimit:10;}
  .st1{fill:#FEF100;}
  .st2{fill:#FEAD00;}
  .st3{fill:#FEFEFE;}
</style>
```

After the `style` instructions follow the graphic elements. The element `<path />` defines a curve consisting of an arbitrary number of subpaths, which in turn consist of a combination of distances, elliptical arcs, square and cubic Bézier curves, which are described by means of relative or absolute coordinates.

Here you can read more about the SVG format:

- https://en.wikipedia.org/wiki/Scalable_Vector_Graphics
- https://www.w3.org/TR/SVG/

2. Create a src/assets/img folder for the SVG

Let's create an `img` folder in `src/assets` and put the SVG file into it.

3. Integrate the SVG

We integrate the SVG in `src/app/components/about/about.component.html`:

```
<div class="ion-text-center ion-padding">
  <!-- <h3>BoB Tours App</h3> -->
  <ion-img src="/assets/img/bob-tours-logo.svg"
           style="margin-bottom: 16px;"></ion-img>
  <small>A tourism app created with love by</small>
  <p>Andreas Dormann</p>
  <small>&copy; 2020</small>
</div>
```

We use the SVG file as source for an `ion-img` element (and replace the old `h3` element). Nothing special. But the special features of an SVG file, we will get to know in the next section.

Here is our app with new built-in SVG logo:

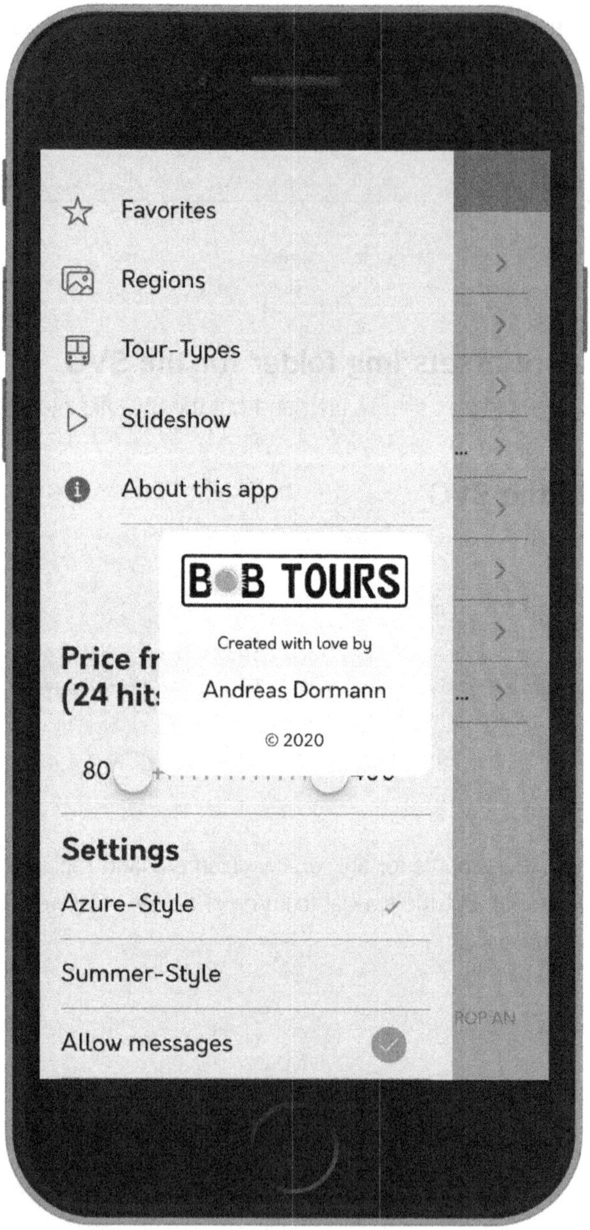

8.8 Ionic Animations

There are animations in each app! You don't believe that? Then take a good look at what happens when you navigate in an app from one side to the other. Do you notice something? Right: the side transition is *animated*! And not just that: loading ads, alerts, menus, modals, popovers - all are animated!

Ionic Animations is a new utility in Ionic 5 that allows developers to build complex animations in a platform agnostic manner. Developers do not need to be using a particular framework such as React or Angular, nor do they even need to be building an Ionic app. As long as developers have access to v5.0 or greater of Ionic Framework, they will have access to all of Ionic Animations.

Building efficient animations can be tricky. Developers are often limited by the libraries available to them as well as the hardware that their apps run on. On top of that, many animation libraries use a JavaScript-driven approach to running animations where they handle the calculation of your animation's values at every step in a requestAnimationFrame loop. This reduces the scalability of your animations as the library is constantly computing values and using up CPU time.

Ionic Animations uses the Web Animations API to build and run your animations. In doing this, we offload all work required to compute and run your animations to the browser. As a result, this allows the browser to make any optimizations it needs and ensures your animations run as smoothly as possible. While most browsers support a basic implementation of Web Animations, we fallback to CSS Animations for browsers that do not support Web Animations.

Admittedly, animations should be more or less discreet and should be perceived as "natural" movements. For example, the lack of animation sometimes appears as "unnatural". So also in our app - namely on the `DetailsPage`.

Simple button animation

If you open and close the social media button on the `DetailsPage`, the options button on the left disappears or appears.

So it's either gone immediately or immediately there. Without animation. We want to change that and subtly animate the options button by fading it in and out.

Open `details.page.html` and add the following (bold formatted) HTML code in the footer area:

```
<ion-header>
  ...
</ion-header>

<ion-content class="ion-padding">
  ...
</ion-content>

<ion-footer class="ion-padding" style="height: 80px;">
  <ion-button id="animatedButton"
              (click)="presentActionSheet()">
    Options
  </ion-button>
  <!-- A (FAB) share button -->
  <ion-fab vertical="bottom" horizontal="end" slot="fixed"
           (click)="toggleSocial()">
    <ion-fab-button>
      <ion-icon name="share-social"></ion-icon>
    </ion-fab-button>
```

```
    <ion-fab-list side="start">
      <ion-fab-button (click)="openSocial('facebook')"
                      color="tertiary">
        <ion-icon name="logo-facebook"></ion-icon>
      </ion-fab-button>
      <ion-fab-button (click)="openSocial('instagram')"
                      color="danger">
        <ion-icon name="logo-instagram"></ion-icon>
      </ion-fab-button>
      <ion-fab-button (click)="openSocial('twitter')"
                      color="secondary">
        <ion-icon name="logo-twitter"></ion-icon>
      </ion-fab-button>
      <ion-fab-button (click)="openSocial('whatsapp')"
                      color="success">
        <ion-icon name="logo-whatsapp"></ion-icon>
      </ion-fab-button>
    </ion-fab-list>
  </ion-fab>
</ion-footer>
```

We now can use the "`animatedButton`" id to address this particular button in the code behind. Don't forget to delete the `*ngIf` directive! It's not needed any more.

Now we use the new Ionic Animations magic in `details.page.ts`:

```
import { Component, OnInit } from '@angular/core';
import { ActivatedRoute } from '@angular/router';
import { BobToursService }
         from 'src/app/services/bob-tours.service';
import { FavoritesService }
         from 'src/app/services/favorites.service';
import _ from 'lodash';
import { ActionSheetController, AlertController,
         ModalController, AnimationController }
         from '@ionic/angular';
import { RequestPage } from './../request/request.page';
import { MapPage } from './../map/map.page';
```

```
@Component({
  selector: 'app-details',
  templateUrl: './details.page.html',
  styleUrls: ['./details.page.scss'],
     })
export class DetailsPage implements OnInit {

  tour = null;
  isFavorite: boolean;

  region: string;
  tourtype: string;

  showSocial: boolean;

  constructor(
    private activatedRoute: ActivatedRoute,
    public btService: BobToursService,
    public favService: FavoritesService,
    private actionSheetCtrl: ActionSheetController,
    private alertCtrl: AlertController,
    private modalCtrl: ModalController,
    private animationCtrl: AnimationController
  ) { }

  ngOnInit() {
    let id = this.activatedRoute.snapshot.paramMap.get('id');
    this.tour = _.find(this.btService.tours,
                       ['ID', parseInt(id)]);
    this.isFavorite = this.favService.favIDs
                      .indexOf(parseInt(id)) != -1;
    this.region = _.find(this.btService.regions,
                         { 'ID': this.tour.Region }).Name;
    this.tourtype = _.find(this.btService.tourtypes,
                           { 'ID': this.tour.Tourtype }).Name;
  }

  async presentActionSheet() {
    ...
  }

  async presentAlert() {
```

```
    ...
  }

  // user clicked share button
  toggleSocial() {

    this.showSocial = !this.showSocial;

    const animatedButton =
      document.getElementById('animatedButton');

    const fadeIn = this.animationCtrl.create()
                   .addElement(animatedButton)
                   .duration(400)
                   .fromTo('opacity', 0, 1);

    const fadeOut = this.animationCtrl.create()
                    .addElement(animatedButton)
                    .duration(300)
                    .fromTo('opacity', 1, 0);

    if (this.showSocial) {
      fadeOut.play();
    } else {
      fadeIn.play();
    }

  }

  openSocial(app) {
    ...
  }

  async presentModal() {
    ...
  }

  async presentMap() {
    ...
  }

}
```

We import the new Animation Controller with

```
import { ..., AnimationController } from '@ionic/angular';
```

and inject it as `animationCtrl` into the constructor:

```
constructor(
    ...,
    private animationCtrl: AnimationController
  ) { }
```

Now we can use this controller in the `toggleSocial()` method to animate our button. With

```
const animatedButton =
  document.getElementById('animatedButton');
```

we first create an `animatedButton` constant to hold a reference to the button.

With

```
const fadeIn = this.animationCtrl.create()
                      .addElement(animatedButton)
                      .duration(400)
                      .fromTo('opacity', 0, 1);
```

we declare a `fadeIn` animation with the help of the `create()` method of Ionic's AnimationController. `addElement` assigns the animation to our button, `duration` sets the length of the animation to `400` milliseconds, `fromTo` defines the actual animation by changing the opacity from `0` to `1`.

It's not surprising that the following `fadeOut` animation is coded in the same manner with the exception of the `fromTo` instruction, which animates the opacity in reverse order.

In the last piece of code

```
if (this.showSocial) {
      fadeOut.play();
    } else {
      fadeIn.play();
    }
```

we play the `fadeIn` or `fadeOut` animation depending on the (`true` or `false`) value of `this.showSocial`.

SVG animation

In the previous section, we got to know the use of an SVG graphic (see "8.7 Scalable Vector Graphics (SVG)" starting on page 362). How would you like it if we let the sun rise in our SVG logo as soon as the user opens the page menu?

For this we open our logo file `bob-tours-logo.svg` and look for the following entry:

```
<g id="sun">
```

It is the identification of a group (`g`), which consists of several path elements and represents the solar part of our logo.

In SVG files, you can animate any group, as well as any path element. So you could also animate each single letter of our logo individually.

Now let's let our logo sun rotate endlessly.

We extend our SVG file `bob-tours-logo.svg` as follows:

```
<?xml version="1.0" encoding="utf-8"?>
<!-- Generator: Adobe Illustrator 21.0.2, SVG Export Plug-In .
SVG Version: 6.00 Build 0)  -->
<svg version="1.1" id="Logo"
xmlns="http://www.w3.org/2000/svg"
xmlns:xlink="http://www.w3.org/1999/xlink" x="0px" y="0px"
        viewBox="0 0 700 160" style="enable-background:new 0 0
700 160;" xml:space="preserve">
<style type="text/css">
       .st0{fill:#FFFFFF;stroke:#000000;stroke-
width:8.8818;stroke-miterlimit:10;}
       .st1{fill:#FEF100;}
       .st2{fill:#FEAD00;}
       .st3{fill:#FEFEFE;}
</style>
<path id="border_1_" class="st0" d="M685.2,155H14.8c-5.4,0-
9.8-5.2-9.8-11.5v-127C5,10.2,9.5,5,14.8,5h670.4

c5.4,0,9.8,5.2,9.8,11.5v126.9C695,149.8,690.5,155,685.2,155z"/
>
<g id="text">
   ...
</g>
```

```
<g id="sun">
  <animateTransform attributeType="xml"
                    attributeName="transform"
                    type="rotate"
                    from="0 139 79"
                    to="360 139 79"
                    dur="6s"
                    repeatCount="indefinite" />
  <path id="light-rays" class="st1" ... />
  <path id="inner-circle" class="st2" ... />
  <path id="high-light" class="st3" ... />
</g>
</svg>
```

The `<animateTransform>` tag allows you to animate one of SVG's transformation attributes over time. Here we set `attributeName` to `transform` and define a `rotate` animation as `type`. The `from` and `to` attributes have three values: degree, the x-position of the rotation point and the y-position of the rotation point. So, guess what we do here: We rotate form 0 to 360 degree around the middle of the sun. One rotation needs 6 seconds, because we defined this in the `dur` attribute. Finally, the value `indefinite` assigned to the `repeatCount` attribute says, that the animation will never end.

There is much more to discover here, such as the `<animateMotion>` tag, which moves an element along a motion path or the `<animateColor>` tag, which modifies the color value of particular attributes or properties over time. But that would be beyond the scope of this book. That's why I've listed quite a few useful links for you on the next page.

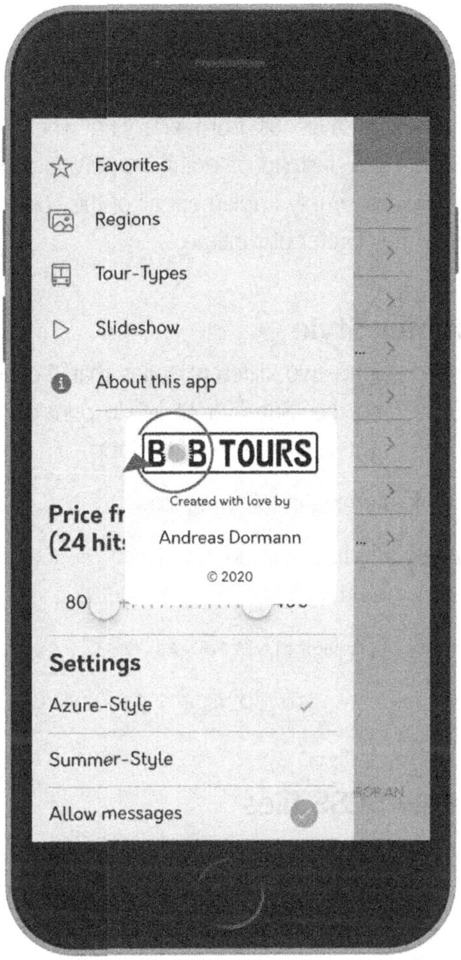

More informations about Ionic and SVG animations you can find here:

- https://ionicframework.com/docs/utilities/animations
- https://en.wikipedia.org/wiki/SVG_animation
- https://css-tricks.com/guide-svg-animations-smil
- https://www.hongkiat.com/blog/svg-animations
- https://theartificial.com/blog/2018/05/23/svg-animation.html

8.9 Dynamic Theming

We can change the complete (!) look of an app at runtime. This is called *Dynamic Theming*. Dynamic theming saves us from worrying whether our chosen color scheme will suit all audiences. Instead of doing numerous mockups with different schemes to evaluate, we can simply implement all of the color schemes and let the user choose which one they prefer at runtime.

Azure and Summer Style

In our app we want to spend two different styles that the user can choose between: the "Azure Style" and the "Summer Style". In principle the latter is already available. It corresponds to the current look of our app.

Let's realize this dynamic theming in following steps:

1. Create two new scss files, named `azure-style.scss` and `summer-style.scss`.
2. Import the new SCSS files in `variables.scss`.
3. Adjust `app.component.html` to use the new styles.

1. Create two new SCSS files

In `src/theme` create a file named `summer-style.scss` with following content:

```
.summer-style {

  --ion-toolbar-background: var(--ion-color-primary);
  --ion-toolbar-color: var(--ion-color-primary-contrast);

  ion-icon {
    color: var(--ion-color-primary);
  }

  ion-back-button ion-icon, ion-fab-button ion-icon, .button {
    color: var(--ion-color-primary-contrast);
  }

}
```

In `src/theme` create a second file named `azure-style.scss` with following content:

```
.azure-style {

  --ion-color-primary: #1877c0;                     // azure
  --ion-color-primary-rgb: 24,119,192;              // rgb
  --ion-color-primary-contrast: #ffffff;            // contrast
  --ion-color-primary-contrast-rgb: 255,255,255;  // cont. rgb
  --ion-color-primary-shade: #1569a9;               // shade
  --ion-color-primary-tint: #2f85c6;                // tint

    --ion-toolbar-background: var(--ion-color-primary);
    --ion-toolbar-color: var(--ion-color-primary-contrast);

    .button {
      color: var(--ion-color-primary-contrast);
    }

    ion-item, ion-card-title, ion-card-content {
      color: var(--ion-color-primary);
    }

    ion-card-subtitle {
      color: rgba(var(--ion-color-primary-rgb), 0.5);
    }

    ion-chip, ion-chip ion-icon {
      color: var(--ion-color-primary-contrast);
      background-color: var(--ion-color-primary-tint);
    }

}
```

In both SCSS files, we set the background and text color for the `toolbar`. At first glance, the definitions seem identical. But beware! In `azure-style.scss` we just swap out the full color palette for the `primary` color. And we know meanwhile: With this we change the appearance of the entire app radically. The seemingly identical instructions in `azure-style.scss` therefore relate to a completely new color palette.

For the rest, in `azure-style.scss` we define the colors of a few more elements, such as `ion-card-title`, `ion-card-content` and `ion-card-subtitle`, as well as `ion-chip` and `ion-chip ion-icon`.

2. Import the new SCSS files

Now we have to import the new SCSS files in `variables.scss`:

```
// Ionic Variables and Theming. For more info, please see:
// http://ionicframework.com/docs/theming/

/** Ionic CSS Variables **/
:root {

  /** Global Theming (BoB Tours Corporate Design) **/

  @import './azure-style.scss';
  @import './summer-style.scss';

  /** Moved to azure-style.scss and summer-style.scss
      in chapter 8.9 **/

  //--ion-toolbar-background:
      var(--ion-color-primary);
  //--ion-toolbar-color:
      var(--ion-color-primary-contrast);

  //.button {
  //  color: var(--ion-color-primary-contrast);
  //}

  /** Individual app font 'Orkney' from fontlibrary.org
      (added in chapter 8.7) **/
  @font-face {
    font-family: 'Orkney';
    font-style: normal;
    src: url('../assets/font/OrkneyRegular.ttf');
  }

  @font-face {
    font-family: 'Orkney';
    font-style: bold;
```

```
    src: url('../assets/font/OrkneyBold.ttf');
  }

  --ion-font-family: 'Orkney';

  /** primary **/
  ...

  /** secondary **/
  ...

  /** tertiary **/
  ...

  /** success **/
  ...

  /** warning **/
  ...

  /** danger **/
  ...

  /** dark **/
  ...

  /** medium **/
  ...

  /** light **/
  ...

}
```

To import the SCSS files we use the `@import` statement.

Be sure to comment out or delete the previous CSS statements here (see above).

3. Use the new styles

Finally, we have to modify `app.component.html` in order to use the new styles in our app:

```
<div [class]="settings.style">

  <ion-app>

    <ion-split-pane>

      <ion-menu>

        <ion-header>
          ...
        </ion-header>

        <ion-content translucent="true">
          ...
        </ion-content>

        <ion-footer>
          ...
        </ion-footer>

      </ion-menu>

      <ion-router-outlet main></ion-router-outlet>

    </ion-split-pane>

  </ion-app>

</div>
```

We wrap the entire content of `app.component.html` into a `div` tag. This gives us access to the highest hierarchical level of our app. We now assign the current style to this new `div` level via

```
[class] = "settings.style"
```

via the class attribute using data binding. That's it!

Let's summarize: We have defined two themes and put them under `src/theme` in their own SCSS file (`azure-style.scss` and `summer-style.scss`). In `variables.scss` we imported these themes. In a `div` layer that encloses our app, a `class` attribute via data binding ensures the change of themes/styles.

The actual change of the style value, we remember, is done by the user tapping one of the two radio buttons "Azure-Style" or "Summer-Style" in the side menu. The buttons are linked to the variable `settings.style` via the entry

```
<ion-list radio-group [(ngModel)] = "settings.style">
```

If their value changes, the class name changes in the `div` tag. This in turn leads to rendering the entire app based on the associated theme.

Here is the result of our work: an app with changeable styles:

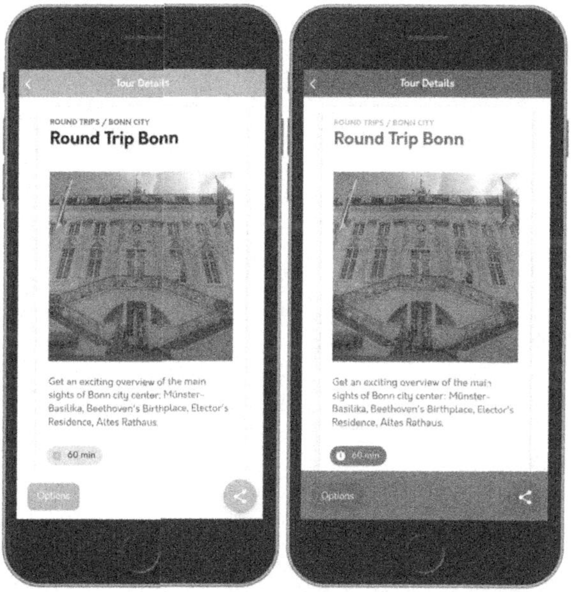

More informations about theming you can find here:

- https://ionicframework.com/docs/theming/themes
- https://ionicframework.com/docs/theming/dark-mode
- https://ionicframework.com/docs/theming/advanced

8.10 UI-Design for Tablets (Split Pane Layout)

Responsive is duty

A responsive design is mandatory! This should not only apply to websites, but also to apps. Unfortunately, there are still apps in the stores that look like a mouse cinema on the tablet. This won't happen with our app, because with Ionic it's easy to bring our app on the big stages of iPads & Co.

Let's (again) have a look at `app.component.html`:

```
<div [class]="settings.style">

  <ion-app>

    <ion-split-pane contentId="main-content">

      <ion-menu contentId="main-content" type="overlay">

        <ion-header>
          ...
        </ion-header>

        <ion-content translucent="true">
          ...
        </ion-content>

        <ion-footer>
          ...
        </ion-footer>

      </ion-menu>

      <ion-router-outlet id="main-content">
      </ion-router-outlet>

    </ion-split-pane>

  </ion-app>

</div>
```

I'm sure you wondered what the hell `ion-split-pane` is doing here, right?

First of all, how does `ion-split-pane` get into our app? That is answered quickly. With

```
$ ionic start bob-tours sidemenu
```

we had chosen the `sidemenu` template, which has generated an app with just this structure (see "3.5 The side menu app for our book project" on page 72). Of course, you can retrofit any differently structured app yourself with an `ion-split-pane`.

An `ion-split-pane` component makes it possible to realize a so-called multi-view layout: menu on the left, content on the right. This layout won't be "unpacked" until a certain display area is available. In other words, a SplitPane is dynamic. If it has enough space (like the tablet or a website), then it shows several areas of an app at the same time, if the area is small (like the smartphone), it remains at a simple representation. Where exactly is the border between small and large? We'll come to that soon.

It's important to note that the element with the `id` matching the `content-id` specified by the split pane will be the main content that is always visible. This can be any element, including an `ion-nav`, `ion-router-outlet`, or an `ion-tabs`.

Breakpoints

By default, the SplitPane will expand when the screen is larger than `768px`. To customize this, pass a breakpoint in the `when` property. The `when` property can accept a boolean value, any valid media query, or one of Ionic's predefined sizes.

```
<!-- can be "xs", "sm", "md", "lg", or "xl" -->
<ion-split-pane when="sm"></ion-split-pane>

<!-- can be any valid media query
     https://developer.mozilla.org/en-US/docs/Web/
     CSS/Media_Queries/Using_media_queries -->
<ion-split-pane when="(min-width: 40px)"></ion-split-pane>
```

Size	Value	Description
`xs`	`(min-width: 0px)`	Show the SplitPane when the min-width is 0px (meaning, always)
`sm`	`(min-width: 576px)`	Show the SplitPane when the min-width is 576px
`md`	`(min-width: 768px)`	Show the SplitPane when the min-width is 768px
`lg`	`(min-width: 992px)`	Show the SplitPane when the min-width is 992px (default break point)
`xl`	`(min-width: 1200px)`	Show the SplitPane when the min-width is 1200px

Our app always adapts perfectly thanks to `ion-split-pane`. Hard to believe that this is so easy, right?

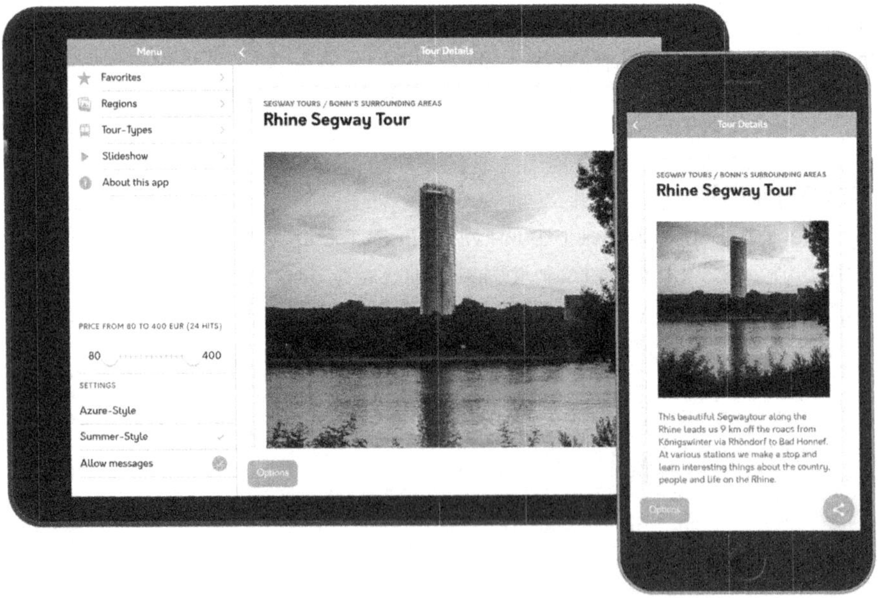

Adjust/centralize logic

Our app has a little flaw – maybe you have already noticed it: The Badge numbers that indicate the number of available tours, appear and update only when we switch from "Tour-Types" to "Regions" or vice versa in the side menu. But an update should take place immediately as soon as the price range is changed. We'll optimize that by removing the filter logic from the regions and tour types pages and centralize them in `bob-tours-service.ts`.

We refactor our logic in the following steps:

1. Extend the central filter function in `BobToursService`.
2. Modify `RegionsPage`.
3. Modify `TourTypesPage`.

1. Extend the central filter funtion

We extend the filter function in `bob-tours.service.ts` as follows:

```
import { Injectable } from '@angular/core';
import { HttpClient } from '@angular/common/http';
import { FavoritesService } from './favorites.service';
import { LoadingController } from '@ionic/angular';
import _ from 'lodash';

@Injectable({
  providedIn: 'root'
})
export class BobToursService {

  public regions: any;
  public tourtypes: any;
  public tours: any;
  public all_tours: any;

  baseUrl = 'https://bob-tours-app.firebaseio.com/';

  constructor(private http: HttpClient,
              public favService: FavoritesService,
              private loadingCtrl: LoadingController) { }
```

```
async initialize() {
  const loading = await this.loadingCtrl.create({
    message: 'Loading tour data...',
    spinner: 'crescent'
  });
  await loading.present();
  await this.getRegions().then(data => this.regions = data);
  await this.getTourtypes().then(data => this.tourtypes
                              = _.sortBy(data, 'Name'));
  await this.getTours().then(data => {
    this.tours = _.sortBy(data, 'Title');
    this.all_tours = _.sortBy(data, 'Title');
    this.filterTours( {lower: 80, upper: 400} );
    this.favService.initialize(this.all_tours);
  });
  await loading.dismiss();
}

getRegions() {
  let requestUrl = `${this.baseUrl}/Regions.json`;
  return this.http.get(requestUrl).toPromise();
}

getTourtypes() {
  let requestUrl = `${this.baseUrl}/Tourtypes.json`;
  return this.http.get(requestUrl).toPromise();
}

getTours() {
  let requestUrl = `${this.baseUrl}/Tours.json`;
  return this.http.get(requestUrl).toPromise();
}

filterTours(price):number {
  this.tours = _.filter(this.all_tours, function(tour) {
    return tour.PriceG >= price.lower
        && tour.PriceG <= price.upper;
  });
  this.regions.forEach(region => {
    const rtours = _.filter(this.tours,
                            ['Region', region.ID]);
    region['Count'] = rtours.length;
```

```
    });
    this.tourtypes.forEach(tourtype => {
      const ttours = _.filter(this.tours,
                              ['Tourtype', tourtype.ID]);
      tourtype['Count'] = ttours.length;
    });
    return this.tours.length;
  }

}
```

In the `initialize()` method with

```
this.filterTours( {lower: 80, upper: 400} );
```

we first make sure that we start with default values.

With implementing the (bold formatted) filter logic for `this.regions` and `this.-tourtypes` in our `filterTours()` method we ensure that these variables are also updated whenever one of the filter parameters is changed by the user.

2. Modify RegionsPage

In `regions.page.ts` we delete the following out-commented lines:

```
import { Component, OnInit } from '@angular/core';
import { BobToursService } from 'src/app/services/bob-
tours.service';
import _ from 'lodash';

@Component({
  selector: 'app-regions',
  templateUrl: './regions.page.html',
  styleUrls: ['./regions.page.scss'],
})
export class RegionsPage implements OnInit {

  //regions: any;

  constructor(public btService:BobToursService) { }
```

```
ngOnInit() {
     /*  this.regions = this.btService.regions;
    this.regions.forEach(region => {
      const tours = _.filter(this.btService.tours,
                              ['Region', region.ID]);
      region['Count'] = tours.length;
    }); */
  }

}
```

We remove the variable `regions` and in `ngOnInit()` its corresponding filter logic, because we centralized it in the BobToursService just now.

In `regions.page.html` we make the following little change:

```
<ion-header>
  <ion-toolbar>
    <ion-buttons slot="start">
      <ion-menu-button></ion-menu-button>
    </ion-buttons>
    <ion-title>Regions</ion-title>
  </ion-toolbar>
</ion-header>

<ion-content class="ion-padding">
  <ion-list>
    <ion-item *ngFor="let region of btService.regions"
              [routerLink]="['/list', { Category: 'Region',
                                         ID: region.ID,
                                         Name: region.Name } ]"
              routerDirection="forward"
              [disabled]="region.Count==0">
      <ion-icon name="{{region.Icon}}" slot="start"></ion-i-
con>
      {{region.Name}}
      <ion-badge slot="end">{{region.Count}}</ion-badge>
    </ion-item>
  </ion-list>
</ion-content>
```

Here we refer directly to the variable `regions` of the BobToursService now.

3. Modify TourTypesPage

In `tour-types.page.ts` we delete the following out-commented lines:

```
import { Component, OnInit } from '@angular/core';
import { BobToursService } from 'src/app/services/bob-
tours.service';
import _ from 'lodash';

@Component({
  selector: 'app-tour-types',
  templateUrl: './tour-types.page.html',
  styleUrls: ['./tour-types.page.scss'],
})
export class TourTypesPage implements OnInit {

  // tourtypes: any;

  constructor(private btService:BobToursService) { }

  ngOnInit() {
   /*  this.tourtypes = this.btService.tourtypes;
    this.tourtypes.forEach(tourtype => {
      const tours = _.filter(this.btService.tours,
                              ['Tourtype', tourtype.ID]);
        tourtype['Count'] = tours.length;
    }); */
  }

}
```

We remove the variable `tourtypes` and in `ngOnInit()` its corresponding filter logic, because we centralized it in the BobToursService.

And in `tour-types.page.html` we make the following little change:

```
<ion-header>
  <ion-toolbar>
    <ion-buttons slot="start">
      <ion-menu-button></ion-menu-button>
    </ion-buttons>
    <ion-title>Tour-Types</ion-title>
  </ion-toolbar>
```

```
</ion-header>
<ion-content class="ion-padding">
 <ion-list>
  <ion-item *ngFor="let tourtype of btService.tourtypes"
           [routerLink]="['/list', { Category: 'Tourtype',
                                     ID: tourtype.ID,
                                     Name: tourtype.Name } ]"
           routerDirection="forward"
           [disabled]="tourtype.Count==0">
    <ion-icon name="{{tourtype.Icon}}" slot="start">
    </ion-icon>
    {{tourtype.Name}}
    <ion-badge slot="end">{{tourtype.Count}}</ion-badge>
  </ion-item>
 </ion-list>
</ion-content>
```

Here we refer directly to the variable `tourtypes` of the BobToursService now.

In multi-view mode, our app now reacts directly to changed user's price filtering:

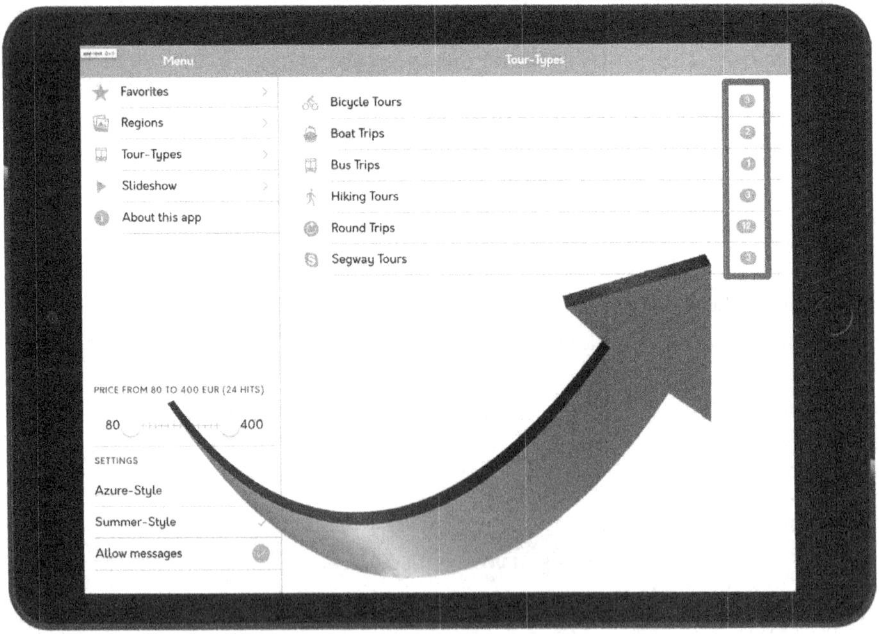

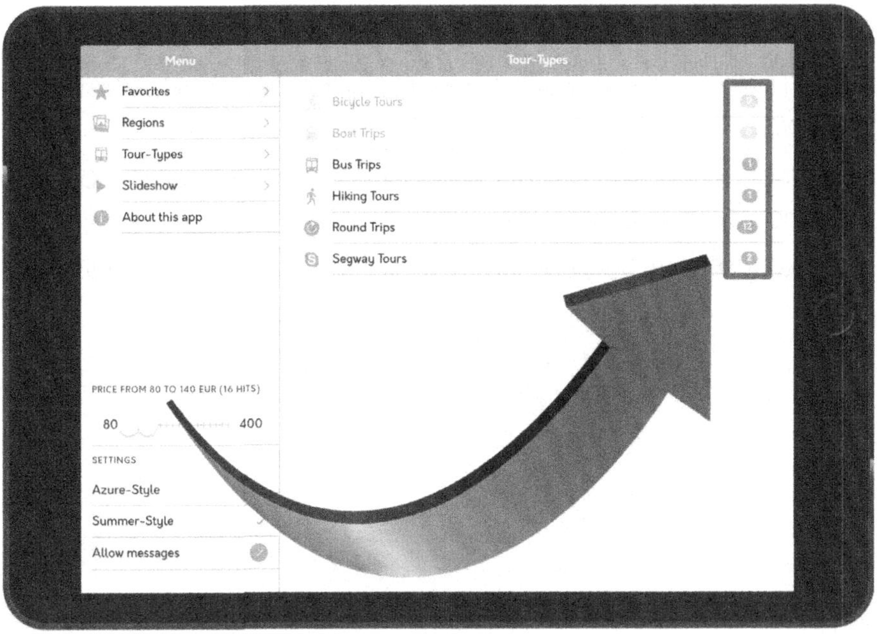

More informations about SplitPane layout you can find here:

- https://ionicframework.com/docs/api/split-pane
- https://ionicframework.com/docs/layout/structure#split-pane-layout

Summary

In this chapter, you have learned the basics of theming, styling and customizing an Ionic app.

From simple theming with the Color Generator to targeted changes using CSS Variables and CSS Utilities to advanced techniques.

You have embedded your own fonts into the app, got to know the handling and the animation of SVG graphics.

Even dynamic theming and responsive designs are no longer secrets for you.

9 Ionic Native

9.1 Introduction

One of the most common misconceptions about Ionic is that as an app developer you have no access to the same native SDK features as native apps. That's not right!

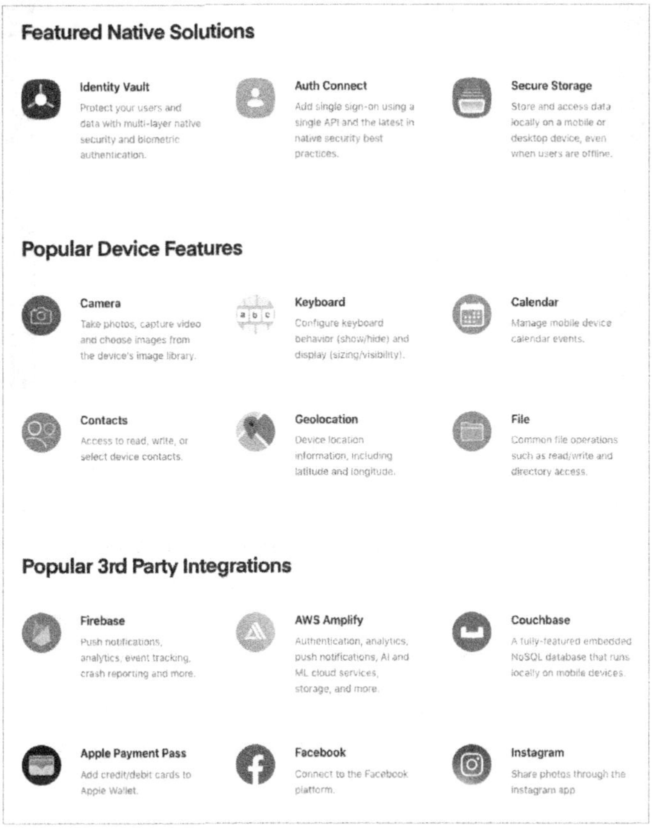

With Ionic Native you have complete native access to the hardware of a mobile device. Taking pictures with the camera, connecting to other devices via Bluetooth, authentication via the fingerprint scanner - all this and much more is possible.

Ionic Native makes it easy to add native device functionality to any Ionic app leveraging Cordova or Capacitor.

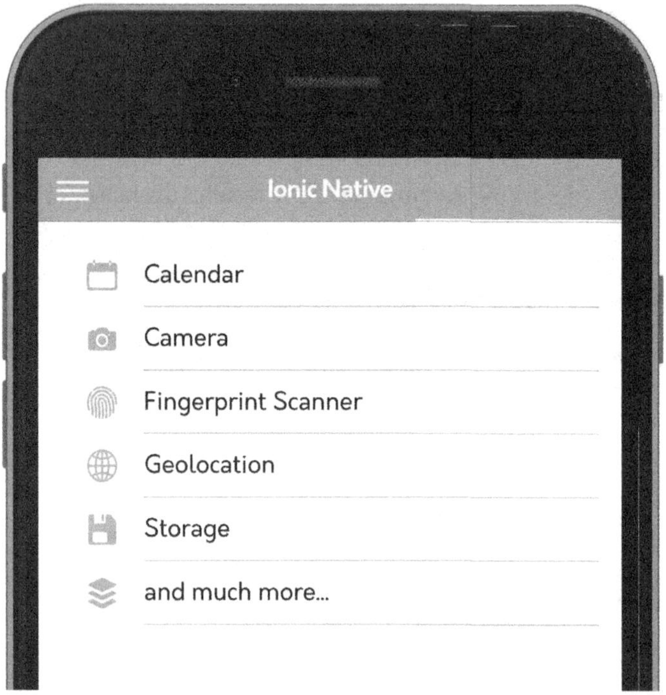

In the next division we'll show the usage of Ionic Native by implementing the Geolocation Cordova plugin in our app. Note that there are *community* and *enterprise/premier* editions of the plugins. Community Plugins are a collection of open source Cordova plugins that make it easy to add native functionality to any Ionic app. They're submitted and maintained by the Ionic community. We'll use the free community edition of the Geolocation plugin.

In addition to Cordova, Ionic Native also works with Capacitor (see chapter "B2. Ionic and Capacitor", starting from page 565). Cordova and Capacitor can be used together in an Ionic project.

More informations about Ionic Native you can find here:

- https://ionicframework.com/docs/native
- https://ionicframework.com/docs/native/community

9.2 Geolocation

The Geolocation plugin provides information about the location of a terminal such as latitude and longitude. Global positioning system (GPS), network information such as the IP address, RFID, WiFi and Bluetooth MAC addresses, as well as GSM / CDMA cell IDs are used to achieve the most accurate results possible.

Geolocation supports the following platforms:

- Amazon Fire OS
- Android
- Browser
- iOS
- Windows

This API is based on the W3C Geolocation API Specification, and only executes on devices that don't already provide an implementation.

For iOS you have to add this configuration to your `config.xml` file:

```
<edit-config file="*-Info.plist"
             mode="merge"
             target="NSLocationWhenInUseUsageDescription">
  <string>
   We use your location for full functionality of certain
   app features.
  </string>
</edit-config>
```

Geolocation in our app

We want to use this plugin in our app to find the user location. With the help of the determined coordinates later a route planning to the starting point of an offered tour should be possible.

Installation

First we install the (community) plugins of Cordova and Ionic Native via terminal:

```
$ ionic cordova plugin add cordova-plugin-geolocation
$ npm install @ionic-native/geolocation
```

Important imports

Now it's important to import (what a wording ;-)) Geolocation in:

1. `app.module.ts`
2. `map.module.ts` and
3. `map.page.ts` and
4. not to forget to append `/ngx` to every import statement.

1. app.module.ts

We start with the import in `app.module.ts`:

```
import { NgModule } from '@angular/core';
import { BrowserModule } from '@angular/platform-browser';
import { RouteReuseStrategy } from '@angular/router';

import { IonicModule, IonicRouteStrategy }
         from '@ionic/angular';
import { SplashScreen }
         from '@ionic-native/splash-screen/ngx';
import { StatusBar } from '@ionic-native/status-bar/ngx';

import { AppComponent } from './app.component';
import { AppRoutingModule } from './app-routing.module';

import { HttpClientModule } from '@angular/common/http';
import { IonicStorageModule } from '@ionic/storage';

import { FormsModule, ReactiveFormsModule }
         from '@angular/forms';
import { AboutComponent }
         from './components/about/about.component';

import { Geolocation } from '@ionic-native/geolocation/ngx';

@NgModule({
  declarations: [AppComponent, AboutComponent],
  entryComponents: [AboutComponent],
  imports: [
    BrowserModule,
    IonicModule.forRoot(),
```

```
    AppRoutingModule,
    HttpClientModule,
    IonicStorageModule.forRoot(),
    FormsModule,
    ReactiveFormsModule
  ],
  providers: [
    StatusBar,
    SplashScreen,
    Geolocation,
    { provide: RouteReuseStrategy, useClass: IonicRouteStrate-
gy }
  ],
  bootstrap: [AppComponent]
})
export class AppModule { }
```

2. map.module.ts

Now we import it – in the same way – to `map.module.ts`:

```
import { NgModule } from '@angular/core';
import { CommonModule } from '@angular/common';
import { FormsModule } from '@angular/forms';

import { IonicModule } from '@ionic/angular';

import { MapPageRoutingModule } from './map-routing.module';

import { MapPage } from './map.page';

import { Geolocation } from '@ionic-native/geolocation/ngx';

@NgModule({
  imports: [
    CommonModule,
    FormsModule,
    IonicModule,
    MapPageRoutingModule
  ],
  declarations: [MapPage],
```

```
  providers: [Geolocation]
})
export class MapPageModule { }
```

3. map.page.ts

Let's finally import Geolocation in `map.page.ts` and also add a function to use the plugin:

```
import { Component, OnInit } from '@angular/core';
import { ModalController, LoadingController }
         from '@ionic/angular';

import { Geolocation } from '@ionic-native/geolocation/ngx';

@Component({
  selector: 'app-map',
  templateUrl: './map.page.html',
  styleUrls: ['./map.page.scss'],
})
export class MapPage implements OnInit {

  currentView = 'map';

  constructor(
              private modalCtrl: ModalController,
              private loadingCtrl: LoadingController,
              private geolocation: Geolocation) { }

  ngOnInit() {
    this.calcRoute();
  }

  // Calculates a route
     from current user position to destination
  async calcRoute() {
    const loading = await this.loadingCtrl.create({
      message: 'Calculate route...',
      spinner: 'crescent'
    });
    await loading.present();
```

```
    const geo = await this.geolocation.getCurrentPosition();
    console.log(geo.coords.latitude, geo.coords.longitude);
    loading.dismiss();
  }

  ...

}
```

We import `Geolocation` and inject it with the variable `geolocation` into the constructor. We also import a `LoadingController` (see "6.19 Progress Indicators", starting from page 240) and inject it with the variable `loadingCtrl` into the constructor.

In `ngOnInit()` we place a call to a method `calcRoute()`.

Within this async method `calcRoute()` we first create a new LoadingController:

```
const loading = await this.loadingCtrl.create({
      message: 'Calculate route...',
      spinner: 'crescent'
    });
```

After finishing the creation process we present it:

```
await loading.present();
```

Now we make use of the native Geolocation component to get the current position of our device:

```
const geo = await this.geolocation.getCurrentPosition();
```

Note that the method `getCurrentPosition()` is asynchronous and we can work with the help of `await` to wait for the result of the coordinate determination.

The coordinates are given (initially) via the console:

```
console.log(geo.coords.latitude, geo.coords.longitude);
```

For our card logic we limit ourselves to latitude and longitude. However, some devices also output other parameters such as altitude.

Finally, the LoadingController is dismissed:

```
loading.dismiss();
```

When first retrieved, the browser, the emulator or the device asks us if we can query the location. If we allow it, after some waiting we'll be rewarded with the rather exact coordinates of our location.

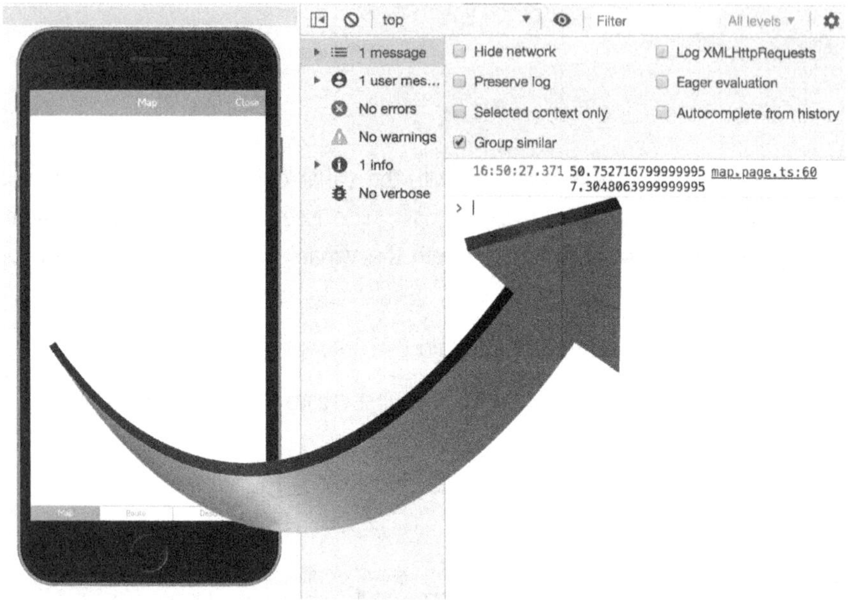

More informations about the Geolocation you can find here:

► https://ionicframework.com/docs/native/geolocation

9.3 A map for our app

Since apps run on mobile devices, they are of course excellent companions and map-based application scenarios that can take advantage of this fact are quickly found.

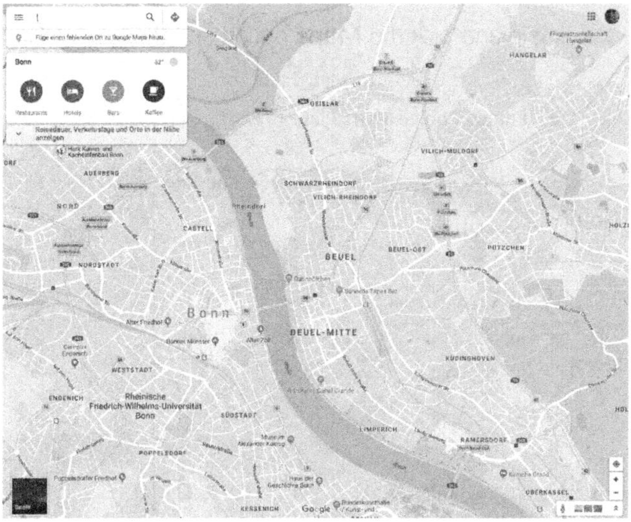

Of course, there's also a native plugin in Ionic Native for the use of maps, namely Google Maps. You can find it here:

► https://github.com/ionic-team/ionic-native-google-maps

This plugin supports Android and iOS only.

In our app, however, we claim to support as many platforms as possible. And we can do that, too. However, we have to do *without* the plugin and instead rely on a JavaScript-based solution using the Google Maps JavaScript API:

► https://developers.google.com/maps/documentation/JavaScript/tutorial

To implement a map functionality in our app, the following steps are required:

1. Generate a Google Maps JavaScript API KEY
2. Add a reference in index.html
3. Prepare the map
4. Add own markers to map and route

1. Generate a Google Maps JavaScript API KEY

Via the aforementioned link you can access the documentation page of the API. To use the API, you need a key that you can get by clicking on the GET STARTED button above.

First you have to log in and pick the **Maps** option and then click CONTINUE.

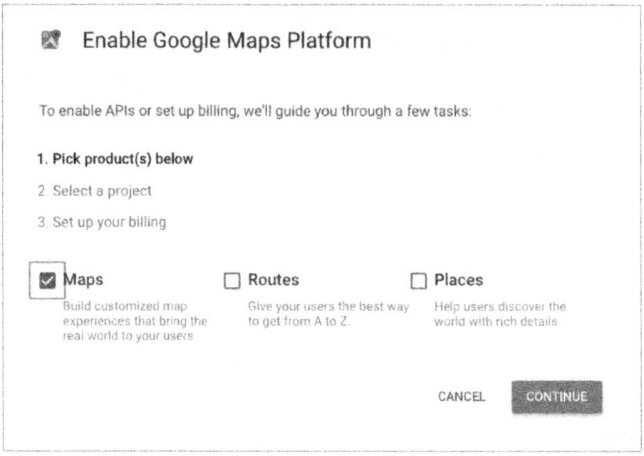

Second you have to select a project. If you followed the database chapter (see "5.1 Database Backend with Google Firebase", starting from page 97), you already have a "BoB-Tours-App" project. Otherwise, you have to create one now.

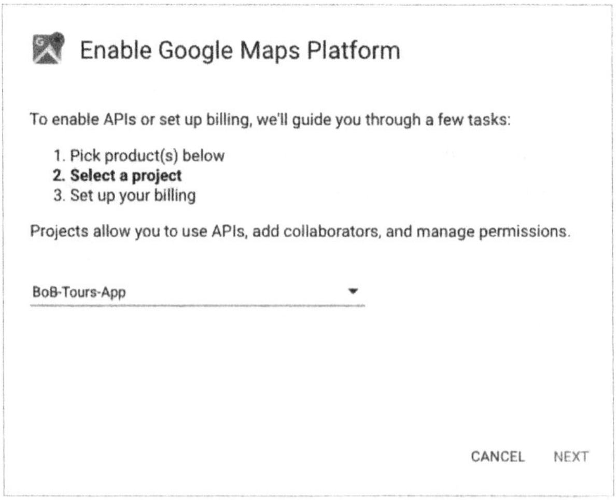

With a click on NEXT the process will be finished and you'll get your API KEY:

Copy this API KEY into the clipboard. We'll need it for the next step.

2. Add a reference in index.html

Add the following script link in `index.html`:

```
<!DOCTYPE html>
<html lang="en">

<head>
  <meta charset="utf-8" />
  <title>Ionic App</title>

  <base href="/" />

  <meta name="viewport"
        content="viewport-fit=cover, width=device-width,
   initial-scale=1.0, minimum-scale=1.0, maximum-scale=1.0,
   user-scalable=no" />
  <meta name="format-detection" content="telephone=no" />
  <meta name="msapplication-tap-highlight" content="no" />

  <link rel="icon"
      type="image/png"
      href="assets/icon/favicon.png" />
```

```
  <!-- add to homescreen for ios -->
  <meta name="apple-mobile-web-app-capable" content="yes" />
  <meta name="apple-mobile-web-app-status-bar-style"
content="black" />

  <!-- Animation with Animate.css /
https://github.com/daneden/animate.css -->
  <link rel="stylesheet"
        href="https://cdnjs.cloudflare.com/ajax/libs/ani-
mate.css/3.7.0/
             animate.min.css">

  <!-- Google Maps JavaScript API -->
  <script src="https://maps.googleapis.com/maps/api/js?
              key=YOUR_API_KEY"
          async defer>
  </script>

</head>

<body>
    <app-root></app-root>
</body>

</html>
```

Now replace `YOUR_API_KEY` with your own API KEY (from the clipboard).

With this script entry, we get access to the Google Maps JavaScript API, and thus a whole range of useful map features, as we'll see shortly. The `async` attribute specifies that the script will execute (asynchronously) as soon as it's available. With the attribute `defer` we make sure that our app is fully rendered *before* the script is executed. In other words: load the script asynchronously (`async`), but don't execute it before the page has been completely rendered (`defer`).

3. Prepare the map

Let's start preparing map.page.html:

```
<ion-header>
  <ion-toolbar>
    <ion-title>{{currentView | titlecase}}</ion-title>
    <ion-buttons slot="end">
      <ion-button (click)="close()">Close</ion-button>
    </ion-buttons>
  </ion-toolbar>
</ion-header>

<ion-content>
  <div id="map"
       [class.hidden]="currentView=='description'">
  </div>
  <div id="description"
       [class.hidden]="currentView!='description'"
       padding>
  </div>
</ion-content>

<ion-footer class="ion-padding">
  <ion-segment [(ngModel)]="currentView"
               (ionChange)="currentViewChanged($event)">
    <ion-segment-button value="map">
      <ion-label>Map</ion-label>
    </ion-segment-button>
    <ion-segment-button value="route">
      <ion-label>Route</ion-label>
    </ion-segment-button>
    <ion-segment-button value="description">
      <ion-label>Description</ion-label>
    </ion-segment-button>
  </ion-segment>
</ion-footer>
```

Within the header/toolbar area in ion-title we write

```
{{currentView | titlecase}}
```

to show the current view value. You remember: we get it from an ion-segmen-t-button when a user clicks on one. So that the values "map", "route" or "description" are not lowercase, we use the built-in pipe titlecase to capitalize the first letter (see "2.8 Pipes", starting from page 41).

In the content area we place two div tags, one for showing the map and one for showing the description of a calculated route:

```
<div id="map"
     [class.hidden]="currentView=='description'">
</div>
<div id="description"
     [class.hidden]="currentView!='description'"
     padding>
</div>
```

We bind a CSS class called hidden (which we define afterwards) to a condition to do the following: If description was selected as currentView, the div with the id "map" will be hidden, otherwise the div with the id "description" will be hidden (and the "map" div will be displayed).

Perhaps you wanna save space in favor of the map or description. Then delete the padding directive in the ion-footer tag.

We now add some styling in map.page.scss:

```
#map, #description {
    height: 100%;
    background-color: white;
}

#description {
  margin: 8px;
}

.hidden {
    display: none;
}
```

We make sure that our divs get the maximum height and a white background and we define the conditionally assigned CSS class "hidden" with display: none.

Now we use Google Maps JavaScript API to draw a map and calculate the route from the user's position to a destination. It would be a good idea to write your own provider for this. But to make it clearer, we do that in map.page.ts:

```
import { Component, OnInit } from '@angular/core';
import { Geolocation } from '@ionic-native/geolocation/ngx';
import { ModalController, LoadingController, NavParams }
         from '@ionic/angular';
declare var google: any;

@Component({
  selector: 'app-map',
  templateUrl: './map.page.html',
  styleUrls: ['./map.page.scss'],
})
export class MapPage implements OnInit {

  currentView = 'map';

  tour:           any = {};
  map:            any;
  position:       any;
  destination:    any;
  isCalculated:   boolean;

  constructor(
              private modalCtrl: ModalController,
              private loadingCtrl: LoadingController,
              private geolocation: Geolocation,
              private navParams: NavParams
             ) { }

  ngOnInit() {
      this.initMap();
      //this.calcRoute();
  }

  // Initialize map
  initMap() {
   this.tour = this.navParams.data;
   this.destination = new google.maps.LatLng(
     this.tour.StartingPoint.Lat,
     this.tour.StartingPoint.Lng
   );
   this.map = new
     google.maps.Map(document.getElementById('map'), {
```

```
      center: this.destination,
      zoom: 16,
      fullscreenControl: false
    });
   this.isCalculated = false;
  }
  // Calculates a route
     from current user position to destination
  async calcRoute() {

    if (this.isCalculated) return;

    // Show calculation process
    const loading = await this.loadingCtrl.create({
      message: 'Calculate route...',
      spinner: 'crescent'
    });
    await loading.present();

    // Get current user position
    const geo = await this.geolocation.getCurrentPosition();
    this.position = new google.maps.LatLng(
      geo.coords.latitude,
      geo.coords.longitude
    );

    // Prepare map and description display
    const dirDisplay = new google.maps.DirectionsRenderer();
    dirDisplay.setMap(this.map);
    dirDisplay.setPanel(
      document.getElementById('description')
    );

    // Calculate route from position to destination
    const dirService = new google.maps.DirectionsService();
    dirService.route({
      origin: this.position,
      destination: this.destination,
      travelMode: 'DRIVING'
    },
    function(result, status) {
      if (status == 'OK') {
```

```
        dirDisplay.setDirections(result);
      }
    });

    // Calculation process finished
    this.isCalculated = true;
    loading.dismiss();
  }

  // User changed a segment
  currentViewChanged(ev) {
    switch (ev.detail.value) {
      case 'map': this.initMap(); break;
      case 'route' : this.calcRoute(); break;
      case 'description': this.calcRoute(); break;
    }
  }

  // User clicked 'close' icon/button
  close() {
    this.modal.dismiss();
  }

}
```

First, to get the tour data in our map popup, we use NavParams, which we import from `'@ionic/angular'` and inject into the constructor as a variable `navParams`.

It is very important to set a variable called google:

```
declare var google: any;
```

It's needed by the referenced Google Maps JavaScript API (see the Google Maps JavaScript API documentation for more information about this topic).

We declare a bunch of variables (`tour`, `map`, `position`, `destination`, `isCalculated`) that we use in the following methods.

In the `initMap()` method we grab the tour from the calling DetailsPage with

```
this.tour = this.navParams.data;
```

Then we create a `LatLng` object for the destination:

```
this.destination = new google.maps.LatLng(
  this.tour.StartingPoint.Lat,
   this.tour.StartingPoint.Lng
);
```

We form it from the starting point of a tour. We get the starting point from the database. Let's have a short look at this:

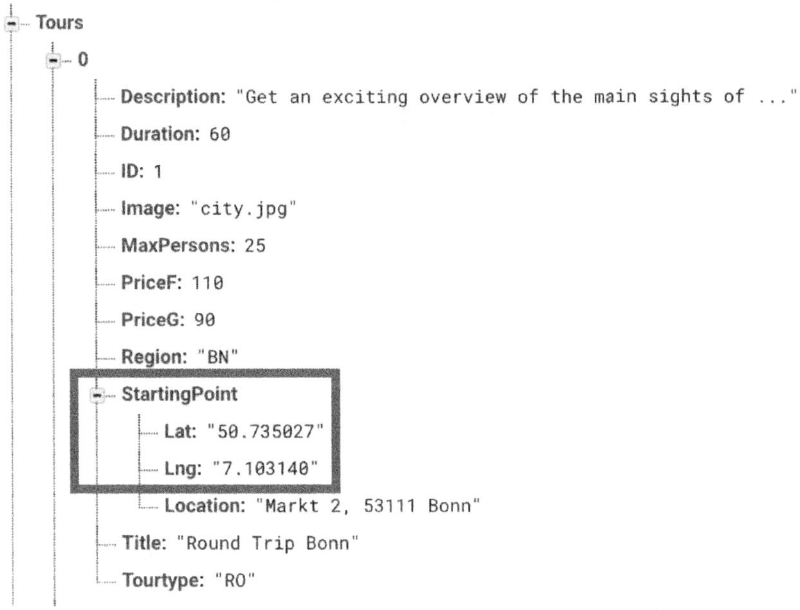

`Lat` contains the latitude and `Lng` the longitude information of the starting point of a tour. With these coordinates we can

With this destination information we can now create our map. This happens with:

```
this.map = new
  google.maps.Map(document.getElementById('map'), {
    center: this.destination,
    zoom: 16,
    fullscreenControl: false
  });
```

The `Maps` method of `google.maps` expects two arguments:

1. an HTML element as the place where the map should be drawn (the `'map'` div in `map.page.html`) and
2. a JSON object to configure the map

Here we center the map to the `LatLng` object `destination` (the starting point of a tour), determine a zoom level of `16` and hide the fullscreen control of the map. You can find these and all other `google.maps.Map` parameters in the Google Maps JavaScript API documentation.

Finally, we set the `isCalculated` flag to `false`. What we need it for, we'll see right away.

In the existing `calcRoute()` method we check, if `isCalculated` is `true` to prevent unnecessary calculations:

```
if (this.isCalculated) return;
```

With

```
this.position = new google.maps.LatLng(
  geo.coords.latitude,
  geo.coords.longitude
);
```

we create a `LatLng` object from the current device position. You remember: we determined this position named `geo` using the Ionic Native Geolocation plugin before (see “9.2 Geolocation” on page 395).

With

```
const dirDisplay = new google.maps.DirectionsRenderer();
```

we assign a so-called `DirectionsRenderer` to a variable `dirDisplay`.

This allows us to draw a map and alternatively a panel (description) on it:

```
dirDisplay.setMap(this.map);
dirDisplay.setPanel(document.getElementById('description'));
```

Now we create a `DirectionsService`:

```
const dirService = new google.maps.DirectionsService();
```

This service owns a `route` method:

```
dirService.route({
  origin: this.position,
  destination: this.destination,
  travelMode: 'DRIVING'
},
function(result, status) {
  if (status == 'OK') {
    dirDisplay.setDirections(result);
  }
});
```

It expects two arguments:

1. a JSON object to configure the route
2. a callback function to handle the result

In the configuration object we determine `this.position` as `origin` and `this.destination` as `destination` for the route. As travel mode we choose `'DRIVING'` (other travel modes are `'Bicycling'`, `'Transit'` and `'Walking'`).

In the callback function we check for `status=='OK'` and use the `SetDirections` method with the `result` as argument for it.

Again: You can find all these parameters and methods in the Google Maps JavaScript API documentation.

Because we now have a calculated route, we set the `isCalculated` flag to `true`.

Finally, in the `currentViewChanged(ev)` method we react to every button:

```
switch (ev.detail.value) {
  case 'map': this.initMap(); break;
  case 'route' : this.calcRoute(); break;
  case 'description': this.calcRoute(); break;
}
```

Our map and route calculation works basically now.

Let's take a look at the whole thing in action:

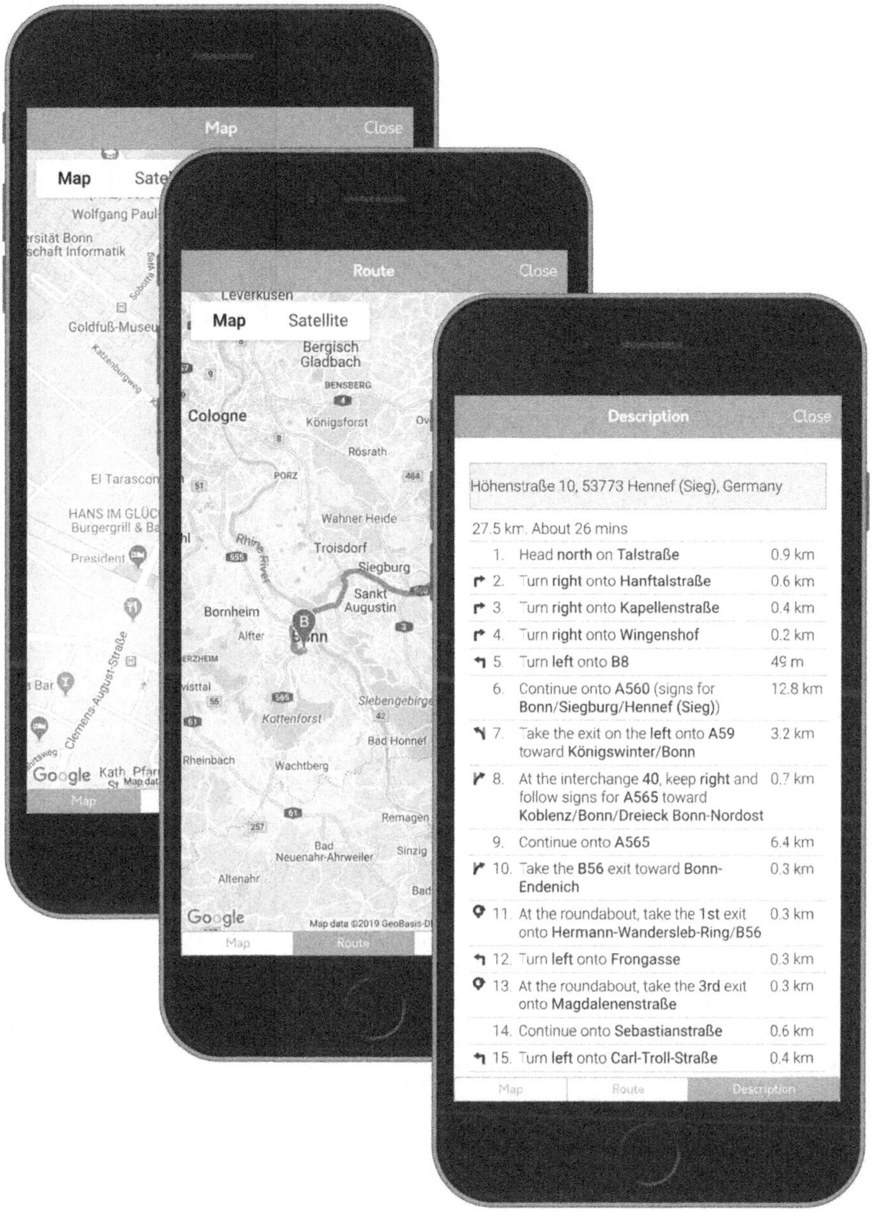

4. Add own markers to map and route

To put the cherry on the cake, we add our own markers to the map and the route display. For this we extend once again and for the last time the code in `map.-page.ts`:

```
import { Component, OnInit } from '@angular/core';
import { Geolocation } from '@ionic-native/geolocation/ngx';
import { ModalController, LoadingController, NavParams }
         from '@ionic/angular';

declare var google: any;

@Component({
  selector: 'app-map',
  templateUrl: './map.page.html',
  styleUrls: ['./map.page.scss'],
})
export class MapPage implements OnInit {

  currentView = 'map';
  modal: Components.IonModal;

  tour:            any = {};
  map:             any;
  position:        any;
  destination:     any;
  isCalculated:    boolean;

  constructor(private navParams: NavParams,
              private geolocation: Geolocation,
              private loadingCtrl: LoadingController) { }

  ngOnInit() {
      this.initMap();
  }

  // Initialize map
  initMap() {
   this.tour = this.navParams.data;
   this.destination = new google.maps.LatLng(
     this.tour.StartingPoint.Lat,
```

```
      this.tour.StartingPoint.Lng
    );
    this.map = new google.maps.Map(
      document.getElementById('map'), {
      center: this.destination,
      zoom: 16,
      fullscreenControl: false
    });
    this.isCalculated = false;
    this.addDestinationMarker();
  }

  // Calculates a route
     from current user position to destination
  async calcRoute() {

    if (this.isCalculated) return;

    // Show calculation process
    const loading = await this.loadingCtrl.create({
      message: 'Calculate route...',
      spinner: 'crescent'
    });
    await loading.present();

    // Get current user position
    const geo = await this.geolocation.getCurrentPosition();
    this.position = new google.maps.LatLng(
      geo.coords.latitude,
      geo.coords.longitude
    );

    // Prepare map and description display
    const dirDisplay = new google.maps.DirectionsRenderer({
      suppressMarkers: true
    });
    dirDisplay.setMap(this.map);
    dirDisplay.setPanel(
      document.getElementById('description'));

    // Calculate route from position to destination
    const dirService = new google.maps.DirectionsService();
```

```
    dirService.route({
      origin: this.position,
      destination: this.destination,
      travelMode: 'DRIVING'
    },
    function(result, status) {
      if (status == 'OK') {
        dirDisplay.setDirections(result);
      }
    });

    // Add position marker
    this.addPositionMarker();

    // Calculation process finished
    this.isCalculated = true;
    loading.dismiss();
  }

  // Add current position marker
  addPositionMarker() {

   // icon
   const iconCar = {
    url: 'https://ionic.andreas-dormann.de/img/car-point.svg',
    scaledSize: new google.maps.Size(96, 96)
   }

    // marker
   const marker = new google.maps.Marker({
     position: this.position,
     map: this.map,
     icon: iconCar
   });

  }

  // Add destination marker
  addDestinationMarker() {

   // icon
   const iconSun = {
```

```
      url: 'https://ionic.andreas-dormann.de/img/sun-point.svg',
      scaledSize: new google.maps.Size(96, 96)
    }

    // marker
    const marker = new google.maps.Marker({
      position: this.destination,
      map: this.map,
      icon: iconSun
    });

    // information window
    const infoWindow = new google.maps.InfoWindow({
       content: '<h3>' + this.tour.Title + '</h3>' +
                '<p>Starting point of the tour:<br />' +
                this.tour.StartingPoint.Location + '</p>',
       maxWidth: 200
    })

    // click handler
    marker.addListener('click', function() {
      infoWindow.open(this.map, marker);
    });

  }

  // User changed a segment
  currentViewChanged(ev) {
    switch (ev.detail.value) {
      case 'map': this.initMap(); break;
      case 'route' : this.calcRoute(); break;
      case 'description': this.calcRoute(); break;
    }
  }

  // User clicked 'close' icon/button
  close() {
    this.modal.dismiss();
  }

}
```

In `initMap()` we call the new method `addDestinationMarker()`. Let's look at this method bit by bit:

```
const iconSun = {
  url: 'http://ionic.andreas-dormann.de/img/sun-point.svg',
  scaledSize: new google.maps.Size(96, 96)
}
```

We define an icon object named `iconSun` and scale it to 96 by 96 pixels.

We use this icon as third of three arguments to create a `Marker` object:

```
const marker = new google.maps.Marker({
  position: this.destination,
  map: this.map,
  icon: iconSun
});
```

The first argument `position` is assigned to `this.destination` and the second argument `map` is assigned to `this.map`.

We want to add an information window to the marker. So we code:

```
const infoWindow = new google.maps.InfoWindow({
  content: '<h3>' + this.tour.Title + '</h3>' +
           '<p>Starting point of the tour:<br />' +
           this.tour.StartingPoint.Location + '</p>',
  maxWidth: 200
})
```

I think that's self-explanatory.

Now we have to link the info window with the marker:

```
marker.addListener('click', function() {
  infoWindow.open(this.map, marker);
});
```

If the user clicks on the marker, the info window will open.

Let's see that in action:

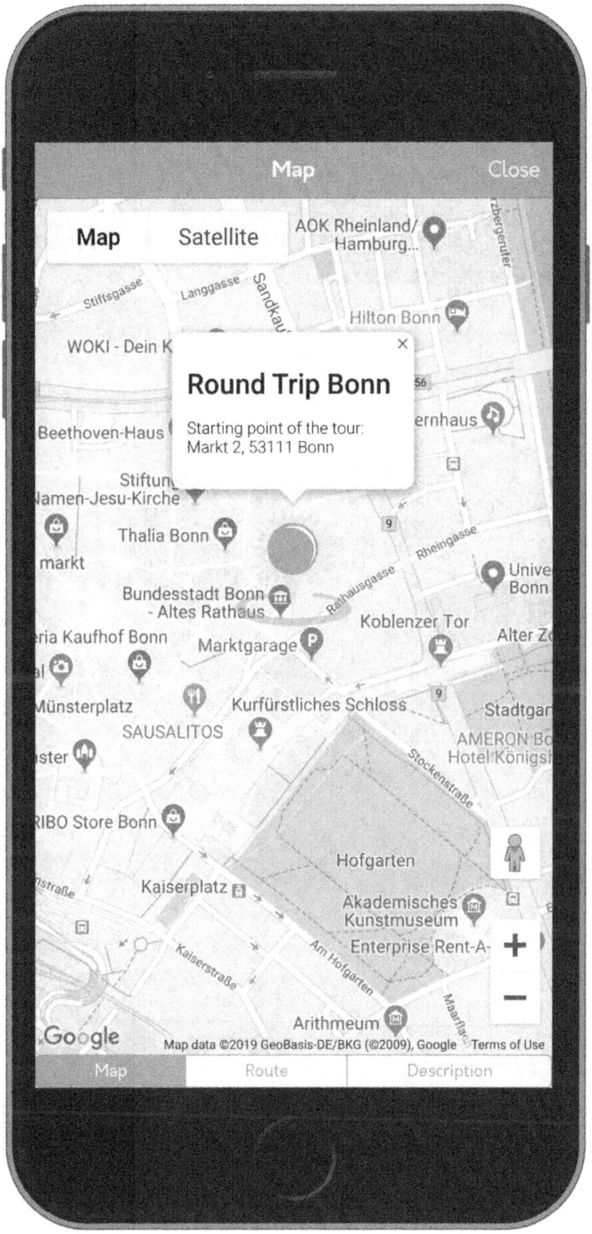

Also Google StreetView works great in our app:

If we plan a route, we need another marker, which we build in the method `addPositionMarker()`. We also want to look at this method bit by bit:

```
const iconCar = {
  url: 'http://ionic.andreas-dormann.de/img/car-point.svg',
  scaledSize: new google.maps.Size(96, 96)
}
```

We define an icon object named `iconCar` and scale it to 96 by 96 pixels.

We use this icon as third of three arguments to create a `Marker` object:

```
const marker = new google.maps.Marker({
  position: this.position,
  map: this.map,
  icon: iconCar
});
```

The first argument `position` is assigned to `this.position` and the second argument `map` is again assigned to `this.map`.

That's it.

The marker is built on every call to the `calcRoute()` method.

One last thing to mention: I extended the call of `DirectionsRenderer`:

```
const dirDisplay = new google.maps.DirectionsRenderer(
  { suppressMarkers: true }
);
```

This little configuration takes care of suppressing the Google Maps default markers "A" and "B". We have our own markers.

Let's marvel at the route display with our own markers at the beginning and end of the route:

9.4 Native Plugins in browsers

In the past, it has always been difficult or impossible to test native functionality in the browser. Nobody passed tests on emulators or even real hardware.

`Geolocation` wasn't a problem, as a browser operated by a desktop PC or Mac provides location coordinates. But a browser doesn't have a built-in camera, sensors or pedometer, etc.

Ionic Native allows us as a developer now to use native plug-ins in the browser and thereby overwrite so that we can "simulate" the sensor data, for example. Such a *mocking* of plugins is easy to implement. Thanks to Chris Griffith and his

Ionic Native Mocks

Ionic Native Mocks are designed to be used as placeholders during development for the actual Ionic Native modules. More about this topic you can find in the last link below.

More informations about Ionic Native and related topics you can find here:

- https://ionicframework.com/docs/native
- https://ionicframework.com/docs/native/native-core
- https://ionicframework.com/blog/ionic-native-mocks/

Summary

In this chapter, you have developed a basic understanding of Ionic Native.

Using the example of Geolocation you have used a native plugin. Furthermore, you have enhanced our app with a great map functionality using the Google Maps JavaScript API.

At the end I gave you a hint how you can develop using native plugins in the browser with Ionic Native Mocks.

10 Communication & Messaging

Today, almost every device communicates with everyone (Internet of Things). But even more than ever, people communicate via special apps and software with family members or on business. Smartphones are handheld messengers rather than phones. They include WhatsApp, Snapchat, Skype, and TeamSpeak. And surely you also have an idea, how the users should communicate with the apps developed by you.

10.1 Mails, SMS & Co

It doesn't take much to send an email from an Ionic app, just the JavaScript call `window.location.href` in conjunction with the `mailto:` directive. In the same way we can send short messages via `window. location.href` and `sms:` or dial a phone number with `tel:`. It couldn't be easier, right?

Here are the variables you can use in `mailto:` links:

mailto:	to set the recipient, or recipients, separate with comma
&cc=	to set the CC recipient(s)
&bcc=	to set the BCC recipient(s)
&sub-ject=	to set the email subject, URL encode for longer sentences, so replace spaces with %20, etc.
&body=	to set the body of the message, you can add entire sentences here, including line breaks. Line breaks should be converted to %0A.

Email a request

In our app, we want to send the request for a tour via email using the path described above.

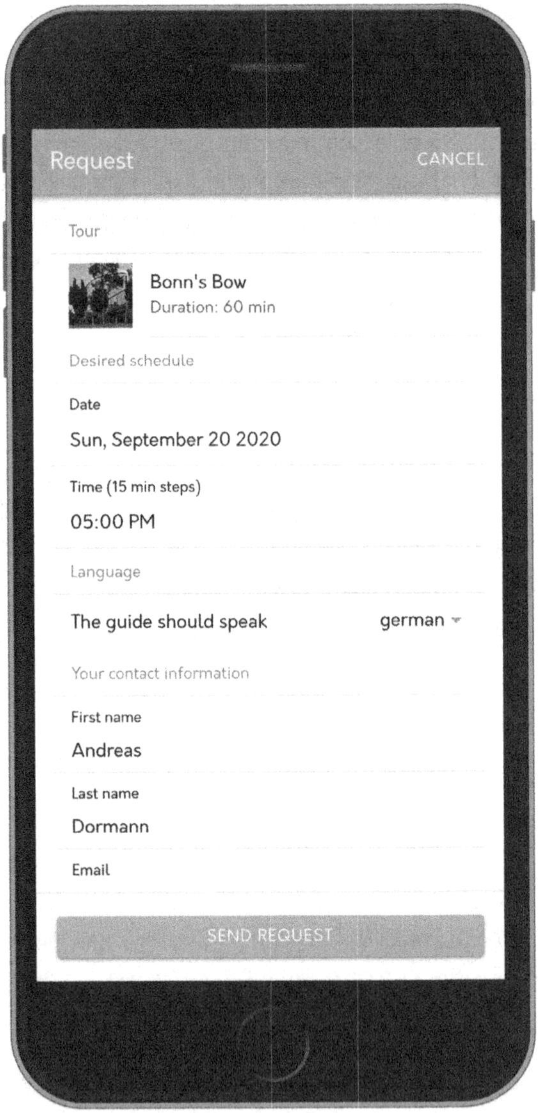

Here is the corresponding code in `request.page.ts`:

```
import { Component, OnInit } from '@angular/core';
import { ModalController, NavParams, ToastController }
        from '@ionic/angular';
import { FormBuilder, FormGroup, FormControl, Validators }
        from '@angular/forms';

@Component({
  selector: 'app-request',
  templateUrl: './request.page.html',
  styleUrls: ['./request.page.scss'],
})
export class RequestPage implements OnInit {

  tour: any = {};
  request: any = { Language: 'english' };
  day_after_tomorrow: string;
  two_years_later: string;
  isBusTrip: boolean;

  validationForm: FormGroup;
  validationMessages: any;

  constructor(
    private modalCtrl: ModalController,
    private navParams: NavParams,
    private toastCtrl: ToastController,
    public formBuilder: FormBuilder
  ) {
    this.tour = navParams.data;
  }

  ngOnInit() {
    ...
  }
  // Prepare form validation & messages
  prepareFormValidation() {
    ...
  }
```

```
// User clicked 'Send request' - so we send an email.
send(request) {

  this.request = request;

  const br = '%0A';

  const recipient = 'request@bob-tours.com'
  const subject = 'Request for BoB Tour "'
              + this.tour.Title + '"';

  const datetime = request.DesiredDate.slice(0, 10) + ' at '
               + request.DesiredTime.sclice(11, 5);
  const language = 'The guide should speak '
               + request.Language + '.';
  const needbus = (request.needBus)
              ? br + 'We need a bus' : '';
  const contact = request.FirstName + ' '
              + request.LastName;

  const body = 'Dear Ladies and Gentlemen,' + br + br
           + 'I hereby ask if you can do the tour
              mentioned in the subject on '
           + datetime + '.' + br
           + language + needbus + br + br
           + 'Yours sincerely' + br + contact;

  const email = 'mailto:' + recipient
            + '?cc=' + request.Email
            + '&subject=' + subject
            + '&body=' + body;

  window.location.href = email;

  this.confirm();
  this.modalCtrl.dismiss();
}
// User clicked 'Cancel'
cancel() {
  this.modal.dismiss();
}
```

```
  // Confirmation after sending the request.
  async confirm() {
    const toast = await this.toastCtrl.create({
      message: 'Thank you for your request!
              We will answer you shortly.',
      duration: 3500
    });
    toast.present();
    this.modal.dismiss();
  }

}
```

I think the code in our `send(request)` method is almost self-explanatory.

We build a complete email text using the request object (the user's input data from the form).

To insert a line break, we use the variable `br` and assign it the URL encoded expression `'%0A'`. URL encoding replaces unsafe ASCII characters with a `'%'` followed by two hexadecimal digits and should be displayed correctly in all mail clients.

At the end we send the email with

```
window.location.href = email;
```

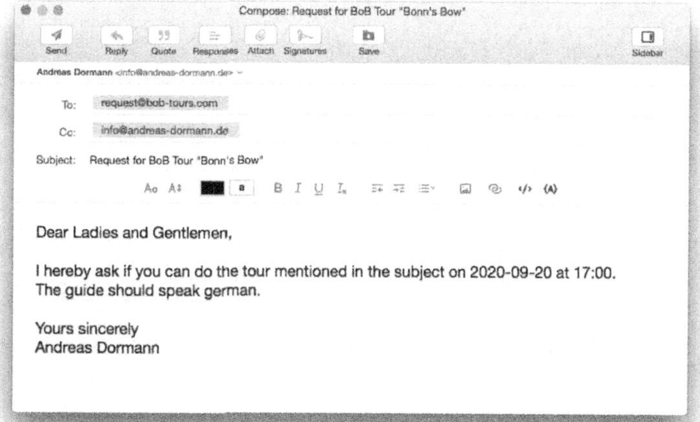

Short message system (SMS)

At the beginning I already mentioned that it is also possible to send an SMS via `href`. The SMS text structure is:

sms:	to set the phone number of the recipient
?body=	to set the body of the message, you can add entire sentences here, including line breaks. Line breaks should be converted to %0A.

Examples:

You know the phone number of a recipient.

```
window.location.href = 'sms:1-234-56789?body=My app is cool!';
```

You want the user to select a phone number himself:

```
window.location.href = 'sms:?body=My app is cool!';
```

In both cases, the app will launch your message app on the smartphone and you can send the prepared SMS.

Phone calls

Via `href` you can also start phone calls. The phone call structure is:

tel:	to set the phone number of the recipient

Example:

```
window.location.href = 'tel:1-234-56789';
```

Geo

Another use of `href` is the use of `geo:`. This allows you to call an external map app with predefined coordinates from your app. The appropriate syntax is:

geo:	Latitude, Longitude (separated by comma)

Example:

```
window.location.href = 'geo:50.941278,6.958281';
```

10.2 Social Sharing

A plugin called Social Sharing allows us to send text, files, pictures and links via social networks, SMS and mail.

Social Sharing supports the following platforms:

- Android
- Browser
- iOS
- Windows
- Windows Phone

Installation

Like the native plugin Geolocation used in the previous chapter (see chapter "9.2 Geolocation" starting on page 395), an installation of the plugins of Cordova and Ionic Native is required.

This is done by entering the following lines in the terminal:

```
$ ionic cordova plugin add cordova-plugin-x-socialsharing
$ npm install @ionic-native/social-sharing
```

Next, we need to import Social Sharing into `app.modules.ts` and enter it as a provider:

```
import ...

import { Geolocation } from '@ionic-native/geolocation/ngx';
import { SocialSharing }
         from '@ionic-native/social-sharing/ngx';

@NgModule({
  declarations: [AppComponent, AboutComponent],
  entryComponents: [AboutComponent],
  imports: [
    BrowserModule,
    IonicModule.forRoot(),
    AppRoutingModule,
    HttpClientModule,
    IonicStorageModule.forRoot(),
```

```
    FormsModule,
    ReactiveFormsModule
  ],
  providers: [
    StatusBar,
    SplashScreen,
    Geolocation,
    SocialSharing,
    { provide: RouteReuseStrategy, useClass: IonicRouteStrate-
gy }
  ],
  bootstrap: [AppComponent]
})
export class AppModule {}
```

Sharing a tour from DetailsPage

We want to be able to share a tour by clicking one of the social media app buttons on the `DetailsPage`. Therefore we expand `details.page.ts` as follows:

```
import ...

import { SocialSharing }
         from '@ionic-native/social-sharing/ngx';

@Component({
  selector: 'app-details',
  templateUrl: './details.page.html',
  styleUrls: ['./details.page.scss'],
})
export class DetailsPage implements OnInit {

  tour = null;
  isFavorite: boolean;

  region: string;
  tourtype: string;

  showSocial: boolean;

  constructor(
    private activatedRoute: ActivatedRoute,
```

```
    public btService: BobToursService,
    public favService: FavoritesService,
    private actionSheetCtrl: ActionSheetController,
    private alertCtrl: AlertController,
    private modalCtrl: ModalController,
    private animationCtrl: AnimationController,
    private socialSharing: SocialSharing
  ) { }

  ngOnInit() {
    ...
  }

  // Action Sheet
  async presentActionSheet() {
    ...
  }

  // Alert
  async presentAlert() {
    ...
  }

  // User clicked "share" FAB button
  toggleSocial() {
    ...
  }

  // User clicked one of the social app buttons
  openSocial(app) {
    const sbj = 'Planning a tour';
    const img = 'http://ionic.andreas-dormann.de/img/big/'
              + this.tour.Image;
    const msg = 'BoB Tours offers a great tour titled "'
              + this.tour.Title
              + '".\n\nAre you in?\n\n'
              + 'Shipped from my BoB Tours app';

    this.socialSharing.canShareVia(app, msg, sbj, img)
    .then(() => {
      switch(app) {
        case 'facebook':
```

```
        this.socialSharing.shareViaFacebook(msg, img);
        break;
      case 'instagram':
        this.socialSharing.shareViaInstagram(msg, img);
        break;
      case 'twitter':
        this.socialSharing.shareViaTwitter(msg, img);
        break;
      case 'whatsapp':
        this.socialSharing.shareViaWhatsApp(msg, img);
        break;
    }
  })
  .catch(() => {
    this.errorOpenSocial(app, msg, sbj, img);
  });
}

// Error trying to open a social app
async errorOpenSocial(app, msg, sbj, image) {
  const alert = await this.alertCtrl.create({
    header: app + ' doesn\'t work',
    message: 'Unfortunately an error occurred
             while sharing via '
            + app + '!\n\n'
            + 'Would you like to try an alternative?',
    buttons: [
      {
        text: 'No'
      },
      {
        text: 'Simple email',
        handler: () => {
         const mailmsg =
           msg.replace(new RegExp('\n','g'),'%0A');
         window.location.href = 'mailto:?subject=' + sbj
                              + '&body=' + mailmsg;
        }
      },
      {
        text: 'Yes, absolutely',
        handler: () => {
```

```
            this.socialSharing.share(msg, subject, image);
          }
        }
      ]
    });
    await alert.present();
  }

  // User clicked 'request' option
  async presentModal() {
    ...
  }

   // User clicked 'map' option
   async presentMap() {
     ...
  }

}
```

We import SocialSharing in our DetailsPage and inject it as variable `socialSharing` into the constructor of the page.

In the `openSocial(app)` method we define a subject (`sbj`), an image (`img`) and a message (`msg`). We'll use these values to inform our social community about great tours.

With

```
this.socialSharing.canShareVia(app, msg, sbj, img)
    .then(() => { … }
```

we first check if a social app is available and we are able to share content about it.

Depending on which app the user has selected, we then use a `switch` construct to use the different methods of SocialSharing to send the message.

In case of an error, the method `errorOpenSocial` is called, in which we use an AlertController to bring the error to the display.

The user can alternatively send a simple email or try to use a different social media channel with the `share` method of SocialSharing.

Here's our social media enabled app in action:

More informations about the Social Sharing native plugin you can find here:

- https://ionicframework.com/docs/native/social-sharing
- https://github.com/EddyVerbruggen/SocialSharing-PhoneGap-Plugin

10.3 Notifications

Notifications are messages sent by apps that pop up on user's device, and their function is to deliver information and improve engagement.

We distinguish two types of notifications:

- Local Notifications
- Push Notifications (also called Server Push Notifications)

Local Notifications

Local Notifications can be easily implemented and are a good introduction to the world of notifications. We'll soon use this kind of notification for our app.

Push Notifications

A Push Notification allows to deliver information from the app to the mobile device (or computer) without a request from the user. Setting up push notifications can be truly frustrating and time consuming. Since this topic would go beyond this basic book, I have listed some links to good tutorials for those who are interested in push notifications at the end of this section.

A weekly reminder notification for our app

We want to add a reminder feature that prompts the user every week to rummage in our app for tours.

We can realize that in the following steps:

1. Install the Local Notifications plugin
2. Import Local Notifications into `app.module.ts`
3. Import Local Notifications into `app.component.ts`
4. Write the Local Notifications functionality in `app.cpomponent.ts`
5. Test in Android emulator

1. Install to Local Notifications plugin

We install the needed plugin via terminal with the following lines:

```
$ ionic cordova plugin add cordova-plugin-local-notification
$ npm install @ionic-native/local-notifications
```

2. Import Local Notifications into app.module.ts

Let's import the package into `app.module.ts`:

```
import ...

import { Geolocation }
        from '@ionic-native/geolocation/ngx';
import { SocialSharing }
        from '@ionic-native/social-sharing/ngx';
import { LocalNotifications }
        from '@ionic-native/local-notifications/ngx';

@NgModule({
  declarations: [AppComponent, AboutComponent],
  entryComponents: [AboutComponent],
  imports: [
    BrowserModule,
    IonicModule.forRoot(),
    AppRoutingModule,
    HttpClientModule,
    IonicStorageModule.forRoot(),
    FormsModule,
    ReactiveFormsModule
  ],
  providers: [
    StatusBar,
    SplashScreen,
    Geolocation,
    SocialSharing,
    LocalNotifications,
    { provide: RouteReuseStrategy,
      useClass: IonicRouteStrategy },
  ],
  bootstrap: [AppComponent]
})
export class AppModule {}
```

3. Import Local Notifications into app.component.ts

Now we import the local notifications package into `app.component.ts`, too. We'll soon write the notification functionality here. For this we'll also need AlertController and Router, which is why we import and inject them, too.

```
import ...
import { Platform, PopoverController, AlertController }
         from '@ionic/angular';

import { Router } from '@angular/router';
import { LocalNotifications, ELocalNotificationTriggerUnit }
         from'@ionic-native/local-notifications/ngx';

@Component({
  selector: 'app-root',
  templateUrl: 'app.component.html',
  styleUrls: ['app.component.scss']
})
export class AppComponent implements OnInit {

  ...

  constructor(
    private platform: Platform,
    private splashScreen: SplashScreen,
    private statusBar: StatusBar,
    public btService: BobToursService,
    private popoverCtrl: PopoverController,
    private storage: Storage,
    private alertCtrl: AlertController,
    private router: Router
    private localNotifications: LocalNotifications,
  ) {
    this.initializeApp();
  }

  ...

}
```

4. Write the Local Notifications functionality

We now add the functionality in `app.component.ts`:

```
import ...

@Component({
  selector: 'app-root',
  templateUrl: 'app.component.html',
  styleUrls: ['app.component.scss']
})
export class AppComponent implements OnInit {

  ...

  // Loading settings
  loadSettings() {
    ...
  }

  // User has changed his/her settings
  updateSettings() {
    this.storage.set('settings', this.settings);
    this.setNotifications();
  }

  // User clicked on 'About this app'
  async about() {
    const popover = await this.popoverCtrl.create({
      component: AboutComponent,
      translucent: true
    });
    await popover.present();
  }

  // User has changed price range.
  filterByPrice() {
    ...
  }

  ngOnInit() {
    ...
  }
```

```
  // A weekly notification is scheduled,
  // if notifications are activated.
  setNotifications() {
    if (this.settings.notifications == true) {
      this.localNotifications.schedule({
        id: 1,
        title: 'BoB Tours recommends:' ,
        text: 'Find a tour and enjoy life! Tap here...',
        data: { path: '/slideshow' },
        trigger: { every: ELocalNotificationTriggerUnit.WEEK }
      });
      this.onNotificationClick();
    // cancels/deactivates notifications.
    } else {
      this.localNotifications.cancelAll();
    }
  }

  // User clicked on the notification. The app shows
  // a message. After user clicked the button, the app shows
  // the slideshow.
  onNotificationClick() {
    this.localNotifications.on('click')
    .subscribe(notification => {
      let path = notification.data
               ? notification.data.path
               : '/';
      this.alertCtrl.create({
        header: notification.title,
        message: 'Be inspired by the following slideshow
                  and book a tour!',
        buttons: [{
          text: 'Good idea!',
          handler: () => this.router.navigateByUrl(path)
        }]
      }).then(alert => alert.present());
    });
  }

}
```

In the existing routine `updateSettings()` we add a call to a new method `setNotifications()`.

In this new method we first check, if notifications are activated in the user settings. You remember? The user can check/uncheck notifications via a checkbox in our side menu (see "6.7 Checkbox" on page 177):

```
if (this.settings.notifications == true) {
```

If this condition is true, we call the `schedule` method of the Local Notifications plugin. This method expects a JSON object with an `id`, a `title`, a `text`, a `data` object and a `trigger`:

```
this.localNotifications.schedule({
  id: 1,
  title: 'BoB Tours recommends:' ,
  text: 'Find a tour and enjoy life! Tap here...',
  data: { path: '/slideshow' },
  trigger: { every: ELocalNotificationTriggerUnit.WEEK }
});
```

While the `id`, `title`, and `text` properties are self-explanatory, I should explain the `data` object. `data` can be everything. Here you can give hidden information to a message, which you would like to use individually in an app. We use `data` here to give a `path` to a particular page, here to our `slideshow` page. Our `trigger every` is a so-called *repeating* trigger. Through the `ELocalNotificationTriggerUnit` enumeration with the value `WEEK`, we specify that a notification is triggered every week (starting from the time the `schedule` method is activated).

Tip: For testing, I used

```
ELocalNotificationTriggerUnit.MINUTE
```

as the value for `every`. I didn't want to wait a whole week, until a message appeared ;-) Be careful with `SECOND` as trigger unit. Maybe this could overwhelm your system.

An interesting trigger variant seems to be the *location based* triggers, where a notification is triggered depending on the position of a mobile device.

The plugin has a set of other properties, all of which are described in the following GitHub link to the Cordova plugin documentation.

Before we turn to the new method `onNotificationClick()`, the `else` branch is explained:

```
} else {
  this.localNotifications.cancelAll();
}
```

When the user turns off the notifications, the `cancelAll()` method of the Local Notifications plugin causes all notifications to be canceled.

Now the method `onNotificationClick()`:

```
this.localNotifications.on('click')
```

sets up an event handler. It's an Observable that we can subscribe to. Whenever the user clicks on a message, we evaluate the content of the notification. At first we are interested in the value of `data`:

```
let path = notification.data
         ? notification.data.path
         : '/';
```

We check if `notification.data` has any value at all. If so, we take the path property, if not, we set an empty path.

Then we create an alert to which we assign the `notification.title` in the `header`, a `message` and a `button`:

```
this.alertCtrl.create({
  header: notification.title,
  message: 'Be inspired by the following slideshow
           and book a tour!',
  buttons: [{
    text: 'Good idea!',
    handler: () => this.router.navigateByUrl(path)
  }]
})
.then(alert => alert.present());
```

The button `handler` ensures that our app changes to the specified path. Finally, after creating the alert, we present it.

That's it.

5. Test on device or Android emulator

Since the Local Notifications plugin only supports the platforms Android and iOS, but not browsers, we now have to test our app on a device or an emulator. Whether you're developing on iOS or Windows, the Android Emulator is available in both environments. Prerequisite is that Android Studio must be installed (see "11.4 Emulator / Simulator" on page 484).

Start the emulation of an Android system via terminal with

```
ionic cordova emulate android
```

If you use this command for the first time, it will take a while, because Ionic/Cordova first has to set up the Android platform with all the necessary plugins.

After starting the emulator we can see the new notifications functionality in action:

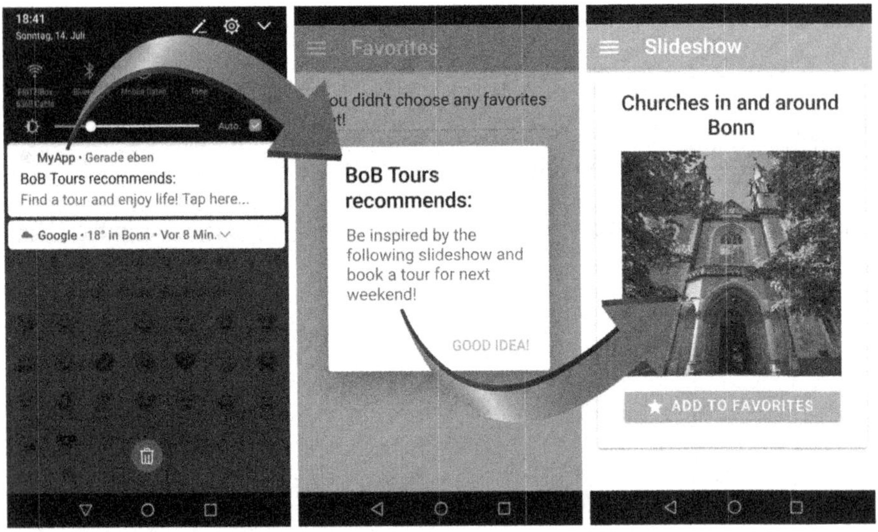

Perhaps your notifications are reported by "MyApp". That's because you probably have not yet added an individual AppID to your app. We will do that in chapter "12 Build, Deploy & Publish" (starting from page 511).

More informations about Local Notifications you can find here:

- https://ionicframework.com/docs/native/local-notifications
- https://github.com/katzer/cordova-plugin-local-notifications

Informations about Push Notifications you can find here:

- https://ionicframework.com/docs/native/push
- https://devdactic.com/push-notifications-ionic-onesignal/
- https://www.freecodecamp.org/news/how-to-get-push-notifications-working-with-ionic-4-and-firebase-ad87cc92394e/

Summary

In this chapter you got to know the basics of Communication & Messaging.

You have seen how to send mails, SMS and more.

You can do social sharing with the help of a plugin now.

Finally, you've taught our app how to use Notifications.

11 Debugging & Testing

11.1 Health Check with Ionic Doctor

Yes, you are reading correctly: You can have the health of your Ionic system checked by a doctor.

Enter the following in the terminal:

```
$ ionic doctor check
```

This command detects problems and provides guidance on how to fix them.

If you've developed our app according to the book, the command should give you the following result:

```
4 Detecting issues: 1 / 1 complete - done!
[WARN] Package ID unchanged in config.xml.

       The Package Identifier (AKA "Bundle ID" for iOS and
       "Application ID" for Android) is a unique ID (usually written
       in reverse DNS notation, such as com.mycompany.MyApp) that
       Cordova uses when compiling the native build of your
       app. When your app is submitted to the App Store or Play
       Store, the Package ID can't be changed. This issue was
       detected because this app's Package ID is "io.ionic.starter",
       which is the default Package ID provided after
       running ionic start.

       To fix, take the following step(s):

       1) Change the id attribute of <widget> (root element) to
          something other than "io.ionic.starter"

       $ ionic config set -g doctor.issues.default-cordova-bundle-id-
         used.ignored true (ignore this issue in the future)

[INFO] Doctor Summary

       - Detected 1 issue.
       - 0 issues can be fixed automatically
```

Please don't alarm, if the doctor also determines a finding in your system.

The issue discovered here is harmless and states that we have not yet assigned an `Application ID` for our app. We will do this later in "12.3 config.xml" (on page 520).

A complete list of all issues can be shown with

```
$ ionic doctor list
```

The result of this command might look like this:

```
id                                  | affected projects | tags
-------------------------------------------------------------------
cordova-platforms-committed         | all               |
default-cordova-bundle-id-used      | all               |
git-config-invalid                  | all               |
git-not-used                        | all               | ignored
ionic-installed-locally             | all               | treatable
ionic-native-old-version-installed  | all               |
npm-installed-locally               | all               | treatable
unsaved-cordova-platforms           | all               |
viewport-fit-not-set                | all
```

This shows more serious issues. Those labeled as `treatable` can be fixed automatically with

```
$ ionic doctor treat [id]
```

For `[id]` then the appropriately named issue must be used, for example

```
$ ionic doctor treat ionic-installed-locally
```

More informations about Ionic Doctor you can find here:

- https://ionicframework.com/docs/cli/commands/doctor-check

11.2 Strictly Typing!

TypeScript and its advantages

The Ionic framework uses TypeScript. As I mentioned at the beginning (see "1 Introduction" on page 13) TypeScript is a strongly-typed superset of JavaScript, which means it adds some syntactical benefits to the language while still letting you write normal JavaScript if you want to.

Most likely, the first thing that comes to mind with TypeScript is the optional static type system that it provides. Types can be added to variables, functions, properties, etc. This will help the compiler and show warnings about any potential errors in code, before an app is ever run. Types also help when using libraries and frameworks, as they let developers know exactly what type of data APIs expect.

One of the biggest advantages of TypeScript is its code completion and IntelliSense. IntelliSense provides active hints as code is added. Since Ionic itself is written in TypeScript as well, editors can present all the methods available and what they expect as arguments. All the best IDE's available today have support for code completion, including VSCode, Atom, WebStorm, Sublime text, and even command line editors, such as Vim/Neovim!

To be honest, for simplicity's sake I haven't taken it so seriously with strict typing in this book so far. I would like to change that now explicitly. And I recommend that you use the advantages of TypeScript in your own Ionic App projects as well! The good reasons for doing this I have told you now.

Create classes

The most obvious typing we should do is create classes for the data supplied by the database: `Tour`, `Tourtype`, `Region` (we can abstract the last two as `Category`).

Let's start. Via terminal type:

```
$ ionic g class models/category/category
$ ionic g class models/tour/tour
```

These commands create the classes `Category`, and `Tour`, each in their own subfolders, within `src/app/models`.

Your project structure should now look like this:

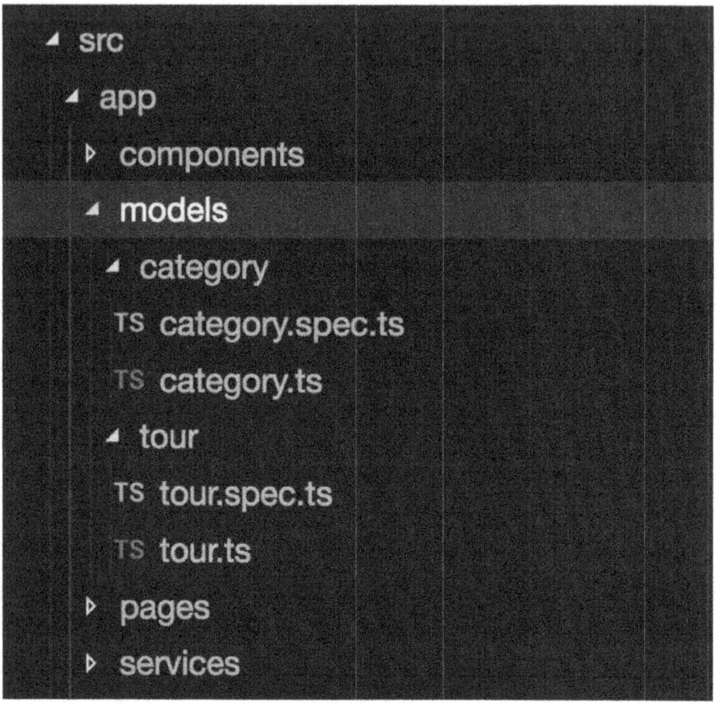

Let's open the file `category.ts` and add the following:

```
export class Category {
  public ID: number;
  public Icon: string;
  public Name: string;
}
```

Then let's open the file `tour.ts` and add:

```
export class Tour {
  public Description: string;
  public Duration: number;
  public ID: number;
  public Image: string;
  public MaxPersons: number;
  public PriceF: number;
```

```
  public PriceG: number;
  public Region: string;
  public StartingPoint: Point;
  public Title: string;
  public Tourtype: string;
}

export class Point {
  public Lat: string;
  public Lng: string;
  public Location: string;
}
```

We've now defined some classes that owns public properties, each of them assigned to a specific data type. If you look closely to the `Tour` class, you'll notice the `StartingPoint` property, which is of type `Point`. JavaScript/TypeScript doesn't know this data type. This type is custom. That's why we have to define it ourselves within `tour.ts` (or maybe in an extra class file).

Use classes

We now want to use the classes in our app code for typing.

Let's start with `favorites.service.ts`: and modify it (see bold formatted code):

```
import { Injectable } from '@angular/core';
import { Storage } from '@ionic/storage';

import { Tour } from '../models/tour/tour';

@Injectable({ providedIn: 'root' })
export class FavoritesService {

  public favIDs: Array<number>;
  public favTours: Array<Tour>;

  constructor(private storage: Storage) { }

  initialize(tours: Array<Tour>) {
    this.favTours = [];
    this.storage.ready().then(() => {
      this.storage.get('FavoritesIDs').then(ids => {
```

```
        this.favIDs = ids;
        if (this.favIDs == null) {
          this.favIDs = [];
        } else  {
          this.favIDs.forEach(favID => {
            let tour = tours.filter(t => t.ID == favID)[0];
            tour.isFavorite = true;
            this.favTours.push(tour);
          });
        }
      });
    });
  }

  add(tour:Tour) {
    this.favIDs.push(tour.ID);
    this.favTours.push(tour);
    this.storage.set('FavoritesIDs', this.favIDs);
  }

  remove(tour:Tour) {
    let removeIndex:number = this.favIDs.indexOf(tour.ID);
    if (removeIndex != -1) {
      this.favIDs.splice(removeIndex, 1);
      this.favTours.splice(removeIndex, 1);
      this.storage.set('FavoritesIDs', this.favIDs);
    }
  }

  reorder(ev) {
    this.favTours = ev.detail.complete(this.favTours);
    this.favIDs = this.favTours.map(tour => tour.ID);
    this.storage.set('FavoritesIDs', this.favIDs);
  }

}
```

We import our newly defined `Tour` class with:

```
import { Tour } from '../models/tour/tour';
```

Wherever we know that an object of the type `Tour` is expected, we typify it explicitly. Now, all parts of the app that use our FavoritesService know exactly where the specific `Tour` data type is expected. The service itself knows that from now on. And now the code checker knows - already before the code execution - that our data type `Tour` doesn't have the property `isFavorite`:

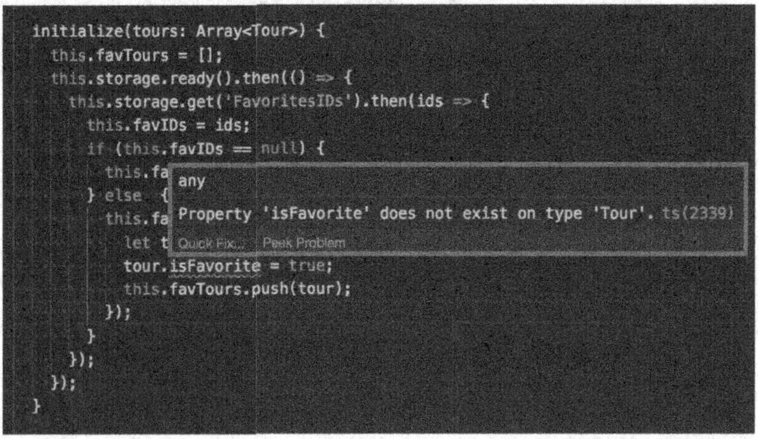

Why hasn't this been noticed so far? Well, in the `initialize` method, `tours` was of the type `any`. This type is very variable and a property can be attached *dynamically* at runtime, which has worked so far. Now we have a *static* data type.

The solution to get rid of this new error is, of course, simple: We extend `tour.ts` by the the property `IsFavorite`:

```
export class Tour {
  public Description: string;
  public Duration: number;
  public ID: number;
  public Image: string;
  public IsFavorite: boolean;
  public MaxPersons: number;
  public PriceF: number;
  public PriceG: number;
  public Region: string;
  public StartingPoint: Point;
  public Title: string;
  public TourType: string;
}
```

In this occasion, I have also made the conventional capitalization of the property. To customize all the codes involved, the function `Find in Files` (see `Edit` Menu) in combination with the `Replace All` button is helpful:

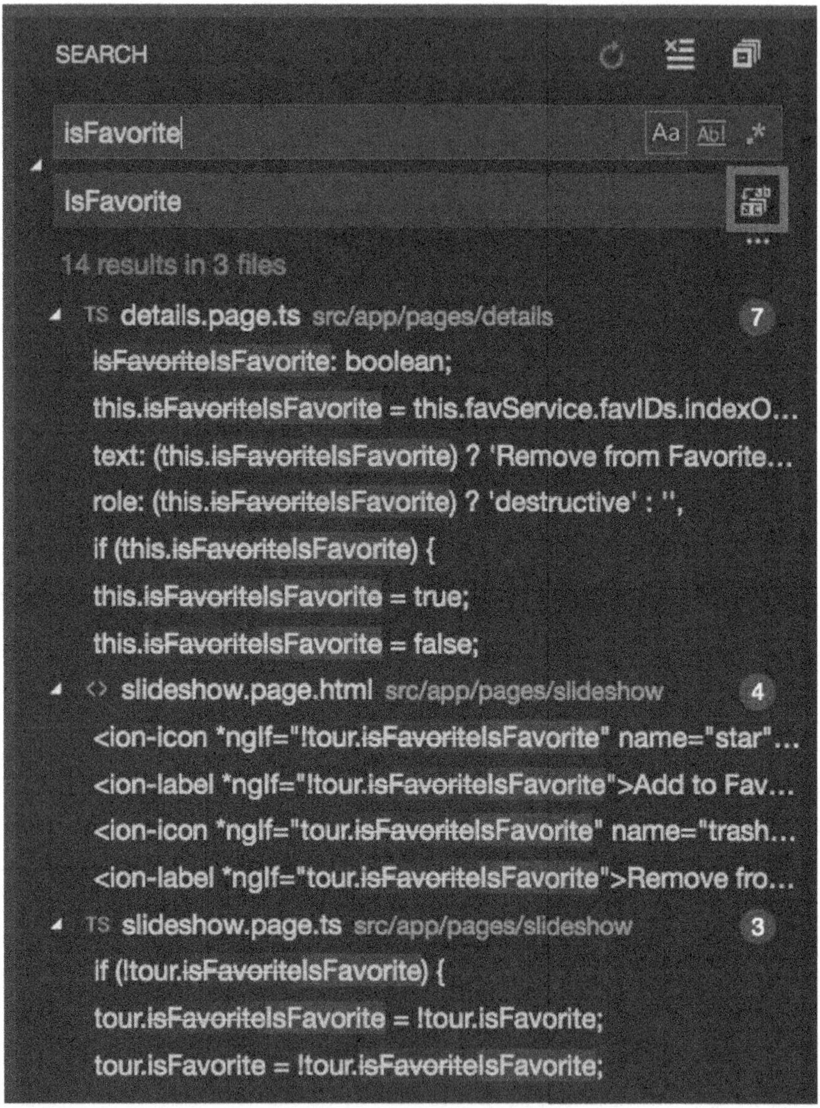

Now the code compiles successfully again.

Let's also type bob-tours.service.ts:

```
import { Injectable } from '@angular/core';
import { HttpClient } from '@angular/common/http';
import { FavoritesService } from './favorites.service';
import { LoadingController } from '@ionic/angular';
import _ from 'lodash';

import { Category } from '../models/category/category';
import { Tour } from '../models/tour/tour';

@Injectable({ providedIn: 'root' })
export class BobToursService {

  public regions: Array<Category>;
  public tourtypes: Array<Category>;
  public tours: Array<Tour>;
  public all_tours: Array<Tour>;

  baseUrl = 'https://bob-tours-app.firebaseio.com/';

  constructor(private http: HttpClient,
              public favService: FavoritesService,
              private loadingCtrl: LoadingController) { }

  async initialize() {
    const loading = await this.loadingCtrl.create({
      message: 'Loading tour data...',
      spinner: 'crescent'
    });
    await loading.present();
    await this.getRegions().then(data => this.regions = data);
    await this.getTourtypes()
      .then(data => this.tourtypes = _.sortBy(data, 'Name'));
    await this.getTours().then(data => {
      this.tours = _.sortBy(data, 'Title');
      this.all_tours = _.sortBy(data, 'Title');
      this.filterTours({lower: 80, upper: 400});
      this.favService.initialize(this.all_tours);
    });
    await loading.dismiss();
  }
```

```
  // Reads regions as JSON formatted data
  // from Google Firebase.
  getRegions(): Promise<Array<Category>> {
    let requestUrl = `${this.baseUrl}/Regions.json`;
    return this.http.get(requestUrl).toPromise() as any;
  }

  // Reads tour types as JSON formatted data
  // from Google Firebase.
  getTourtypes(): Promise<Array<Category>> {
    let requestUrl = `${this.baseUrl}/Tourtypes.json`;
    return this.http.get(requestUrl).toPromise() as any;
  }

  // Reads tours as JSON formatted data from Google Firebase.
  getTours(): Promise<Array<Tour>> {
    let requestUrl = `${this.baseUrl}/Tours.json`;
    return this.http.get(requestUrl).toPromise() as any;
  }

  // Filtering tours by Price.
  filterTours(price): number {
   this.tours = _.filter(this.all_tours, function(tour:Tour){
      return tour.PriceG >= price.lower
          && tour.PriceG <= price.upper;
    });
    this.regions.forEach(region => {
      const rtours = _.filter(this.tours,
                              ['Region',
                              region.ID]);
      region['Count'] = rtours.length;
    });
    this.tourtypes.forEach(tourtype => {
      const ttours = _.filter(this.tours,
                              ['Tourtype',
                               tourtype.ID]);
      tourtype['Count'] = ttours.length;
    });
    return this.tours.length;
  }

}
```

All of our variables (`regions`, `tourtypes`, `tours` and `all_tours`) had been typed as any so far. Again, it is better to type this strict. We do this by stating that the first two are Arrays with elements of type `Category` and the other two are Arrays with elements of type `Tour`.

We also typify the return types of the methods `getRegions()`, `getTourtypes()`, and `getTours()` by specifying that these are Promises that return Arrays with the certain element types `Category` and `Tour`.

If we omitted in each return `as any`, we got the following error:

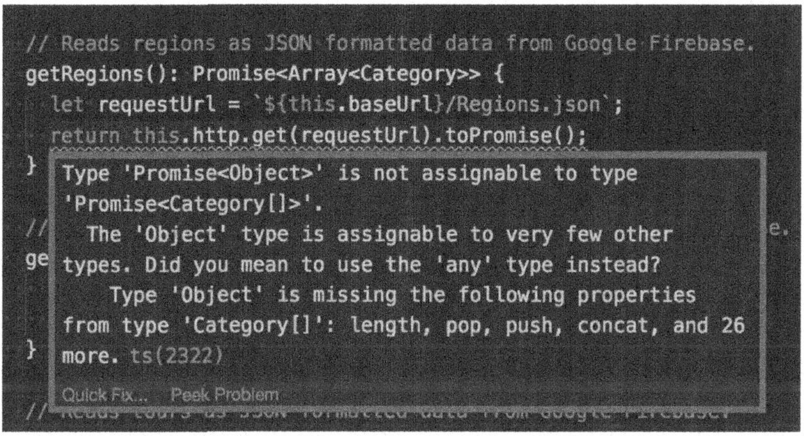

The solution is to cast the Promise return value `as any`.

Finally we also typify the `tour` parameter of the callback function within the filter function of type `Tour`.

You like to do some more typing? Feel free to find more code that needs typing. This is a good exercise in preparation for real live app projects.

More informations about typing with classes in TypeScript you can find here:

► https://www.typescriptlang.org/docs/handbook/classes.html

11.3 Browser Debugging

Google Chrome: Developer Tools

The most important tools – as we also use them regularly in this book – are Chrome's Developer Tools, of course.

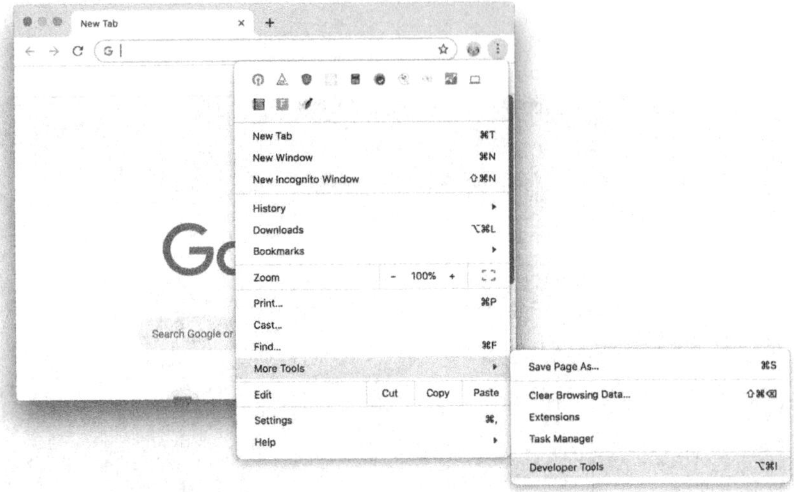

There are many ways to open DevTools, because different users want quick access to different parts of the DevTools UI.The most common way is via the menu: Click `Customize and control Google Chrome` (the symbol with the three vertically arranged dots at the top right) and then select `More Tools > Developer Tools`.

There are keyboard shortcuts, of course: Use the keyboard shortcut `CTRL+Shift+J` (on Windows) or `CMD+Option+J` (on Mac).

The DevTools have nine different areas. Here is an overview in alphabetical order:

- Application
- Audits
- Console
- Elements
- Memory
- Networks

- Performance
- Security
- Sources

We'll take a look at each of these areas in the context of our app.

Application

In the `Application` area you'll find various useful functions such as `Clear storage > Clear site` data for resetting the app storage.As we have already seen in chapter "5 Services & Storage" (see divisions "5.8 Local Storage" starting from page 136 and "5.9 Ionic Storage" starting from page 146), we can also see the storage here and read out its keys and values. And we can also edit these with a little knowledge about Web SQL queries.

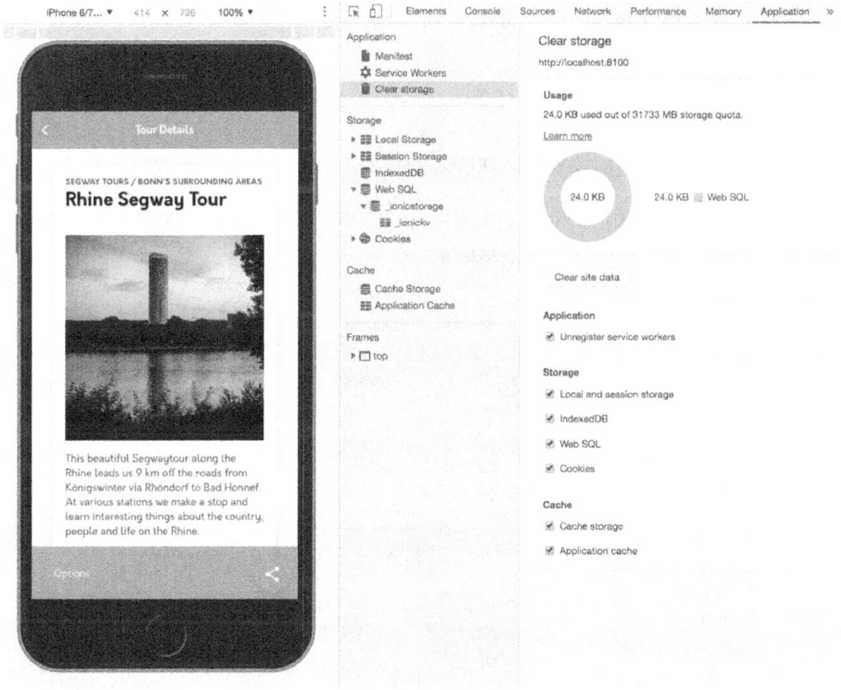

In the `Storage` section we expand the storage engine, which is displayed on the `Clear storage` page (see previous figure). That's `Web SQL` for me. We click the corresponding domain table (for me `_ionicstorage > _ionickv`) to show the keys and values within the storage. For me it looks like that:

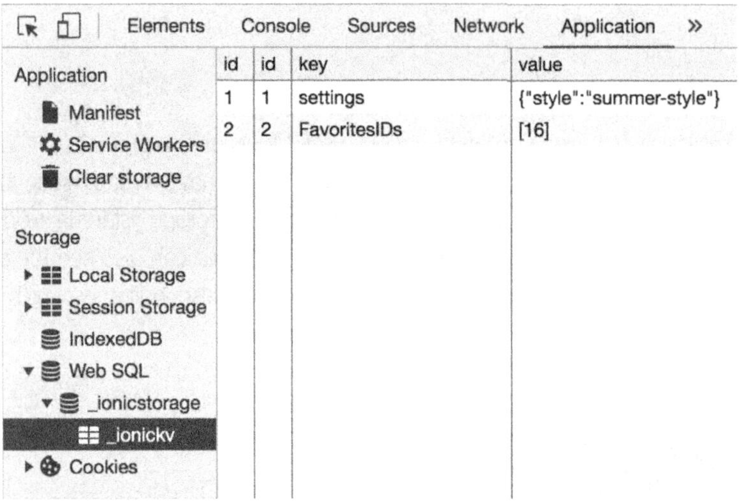

Let's say, we want to add a whole bunch of `FavoritesIDs` to the storage.

We now click on the domain level (`_ionicstorage`). Here's the Web SQL Console where we can type Web SQL statements.

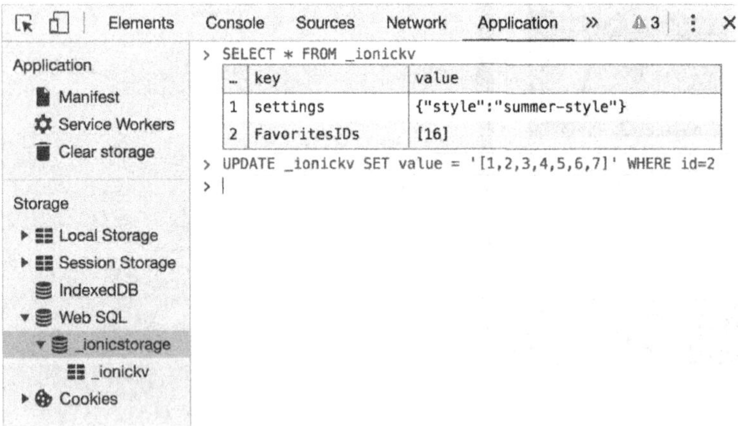

With

```
SELECT * FROM _ionickv
```

we display the contents of the `_ionickv` table. With

```
UPDATE _ionickv SET value = '[1,2,3,4,5,6,7]' WHERE id=2
```

we set our new bunch of `FavoritesIDs`. You have to admit, that this way is faster than making all the input manually via the app, right?

Note: Successfully executed queries are colored *blue*. Errors are colored *red*.

If you switch back to the table view, you will find the new `FavoritesIDs` here. And after a browser refresh, the corresponding tours are also listed in the app.

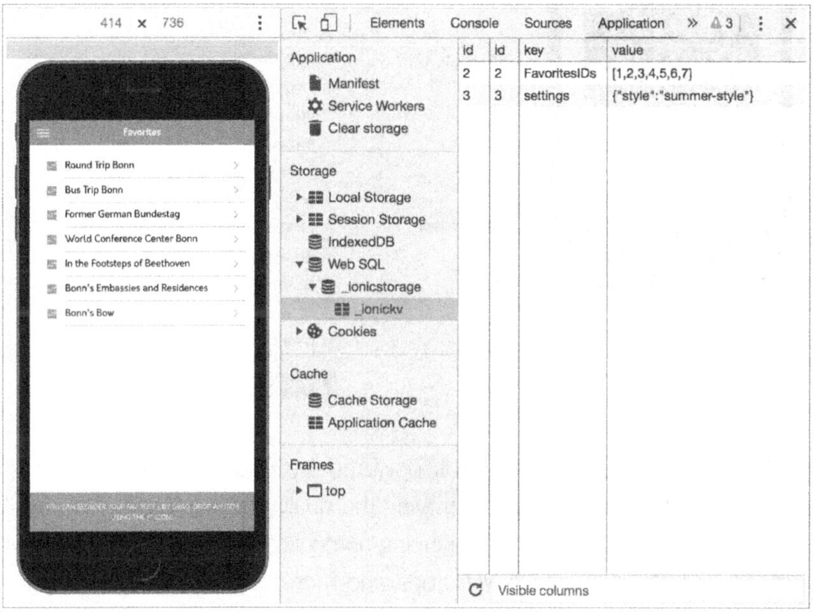

Audits

Via the audit panel you can identify and fix common problems that affect your app's performance, accessibility and user experience.

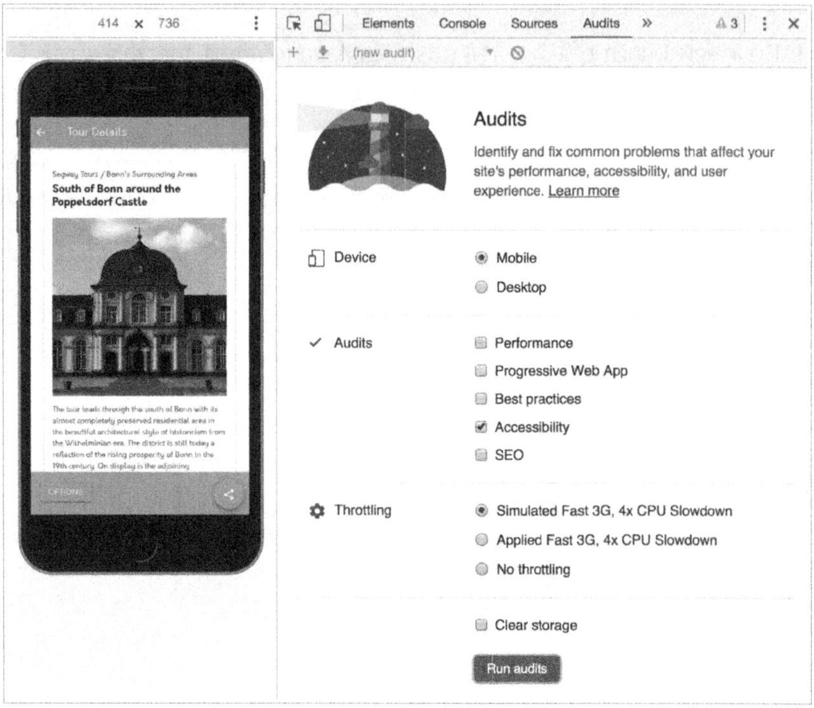

Since Chrome 60 the Audit panel is powered by Lighthouse. Lighthouse is an open-source, automated tool for improving the quality of web pages. You can run it against any web page, public or requiring authentication. It has audits for performance, accessibility, progressive web apps, and more.

Let's activate all audit options and start a first run by clicking "Run audits".

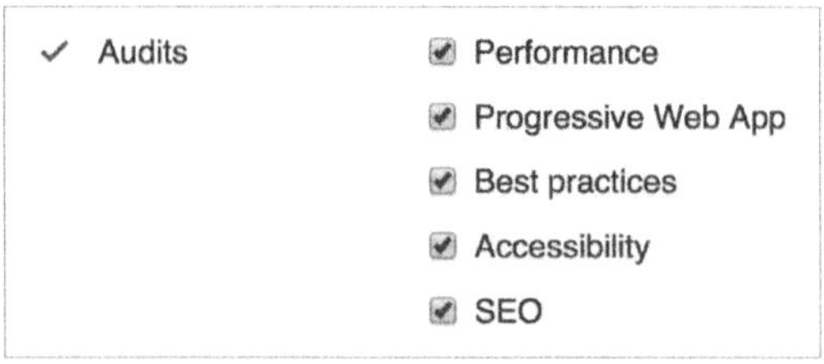

We get about the following result:

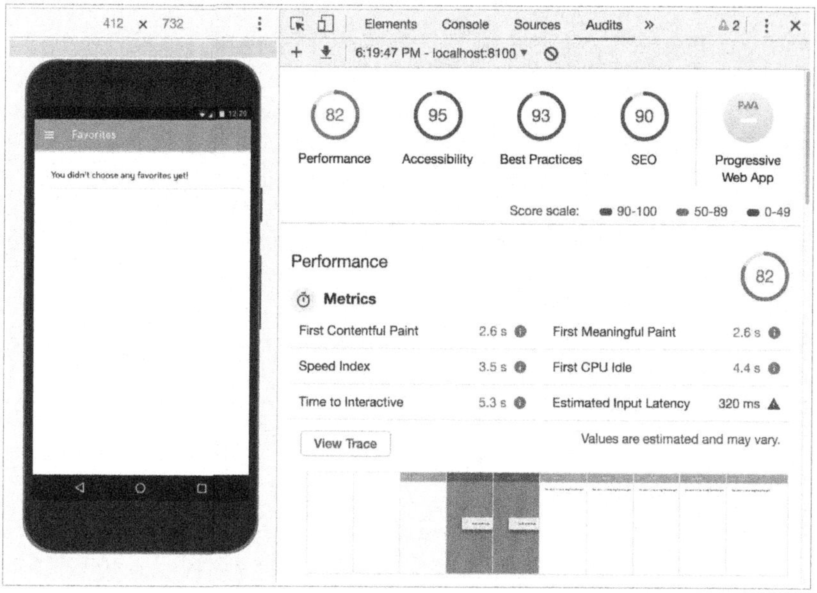

While the Performance metrics of our app leaves something to be desired, at Accessibility, Best Practices and SEO we already have decent values. In the Diagnostics section, you can view more detailed information and suggestions for improving the various parameters.

The Progressive Web App section hasn't been measured yet because, among other things, there is no Web App Manifest file yet. We'll change that later.

Console

The Console is probably the most used area of DevTools. The Console has two main uses: viewing logged messages and running JavaScript.

In this book we've often logged messages to the Console to make sure that our code is working as expected.

Let's do this one more time and open `src/app/pages/map/map.page.ts` to add the following lines to the `calcRoute()` method:

```
// Calculates a route from user position to destination
async calcRoute() {

 if (this.isCalculated) return;

 // Show calculation process
 const loading = await this.loadingCtrl.create({
   message: 'Calculate route...',
   spinner: 'crescent'
 });
 await loading.present();
 console.log(loading);

 // Get current user position
 const geo = await this.geolocation.getCurrentPosition();
 this.position = new google.maps.LatLng(geo.coords.latitude,
                                        geo.coords.longitude);
 console.log(geo);

 // Prepare map and description display
 const dirDisplay = new google.maps.DirectionsRenderer(
   { suppressMarkers: true } );
 dirDisplay.setMap(this.map);
 dirDisplay.setPanel(document.getElementById('description'));

 // Calculate route from position to destination
 const dirService = new google.maps.DirectionsService();
 dirService.route({
   origin: this.position,
   destination: this.destination,
   travelMode: 'DRIVING'
 },
 function(result, status) {
   if (status == 'OK') {
     dirDisplay.setDirections(result);
     console.log(result);
   }
 });
```

```
  // Add position marker
  this.addPositionMarker();

  // Calculation process finished
  this.isCalculated = true;
  loading.dismiss();
}
```

Let's start the app, search for a tour, switch to it's details, open the map page and calculate the route from our current position to the starting point of the tour.

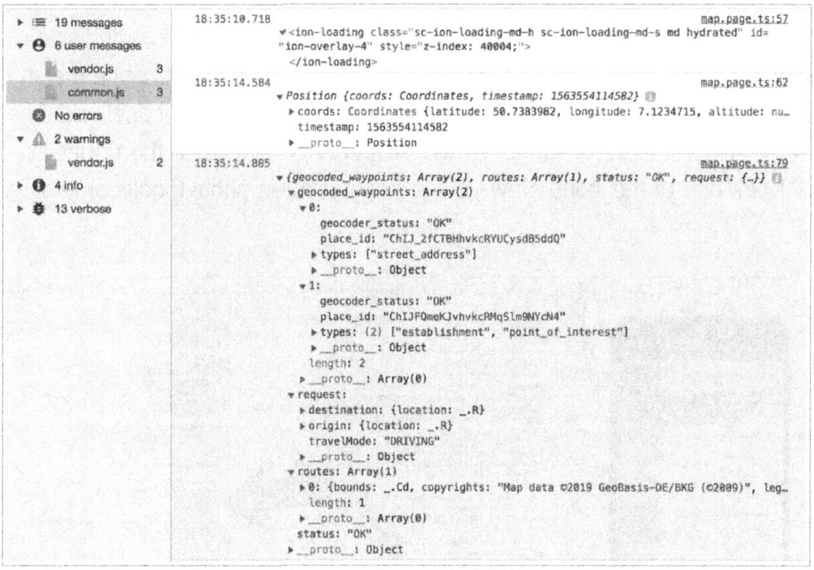

At the desired positions, the respective console logs are output and provide detailed information about the objects to be inspected.

In addition, each output is time-stamped, so you also get important information about the duration of certain processes. In my example, it takes more than three seconds to calculate the route. This may be a symptom that needs further investigation.

There are a number of ways to configure the information that the Console issues, for example, to hide warnings. Since this isn't a book on Chrome DevTools, please refer to the documentation provided by Google for details, which I have listed as a link at the end of this section.

Elements

The Elements panel has excellent tools to inspect and edit pages and styles and offers the following options:

- inspect and edit on the fly any element in the DOM tree
- view and change the CSS rules applied to any selected element in the Styles pane
- view and edit a selected element's box model in the Computed pane
- view any changes made to your page locally in the Sources panel

Let's try a few of these options to introspect the style of the icons in the side menu and invert their colors. Start our app and open the side menu. Change the style to "Summer-Style" With DevTools activated switch to the Elements panel and click the `Select an element in the page to inspect it` button (at the upper left corner). Mark one of the icons. Now your element window should look something like this:

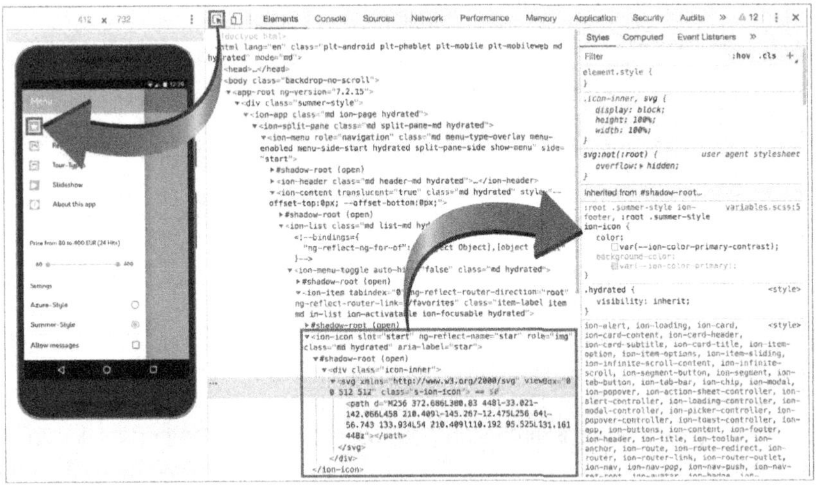

Within the Document Object Model (DOM) of the page, the `svg` element (icon) is highlighted. It's surrounded by a `div` tag, which in turn is integrated into an `ion-item` tag. So we can see well what the Ionic framework rendered from the original

```
<ion-icon slot="start" [name]="p.icon"></ion-icon>
```

in `app.component.html`. Such insights can help you better understand Ionic.

In the Style Panel on the right, we can also see the CSS instructions applied to the element:

```
ion-icon {
   color:
      var(--ion-color-primary-contrast);
   background-color:
      var(--ion-color-primary);
}
```

We can easily change these values by first editing the `color` and then deactivate the `background-color` - directly in the Style pane:

```
ion-icon {
   color: var(--ion-color-primary);
   background-color:
      var(--ion-color-primary);
}
```

Now the icons in the side menu look like this:

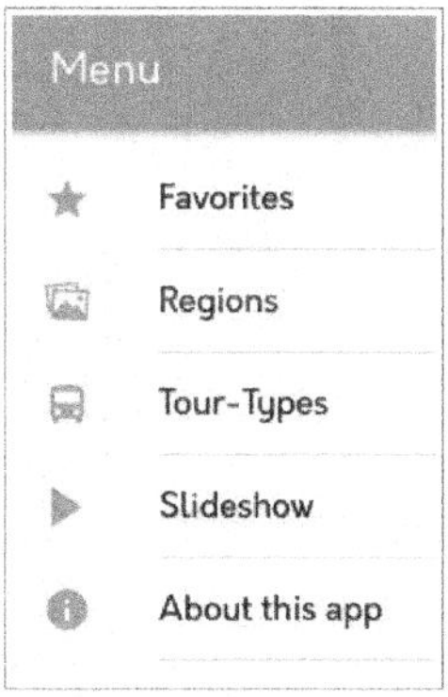

These CSS modifications are not permanent, changes are lost when you reload the page. But as you know from chapter "8 Theming, Styling, Customizing" (see division "8.9 Dynamic Theming" starting from page 376), you can add some code to `summer-style.scss`:

```
ion-content ion-icon {
  color: var(--ion-color-primary);
  background-color: var(--ion-color-primary-contrast);
}
```

This makes the style changes permanent.

Memory

Do you have any idea how much memory an Ionic App consumes? No? That doesn't matter. Soon you will know! With Chrome's Memory tools you can

- find out how much memory your page is currently using with the Chrome Task Manager
- visualize memory usage over time with Timeline recordings
- identify detached DOM trees (a common cause of memory leaks) with Heap Snapshots
- find out when new memory is being allocated in your JavaScript heap with Allocation Timeline recordings

Let's use the Chrome Task Manager as a starting point to our memory issue investigation. The Task Manager is a realtime monitor that tells us how much memory a page is currently using.

Via the Chrome main menu we select `More tools > Task Manager`. On the table header we right-click and enable `JavaScript Memory`.

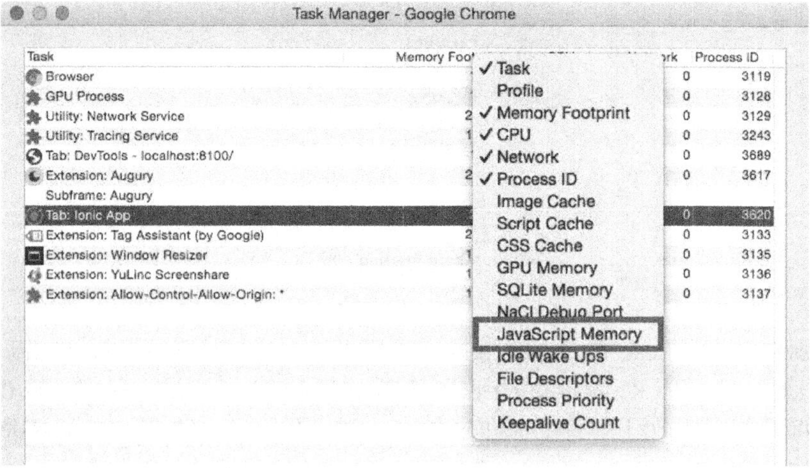

The `Memory Footage` column represents native memory. DOM nodes are stored in native memory. If this value is increasing, DOM nodes are getting created.

The `JavaScript Memory` column represents the JS heap. This column contains two values. The value we're interested in is the live number (the number in parentheses). The live number represents how much memory the reachable objects in our app are using. If this number is increasing, either new objects are being created, or the existing objects are growing.

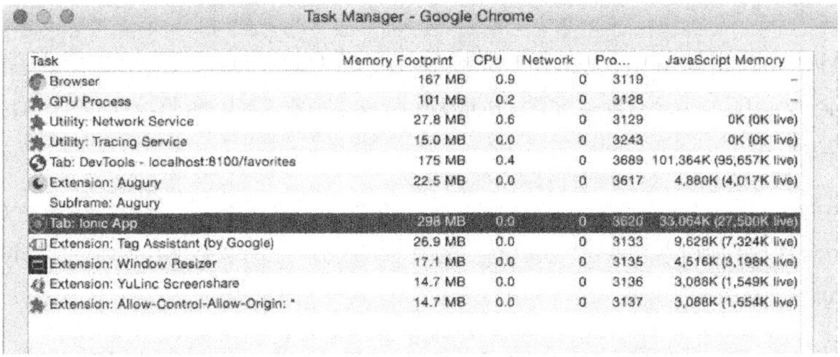

For me the Task Manager shows a live memory usage of 27,500K after starting the app. If you do actions in the app, this value will increase. With me the memory usage levels off at 34,000K to 36,000K, but after the the slideshow starts, it temporarily rises over 40,000K.

The Memory panel has sophisticated tools for profiling memory problems.

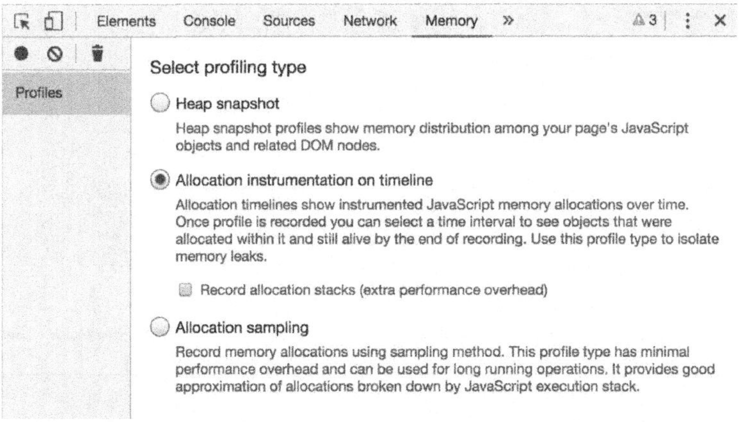

In order to be able to use these in a targeted manner, a basic knowledge of storage terminology and analysis is required, the mediation of which would exceed the scope of this book. For details to these topics you can read the Chrome DevTool documentation, which I listed as a link at the end of this section.

Networks

Use the Network panel when you need to make sure that resources are being downloaded or uploaded as expected. The most common use cases for the Network panel are:

- making sure that resources are actually being uploaded or downloaded at all
- inspecting the properties of an individual resource, such as its HTTP headers, content, size, and so on

We already used the Network panel in chapter "5 Services & Storage" (see division "5.2 An HTTPClient Service", starting from page 101) to see, what our newly created service does.

Let's activate the DevTools and switch to the Network panel, click the `Show overview` button and see, what happens during the app start.

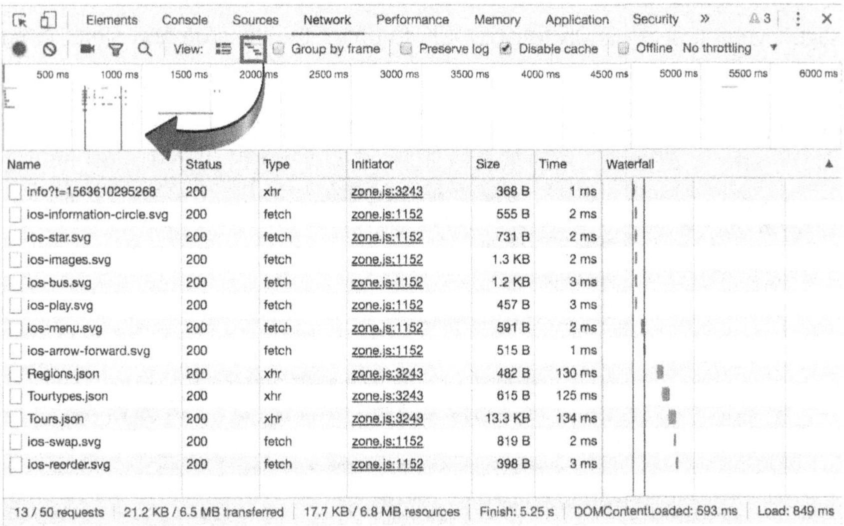

For me, at the application start 13/50 requests were executed, 6.8 MB data transferred and 6.8 MB of resources loaded. The whole thing took 5.25 s, with the DOMContent having taken 593 ms load time (blue) and the remaining load (red) 849 ms. These details you can find in the footer of the Network panel.

In the overview timeline, mark the green bar so that the start mark is just before the bar and the end marker is just behind the bar (see next figure – red frame):

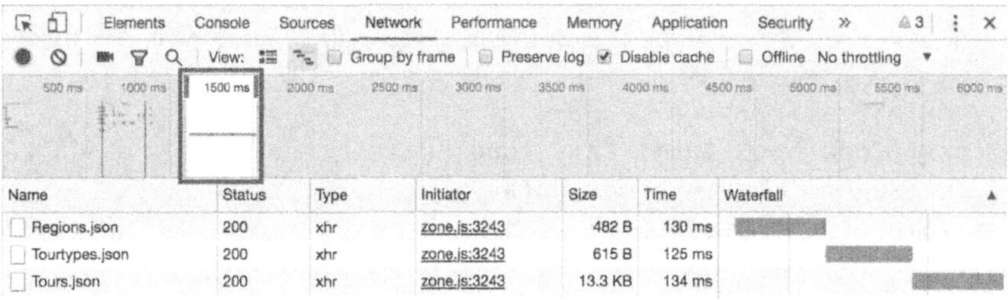

We have hereby selected a temporal excerpt of the charging process of the app, which we can take a closer look at. In the so-called `Waterfall` (on the right) we see very well that first `Regions.json`, then `Tortypes.json` and then `Tours.json` are loaded from the database. Sequential processes.

This is exactly what we coded in the `initialize()` method within `bob-tours.service.ts`:

```
async initialize() {

  ...

  await this.getRegions()
    .then(data => this.regions = data);
  await this.getTourtypes()
    .then(data => this.tourtypes = _.sortBy(data, 'Name'));
  await this.getTours()
    .then(data => {
      this.tours = _.sortBy(data, 'Title');
      this.all_tours = _.sortBy(data, 'Title');
      this.filterTours({lower: 80, upper: 400});
      this.favService.initialize(this.all_tours);
    });

  ...

}
```

By using the `async/await` concept, we wait to load the next data until the previous ones are fully loaded. Is that optimal? No.

If you've read chapter "2 Angular Essentials" (see division "2.11 Async / Await", starting from page 51), you may remember the ability to parallelize loads. That's exactly what we want to do here now.

In `bob-tours.service.ts` we modify our code as follows:

```
async initialize() {
  const loading = await this.loadingCtrl.create({
    message: 'Loading tour data...',
    spinner: 'crescent'
  });
  await loading.present();
  await this.loadAllData();
  await loading.dismiss();
}

// Parallelized loading of all database data.
async loadAllData() {
  let regions = this.getRegions()
    .then(data => this.regions = data);
  let tourtypes = this.getTourtypes()
    .then(data => this.tourtypes = _.sortBy(data, 'Name'));
  let tours = this.getTours()
    .then(data => {
      this.tours = _.sortBy(data, 'Title');
      this.all_tours = _.sortBy(data, 'Title');
      this.filterTours({lower: 80, upper: 400});
      this.favService.initialize(this.all_tours);
  });
  let regions_loaded = await regions;
  let tourtypes_loaded = await tourtypes;
  let tours_loaded = await tours;
}
```

We outsource the load code from `initialize()` to a separate `loadAllData()` method. We start all loading processes there in parallel. At the end of the routine, we wait until all processes are completed.

Now it will be exciting to see what the Network Panel will record, when we start the app. Let's again take a closer look at the time span in which the data is loaded from the database (green bars):

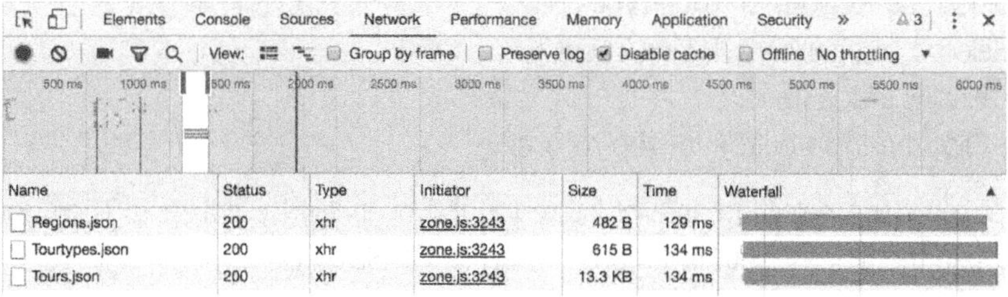

Whereas the previous serial load lasted 389 ms (130+125+134 ms), the parallel loading of the data is done in 134 ms now - almost a third of the time.

You see, the Network Panel is a good helper to make loading processes visible and perhaps pointing out ways to optimize it.

A tip on this topic: If you're looking for ways to improve *page* (not *data*) load performance, don't start with the Network panel. There are many types of load performance issues that aren't related to network activity. Start with the Audits panel because it gives you targeted suggestions on how to improve your page.

Performance

With the help of the Performance panel yo can:

- record runtime performance
- simulate a mobile CPU
- analyze the results as frames per seconds (FPS)
- find bottlenecks

To get more comfortable with the Performance panel, practice makes perfect. So let's try to profile our app and analyze the results. We do this step by step:

1. Start our app with `ionic serve`.
2. Activate the DevTools and switch to the Performance panel.
3. Make sure that the `Screenshots` checkbox is enabled.
4. Click `Capture settings` (gearwheel symbol top right).

5. For `CPU`, select `4x` slowdown. This simulates a mobile CPU.
6. Click the `Record` button.
7. In our app, open the side menu.
8. Select the Regions or Tour-Types page.
9. Select a category, e.g. Hiking Tours.
10. Finally, pick a tour.
11. Click the `Stop` button to stop recording.

After recording, select an area of interest in the overview by dragging. Then, zoom and pan the timeline with the mouse wheel or WASD keys.

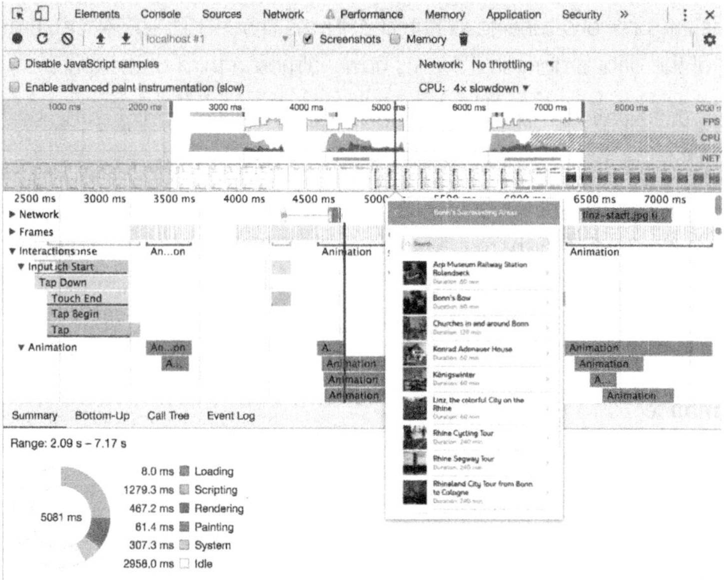

It's pretty cool to move your mouse over the timeline and watch the operation like a video and to get so much information about your app's performance. Some people think that's a bit overwhelming. And yes, admittedly, to be able to do a targeted analysis, I strongly recommend the DevTools documentation on this topic:

► https://developers.google.com/web/tools/chrome-devtools/evaluate-performance/

Security

Use the Security Panel in Chrome DevTools to make sure HTTPS is properly implemented on a page. Every website should be protected with HTTPS, even sites that don't handle sensitive user data.

To easily check which HTTP(S) addresses an app is calling, all you need to do is start the app, enable DevTools, and switch to the Security panel:

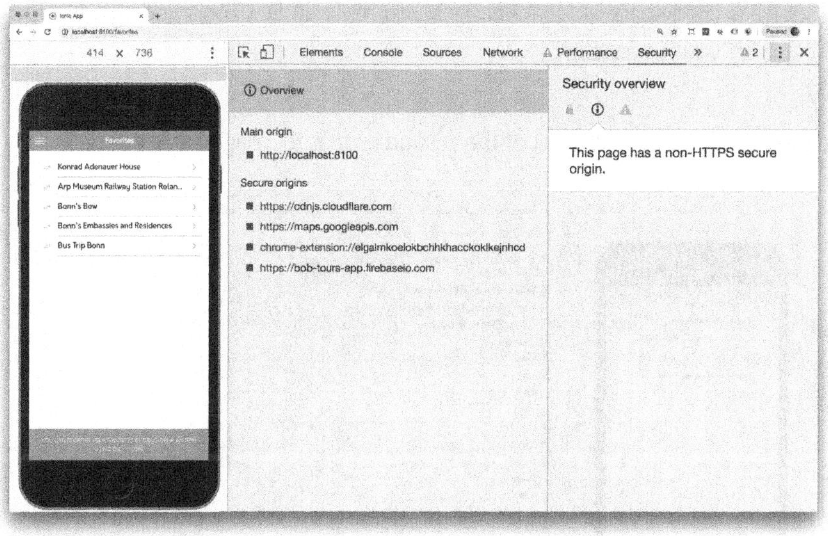

Sources

Use the Chrome DevTools Sources panel to:

- view files.
- edit CSS and JavaScript.
- create and save Snippets of JavaScript, which you can run on any page. Snippets are similar to bookmarklets.
- debug JavaScript.
- set up a Workspace, so that changes you make in DevTools get saved to the code on your file system.

Use the `Page` pane to view all of the resources that the page has loaded.

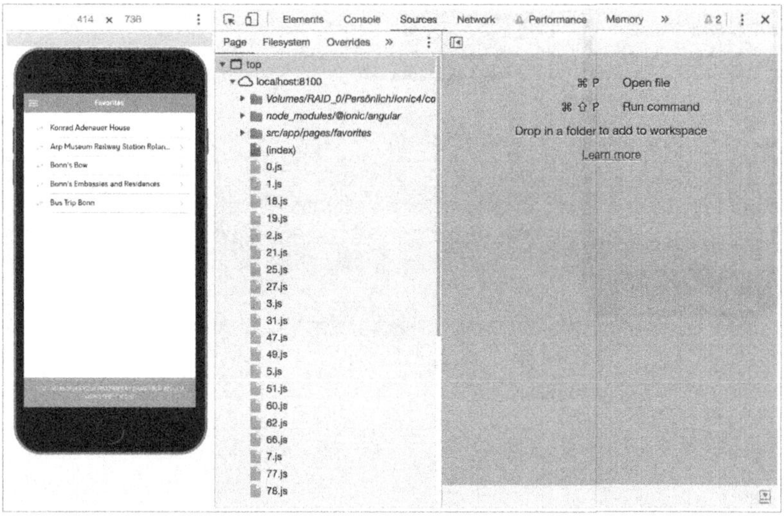

How the Page pane is organized:

- The top-level, such as `top` in the figure above, represents an HTML frame. You'll find `top` on every app/page that you visit. `top` represents the main document frame.
- The second-level, such as `localhost:8100` in the figure above, represents an origin.
- The third-level, fourth-level, and so on, represent directories and resources that were loaded from that origin.

As you can see, in the domain `localhost:8100` the precompiled JS files like `0.js`, `1.js`, `2.js` etc. can be found.

For example, if you dare to take a closer look at `0.js`, you'll begin to suspect something about how Ionic and Webpack will neatly transform your original TypeScript code in the background.

A very useful way to use the Sources area is using the keyword `debugger`. When most browsers encounter a `debugger` statement, running of JavaScript is stopped, and the browser will load its debugger, so does Chrome. This can be used to set "breakpoints" in the app. For example, if a function that isn't returning the correct value, the debugger can be used to step through the code and inspect variables.

When an app runs, it will pause at this function. From there, the developer tools can be used to run pieces of JavaScript, line by line, and inspect where exactly the function breaks.

Let's try this. Again we use open `src/app/pages/map/map.page.ts`. Change the first console log directive `console.log(loading)` to `debugger`:

```
// Calculates a route from user position to destination
async calcRoute() {

 if (this.isCalculated) return;

 // Show calculation process
 const loading = await this.loadingCtrl.create({
   message: 'Calculate route...',
```

```
    spinner: 'crescent'
  });
  await loading.present();
  debugger;
  ...
}
```

Start our app, activate DevTools and switch to the Sources panel. Now pick a tour, click `Options > Map` and then `Route`.

Execution of the app is now interrupted:

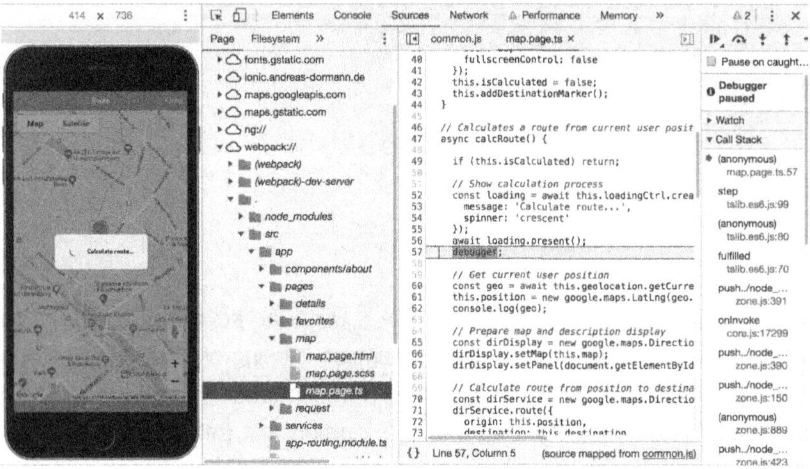

Here we end up exactly at the point in the code that we have set with the `debugger` instruction.

When we unfold the tree in the Page pane, we see that we are in the second level, in the origin `webpack://`. Here we find our project structure with our ts files.

What can we do here now?

By moving the mouse over a variable, we can see their current content. This is of course very helpful and is a good alternative to generating output via `console.log`.

But we now have several options to continue executing the code. You can use the little toolbar on the top right to:

- Resume script execution
- Step over next function call
- Step into next function call
- Step out of current function
- Step (to next line)

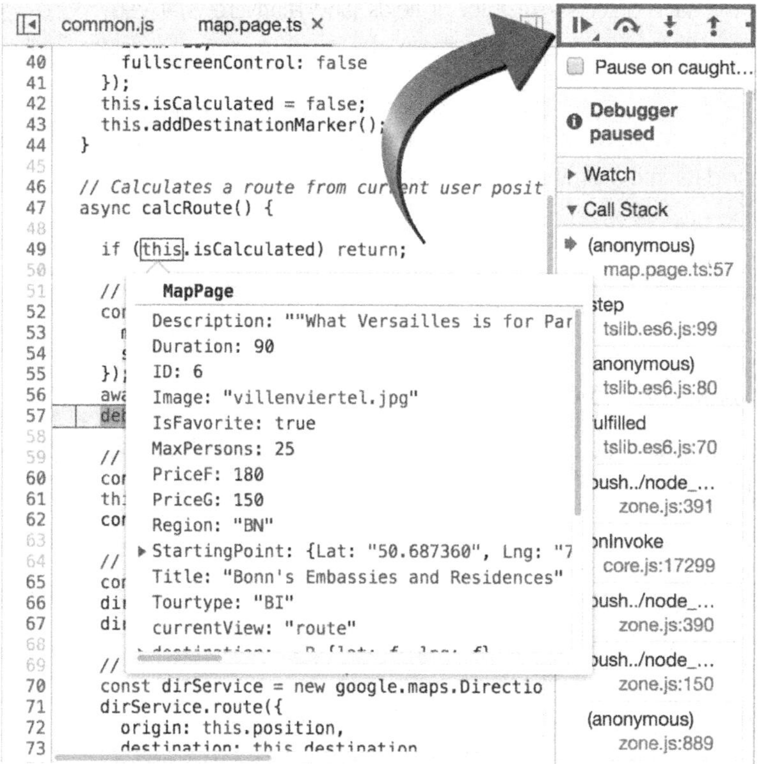

An alternative to the `debugger` statement is to set a breakpoint. You can do that by clicking on a row number within the code window. Then a blue arrow appears.

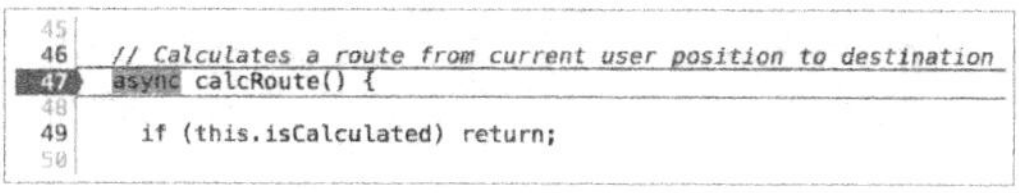

Chrome now breaks the code execution at this line.

Chrome DevTools tips

I want to share a few Chrome DevTools tips I recently got from Nate Murray from ng-book that will make your life easier when writing Ionic/Angular apps. Thanks, Nate!

Tip 1: Use console.table for large data sets

When we have objects with a lot of fields (and many rows) if you `console.log` it out, you have to dig deep within these objects to uncover the values you're looking for.

However, Chrome provides a handy function `console.table`, which will nicely format our data into a pretty table! Example:

```
console.table(geo);
```

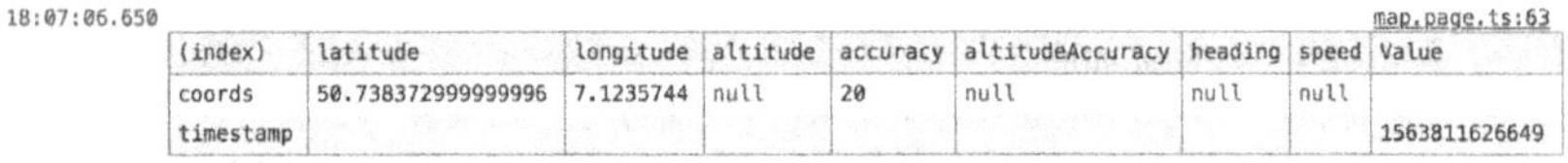
18:07:06.650 map.page.ts:63

(index)	latitude	longitude	altitude	accuracy	altitudeAccuracy	heading	speed	Value
coords	50.738372999999996	7.1235744	null	20	null	null	null	
timestamp								1563811626649

Tip 2: Add color to console.log

Try this out. Start our app, open the DevTools and switch to the Console panel. Then type:

```
console.log(
  "%cWelcome to the world of Ionic!",
  "font-size:600%;color:salmon;font-weight:bold; font-
family:Orkney; text-transform: uppercase;"
);
```

And you should see something that looks like this:

... cool, right!?

How it works: You'll notice that the first argument to `console.log` is a string, as normal, but with a special `%c`, which is where the CSS will be placed. We pass the CSS as a string as the second argument.

You can even load images this way - if you use a background image.

Try the following:

```
let src = "https://i.imgur.com/UYkfHNy.png";
let img = new Image();
img.onload = () =>
  console.log(
    "%c+",
    "background: url(" +
      src +
      "); background-size: 473px 315px; color transparent;
padding: 150px 200px"
  );
img.src = src;
```

And you should see something like this:

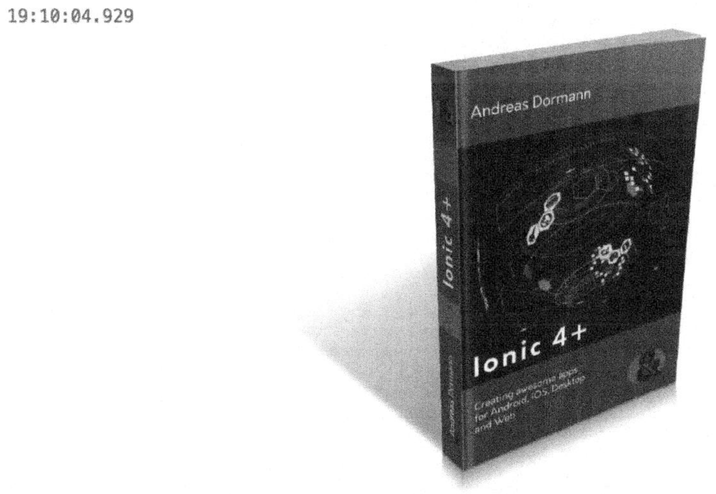

How it works: We're using a background URL within the CSS. You might notice that getting the sizing right is a little tricky. If you're going to be doing this a lot, checkout `console.image`.

Tip 3: Using await in the console

Did you know that Chrome supports a top-level `await` keyword for async functions? It's super helpful.

```
const url =
"https://world.openfoodfacts.org/api/v0/product/737628064502.json";
// Get product informations from Open Food Facts
fetch(url)
  .then(response => response.json())
  .then(body => console.log(body));

// let's try using await
let response = await fetch(url).then(response => response.json());
```

And here's what it looks like in our console:

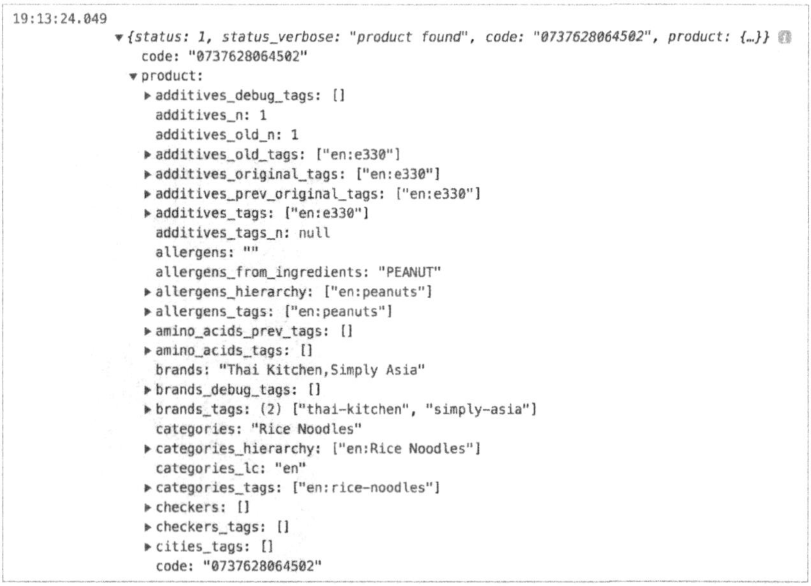

And if we wanted to inspect this product's ingredients? We can again use `console.table`!

```
let product = response.product;
product.ingredients; // ugly
console.table(product.ingredients);
```

19:19:39.996 VM11065:3

(index)	text	id	rank	vegan	vegetarian	from_palm_oil
0	"RICE NOODLES"	"en:RICE NOOD…	1			
1	"SEASONING PA…	"en:SEASONING…	2			
2	"RICE"	"en:rice"		"yes"	"yes"	
3	"WATER"	"en:water"		"yes"	"yes"	
4	"PEANUT"	"en:peanut"		"yes"	"yes"	
5	"SUGAR"	"en:sugar"		"yes"	"yes"	
6	"SALT"	"en:salt"		"yes"	"yes"	
7	"CORN STARCH"	"en:corn-star…		"yes"	"yes"	
8	"SPICES"	"en:spice"		"yes"	"yes"	
9	"CHILI"	"en:chili-pep…		"yes"	"yes"	
10	"CINNAMON"	"en:cinnamon"		"yes"	"yes"	
11	"PEPPER"	"en:bell-pepp…		"yes"	"yes"	
12	"CUMIN"	"en:cumin-see…		"yes"	"yes"	
13	"CLOVE"	"en:clove"		"yes"	"yes"	
14	"HYDROLYZED S…	"en:HYDROLYZE…				
15	"GREEN ONIONS"	"en:green-oni…		"yes"	"yes"	
16	"CITRIC ACID"	"en:e330"		"yes"	"yes"	
17	"PEANUT OIL"	"en:peanut-oi…		"yes"	"yes"	"no"
18	"SESAME OIL"	"en:sesame-oi…		"yes"	"yes"	"no"
19	"NATURAL FLAV…	"en:natural-f…		"maybe"	"maybe"	

Hope this makes your day a little easier!

More informations about the Chrome DevTools you can find here:

▶ https://developers.google.com/web/tools/chrome-devtools/

11.4 Emulator / Simulator

Not every app developer can (and wants to) afford multiple smartphones and tablets for Android and iOS, just to test and debug his own apps on mobile devices. However, judging an app in the context of a concrete platform is indispensable. And for that emulators/simulators are quite practical.

Emulators/simulators strive to simulate a target operating system as realistically as possible. This goes so far that actually many hard-close functions can be tested and debugged on an emulator.

Using the Android Emulator

In order to use the Android emulator Android Studio or the Android SDK must be installed. Here is the download link:

- https://developer.android.com/studio

We start the emulator in the terminal with

```
$ ionic cordova emulate android [--livereload]
```

After an extensive build process an `apk` file is created. This is executed immediately in the emulator after it has been started. The optionally specified `--livereload` option makes use of the dev server from `ionic serve` for live reload functionality.

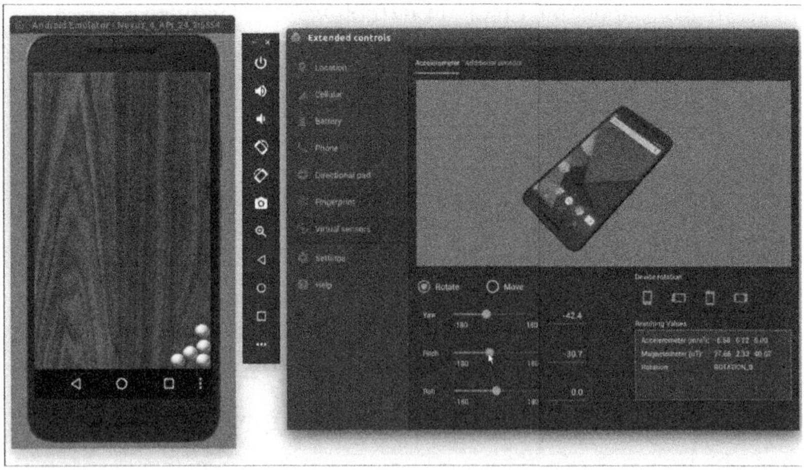

Maybe you get the following error during the build process:

```
[ERROR] native-run wasn't found on your PATH.
Please install it globally:

npm i -g native-run
```

In this case install `native-run` and then repeat the `emulate` statement.

The emulator provides almost all of the capabilities of a real Android device. You can simulate incoming phone calls and text messages, specify the location of the device, simulate different network speeds, simulate rotation and other hardware sensors, access the Google Play Store, and much more.

Testing your app on the emulator is in some ways faster and easier than doing so on a physical device. For example, you can transfer data faster to the emulator than to a device connected over USB.

The emulator comes with predefined configurations for various Android phone, tablet, Wear OS, and Android TV devices.

More informations about the Android emulator you can find here:

- https://ionicframework.com/docs/installation/android
- https://developer.android.com/studio/run/emulator

Android Studio

Android Studio can also be used to launch the emulator and debug an app. Open up Android Studio and choose `File > Open` from menu to open `../path-to-app/platforms/android/`. After creating a virtual device for the emulator via the Android Virtual Device (AVD) Tools you can click `Run > Debug...` from menu to launch the app. Console output and device logs will be printed inside of Android Studio's Gradle Console and Event Log windows.

More informations about this topic you can find here:

- https://developer.android.com/studio/debug
- https://developer.android.com/studio/run/managing-avds

Using the Genymotion Android Emulator

While the Android SDK comes with a stock emulator, it can be slow and unresponsive at times. `Genymotion` is an alternate emulator that is faster, and still allows accesses to native functionality like GPS, camera, network and WiFi. Genymotion requires Oracle VirtualBox:

- https://www.virtualbox.org/

You're able to download and install a free version of Genymotion for personal use (after registration) from here:

- https://www.genymotion.com/

Within Genymotion you can install various virtual mobile devices like a Samsung Galaxy S3, for example. You can determine a specific Android version, the number of processors, memory size, to show Android navigation bar, to use virtual keyboard for text input and much more. A virtual device is started as a virtual machine in VirtualBox.

Now you just need to drag-and-drop the `apk` file created in the `build/emulate` process (see `platforms/android/app/build/outputs/apk/debug/app-debug.apk`) to the virtual device and our app starts within the Genymotion environment.

The cloud option of Genymotion may also be interesting for you:

- https://cloud.geny.io/

Compatible with Android SDK tools and Android Studio

Works on multiple OS

Test your website in various Android browsers

Using the iOS Simulator

The iOS simulator enables testing and debugging of an app before it reaches an actual device. Before it can be used, Xcode, Apple's IDE, must be installed. The Ionic CLI can then be used to run the app in the current directory on the simulator:

```
$ ionic cordova emulate ios [--livereload]
```

After an extensive build process an `apk` file is created. Passing in the optional `--livereload` flag will enable live reload.

Maybe you get the following error during the build process:

```
[ERROR] native-run wasn't found on your PATH.
Please install it globally:

npm i -g native-run
```

In this case install `native-run` and then repeat the `emulate` statement.

When I wrote this book, there was an issue with the build process - related to Xcode's new 'Modern' build system - that I solved by creating the following `build.json` file in the root directory of the app project:

```
{
  "ios": {
    "debug": {
      "buildFlag": [
        "-UseModernBuildSystem=0"
      ],
      "developmentTeam": "YOUR_DEV_TEAM_ID"
    },
    "release": {
      "buildFlag": [
        "-UseModernBuildSystem=0"
      ],
      "developmentTeam": "YOUR_DEV_TEAM_ID"
    }
  }
}
```

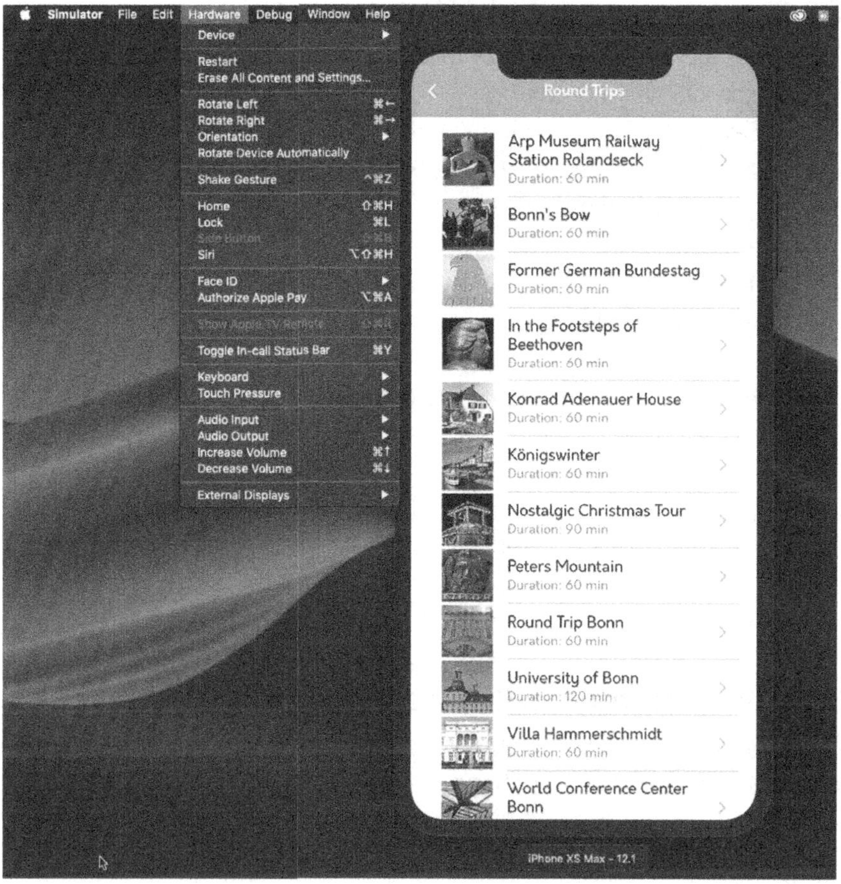

Xcode

Xcode can be used to launch the emulator and debug an app. Open up Xcode and open `../path-to-app/platforms/ios/myApp.xcodeproj`. After the app loads, console output and device logs will be printed inside of Xcode's output window.

More informations about the iOS Simulator and Xcode you can find here:

► https://developer.apple.com/library/archive/documentation/IDEs/Conceptual/iOS_Simulator_Guide/Introduction/Introduction.html

iOS Simulator and Safari / Web Inspector

You can use the Safari Browser on a Mac to debug an iOS simulator session:

1. Launch an iOS simulator session.
2. Open Safari.
3. Select `Develop > Show Web Inspector` in the Safari menu.
   (If `Develop` isn't in the menu, goto `Preferences > Advanced` and activate `Show Develop menu in menu bar`.)
4. Check to see if the web inspector is active for the iOS Simulator (it should be enabled by default):
   Select `Settings (for iOS Simulator) > Safari > Advanced` (scroll to the bottom of the Settings page) and turn on web inspector.
5. Select `iOS Simulator > Quit iOS Simulator`. (Important)
6. Re-launch the iOS Simulator.
   (This can usually be done from the Apple menu > `Recent Items`.)
7. Open the app in the iOS Simulator.
8. In Safari, select `Develop > iOS Simulator > your-app`.

Emulator/Simulator vs Browser Debugging

The advantages of emulator/simulator debugging over pure browser debugging, which I have described in the previous section, are the following:

- Functions can now be tested in the context of the respective device platform, in particular in conjunction with native plug-ins (as far as they are suitable for emulators/simulators).
- The code execution takes place in the transpiled/packed Java script code within the folder `www` (and no longer in the original source code files).
- The emulator/simulator can also be used to test the termination and (re)launch of an app. This can be useful for checking initial or final functions, as well as icon and splash screen ratings.

More informations about Ionic and emulators/simulators you can find here:

► https://ionicframework.com/docs/cli/commands/cordova-emulate

App and Browser testing with BrowserStack

Testing with Android Emulator and iOS Simulator can also be awkward. In the recent past, more and more cloud-based services have taken care of this topic and make interesting offers, so BrowserStack, too. BrowserStack promotes having more than 2000 real devices ready for debugging and testing.

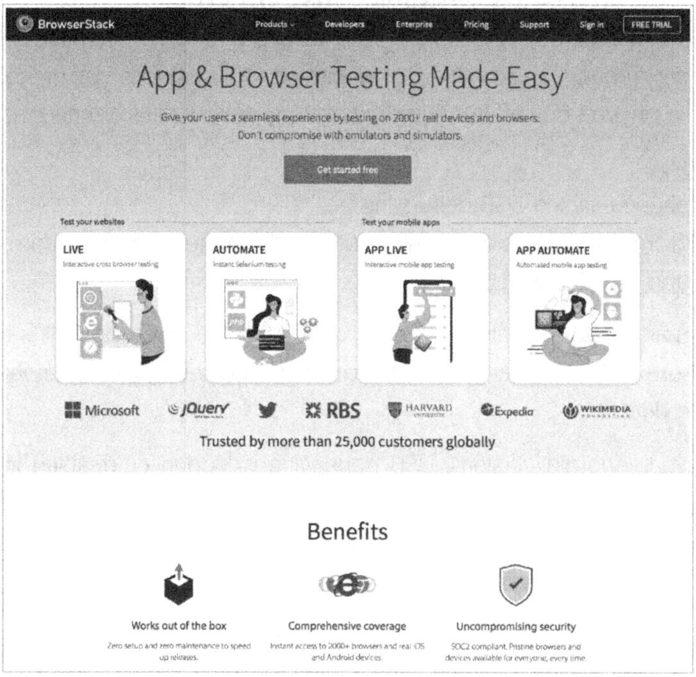

The following areas are supported:

- Live - Interactive cross browser testing
- App Live - interactive native & hybrid app testing
- Automate - Selenium testing at scale
- App Automate - Test automation for native & hybrid mobile apps

During the creation of this book, prices ranged from $29 to $199 per month (enterprise fees on request).

You can find the BrowserStack website here:

▶ https://www.browserstack.com

11.5 Live Device / Remote Debugging

You can live debug our app on your device directly from Ionic! Below I describe the required steps for Android and iOS.

Android Remote Debugging with Chrome

Chrome's `Developer Tools` can be used to debug an app when it is running in the browser through `ionic serve`, or deployed to an emulator (as mentioned before) - or a physical device! For this, the following prerequisites are necessary:

- USB cable
- Smartphone enabled USB debugging
- The Chrome browser in a current version both on the desktop platform as well as an app on the smartphone

1. The smartphone is initially connected via USB to the desktop PC. It is important to ensure that the drivers of the device are properly installed, otherwise it could not be detected.
2. In current Android versions, USB debugging is hidden or disabled in the options of the mobile device. It must first be activated via a simple procedure. The instructions for enabling USB debugging options may vary from device to device. The basic procedure is as follows:

   Under `Settings > About <device>` you'll find a Build Number. This is tapped several times (usually 7 times) until a message appears that you have now enabled the Developer options. Here you can turn on the USB Debugging.
3. We open Chrome on the desktop and add the following line to the address bar: `chrome://inspect/#devices`

4. Here you can activate the detection of USB devices. After activation, the smartphone connected via USB cable should now also be recognized and a dialog for authorization should be displayed. Now we are ready for debugging!

5. Write the following command in terminal:

```
$ ionic cordova run android
```

   After finishing the building process our app appears on the display of the Android device.

6. In Chrome we have a new entry for the running app. We can click on `inspect` to start our live debugging now:

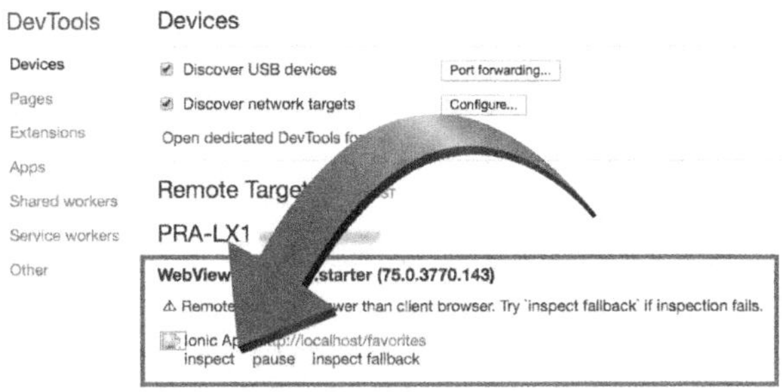

   In a separate Chrome window, we can now follow all actions that we make on the Android device:

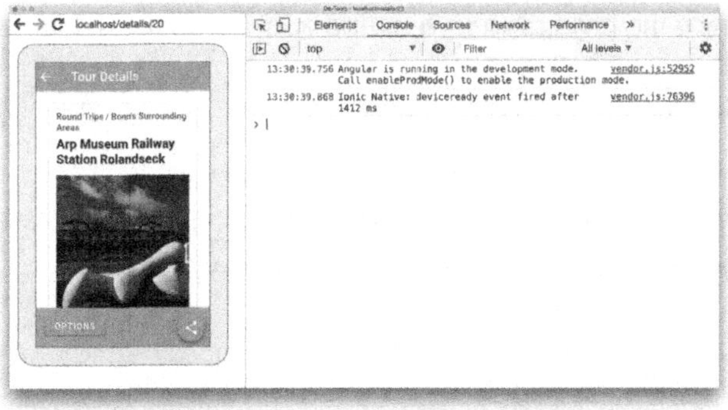

More informations about Remote Debugging Android Devices you can find here:

- https://developers.google.com/web/tools/chrome-devtools/remote-debugging/

iOS Remote Debugging with Safari (MacOS only)

You can use the Safari Browser on a Mac for live debugging an iOS app:

1. Open Safari.
2. Select `Develop > Show Web Inspector` in the Safari menu.
   (If `Develop` isn't in the menu, goto `Preferences > Advanced`
   and activate `Show Develop menu in menu bar`.)
3. Connect your iOS device to your Mac with
   a) an USB cable.
   b) wirelessly (since macOS 10.12.4+, Xcode 9+ and iOS 11+):
    - In Xcode' menu select `Window > Devices and Simulators > Devices > Connect via network`.
    - Unplug the USB cable, a "globe" icon next to your device name indicates that it is now connected wirelessly.
    - Install Safari Technology Preview.
    - Follow the next instructions, use Safari Technology Preview in place of Safari.

   Now Safari on your Mac should be able to see your app running on your device.
4. Write the following command in terminal:

```
$ ionic cordova run ios
```

   After finishing the build process your app appears on the display of the device.

5. Navigate to the `Develop` menu in Safari, and select your device.
6. Click on your app running on the device that you want to debug.
   It will open a Web Inspector window for your app, showing the usual developer tools.

Visual Studio Code Extensions

There are a number of plugins for Visual Studio code that can make developing and debugging with Ionic/Angular a lot easier.

For example there's a dedicated plugin for debugging apps built with Cordova. The plugin creates a bridge between the device and the VSCode Devtools and allows debugging to be done right in the editor. You can find the plugin and a tutorial here:

- https://developers.google.com/web/tools/chrome-devtools/remote-debugging/
- https://geeklearning.io/live-debug-your-cordova-ionic-application-with-visual-studio-code/

Here is a small overview of the plugins that I use:

Further links on this topic can be found here:

- https://ionicframework.com/blog/10-awesome-vs-code-extensions/

11.6 Testing

Testing Principles

When testing an application, note that testing can determine if a system is malfunctioning. However, it's impossible to prove that a nontrivial system is completely error free. For this reason, the goal of testing isn't to check the correctness of the code, but to find problems in the code. This is a subtle but important distinction.

An Ionic/Angular app project is automatically set up for unit testing and end-to-end testing of the app. Ionic uses the same setup that is used by the Angular CLI. So, for detailed information on testing Ionic/Angular apps refer to:

- https://angular.io/guide/testing

If we go to prove that the code is correct, we will stick to the happy path through the code. If we look for problems, we are more likely to be more verbose and find the errors that are lurking there.

It's also best to test an application from the beginning. This allows errors to be detected early if they are easier to fix. In this way, the code can also be safely redesigned as new features are added to the system.

What we can achieve with testing:

- Describe the intended functionality
- Ensure that code is behaving the way we intended
- Enlarge the chance to find broken code by re-running tests after changes
- Write better code

Testing Practices

With unit testing we take an isolated look at a single unit of code (component, page, service etc.). We can achieve isolation from the rest of the system by injection of mock objects in place of the code's dependencies.

We use Jasmine (https://jasmine.github.io/) to create such mock objects, TestBed (https://angular.io/api/core/testing/TestBed) to write tests and Karma (https://karma-runner.github.io) to run tests. Don't worry: With Ionic 5 everything we need for automated testing is included by default.

Let's start with Karma. In terminal we write:

```
$ npm test
```

This runs unit tests in our current project. Let's see what happens...

In my project the following is output in the terminal (severely shortened):

```
12% building 19/19 modules 0 active
29 07 2019 17:48:01.629:WARN [karma]:
No captured browser, open http://localhost:9876/
29 07 2019 17:48:01.634:INFO [karma-server]:
Karma v4.1.0 server started at http://0.0.0.0:9876/
29 07 2019 17:48:01.634:INFO [launcher]:
Launching browsers Chrome with concurrency unlimited
 12% building 22/22 modules 0 active
29 07 2019 17:48:01.679:INFO [launcher]:
Starting browser Chrome
29 07 2019 17:48:06.562:WARN [karma]:
No captured browser, open http://localhost:9876/
29 07 2019 17:48:06.688:INFO [Chrome 75.0.3770 (Mac OS X 10.10.5)]:
Connected on socket vWkCY8uBd2xIWdZTAAAA with id 16782258
Chrome 75.0.3770 (Mac OS X 10.10.5) AppComponent should create the
app FAILED
        Error: StaticInjectorError(DynamicTestModule)[HttpClient]:
          StaticInjectorError(Platform: core)[HttpClient]:
            NullInjectorError: No provider for HttpClient!
            at
NullInjector.push../node_modules/@angular/core/fesm5/core.js.NullInje
ctor.get (node_modules/@angular/core/fesm5/core.js:8896:1)
            at resolveToken
(node_modules/@angular/core/fesm5/core.js:9141:1)
            at tryResolveToken
(node_modules/@angular/core/fesm5/core.js:9085:1)
            at StaticInjector.push../node_modules/@angular/core/fes-
m5/core.js.StaticInjector.get
(node_modules/@angular/core/fesm5/core.js:8982:1)

...

Chrome 75.0.3770 (Mac OS X 10.10.5): Executed 17 of 17 (14 FAILED)
(0.434 secs / 0.353 secs)
TOTAL: 14 FAILED, 3 SUCCESS
TOTAL: 14 FAILED, 3 SUCCESS
```

We've started a test process. Karma has started a server (at the address `http://0.0.0.0:9876`) and has completed 17 tests, 14 of which failed.

After completion of the test, this is also displayed in a separate browser window from the Karma server:

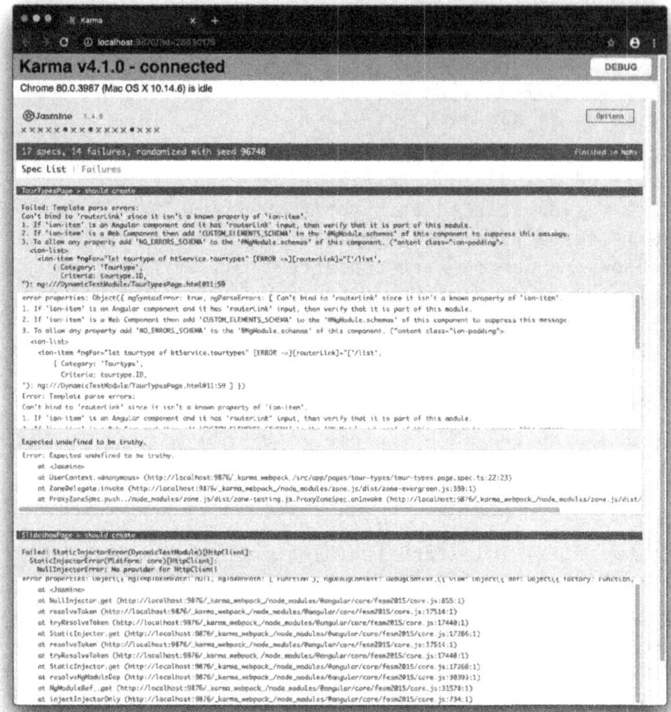

What does all this mean? Do you remember the `spec` files automatically generated by Ionic when creating a page/component? These `spec` files contain a whole series of so-called *test cases*, at least one case per file.

A spec file is constructed by Ionic/Angular according to the following scheme given by Jasmine:

```
describe (COMPONENT_NAME, () => {
   ...
   it (TEST_CASE_NAME, ())> {
     ...
    expect ...
   });
});
```

`describe()` defines a suite (e.g. a "collection") of tests (or "specs").

`it()` defines a specific test or "spec", and it lives inside of a suite (`describe()`). This is what defines the expected behavior of the code you are testing, e.g. "it should do this", "it should do that".

`expect()` defines the expected result of a test and lives inside of `it()`.

Back to the previous picture of our first test run: There were 17 test cases tested, of which 14 failed. Of course that's not a good result. We will now apply and/or adapt and skip some of these test cases to improve our test results.

First, we fix some `No provider` errors in `app.component.spec.ts` by adding some missing imports (bold formatted):

```
import { CUSTOM_ELEMENTS_SCHEMA } from '@angular/core';
import { TestBed, async } from '@angular/core/testing';

import { Platform } from '@ionic/angular';
import { SplashScreen }
          from '@ionic-native/splash-screen/ngx';
import { StatusBar } from '@ionic-native/status-bar/ngx';
import { RouterTestingModule } from '@angular/router/testing';

import { AppComponent } from './app.component';

import { PopoverController } from '@ionic/angular';
import { IonicStorageModule } from '@ionic/storage';
import { HttpClientTestingModule }
         from '@angular/common/http/testing';
import { LocalNotifications }
         from '@ionic-native/local-notifications/ngx';

describe('AppComponent', () => {

  let statusBarSpy, splashScreenSpy, platformReadySpy,
      platformSpy, popoverSpy, localNotifySpy;

  beforeEach(async(() => {
    statusBarSpy
      = jasmine.createSpyObj('StatusBar', ['styleDefault']);
    splashScreenSpy
```

```
      = jasmine.createSpyObj('SplashScreen', ['hide']);
    platformReadySpy = Promise.resolve();
    platformSpy
      = jasmine.createSpyObj('Platform',
                             { ready: platformReadySpy });
    popoverSpy
      = jasmine.createSpyObj('Popover', ['']);
    localNotifySpy
      = jasmine.createSpyObj('LocalNotify', ['']);

    TestBed.configureTestingModule({
      declarations: [AppComponent],
      schemas: [CUSTOM_ELEMENTS_SCHEMA],
      providers: [
     { provide: StatusBar, useValue: statusBarSpy },
     { provide: SplashScreen, useValue: splashScreenSpy },
     { provide: Platform, useValue: platformSpy },
     { provide: PopoverController, useValue: popoverSpy },
     { provide: LocalNotifications, useValue: localNotifySpy }
      ],
      imports: [
        RouterTestingModule.withRoutes([]),
        HttpClientTestingModule,
        IonicStorageModule.forRoot()
      ],
    }).compileComponents();
  }));

  ...

});
```

With this additions we ensure that the test unit `AppComponent` includes all referenced providers. To eliminate all other `No provider` errors, I have modified the following test files:

- `bob-tours.service.spec.ts`
- `favorites.service.spec.ts`

And - for reasons of simplification – I simply deleted the following files:

- `details.page.spec.ts`
- `favorites.page.spec.ts`

- `list.page.spec.ts`
- `map.page.spec.ts`
- `regions.page.spec.ts`
- `request.page.spec.ts`
- `slideshow.page.spec.ts`
- `tour-types.page.spec.ts`

To be able to test on the same level as me now, you can download the code of the current project status from the book website (see "1.4 The book's website" on page 20) in section 11.06.01.

A new Karma test with `npm test` should yield something like the following now:

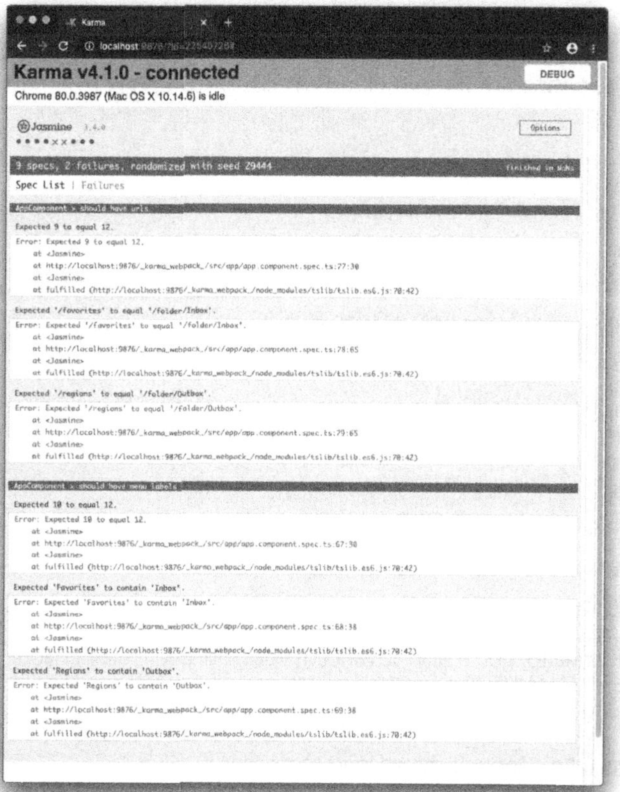

There are still nine tests, of which only two fail.

Let's take a closer look at `app.component.spec.ts` and its `it` methods:

```
it('should create the app', async () => {
  const fixture = TestBed.createComponent(AppComponent);
  const app = fixture.debugElement.componentInstance;
  expect(app).toBeTruthy();
});
```

We open a single test case with the callback method `it`. In this case we check if the app can be created. We use TestBed's `createComponent` method in combination with `debugElement.componentInstance` to get the apps' instance. With `expect` we check the result by using a so-called *matcher* function, in this case `toBeTruthy()`. This Boolean matcher is used in Jasmine to check whether the result is equal to true or false.

There's a whole range of these methods available for testing different scenarios, for example:

- `expect(fn).toThrow(e);`
- `expect(instance).toBe(instance);`
- `expect(mixed).toBeDefined();`
- `expect(mixed).toBeFalsy();`
- `expect(number).toBeGreaterThan(number);`
- `expect(number).toBeLessThan(number);`
- `expect(mixed).toBeNull();`
- `expect(mixed).toBeTruthy();`
- `expect(mixed).toBeUndefined();`
- `expect(array).toContain(member);`
- `expect(string).toContain(substring);`
- `expect(mixed).toEqual(mixed);`
- `expect(mixed).toMatch(pattern);`

And if you want to get really advanced you can even define your own custom matchers.

But now let's take a look at the second test case:

```
it('should initialize the app', async () => {
  TestBed.createComponent(AppComponent);
  expect(platformSpy.ready).toHaveBeenCalled();
```

```
    await platformReadySpy;
    expect(statusBarSpy.styleDefault).toHaveBeenCalled();
    expect(splashScreenSpy.hide).toHaveBeenCalled();
});
```

Here we check if the platform is ready. Because it's an asynchronous call, we use a `platformSpy` and a `platformReadySpy`. We have defined these before in the `beforeEach()` part of the test description. With `await` we wait for the result and then check whether Statusbar and SplashScreen have been called. For this we use the matcher function `toHaveBeenCalled()`.

At this point we should complete the test case with the two following checks:

```
expect(popoverSpy).toBeDefined();
expect(localNotifySpy).toBeDefined();
```

With that we check, if also the objects `popoverSpy` and `localNotifySpy` we have just added have been defined.

The third test case:

```
it('should have menu labels', async () => {
    const fixture = await TestBed.createComponent(AppComponent);
    await fixture.detectChanges();
    const app = fixture.nativeElement;
    const menuItems = app.querySelectorAll('ion-label');
    expect(menuItems.length).toEqual(12);
    expect(menuItems[0].textContent).toContain('Inbox');
    expect(menuItems[1].textContent).toContain('Outbox');
});
```

Here it's checked if the application has the expected menu labels. As Karma showed, this automatically generated test case *failed*!

Let's formulate the requirement for our menu labels ourselves: We expect the menu items `'Favorites'`, `'Regions'`, `'Tour-Types'` and `'Slideshow'`, a total of four entries. They entries can be found by the tag `ion-menu-toggle`.

Formulated as a test case for Jasmine:

```
it('should have menu labels', async () => {
    const fixture = await TestBed.createComponent(AppComponent);
    await fixture.detectChanges();
    const app = fixture.nativeElement;
```

```
  const menuItems = app.querySelectorAll('ion-menu-toggle');
  expect(menuItems.length).toEqual(4);
  expect(menuItems[0].textContent).toContain('Favorites');
  expect(menuItems[1].textContent).toContain('Regions');
  expect(menuItems[2].textContent).toContain('Tour-Types');
  expect(menuItems[3].textContent).toContain('Slideshow');
});
```

After `TestBed.createComponent` has returned the app component to the variable `fixture`, we can wait with `detectChanges()` until we see changes in the component. Now we can access the HTML DOM via `nativeElement` and get all `ion-menu-toggle` tags via the `querySelectorAll` method. With `toEqual(4)` we check if there are four entries and with `toContain(...)` we check if they each have the expected text entry.

If we save these changes and Karma is run again, this test case should now pass successfully.

Our fourth test case in `app.component.spec.ts`:

```
it('should have urls', async () => {
  const fixture = await TestBed.createComponent(AppComponent);
  await fixture.detectChanges();
  const app = fixture.nativeElement;
  const menuItems = app.querySelectorAll('ion-item');
  expect(menuItems.length).toEqual(12);
  expect(menuItems[0]
    .getAttribute('ng-reflect-router-link'))
      .toEqual('/folder/Inbox');
  expect(menuItems[1]
    .getAttribute('ng-reflect-router-link'))
      .toEqual('/folder/Outbox');
});
```

This test case checks if all expected menu urls or better said, routes are present in the component. As Karma showed, this automatically generated test case failed, too.

Again, let's formulate the test conditions for the required routes ourselves: The appropriate routes to the menu items are `'/favorites'`, `'/regions'`, `'/tour-types'` and `'/slideshow'`, a total of four routes.

Formulated as a test case for Jasmine:

```
it('should have routes', async () => {
  const fixture = await TestBed.createComponent(AppComponent);
  await fixture.detectChanges();
  const app = fixture.nativeElement;
  const menuItems
    = app.querySelectorAll('ion-menu-toggle ion-item');
  expect(menuItems.length).toEqual(4);
  expect(menuItems[0].getAttribute('ng-reflect-router-link'))
                     .toEqual('/favorites');
  expect(menuItems[1].getAttribute('ng-reflect-router-link'))
                     .toEqual('/regions');
  expect(menuItems[2].getAttribute('ng-reflect-router-link'))
                     .toEqual('/tour-types');
  expect(menuItems[3].getAttribute('ng-reflect-router-link'))
                     .toEqual('/slideshow');
});
```

To illustrate how to get the correct query selector for the `querySelectorAll(...)` method and the correct name for the `getAttribute(...)` method, here's the `DevTools > Elements` panel with all the information we need:

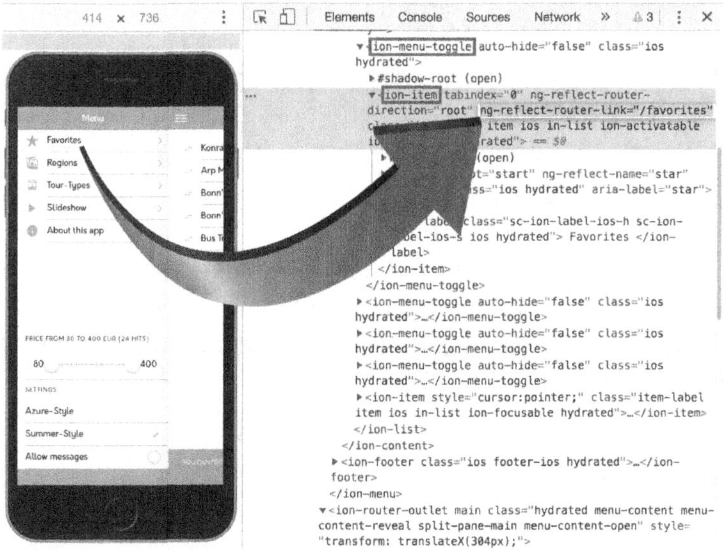

If we save these changes and Karma is run again, this test case should now pass successfully, too.

All our tests were successful, which karma acknowledged with nine green dots, the summary "9 specs, 0 failures" and the corresponding text information about each test unit and its test cases:

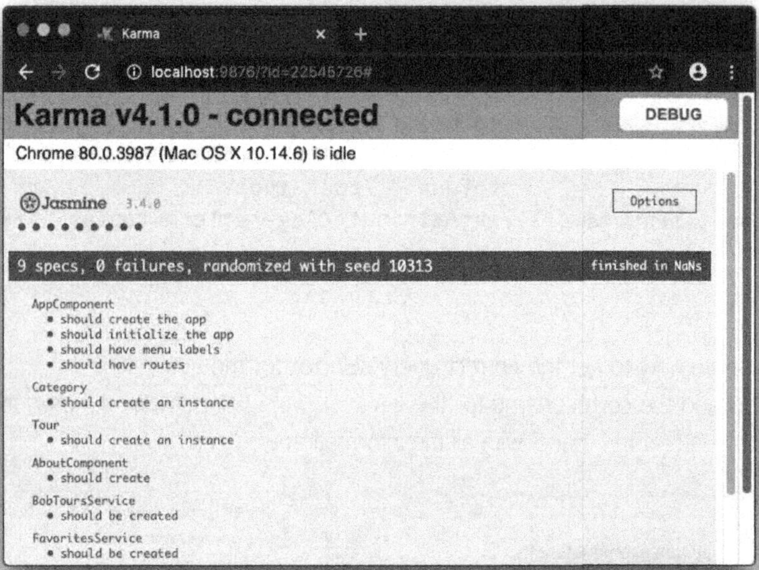

Congratulation! You have successfully created and performed some unit tests.

We won't go deeper into the topic of testing, because it isn't really an *Ionic* topic. The concrete implementation of tests depend heavily on the respective JS framework, in our case, on Angular. But I'd like to finally share a few words about of two other types of tests:

- Testing Services
- End-to-End Testing

Testing Services

Testing services can be a challenge and that has a specific reason: In most cases, JavaScript doesn't get information in sync - and that's the same with most services. Either they return you an observable or a promise object, and only later will you provide the information you requested. To solve this problem, refer to Jasmine's *test doubles*. These are wrapper objects and functions that are used to read function calls (spy) as well as to control behavior (stubs).

So you get a reference to the service stub via the injector and create a Jasmine stub using the get method of the service. This stub returns a promise, which is immediately resolved with an array of two task objects. Despite this immediate resolution, this is an asynchronous operation.

Ionic has already automatically generated the basic framework for testing for our services.

Here's the code skeleton from `bob-tours.service.spec.ts`:

```
import { TestBed } from '@angular/core/testing';

import { BobToursService } from './bob-tours.service';
import { IonicStorageModule } from '@ionic/storage';

import { HttpClientTestingModule }
         from '@angular/common/http/testing';

describe('BobToursService', () => {
  beforeEach(() => TestBed.configureTestingModule({
    imports: [
      HttpClientTestingModule,
      IonicStorageModule.forRoot()
    ]
  }));

  it('should be created', () => {
    const service: BobToursService
      = TestBed.get(BobToursService);
    expect(service).toBeTruthy();
  });
});
```

End-to-End Testing

End-to-end tests - short E2E tests - use Protractor (https://www.protractortest.org).

With E2E testing, you no longer only check units such as classes or individual functions, but entire workflows in your application.

The setup and the configuration are easy and if you master JavaScript, you have a very easy start. There is good material for the training and so the tool is ready to use.

There are some technical requirements for testing an application with Protractor:

- The Angular application must be executable, only then Protractor can run the tests.
- The screen elements should be well and - if possible - logically defined with ID and name.

This is necessary in order to be able to access certain elements in the test code in order to query their state, for example. If this is ignored during development, the application's front-end code must first be adapted by assigning IDs and names for the corresponding elements.

When to test how?

In which cases do you go for unit tests, and when should you prefer to do an E2E test? As you delve deeper into the subject of testing, you'll quickly realize that it's the user interactions and workflows that are becoming cumbersome to cover with unit testing. This is the classic use case for E2E tests: a keyboard input, a click on a button and then wait for the application to respond with the correct output.

With unit tests, on the other hand, you back up individual methods: Does the observable supply the correct values for a given value constellation of an injected service, and is the correct exception triggered when an incorrect entry is made? All these are things that you cover with unit tests.

Although we only scratched the surface of the topic testing, I'm sure, this entry gives you a first idea on how useful it is to test an app.

More informations about Testing an Ionic/Angular app you can find here:

► https://angular.io/guide/testing

Summary

In this chapter you've learned a lot of different new things:

You've learned to play doctor and give your Ionic environment a health check.

You've learned a bit about strict typing and how helpful that can be, not only to support a very convenient code completion.

When debugging your app, you now know how to use Chrome and its DevTools.

You can watch your app in the Android Emulator and/or iOS Simulator and test native features in it.

Finally, you got into unit testing with Jasmine, TestBed and Karma and understand why tests can be the way to improve software quality and prevent software defects.

12 Build, Deploy & Publish

12.1 Introduction

If you've read this book attentively and followed the origins of the Bob Tours app step by step, you've gone through a whole series of typical phases of an app life-cycle: from planning to development to debugging and testing.

Now the final spurt begins with the phases Build, Deploy and Publish. Let us first find a common understanding of the terms.

Build

means: Process all of my code/artifacts and prepare them for deployment. Meaning compile, generate code, package, etc. The process of creating executable software packages is usually automated by build tools, which also ensure the consistency of frameworks between different builds.

Deploy

means: Take all of my artifacts and either copy them to a server/mobile device, or execute them on a server/mobile device. It should truly be a simple process.

Publish

is just a method of deployment. In the context of an app publication, we bring the stores of Apple (App Store) and Google (Google Play) to the scene. We will discuss this in more detail later in own sections. So much in advance: When you publish an application you perform two main tasks:

- You prepare the application for release.
- You release the application to users.

12.2 The web build process

Building web files

To build our app as a simple website, just enter the following in the terminal:

```
$ ionic build
```

As the Ionic documentation says, `ionic build` (without any options) performs an Ionic build, which compiles web assets and prepares them for deployment. It uses the Angular CLI, what you can easily tell from the first line of output after starting the command:

```
> ng run app:build
```

Use `ng build --help` to list all Angular CLI options for building your app. See the `ng build` docs for explanations:

► https://angular.io/cli/build

The `build` command causes the following:

- Transforming the TypeScript and SCSS files located in the `src` folder to JavaScript and CSS files
- Moving the transformed files to the `www` folder

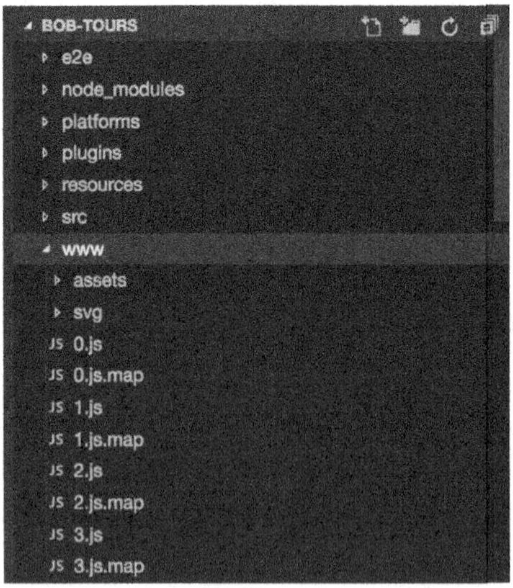

We could grab the files in the `www` folder to put them on a web server and start a web application. But we shouldn't do that because the code isn't yet optimized for production!

Take a look at the files of the www folder, for example `main.js`:

As you can see, there is (in my file from line 602) in a slightly different, but readable form, our source code. I don't think that you want to publish the readable version of it for everyone on a web server - unless you want to share your app as open source with the world.

So, what to do?

For productive deployment we create a build with the `--prod` flag:

```
$ ionic build --prod
```

The `build --prod` command *additionally* causes the following:

- Compiling, concatenating and minifying the `src` TypeScript files into `www/build/main.js.`
- Compressing (nearly) all the node_module libraries and looking for some dead code (a library, that isn't exported anywhere, won't be added)
- Importing all SCSS code into one big `css` file

Ok, let's do it!

Little code re-organization

Unfortunately, the build process with the option `--prod` ran into an error:

```
ERROR in Type RequestPage in /Volumes/Data/Ionic5/code/bob-
tours/src/app/pages/request/request.page.ts is part of the declara-
tions of 2 modules: DetailsPageModule in
/Volumes/Data/Ionic5/code/bob-tours/src/app/pages/details/details.-
module.ts and RequestPageModule in /Volumes/Data/Ionic5/code/bob-
tours/src/app/pages/request/request.module.ts! Please consider moving
RequestPage in /Volumes/Data/Ionic5/code/bob-tours/src/app/pages/re-
quest/request.page.ts to a higher module that imports
DetailsPageModule in /Volumes/Data/Ionic5/code/bob-
tours/src/app/pages/details/details.module.ts and RequestPageModule
in /Volumes/Data/Ionic5/code/bob-tours/src/app/pages/request/re-
quest.module.ts. You can also create a new NgModule that exports and
includes RequestPage in /Volumes/Data/Ionic5/code/bob-
tours/src/app/pages/request/request.page.ts then import that NgModule
in DetailsPageModule in /Volumes/Data/Ionic5/code/bob-
tours/src/app/pages/details/details.module.ts and RequestPageModule
in /Volumes/Data/Ionic5/code/bob-tours/src/app/pages/request/re-
quest.module.ts.
Type MapPage in /Volumes/Data/Ionic5/code/bob-
tours/src/app/pages/map/map.page.ts is part of the declarations of 2
modules: DetailsPageModule in /Volumes/Data/Ionic5/code/bob-
tours/src/app/pages/details/details.module.ts and MapPageModule in
/Volumes/Data/Ionic5/code/bob-tours/src/app/pages/map/map.module.ts!
Please consider moving MapPage in /Volumes/Data/Ionic5/code/bob-
tours/src/app/pages/map/map.page.ts to a higher module that imports
DetailsPageModule in /Volumes/Data/Ionic5/code/bob-
tours/src/app/pages/details/details.module.ts and MapPageModule in
/Volumes/Data/Ionic5/code/bob-tours/src/app/pages/map/map.module.ts.
You can also create a new NgModule that exports and includes MapPage
in /Volumes/Data/Ionic5/code/bob-tours/src/app/pages/map/map.page.ts
```

```
then import that NgModule in DetailsPageModule in /Volumes/Data/Ion-
ic5/code/bob-tours/src/app/pages/details/details.module.ts and
MapPageModule in /Volumes/Data/Ionic5/code/bob-
tours/src/app/pages/map/map.module.ts.

[ERROR] An error occurred while running subprocess ng.

        ng run app:build:production exited with exit code 1.
```

Sometimes it can happen that a project `with ionic serve/build` runs smoothly, but generates errors with ionic `build --prod`. In Angular this particular error is considered as `ng run/serve` run time cache issue and is related to the Ionic/Angular Lazy Loading mechanism (see "2.5 Routing and Lazy Loading", starting from page 36).

An indication of the solution is already given in the terminal text above. We need to take the declaration and import of RequestPage to a higher level. Of course, we should use the app level, `app.module.ts`, for that. And we should do the same for MapPage.

We proceed as follows:

1. Remove the entries from MapPage and RequestPage in `details.module.ts`
2. Add entries to MapPage and RequestPage in `app.module.ts`

Let's start with `details.module.ts` and remove the bold formatted parts:

```
import { NgModule } from '@angular/core';
import { CommonModule } from '@angular/common';
import { FormsModule, ReactiveFormsModule } from
'@angular/forms';
import { Routes, RouterModule } from '@angular/router';
import { IonicModule } from '@ionic/angular';
import { DetailsPage } from './details.page';
import { RequestPage } from './../request/request.page';
import { MapPage } from './../map/map.page';

const routes: Routes = [
  {
    path: '',
    component: DetailsPage
  }
];
```

```
@NgModule({
  imports: [
    CommonModule,
    FormsModule,
    ReactiveFormsModule,
    IonicModule,
    RouterModule.forChild(routes)
  ],
  declarations: [DetailsPage, RequestPage, MapPage],
  entryComponents: [RequestPage, MapPage]
})
export class DetailsPageModule {}
```

Now we add the bold formatted parts in `app.module.ts`:

```
import { NgModule } from '@angular/core';
import { BrowserModule } from '@angular/platform-browser';
import { RouteReuseStrategy } from '@angular/router';

import { IonicModule, IonicRouteStrategy }
         from '@ionic/angular';
import { SplashScreen }
         from '@ionic-native/splash-screen/ngx';
import { StatusBar } from '@ionic-native/status-bar/ngx';

import { AppComponent } from './app.component';
import { AppRoutingModule } from './app-routing.module';
import { HttpClientModule } from '@angular/common/http';
import { IonicStorageModule } from '@ionic/storage';

import { FormsModule, ReactiveFormsModule }
         from '@angular/forms';

import { AboutComponent }
         from './components/about/about.component';

import { Geolocation } from '@ionic-native/geolocation/ngx';
import { SocialSharing }
         from '@ionic-native/social-sharing/ngx';
import { LocalNotifications }
         from '@ionic-native/local-notifications/ngx';
```

```
import { MapPage } from './pages/map/map.page';
import { MapPageModule } from './pages/map/map.module';
import { RequestPage } from './pages/request/request.page';
import { RequestPageModule }
         from './pages/request/request.module';

@NgModule({
  declarations: [AppComponent, AboutComponent],
  entryComponents: [AppComponent, AboutComponent,
                    RequestPage, MapPage],
  imports: [
    BrowserModule,
    IonicModule.forRoot(),
    AppRoutingModule,
    HttpClientModule,
    IonicStorageModule.forRoot(),
    FormsModule,
    ReactiveFormsModule,
    RequestPageModule,
    MapPageModule
  ],
  providers: [
    StatusBar,
    SplashScreen,
    Geolocation,
    SocialSharing,
    LocalNotifications,
    { provide: RouteReuseStrategy,
      useClass: IonicRouteStrategy },
  ],
  bootstrap: [AppComponent]
})
export class AppModule {}
```

Here we import both the *pages* and the *modules* of MapPage and RequestPage, enter the pages as `entryComponents` and the modules as `imports` into `@NgModule`.

Let's again build a production build with

```
$ ionic build --prod
```

We now see a successful, error free build process. And also `ionic serve` works already fine after this little refactoring.

Now let's take a look at the www folder:

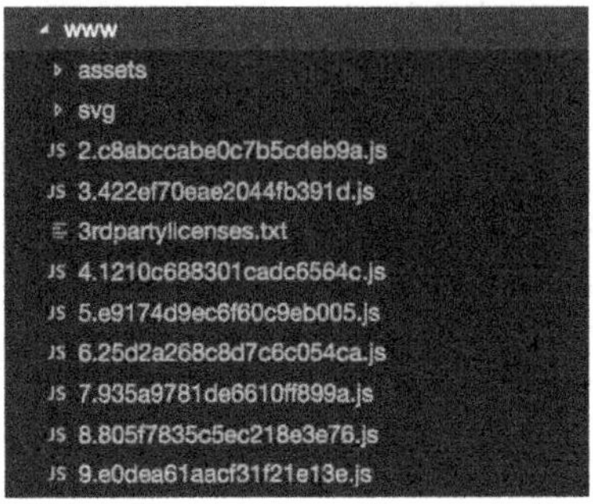

We've received a collection of more than two hundred small JS files. This has been done with the help of Webpack (see "1.1 The idea behind Ionic", section "WebPack" on page 14). The JS files have been split into "chunks" which are only loaded when needed. And when we look at one of them, it's easy to see what compiling, concatenating and minifying have done:

```
(window.webpackJsonp=window.webpackJsonp||[]).push([[9],
{0:function(t,e,n){t.exports=n("zUnb")},"0AIG":function(t,e,n)
{"use strict";n.d(e,"a",(function(){return r}));const
r=(t,e,n,r,s)=>o(t[1],e[1],n[1],r[1],s).map(o=>i(t[0],e[0],n[0
],r[0],o)),i=(t,e,n,r,i)=>i*(3*e*Math.pow(i-1,2)+i*(-
3*n*i+3*n+r*i))-t*Math.pow(i-1,3),o=(t,e,n,r,i)=>s((r-=i)-
3*(n-=i)+3*(e-=i)-(t-=i),3*n-6*e+3*t,3*e-
3*t,t).filter(t=>t>=0&&t<=1),s=(t,e,n,r)=>{if(0===t)return((t,
e,n)=>{const r=e*e-4*t*n;return r<0?[]:[(-e+Math.sqrt(r))/
(2*t),(-e-Math.sqrt(r))/(2*t)]})(e,n,r);const i=(3*(n/=t)-
(e/=t)*e)/3,o=(2*e*e*e-
9*e*n+27*(r/=t))/27;if(0===i)return[Math.pow(-
o,1/3)];if(0===o)return[Math.sqrt(-i),-Math.sqrt(-i)];const
s=Math.pow(o/2,2)+Math.pow(i/3,3);if(0===s)return[Math.pow(o/2
,.5)-e/3];if(s>0)return[Math.pow(-o/2+Math.sqrt(s),1/3)-Math-
.pow(o/2+Math.sqrt(s),1/3)-e/3];const a=Math.sqrt(Math.pow(-
i/3,3)),l=Math.acos(-o/(2*Math.sqrt(Math.pow(-
i/3,3)))),u=2*Math.pow(a,1/3);return[u*Math.cos(l/3)-
```

```
e/3,u*Math.cos((l+2*Math.PI)/3)-
e/3,u*Math.cos((l+4*Math.PI)/3)-e/3]}},"1M1q":function(t,e,n)
{"use strict";n.d(e,"a",(function(){return c}));var
r=n("mrSG"),i=n("U8oy"),o=n("LvDl"),s=n.n(o),a=n("8Y7J"),l=n("
IheW"),u=n("sZkV");let c=(()=>{class t{constructor(t,e,n)
{this.http=t,this.favService=e,this.loadingCtrl=n,this.baseUrl
="https://bob-tours-app.firebaseio.com/"}initialize(){return
r.a(this,void 0,void 0,(function*(){yield this.loadingCtr-
l.create({message:"Loading tour
data...",spinner:"crescent"}),yield
this.getRegions().then(t=>this.regions=t),yield this.getTour-
types().then(t=>this.tourtypes=s.a.sortBy(t,"Name")),yield
this.getTours().then(t=>{this.tours=s.a.sortBy(t,"Title"),this
.all_tours=s.a.sortBy(t,"Title"),this.filterTours({lower:80,up
per:400}),this.favService.initialize(this.all_tours)})}))}ge-
tRegions(){return this.http.get(`$
{this.baseUrl}/Regions.json`).toPromise()}getTourtypes(){re-
turn this.http.get(`$
{this.baseUrl}/Tourtypes.json`).toPromise()}getTours(){return
this.http.get(`${this.baseUrl}/Tours.json`).toPromise()}fil-
terTours(t){return this.tours=s.a.filter(this.all_tours,
(function(e){return
e.PriceG>=t.lower&&e.PriceG<=t.upper})),this.regions.forEach(t
=>{const e=s.a.filter(this.tours,
["Region",t.ID]);t.Count=e.length}),this.tourtypes.forEach(t=>
{const e=s.a.filter(this.tours,
["Tourtype",t.ID]);t.Count=e.length}),this.tours.length}}re-
turn t.ngInjectableDef=a.Pb({factory:function(){return new
t(a.Qb(l.c),a.Qb(i.a),a.Qb(u.Fb))},token:t,providedIn:"root"})
,t})()},"2QA8":function(t,e,n){"use strict";n.d(e,"a",(func-
tion(){return r}));const r=(()=>"function"==typeof Symbol?
Symbol("rxSubscriber"):"@@rxSubscriber_"+Math.random())
()},"2Vo4":function(t,e,n){"use strict";n.d(e,"a",(function()
{return o}));var r=n("XNiG"),i=n("9ppp");class o extends
r.a{constructor(t){super(),this._value=t}get value(){return
this.getValue()}_subscribe(t){const e=super._subscribe(t);re-
turn e&&!e.closed&&t.next(this._value),e}getValue())) [...]
```

The data volume of the entire `www` folder is now 15.3 MB after `ionic build --prod`. For comparison: After a simple `ionic build` it is 46.9 MB.

12.3 config.xml

Numerous aspects of the behavior of an app can be controlled through the global configuration file `config.xml`. It also provides advanced Cordova API functions, plug-ins and platform-specific settings.

The structure of the `config.xml` file as a platform-independent XML file was specified here in detail by the W3C under the title *Packaged Web Apps (Widgets)*:

- https://www.w3.org/TR/widgets/

Although the specification has been marked as obsolete since October 2018, it still has significance for Ionic/Cordova projects. In that regard, reference should also be made to the following document:

- https://cordova.apache.org/docs/en/9.x/config_ref/index.html

Mandatory entries

You have to make the following adjustments in the `config.xml` of an Ionic project:

widget id

In the `<widget>` element, you create an App Reverse Domain ID in the `id` attribute, which is a globally unique identifier for your app. By default, an Ionic app has the ID `io.ionic.starter`. Change this into something like `com.example.myapp`!

version

In the `version` attribute, you assign a full version number in major/minor/patch notation (for example, `1.0.0`). You need to count this version number up every time you update to a Store.

name

In the `<name>` element, give the app a formal name, as it appears on the home screen of a device and in the App Store interfaces, fore example `BoB Tours`.

description / author

The `<description>` and `<author>` elements provide metadata and contact information that can be viewed in the App Store.

Here is an excerpt from the `config.xml` of my BoB Tours app:

```
config.xml
<?xml version='1.0' encoding='utf-8'?>
<widget id="de.dormann.bobtours"
        version="0.0.1"
        xmlns="http://www.w3.org/ns/widgets"
        xmlns:cdv="http://cordova.apache.org/ns/1.0">
    <name>BoB Tours</name>
    <description>The app for the Book "Ionic 5"</description>
    <author email="ionic@andreas-dormann.de" h
            ref="https://ionic.andreas-dormann.de/">Andreas Dormann</author>
    <content src="index.html" />
```

Intent Whitelist

In the `config.xml` you'll find some `allow-intent` elements by default. It is advised to narrow this down based on each app's needs. Without any `<allow-intent>` tags, no requests to external URLs are allowed.

On Android, this equates to sending an intent of type BROWSEABLE.

This whitelist doesn't apply to plugins, only hyperlinks and calls to `window.open()`.

Global Preferences

You can find some `preference` elements. Here you can set different default settings for the app, such as the display duration of the SplashScreen (default is 3000 ms). Details can be found here:

▶ https://cordova.apache.org/docs/en/9.x/config_ref/index.html

Platform elements

When using the CLI to build applications, it is sometimes necessary to specify preferences or other elements specific to a particular platform. Use the `element` to specify configuration that should only appear in a single platform-specific `config.xml` file. A multitude of standard values for icons and splash screens for Android and iOS are already listed there.

12.4 Resources: Icons and Splash Screens

No app without own icon and splash screen. Anyone who has already developed apps with other programming languages knows that creating icons and splash screens for each target platform can be a time-consuming task in all resolutions required. And with the growing number of new different-format devices, this effort has increased even more.

Of course, there are Photoshop templates with automated format output or similar.

With Ionic, that's all a thing of the past. Because the framework itself offers a terminal command with which the creation of icons and splash screens for Android and iOS can be done quickly.

Prerequisite is the following:

- A 1,024x1,024 pixel icon image stored in `resources/icon.png`
- A splash screen graphic with 2,732 x 2,732 pixels, which is stored in `resources/splash.png`. Care must be taken to ensure that the artwork (text and/or logo) is centered within a range of 1,200 x 1,200 pixels within the splash screen graphic.

I have made two downloads for you here:

- https://ionic.andreas-dormann.de/resources/icon.png
- https://ionic.andreas-dormann.de/resources/splash.png

You can copy these files into the project's `resources` folder.

With the terminal command

```
$ ionic cordova resources
```

the generation of the resources is done in seconds.

```
> cordova-res
[cordova-res] Generated 18 resources for android
[cordova-res] Generated 45 resources for ios
[cordova-res] Wrote to config.xml
```

For me that was 18 graphics for the target platform Android and 45 graphics for iOS, which were generated from the two PNG files and then updated `config.xm` to reflect the changes in the generated images.

If you're testing our app in the emulator or on the device, you can be surprised by our new icon and splash screen:

More informations about creating resources for Ionic apps you can find here:

► https://ionicframework.com/docs/cli/commands/cordova-resources

12.5 Deploy & publish for Android

Let's start by typing

```
$ ionic cordova platform add android
```

Similarly to the web build process (see "12.2 The web build process", starting from page 512), this command creates a new folder for Android in the `platforms` folder.

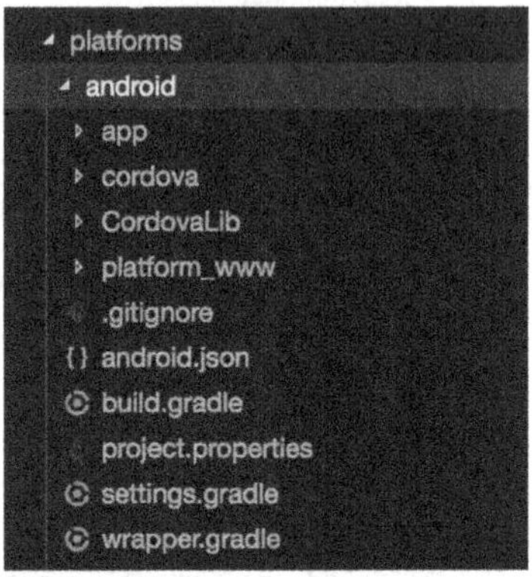

We can now build for the device:

```
$ ionic cordova build android
```

We get more new folders and files. We are especially interested in the APK file:

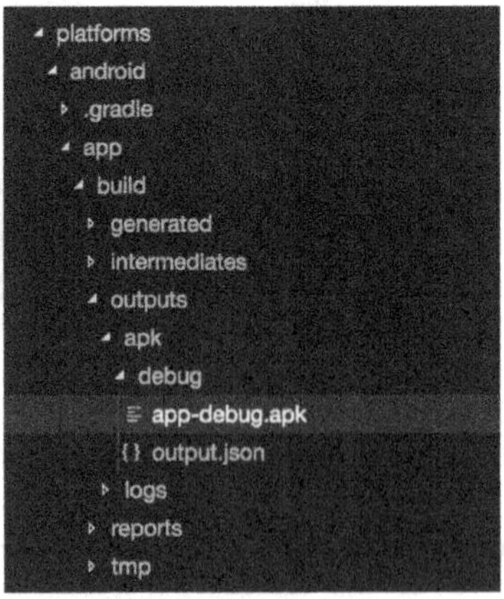

Under the path `platforms/android/app/build/outputs/apk/debug/` we get the `app-debug.apk` file. That's the debug version of our app.

Production build

To get a release build we use additionally the `--prod` and `-release` options:

```
$ ionic cordova build android --prod --release
```

Under `platforms/android/app/build/outputs/apk/` we now find the folder `release` with a file named `app-release-unsigned.apk`:

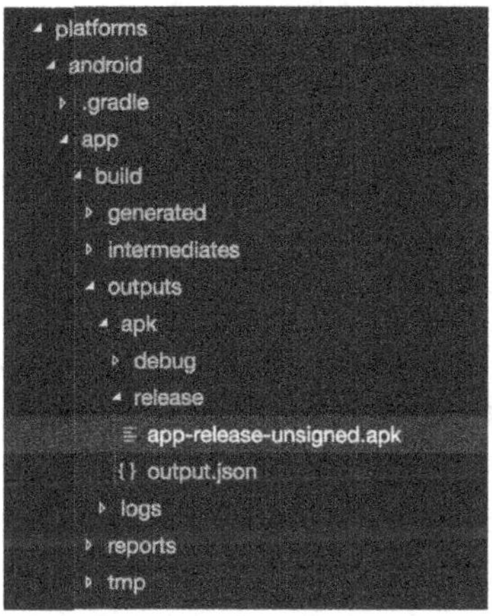

This will minify our app's code as Ionic's source and also remove any debugging capabilities from the APK (short for: Android Package Kit). This is generally used when deploying an app to the Google Play Store.

Hint: An alternative workflow is the use of Ionic's new Capacitor (see "B2. Ionic and Capacitor", starting from page 565).

Sign Android APK

If we want to release our app in the Google Play Store, we have to sign our APK file. To do this, we have to create a new `certificate/keystore`.

Let's generate your private key using the `keytool` command that comes with the Java Development Kit:

```
keytool -genkey -v -keystore my-release-key.jks -keyalg RSA
-keysize 2048 -validity 10000 -alias my-alias
```

You'll first be prompted to create a password for the keystore. Then answer the rest of the questions and when it's all done, you should have a file called `my-release-key.jks` created in the current directory.

Make sure to save this file somewhere safe, if you lose it you won't be able to submit updates to your app!

To sign the unsigned APK, we run the `jarsigner` tool which is also included in the JDK:

```
jarsigner -verbose -sigalg SHA1withRSA -digestalg SHA1 -key-
store my-release-key.jks app-release-unsigned.apk my-alias
```

This signs the APK in place. Finally, we need to run the `zipalign` tool to optimize the APK. The `zipalign` tool can be found in `/path/to/Android/sdk/build-tools/VERSION/zipalign`. For example, on OS X with Android Studio installed, `zipalign` is in `~/Library/Android/sdk/build-tools/VERSION/zipalign`:

```
zipalign -v 4 app-release-unsigned.apk BobTours.apk
```

To verify that our APK is signed we run `apksigner`. The `apksigner` can be also found in the same path as the `zipalign` tool:

```
apksigner verify BobTours.apk
```

Now we have our final release binary called `BobTours.apk` and we can release this on the Google Play Store!

Publish on Google Play

The publishing of an app on Google Play follows these steps:

1. Create a Developer Account
2. Open Play Console
3. Create an Application entry
4. Prepare the Store Listing
5. Create an App Release (to upload the APK)
6. Provide a Content Rating
7. Set up Pricing & Distribution
8. Roll out the app

1. Create a Developer Account

If you don't have one, you need to create a Developer Account. You can easily sign up for one using your existing Google Account. The sign up process is fairly straightforward, and you'll need to pay a one-time registration fee of $25. After you've reviewed and accepted the Developer Distribution Agreement, you can proceed to make the payment using your credit or debit card. To finish the sign up process, fill out all your necessary account details, including your Developer Name, which will be visible to your customers on Google Play.

2. Open Play Console

Sign in to your Play Console at

► https://play.google.com/apps/publish/

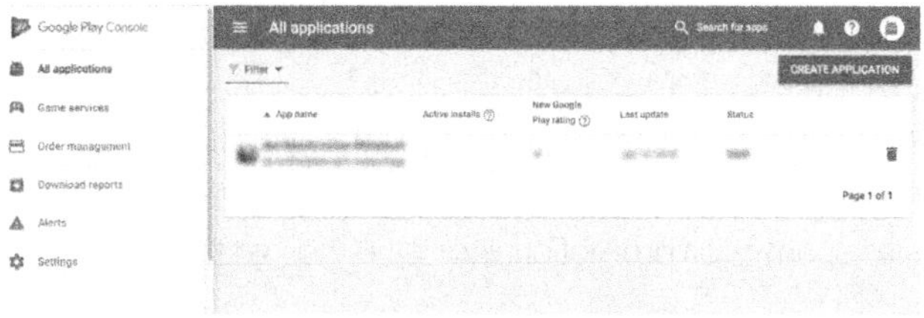

If you want to publish a paid app or plan to sell in-app purchases, you need to create a payments center profile, i.e. a merchant account. You can do that via `Download reports > Financial > Set up a merchant account`. A merchant account will let you you manage your app sales and monthly payouts, as well as analyze your sales reports right in your Play Console.

3. Create an Application entry

Now that you have set up your Play Console, you can finally add your app. Navigate to `All applications` (preselected), click on `Create Application`, select your app's `Default language`, type in a `Title` for your app and click on `Create`.

4. Prepare the Store Listing

Before you can publish your app, you need to prepare its store listing. These are all the details that will show up to customers on your app's listing on Google Play. You don't necessarily have to complete this step before moving on to the next one. You can always save a draft and revisit it later when you're ready to publish.

The information required for your store listing is divided into several categories:

Product details

There are three fields here that you need to fill out:

Field	Description	Character Limit	Notes
Title	Your app's name on Google Play.	50 character limit	You can add one localized title per language.
Short description	The first text users see when looking at your app's detail page on the Play Store app.	80 character limit	Users can expand this text to view your app's full description.
Full description	Your app's description on Google Play.	4000 character limit	

Your app's title and description should be written with a great user experience in mind. Use the right keywords, but don't overdo it. Make sure your app doesn't come across as spam-y or promotional, or it will risk getting suspended.

Graphic assets

Under graphic assets, you can add screenshots, images, videos, promotional graphics, and icons that showcase your app's features and functionality. Some parts under graphic assets are mandatory, like screenshots, a feature graphic, and a high resolution icon. Others are optional, but you can add them to make your app look more attractive to users.

Here are some hints for creating the many graphical assets: Screenshots are easiest to create from the Chrome DevTools (`More options > Capture full size screenshot`). Note the maximum aspect ratio of 2:1! A helpful tool for creating icons is certainly Image Asset Studio, which is part of Android Studio.

Make sure that the collection of your screenshots provides a good overview of the different features of your app. For our BoB Tours app I did it like this (using Dev-Tools' `Pixel 2` settings):

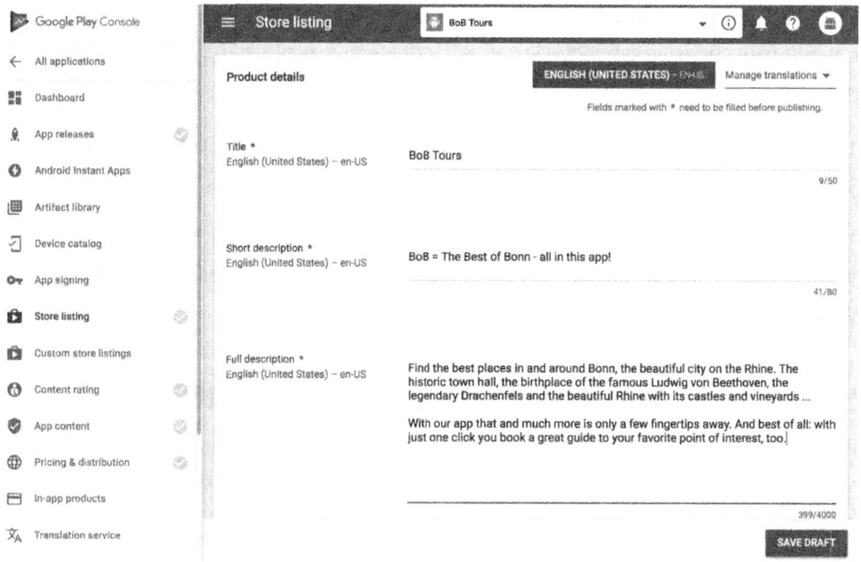

You can read more about the specific requirements for each graphic asset here:

► https://play.google.com/apps/publish/

Categorization

This part requires you to select the appropriate type and category your app belongs to. From the drop-down menu, you can pick either `Application` or `Game` for the application type. There are various categories for each type of app available on the Play Store. Pick the one your app fits into best. In order to rate your content, you'll need to upload an APK first. You can skip this step for later.

Contact Details

This part requires you to enter contact details to offer your customers access to support regarding your app. You can add multiple contact channels here, like an email, website, and phone number, but providing a contact email is mandatory for publishing an app.

Privacy Policy

For apps that request access to sensitive user data or permissions, you need to enter a comprehensive privacy policy that effectively discloses how your app collects, uses, and shares that data.

You must add a URL linking to your privacy policy in your store listing and within your app. Make sure the link is active and relevant to your app.

You're now done with the store listing. Go ahead and click on `Save Draft` to save your details. You can always skip some steps and come back to them later before you publish your app.

5. Create an App Release (to upload the APK)

Now that you have prepared the ground to finally upload your app, it's time to upload our signed APK file. Google offers you multiple ways to upload and release an APK.

Our starting point is the menu entry `App release` on the left side.

Here, you need to select the type of release you want to upload your first app version to. You can choose between

- an internal test track
- a closed track
- an open track
- a production release.

The first three releases allow you to test out your app among a selected group of users before you make it go live for everyone to access. This is a safer option because you can analyze the test results and optimize or fix your app accordingly if you need to before rolling it out to all users.

However, if you create a production release, your uploaded app version will become accessible to everyone in the countries you choose to distribute it in.

Once you've picked an option, click on `Manage` and then `Create release`.

Next, follow the on-screen instructions to add your APK files, and name and describe your release.

6. Provide a Content Rating

If you don't assign a rating to your app, it will be listed as 'Unrated'. Apps that are 'Unrated' may get removed from Google Play. To rate your app, you need to fill out a content rating questionnaire. You can access it when you select your app in the Play Console, and navigate to 'Store presence' – 'Content rating' on the left menu.

Make sure you enter accurate information. Misrepresentation of your app's content can lead to suspension or removal from the Play Store. An appropriate content rating will also help you get to the right audience, which will eventually improve your engagement rates.

7. Set up Pricing & Distribution

Before you can fill out the details required in this step, you need to determine your app's monetization strategy. Once you know how your app is going to make money, you can go ahead and set up your app as free or paid. Remember, you can always change your app from paid to free later, but you cannot change a free app to paid. For that, you'll need to create a new app and set its price. You can also choose the countries you wish to distribute your app in, and opt-in to distribute to specific Android devices and programs too.

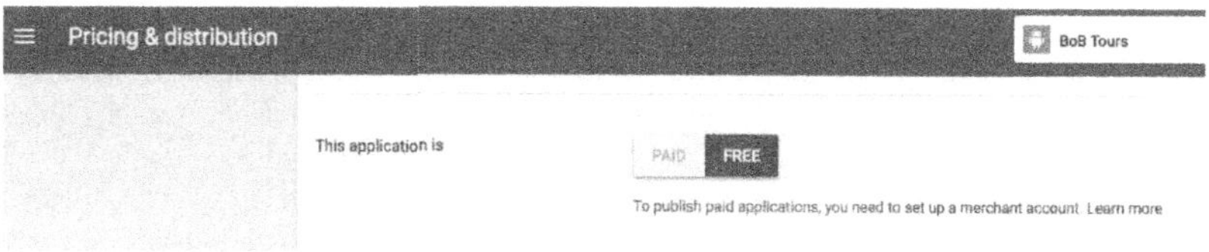

8. Roll out the app

You're almost done. The final step involves reviewing and rolling out your release after making sure you've taken care of everything else. Before you review and roll-out your release, make sure the store listing, content rating, and pricing and distribution sections of your app each have a green check mark next to them.

Once you're sure you've filled out those details, select your app and navigate to `App releases`, press `Manage` and `Edit release` next to your desired release, for example `Production`, and review it.

Next, click on `Review` to be taken to the `Review and rollout release` screen. Here, you can see if there are any issues or warnings you might have missed out on.

Finally, select `Confirm rollout`. This will publish your app to all users in your target countries on Google Play.

More about publishing an Android app on Google Play you can read here:

- https://support.google.com/googleplay/android-developer

12.6 Deploy & publish for iOS (on a Mac)

Open terminal on a Mac and type

```
$ ionic cordova platform add ios
```

Similarly to the web build process (see "12.2 The web build process", starting from page 512), this command creates a new folder for iOS in the `platforms` folder. It takes a few minutes to install and configure the iOS platform.

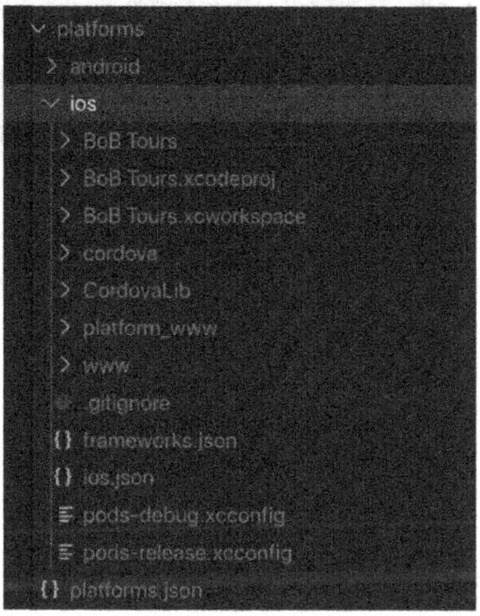

From here, you can open the `.xcworkspace` file in `./platforms/ios/` to start Xcode and debug the app within this IDE.

We can also build for the device:

```
$ ionic cordova build ios
```

Maybe you get an error like this:

```
CordovaError: Promise rejected with non-error:
'Cordova needs xcodebuild version 9.0.0 or greater,
you have version 8.1.0.
Please install version 9.0.0 or greater from App Store'
    at cli.catch.err (/usr/local/lib/node_modules/cordova/bin/
    cordova:29:15)
    at process._tickCallback (internal/process/next_tick.js:68:7)
```

Then you use an older version of Xcode and should update to version 9.0.0 or greater, as this message says.

If everything goes well, we get a new `build` folder.

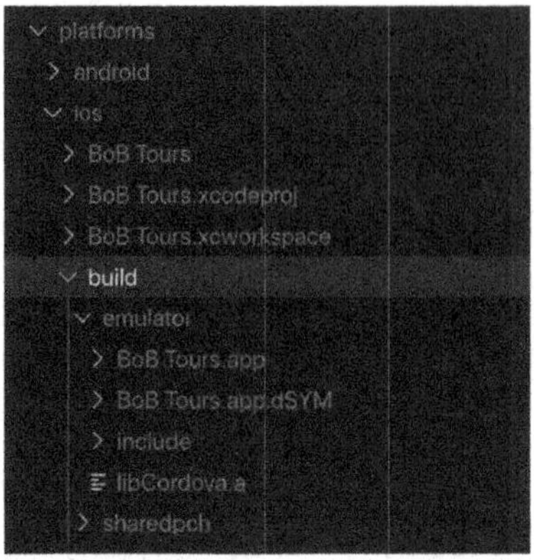

Under the path `platforms/ios/build/emulator/` we get the `BoB Tours.app` file. That's the version of our app we can test and debug in the emulator (see "11.4 Emulator / Simulator", starting from page 484). Because we previously ran the platform add and build processes, with typing

```
$ native-run ios --app "platforms/ios/build/emulator/BoB Tours.app"
```

we can directly start the app on the iOS simulator.

Production build

To get a release build we use additionally the `--prod` option:

```
$ ionic cordova build ios --prod
```

This will generate the minified code for the web portion of an app and copy it over the iOS code base.

From here, you can open the `.xcworkspace` file in `./platforms/ios/` to start the app in Xcode to prepare it for publication. For details read the next division.

Hint: An alternative workflow is the use of Ionic's new Capacitor (see "B2. Ionic and Capacitor", starting from page 565).

Publish on App Store

To publish an app on Apple's App Store, follow these steps:

1. Create a Developer Account
2. Create development and distribution certificates in Xcode
3. Create an App ID in the Developer Account
4. Create a new App Store entry in App Store Connect
5. Register a new Provisioning Profile
6. Download the Provisioning Profile with Xcode
7. Create an archive and uploading the app
8. Wait for Review

1. Create a Developer Account

First, make sure you are an Apple developer. To become one, you need an Apple ID and $99 for a single license (Apple Developer Program) or $299 for a corporate license (Enterprise Program).

More informations about Apple's developer memberships you can find here:

► https://developer.apple.com/de/support/compare-memberships

2. Create development and distribution certificates

Open the `.xcworkspace` file in `./platforms/ios/` to open your Xcode project generated by `ionic cordova build ios -prod`.

Go to `Xcode > Preferences... > Accounts`. If you see no account currently, add one by clicking on the + button in the lower left corner and login to your Apple developer account with your Apple ID.

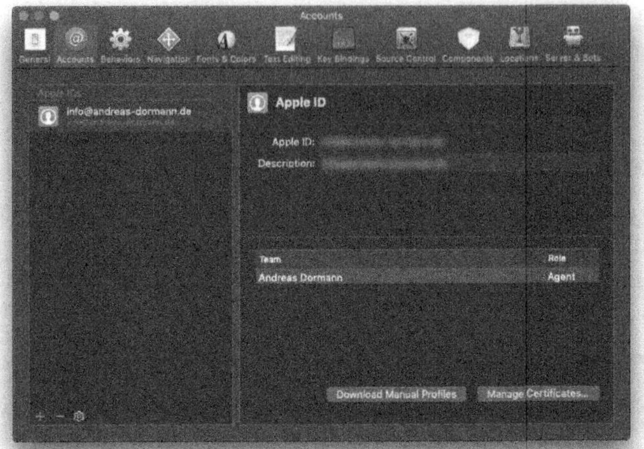

Click on `Manage Certificates...`, then on the + button in the lower left corner and then click on `iOS Distribution`. You can repeat this step for `iOS Development` for the dev build of your app.

After finishing these step you can close this Xcode dialog.

3. Create an App ID in the Developer Account

Open your Apple Developer Account and switch to the section `Identifiers`. Click the blue + icon in the header, choose `App IDs` and click `Continue`.

Give your new app a descriptive name and put in the `Bundle ID`. This must necessarily be exactly the same reverse domain name you set up in your Ionic `config.xml` file (see "Fehler: Referenz nicht gefunden12.3 config.xml", starting from page 520). Then hit the `Continue` button. In the next screen, make sure everything is correct and click the `Register` button.

4. Create a new App Store entry in App Store Connect

Switch to App Store Connect. If you're already within your Apple Developer Account simply select `AppStore Connect` (in the navigation area on the left) and click `Go to App Store Connect`.

App Information

In App Store Connect, from the upper menu select `My Apps`.

In the `My Apps` area click the + button on the top left corner to add a new entry.

As platform select `iOS`. Type in the `Name` for the app as it will appear on the App Store. This can't be longer than 30 characters. Choose the `Primary Language`. If localized app information isn't available in an App Store territory, the information from your primary language will be used instead. More informations about localizing can read here:

▶ https://help.apple.com/app-store-connect/#/deve6f78a8e2

Select your app's `Bundle ID` (see step 3). Type in a `SKU` (Stock Keeping Unit). It's a unique ID for your app that isn't visible on the App Store. Maybe you use the Bundle ID again.

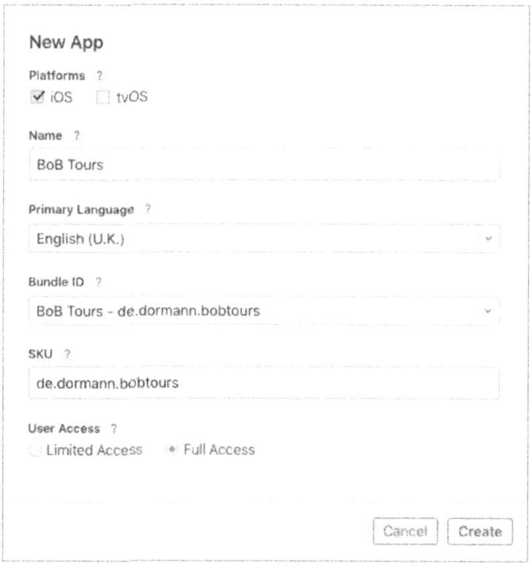

Click `Create`. On the next page you can correct the entries, if necessary.

A word to the app's rating: Based on your application's content and functionality, it is given a rating. This rating isn't only useful for telling users about your application's content and features, but is also used by the operating system for the parental controls features.

It's strongly recommended that you don't try to outsmart the rating system. Apple is well aware of this strategy and will reject your application if it doesn't agree with the rating that you have set. There are many other things here that you may need to adjust based on your app, but we won't go over them since they are pretty self-explanatory.

Pricing and Availability

Switch to `Pricing and availability`. In this area you specify your application's price and availability. Apple works with price tiers so that you don't have to specify a price for each country that Apple operates in. You can also specify in which stores your application should - or shouldn't - be available.

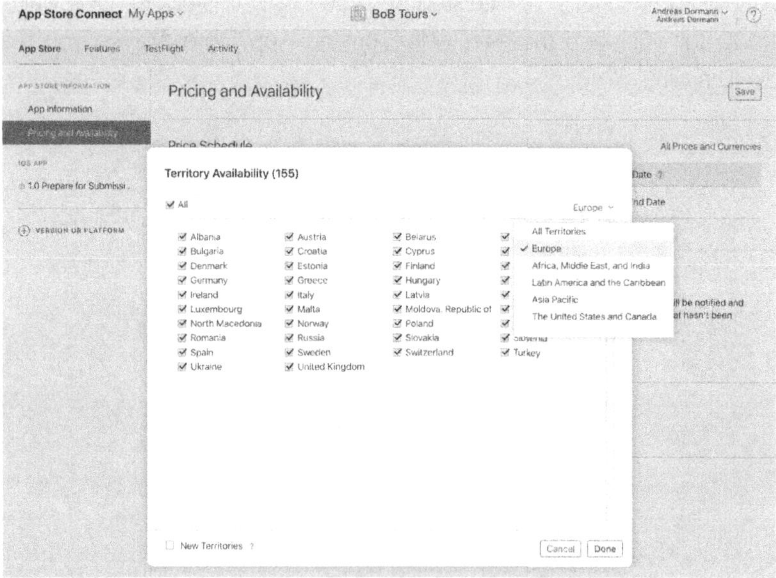

The information that you enter in this step can be modified once your application is live in the App Store. In other words, you can change the price and availability of an application without having to submit an update.

Prepare for Submission

Switch to the `Prepare for Submission` section.

Here you add app previews and screenshots. Screenshots must be in the `JPG` or `PNG` format, and in the RGB color space. App previews (videos) must be in the `M4V`, `MP4`, or `MOV` format and can't exceed 500 MB.

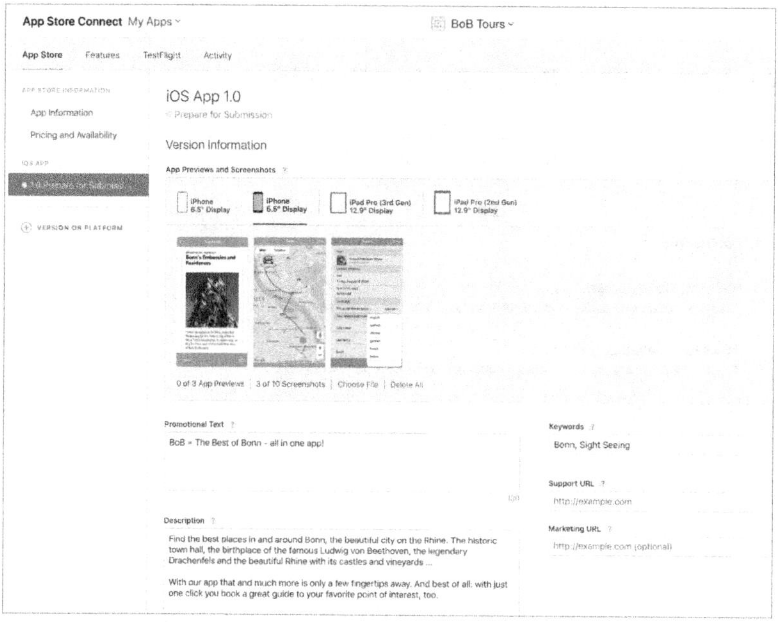

Hint: Starting March 2019, all new apps and app updates for iPhone, including universal apps, will require `iPhone 11/Pro and XS/XR Max` screenshots.

Device	Screenshots	App Previews
6.5-Inch Super Retina Display (iPhone XS Max, iPhone XR)	1242 x 2688 pixels (portrait) 2688 x 1242 pixels (landscape)	886 x 1920 pixels (portrait) 1920 x 886 pixels (landscape) (19.5:9 apect ratio)

Here you can read more about the specifications for all screenshot and preview formats:

- https://help.apple.com/app-store-connect/#/devd274dd925
- https://help.apple.com/app-store-connect/#/dev4e413fcb8

Fill in all other informations, such as `Promotional Text`, `Description` and `Keywords`.

You must also provide an App Store icon, which is used to represent your app in different sections of the App Store. Follow the Human Interface Guidelines when creating your App Store icon:

▶ https://developer.apple.com/design/human-interface-guidelines/

5. Register a new Provisioning Profile

Switch to the section `Profiles`. Click the blue + icon in the header and select the desired profile. You can choose between:

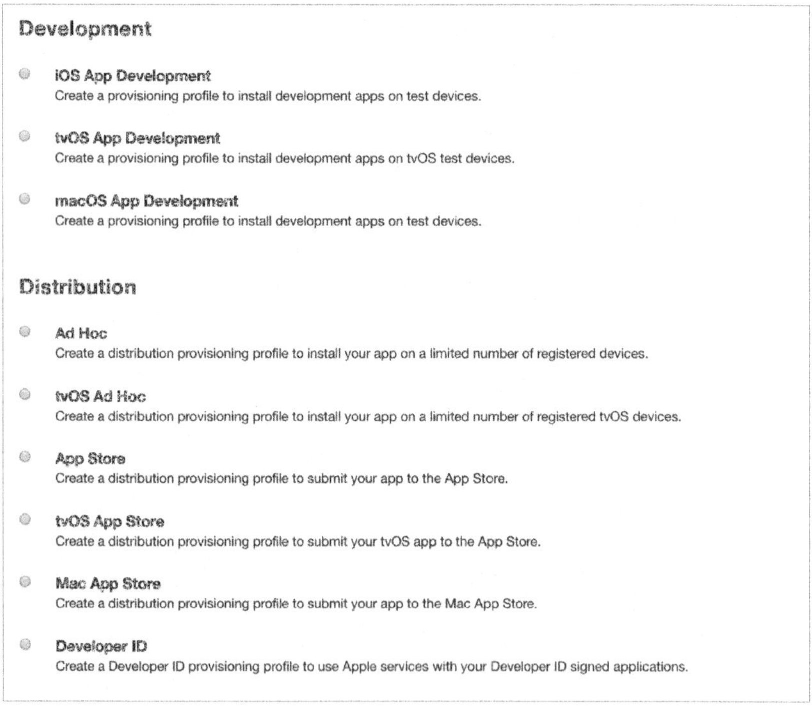

The individual options are briefly explained on the page. For testing you can use `iOS App Development` (without registration of the devices) or `Ad Hoc` (with registration of a limited number of test devices). For a publication in the store, of course, fits the option `AppStore`.

Click `Continue`.

Then select the matching `App ID` and click `Continue`.

Now select the matching certificate and click `Continue`.

Then select devices (only after choosing a development option above) and click `Continue`.

Finally type in a `Provisioning Profile Name` and click `Generate`.

6. Download the Provisioning Profile with Xcode

Go back to Xcode or re-start it. Select `Xcode > Preferences... > Accounts`.

Select your Apple ID and your team, then select `Download Manual Profiles`.

Go to `~/Library/MobileDevice/Provisioning Profiles/` and your profiles should be there. Install the particular profile with a double click on your Mac.

7. Create an archive and uploading the app

In Xcode, choose a target from the Scheme toolbar. For iOS, choose `Generic iOS Device`. Otherwise, choose a real device from the `Scheme` toolbar menu and connect your Mac with this real device.

Important: You can't create an archive if the device is set to a simulator!

Choose `Product > Archive`. If the archive builds successfully, it appears in the `Archives organizer`. (To open the `Archives organizer`, choose `Window > Organizer` and click `Archives`.)

Then, you can click `Distribute App` to submit your app.

Select a method of distribution:

- **iOS App Store** – Distribute through the App Store
- **Ad Hoc** – Install on designated devices
- **Enterprise** – Distribute to your organization
- **Development** – Distribute to members of your team

Click `Next` and select `Upload` (to send the app to the App Store Connect) or `Export` (to sign and export the app without uploading). Click `Next` again and follow the further instructions.

8. Wait for Review

If all went well so far, the application binary is then uploaded to Apple's servers. During this process, your application is also validated. If an error occurs during the validation, the submission process will fail. The validation process is very useful as it will tell you if there is something wrong with your application binary that would otherwise result in a rejection by the App Store review team.

If the submission process went without problems, your application's status will change to `Waiting for Review`. It takes several days for Apple to review your app, and the time it takes tends to fluctuate over time.

Conclusion

The submission process is quite lengthy for a new application, but submitting an update to the App Store is much less cumbersome. Keep in mind that the submission process is much more involved if your application is localized in various languages as your application's metadata needs to be localized as well. However, localizing your application is well worth the effort as it often results in higher sales and positive customer feedback.

12.7 Deploy & publish for Desktop with Electron

Building a desktop app with Ionic allows developers to reuse 100% of their code and ship a traditional desktop app while still having access to all the native device features, like push notifications.

The connection of Ionic to the desktop world is created by *Electron*.

▶ https://electronjs.org/

Electron enables you to create desktop applications with pure JavaScript by providing a runtime with rich native (operating system) APIs. You could see it as a variant of the Node.js runtime that is focused on desktop applications instead of web servers.

This doesn't mean Electron is a JavaScript binding to graphical user interface (GUI) libraries. Instead, Electron uses web pages as its GUI, so you could also see it as a minimal Chromium browser, controlled by JavaScript.

Creating a typical Electron app is platform dependent, which means that a Windows desktop app can only be created on a Windows system, a MacOS desktop app on a Mac only.

The following hints assume familiarity with Electron, and don't go into "how" to build an electron app. For that, check out the official Electron guide:

► https://electronjs.org/docs/tutorial/first-app

MacOS App

Requirements

There are two hard requirements for publishing an app on the macOS app store

- latest version of Xcode
- an active developer account (see "12.6 Deploy & publish for iOS (on a Mac)", section "1. Create a Developer Account", on page 535).

Publishing

The Electron team has a detailed guide on how to publish an app for macOS. Please review the docs here:

► https://electronjs.org/docs/tutorial/mac-app-store-submission-guide

Windows App

Requirements

There are two hard requirements for publishing an app on the Windows app store

- Windows 10 with Anniversary Update (released August 2nd, 2016)
- Windows 10 SDK, download here:
  - ► https://developer.microsoft.com/en-us/windows/downloads/windows-10-sdk
- Node
- electron-windows-store CLI

`electron-windows-store` can be installed via `npm`:

```
$ npm install -g electron-windows-store
```

Publishing

Like MacOS, Electron has a detailed guide on how to publish an app for Windows. Please review the docs here:

- https://electronjs.org/docs/tutorial/windows-store-guide

Building Electron Apps with Capacitor

A whole new way (at the time of going to print this book) to create Electron desktop apps is *Capacitor* (see also "B2. Ionic and Capacitor", starting from page 565).

- https://capacitor.ionicframework.com/docs/

Capacitor is a cross-platform app runtime that makes it easy to build web apps that run natively on iOS, Android, Electron, and the web. It was created by the Ionic team. They call these apps "Native Progressive Web Apps" and want them to represent the next evolution beyond Hybrid apps.

Capacitor has preliminary support for Electron. At the time of going to print this book, Electron support for Capacitor was in preview, and lagged behind iOS, Android, and Web support.

I recommend to read the documentation of the Ionic team here:

- https://capacitor.ionicframework.com/docs/electron

12.8 Deploy & publish Progressive Web Apps

Because Ionic Apps are built with web technologies, they can run just as well as a Progressive Web App (PWA) as they can a native app.

A few words about PWAs

Many experts say PWAs are the future of web and apps because they combine the best of both worlds: fast and powerful web applications that offer the benefits of native apps and can be installed on mobile devices and desktops.

A PWA is a website that has been programmed in a very specific way and can offer certain functions that normal websites can't offer: they can be installed on a mobile phone, tablet or desktop; they load much faster than normal websites and they also work offline.

The concept has existed since 2003, but only in recent years, thanks to the latest standards in web development, are Progressive Web Apps actually being used - and growing!

Especially for someone who doesn't come from the field of web development or programming, it can be difficult to understand the functionality and meaning behind a Progressive Web App (PWA). Therefore, in the following I'll try to explain everything about the PWA, its functions and its advantages as simply as possible.

What are the advantages of a PWA?

Mainly a PWA has the following three advantages:

- **Installable**: PWAs can be installed with one or two clicks on cell phones, tablets or desktops, making them work (almost) like normal apps.
- **Offline**: PWAs also work offline. Even if you don't have internet, you can easily work with the PWA. The PWA doesn't run like other web apps on the server, but directly on your device.
- **Faster**: The PWA loads everything or almost everything that it needs to work, the very first time you call or install it. Thus, it can be loaded much faster for any further use. The data that needs to be retrieved from the Internet and that can't be stored is retrieved in the background so that the user can continue working while the data is being synchronized.

What's the difference between PWA and app?

In short, the big difference is that PWAs are executed in the browser (just like normal websites). Even if a PWA is installed on a device like a smartphone and the look and feel exactly matches that of an app - it runs in the background in the browser.

The fact that a PWA is executed in the browser has some consequences. For example, there are often limits to the amount of disk space you can use on the device, or there are limits to what features of the device you can access.

With better standards and developments in web and app development, the differences between PWAs and apps are shrinking. Nowadays, many apps are no longer "normal" apps, but so-called "apps", which are ultimately executed in the browser, but in a different way so that they don't have such limitations as a PWA.

What's the difference between PWA, a website or a web app?

A PWA is a website or web app. So there is no difference at first. However, PWAs can offer *extra features* like the ones I've already mentioned about the benefits.

What is the difference between a PWA and a hybrid app?

Above, I said that hybrid apps are also running in the browser. What is the difference between the two? Very easily:

PWAs only need a browser for them to work, since they are ultimately websites. They use only "web technologies". They have certain restrictions on what they can do with the device and can't be installed through the App Store.

Hybrid apps, on the other hand, are websites that are programmed in combination with certain native app technologies and combined in one app. They use "web and native app technologies" and are thus hardly distinguishable from normal apps. They barely have any restrictions on what they can do on the device they're installed on and can be installed through their app store.

Why should I choose a PWA?

An overview of the statistics clearly shows why PWAs are the best option for certain projects. According to a comScore Mobile Metrix study in 2017, tablet and mobile users spend 87% of their time on apps and 13% on websites. This means that users clearly prefer apps to websites. The problem is, that statistics also show that 80% of the time people spend on apps, they spend with the top 3 apps. Likewise, on average, each user installs almost no new apps a month, but visits over 100 websites.

Here's what we can conclude: Users want an app, but it's hard to get them to install it. Therefore, a PWA is the absolute right solution! They may not be able to search and install the App in the App Store, but they will definitely visit your website shortly. And then, as soon as they visit them, the browser shows a button to install the app or PWA. With just a quick visit to your website and with no more than 1 or 2 clicks, the user already has the app!

And even if the users don't install the app, the PWA will be stored in the browser's cache, so everything will go super fast for future visits. And here I come to other statistics: According to a study by Google 40% of users leave sites that take more than 3 seconds to load before they are fully loaded.

Who supports the technologies behind PWAs?

Almost all "Internet Big Players" are behind PWAs:

- **Google** is very strong in the use of PWAs with many tutorials and open source docs to support the developers:
  ▶ https://developers.google.com/web/progressive-web-apps/
- In the meantime, **Microsoft** has made it possible to install PWAs under Windows 10 directly via the Microsoft Store, but it also supports developers with its own tools:
  ▶ https://developer.microsoft.com/en-us/windows/pwa
- And last but not least, Apple has silently added basic support for PWAs on iOS:
  ▶ https://brainhub.eu/blog/pwa-on-ios-13/

Also check out Ionic's PWA overview for more info:

▶ https://ionicframework.com/pwa

Starting a new app with the PWA Toolkit

Starting an app with the PWA Toolkit is incredibly easy:

```
npx create-stencil ionic-pwa
```

Congrats! You now have a high performing, great looking PWA starter app that scores 100 on Lighthouse, right out-of-the-box!

Making an Ionic app a PWA

The two main requirements of a PWA are a *Service Worker* and a *Web Manifest*. While it's possible to add both of these to an app manually, the Angular team has an `@angular/pwa` package that can be used to automate this.

The `@angular/pwa` package will automatically add a service worker and a app manifest to the app. To add this package to the app run:

```
$ ng add @angular/pwa
```

Once this package has been added run `ionic build --prod` and the `www` directory will be ready to deploy as a PWA.

Note: By default, the `@angular/pwa` package comes with Angular logo for the app icons. Be sure to update the manifest to use the correct app name and also replace the icons.

If an app is being deployed to other channels such as Cordova or Electron, you can remove the `"serviceWorker": true` flag from the `angular.json` file. The service worker can be generated though by running:

```
$ ionic build --prod --service-worker
```

Note: Features like Service Workers and many JavaScript APIs (such as geolocation) require the app be hosted in a secure context. When deploying an app through a hosting service, be aware that HTTPS will be required to take full advantage of Service Workers.

Deploying via Firebase

Firebase hosting provides many benefits for Progressive Web Apps, including fast response times thanks to CDN's, HTTPS enabled by default, and support for HTTP2 push.

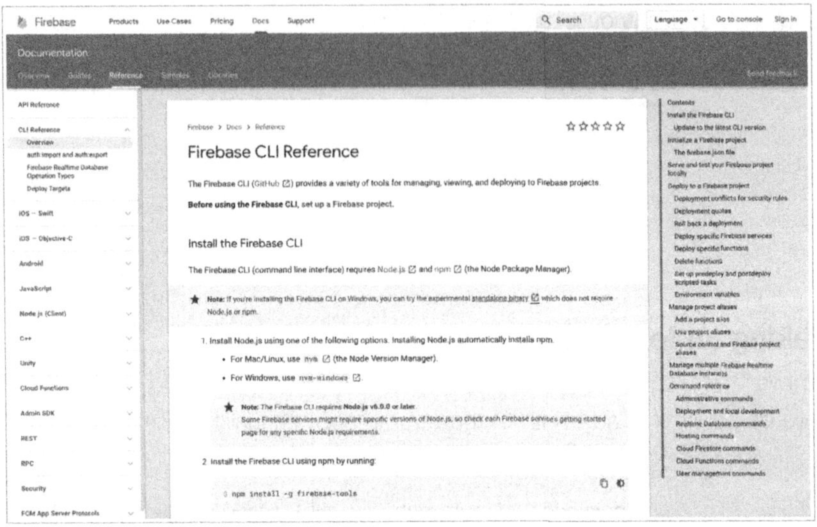

First, install the Firebase CLI:

```
$ npm install -g firebase-tools
```

The Firebase CLI provides a variety of tools for managing, viewing, and deploying to Firebase projects.

With the Firebase CLI installed run

```
$ firebase init
```

in the project. This will generate a `firebase.json` config file and configure the app for deployment.

Note: `firebase init` will present a few questions, including one about redirecting URLs to `/index.html`. Make sure to choose `yes` for this option, but `no` to over-writing your `index.html`. This will ensure that routing, hard reload, and deep linking work in the app.

The last thing needed is to make sure caching headers are being set correctly. To do this, add the following snippet to the `firebase.json` file to the hosting property:

```
"headers": [
  {
    "source": "/build/app/**",
    "headers": [
      {
        "key": "Cache-Control",
        "value": "public, max-age=31536000"
      }
    ]
  },
  {
    "source": "sw.js",
    "headers": [
      {
        "key": "Cache-Control",
        "value": "no-cache"
      }
    ]
  }
]
```

The app can now be deployed by running

```
$ firebase deploy
```

After this the app will be live.

For more information about the Firebase CLI and all `firebase.json` properties, see the Firebase documentation:

- https://firebase.google.com/docs/cli
- https://firebase.google.com/docs/hosting/full-config#section-firebase-json

Will someone be able to easily copy-paste the build code and create the same web app in a few clicks?

In my seminars, I am asked this question again and again. So a few words in reply: When somebody accesses a web app with a browser, they can read all the JavaScript files that the browser downloads to run that application.

The most popular way to use app development frameworks is with a compiler/transpiler such as Babel (https://babeljs.io/) or Closure Compiler (see "1.1 The idea behind Ionic" on page 8). What this means is that when deployed the web application's JavaScript files undergo a deep transformation to be compatible with earlier standards of the language. There are other typical transformations in the build phase, such that the resulting JavaScript files are very obfuscated and extremely hard to read for humans.

For example, look at this JS file excerpt created by `ionic build --prod`:

```
(window.webpackJsonp=window.webpackJsonp||[]).push([[2],
{FH5X:function(t,e,i){"use strict";i.r(e),i.d(e,"create",func-
tion(){return h});var s=/(^-?\d*\.?\d*)(.*)/,r={translateX:1,t
ranslateY:1,translateZ:1,scale:1,scaleX:1,scaleY:1,scaleZ:1,ro
tate:1,rotateX:1,rotateY:1,rotateZ:1,skewX:1,skewY:1,perspecti
ve:1},n="undefined"!=typeof window?window:{},o=n.requestAnima-
tionFrame?n.requestAnimationFrame.bind(n):function(t){return t
(Date.now())} [...]
i=t;e<i.length;e++)i[e].destroy();this._clearAsync(),this._el-
ements&&(this._elements.length=0),this._readCallbacks&&(this._
readCallbacks.length=0),this._writeCallbacks&&(this._writeCall
backs.length=0),this.parent=void 0,this._childAnimations&&(thi
s._childAnimations.length=0),this._onFinishCallbacks&&(this._o
nFinishCallbacks.length=0),this._onFinishOneTimeCallbacks&&(th
is._onFinishOneTimeCallbacks.length=0)},t.prototype._transEl=f
unction(){var t=this._childAnimations;if(t)for(var e=0,i=t;e<i
.length;e++){var s=i[e]._transEl();if(s)return s}return this._
hasTweenEffect&&this._hasDur&&void 0!==this._elements&&this._e
lements.length>0?this._elements[0]:null},t}();function h(t,e,i
){return t?t(a,e,i):Promise.resolve(new a)}}}]); [...]
```

Also note that only client-side code is visible to your users. All the logic of an application which is server-side won't be exposed.

12.9 Ionic Appflow

Ionic Appflow is a continuous integration (CI) and continuous deployment (CD) platform for Ionic development teams. Appflow helps development teams continuously build and ship their iOS, Android, and web apps faster than ever.

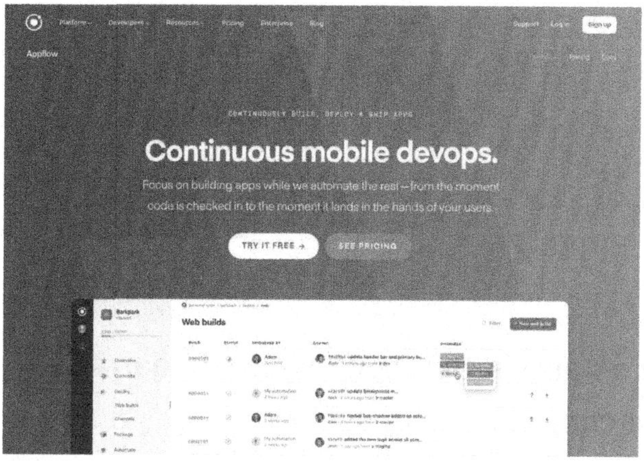

Appflow is offered in several paid versions:

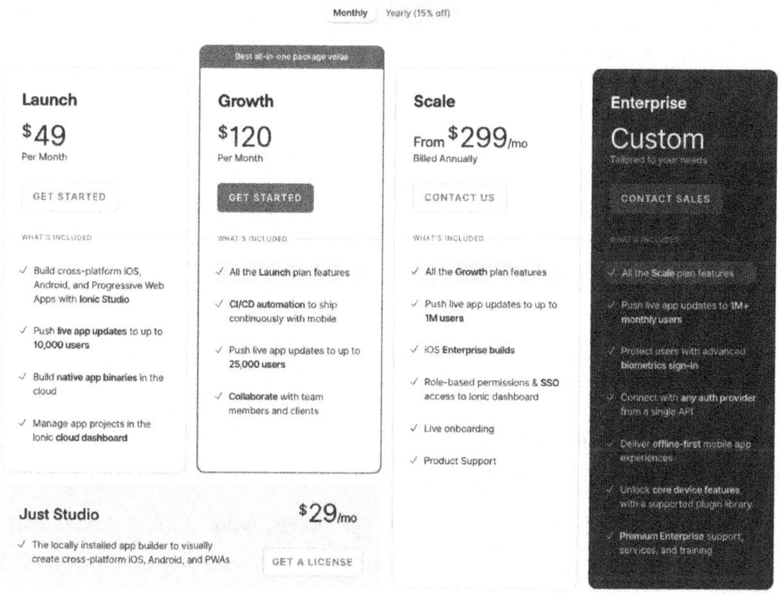

The following pages walks you through the process of setting up your application with Ionic Appflow (free Starter version), including how to connect your application to Appflow, how to set up the Appflow SDK (Deploy plugin) for live updates, and how to configure your first automated Android and iOS builds using native build environments.

I describe the whole thing using our already created BoB Tours app.

What we'll do:

1. Create an app in the Appflow Dashboard and connecting it to a repository
2. Install the Appflow SDK
3. Commit to Appflow
4. Deploy a Live Update

1. Create an app in the Appflow Dashboard and connecting it to a repository

First, log in to the Appflow Dashboard. You can reach this via the following page:

► https://dashboard.ionicframework.com/login

Switch to the `Apps` section. Click `Create a New App` (on the bottom – you'll only see this button, if you don't have any apps yet) or `Add App` (on the right side).

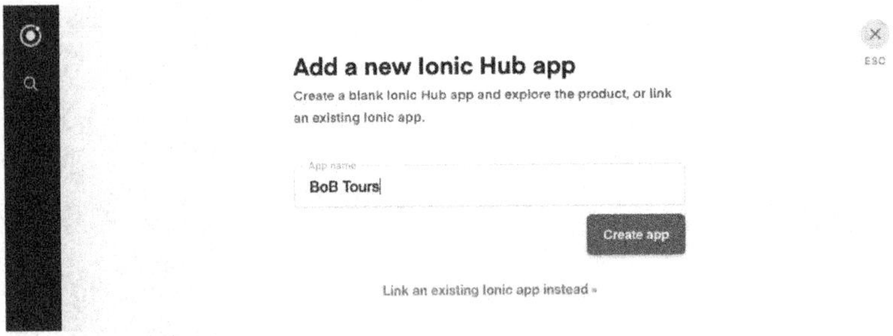

Enter a name for your app and click `Create app` (if you want to create a blank Ionic Hub app) or `Link an existing Ionic app instead`. I click the latter here.

Now we'll need to decide how Appflow will access your source code. The Ionic team suggests using GitHub, Bitbucket, or Bitbucket Server if you're using them already. The integration with these services are easy to configure and you'll get some additional benefits like being able to view the commits your builds came from and the changes on your Git remote.

If you're not using one of these providers, you can also choose to push directly to Ionic. But: Ionic git isn't intended to be a Git host and the Ionic team strongly suggests using GitHub, Bitbucket or another official git hosting service to backup your source code repository.

To keep it simple here, I use GitHub. There I've already created a repository for the BoB Tours app (you'll find many instructions on how to create a GitHub repository on the web).

I navigate to `Settings > Git > GitHub` on the Appflow Dashboard. If this is your first time connecting (like me) you'll need to click the `Connect to GitHub` button.

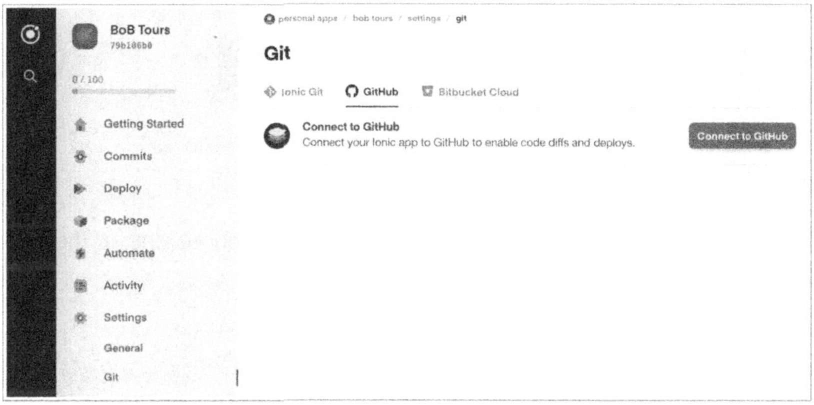

Then I choose the repository to link from the list of available repos.

Linking the repository creates a web-hook for the repository and sends events to Appflow. So Appflow has access to any commits that are pushed to this repository.

Here you can read more about connecting your repo:

► https://ionicframework.com/docs/appflow/quickstart/connect

2. Install the Appflow SDK

In order to take advantage of some of the best Appflow features, like deploying live updates to your app and bypassing the app stores, we'll need to install the Appflow SDK (also known as the Ionic Deploy plugin). The Appflow SDK comes with Ionic Appflow's Deploy feature for detecting and syncing an app with updates that you've pushed to channels. Channels make it easy to deploy different versions of your app in different places. They're useful for testing and sharing early builds with stakeholders, as well as updating devices with new versions of code on the fly.

We switch to `Deploy > Channels` on the Appflow Dashboard. There are already to channels created: **Master** and **Production**.

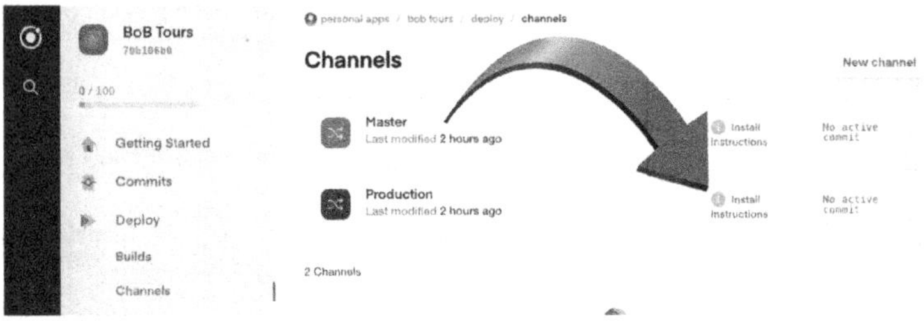

In the next dialog I click `Install Instructions` and choose one of the offered update options for my app:

I copy the code form the dialog and run it in terminal in my apps directory.

```
$ ionic deploy add \
$ --app-id="MY_APP_ID" \
$ --channel-name="Production" \
$ --update-method="background"
```

A little explanation of the code:

`--app-id` is the ID of the app in Ionic Appflow.

`--channel-name` is the name of the Channel you'd like the app to listen to for updates.

`--update-method` is one of `background | auto | none`. This determines how your application responds when a new live update is available for download.

Here you can read more about the available plugin variables:

▶ https://ionicframework.com/docs/appflow/deploy/api#plugin-variables

Now I've installed the plugin and commit the changes to `config.xml` and `package.json`:

```
$ git add .
$ git commit -m "Added Appflow SDK"
```

Here you can read more about installing the Appflow SDK:

▶ https://ionicframework.com/docs/appflow/quickstart/installation

3. Commit to Appflow

In order for Appflow to access your code base you'll need to push a commit so that it shows up in your Dashboard.

If you are using an integration with GitHub, Bitbucket or Bitbucket Server, a new commit will show up every time you push to your git host.

If you are using Ionic as your git remote, you'll need to push to your commit to Appflow directly to see your commit in the Dashboard.

To transfer my changes (from the master branch) to my GitHub repo, I type:

```
$ git push origin master
```

Once you've done a `git push`, you should see your commit available in the `Commits` tab of the Dashboard:

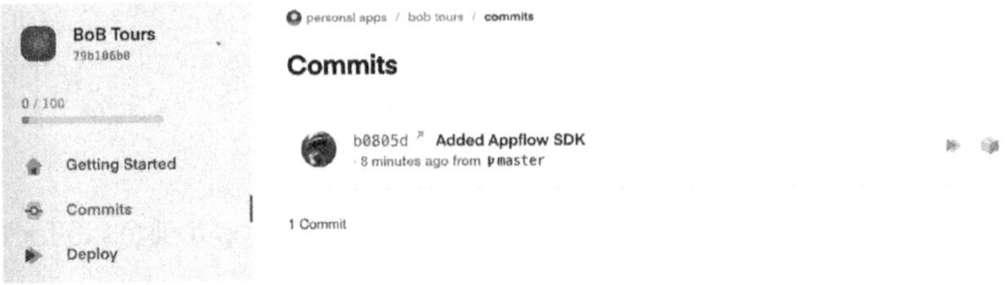

4. Deploy a Live Update

The Deploy feature works by using the installed Appflow SDK in a native application to listen to a particular Deploy Channel.

When a Deploy build is assigned to a Channel, that update will be deployed to user devices running binaries that are configured to listen to the specified Channel.

In order to deploy a live update, we'll first need to create a Deploy build.

To do this, in the `Commit` tab click the `Start web build` icon:

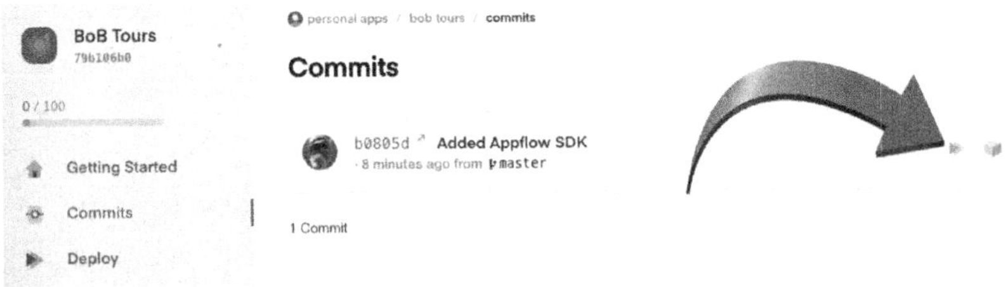

We can pick a Channel to automatically assign the build to once it completes successfully. I leave this option blank now.

Once the build begins we'll be able to watch it's progress and look at the logs if we encounter errors. If you have trouble getting a successful build in this step, here you can find answers to common Deploy build errors:

▶ https://ionic.zendesk.com/hc/en-us/categories/360000410494-Appflow-Builds

My Deploy was, fortunately, successfully built. Now I can assign it to the `Production` channel (I configured the Appflow SDK for; see step 2) by clicking `Assign to channel` (in the top right corner).

For an application to receive a live update from Deploy, we'll need to run the app on a device or an emulator. The easiest way to do this is simply to use the `ionic cordova run` command to launch a local app in an emulator or a device connected to your computer.

If the app is configured correctly to listen to the channel you deployed it to, the application should update immediately on startup if you're using the *auto* update method.

If you're using the *background* update method, just stay in the app for 30 seconds or so while the update is downloaded in the background. Then, close the application, reopen it again and you should see your update applied!

Here you can read more about deploying a Live Update:

▶ https://ionicframework.com/docs/appflow/quickstart/deploy

Conclusion

Here ends our entry into Ionic Appflow.

Of course, the platform has a lot more to offer, such as Building Native Binaries and Automation. But the advanced features are reserved for an Add-On ($49/month) or higher versions like Growth ($120/month). For businesses that need to manage multiple apps and regularly publish updates, it can be a good investment.

The Ionic team keeps its promise with Appflow, to help development teams continuously build and ship their iOS, Android, and web apps faster than ever.

The excellent documentation for Ionic Appflow is also not objectionable:

▶ https://ionicframework.com/docs/appflow

Summary

In this chapter you've learned a lot again:

You've created different builds to deploy and publish apps for iOS, Android, Desktop (with Electron) and PWAs for the Web and got to know the difference between Debugging and Production Builds.

You have learned that the `config.xml` plays an important role.

You've created icons and splash screens in all required resolutions for the various platforms.

You've got an overview of the publishing workflows for Google Play and App Store.

Finally, you got to know and use Ionic's new DevOps and Continuous Delivery platform Appflow.

Bonus: Ionic and other frameworks

B1. Ionic without any framework

Yes, you read correctly: we can use Ionic without any framework! This will not create apps for the stores, of course, but cool, lightweight web applications that you can deploy to a web server.

Web Components

Ionic has achieved its independence from frameworks by rebuilding its components as web components. It's a W3C specification that is supported by nearly all modern browsers like Google Chrome, Mozilla Firefox, Microsoft Edge, Safari and Opera..

The goal of web components is to build reusable components for the Web. So that they are cleanly reusable, the focus is primarily on *encapsulation*. Web Components primarily consists of three Web APIs to achieve these goals:

- Custom Elements
- Shadow DOM
- HTML Templates

With *Custom Elements*, web developers can create new HTML tags, beef-up existing HTML tags, or extend the components other developers have authored.

Shadow DOM is a functionality that allows the web browser to render DOM elements without putting them into the main document DOM tree. This makes it possible to attach a parallel and hidden DOM tree to any element. This creates a high encapsulation between this Shadow DOM and the actual DOM.

HTML Template is a way to insert chunks of HTML that are stamped at will.

Ionic's web components were built with *Stencil*, a very cool toolchain for creating web components and PWAs developed by the Ionic team:

► https://stenciljs.com/

Using Ionic without any framework

Ok, let's start building a little web page with pure Ionic. Everything we need:

- an `index.html` file
- a Content Delivery/Distribution Network (CDN) link to the Ionic framework (Ionic recommends to use `jsdelivr` to access the framework from a CDN)

We code our `index.html`:

```
<!doctype html>

<html lang="en">

<head>

  <meta charset="utf-8">

  <title>Using Ionic without any framework</title>

  <!-- Import Ionic from cdn.jsdelivr.net -->
  <script type="module"
   src="https://cdn.jsdelivr.net/npm/@ionic/core@latest/dist/
        ionic/ionic.esm.js"></script>
  <script nomodule
   src="https://cdn.jsdelivr.net/npm/@ionic/core@latest/dist/
        ionic/ionic.js"></script>
  <link rel="stylesheet"
   href="https://cdn.jsdelivr.net/npm/@ionic/core@latest/css/
         ionic.bundle.css" />

  <!-- Import Ionic icons -->
  <script type="module" src="https://cdn.jsdelivr.net/npm/
   ionicons@latest/dist/ionicons/ionicons.esm.js"></script>
  <script nomodule src="https://cdn.jsdelivr.net/npm/
   ionicons@latest/dist/ionicons.js"></script>

</head>

<body>

  <script>
    hello = async function () {
```

```
      alert('Hello World!');
    };
  </script>

  <ion-app>

    <ion-content text-center>

      <h1>Ionic without any framework</h1>

      <ion-button expand="round" onclick="hello()">
        Say hello
        <ion-icon slot="end" name="hand"></ion-icon>
      </ion-button>
    </ion-content>

  </ion-app>

</body>

</html>
```

Within the `head` section of the `index.html` file we do all the imports from `cdn.jsdelivr.net` to be able to use Ionic, its stylesheet and even the icons.

Within the `body` part we first create a simple JavaScript function to call an `alert`.

Then we declare an Ionic app using the `<ion-app>` element. Within this element we place the `<ion-content>` area. We can use Ionic's CSS Utilities (see "8.4 CSS Utilities", starting from page 350) to center all the content.

We add a `<h1>` heading and a button, more precisely, of course, an `<ion-button>`.

As you can see, here we can also assign the usual attributes like `expand=round` to the button. The button also has an `onclick` event that references our `hello` function.

And because we have also imported the Ionicons (see "6.12 Icons", starting from page 200), we can spend the button a nice `hand` icon next to the caption.

Here is our little Ionic web app without any framework in action:

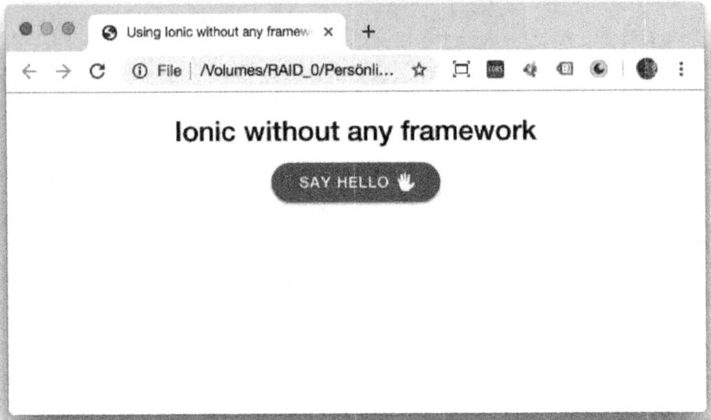

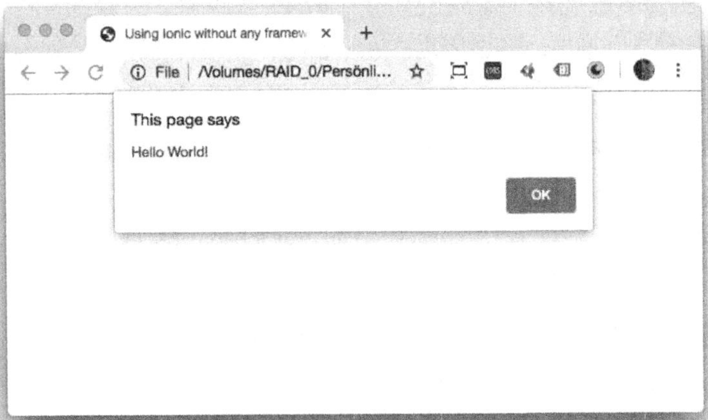

You see that the application looks the same as if we had set it up within an Angular environment – we've just embedded the web components directly into the `index.html` file.

B2. Ionic and Capacitor

In order to build hybrid apps, HTML, JavaScript and CSS are needed as well as a native partner, who takes care of the respective platform-specific connection of things like accelerometer, camera, geolocation and so on.

Such a reliable partner exists since 2008 and belongs to the name Cordova (see "1 Introduction", section "Cordova" on page 9 and also "9 Ionic Native", starting from page 393).

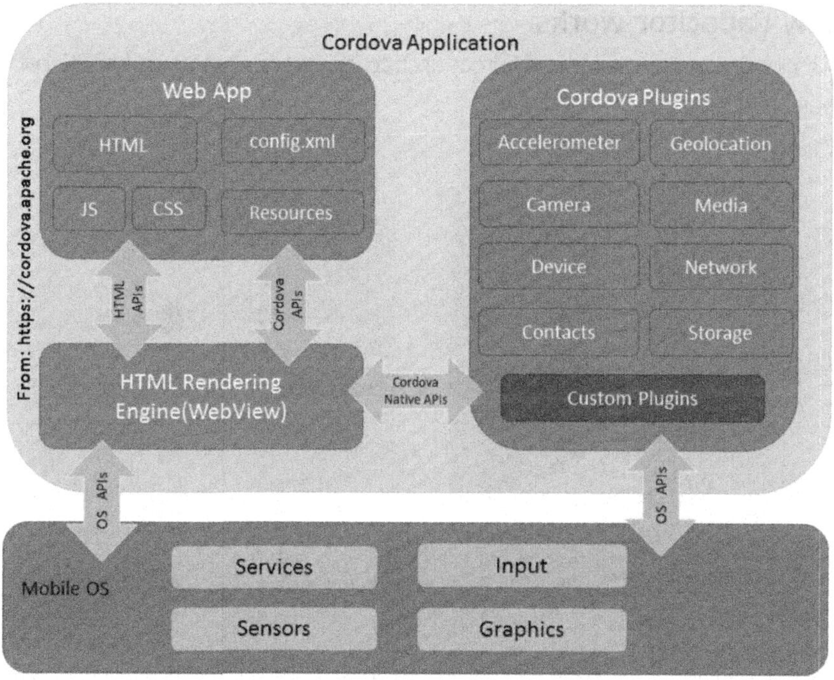

But native platforms continue to evolve faster and faster. Whether it's new OS versions of iOS and Android, new modern plugin systems like CocoaPods and Gradle or simply new hardware. Cordova sometimes has problems to come along.

With Capacitor, the Ionic team claims to have the "spiritual successor to Cordova" that makes use of all the new modern native tools. Ionic calls such apps built with Capacitor "Native Progressive Web Apps" and in their opinion they "represent the next evolution beyond hybrid apps". A statement that makes one sit up. And that's why I decided to take a closer look at Capacitor in this book.

The goals of Capacitor are to provide:

- a runtime environment that runs on all platforms: iOS, Android, Desktop and the Web
- backward-compatibility to support Cordova
- web-focused APIs that stay close to the standards
- modern native tooling for easy native project management

How Capacitor works

This nice figure illustrates the different abstraction layers of modern Ionic/Capacitor apps:

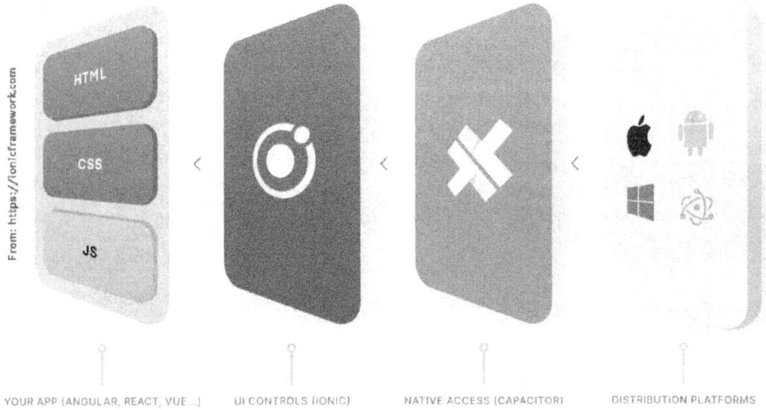

Layer 1 contains your code, written in HTML, CSS and JavaScript, usually using a JS framework like Angular, React or Vue.

Layer 2 makes up the set of UI Controls, in our case, of course, Ionic.

Layer 3 is the job of Capacitor. It containerizes your web app and puts it into a managed native WebView (if running natively), then it exposes native functionality to your web app in a cross-platform way. Capacitor then provides a simple way to expose custom native functionality to your web app (through plugins).

Layer 4 are the distribution platforms.

How is Capacitor different from Cordova?

Web support was not Cordova's strength. Capacitor promises more on this point. But that's not all. Here is a brief overview of the differences between Capacitor and Cordova:

Native Project Management

CHANGE	BENEFIT
Source assets (vs. build time assets)	Native mobile teams can work alongside web teams Add custom native code without creating a new plugin
No custom configuration (i.e. config.xml)	More visibility into native project changes & better app maintainability Easier to troubleshoot native issues Easier upgrades via step-by-step upgrade instructions
Use Platform-specific IDEs	Faster, more typical app dev experience for each platform

Plugin & CLI Management

CHANGE	BENEFIT
Built as Frameworks (iOS) & Libraries (Android) Installed via lead dependency management tools (CocoaPods & Gradle/Maven)	No copying of plugin files directly into the project. Develop plugins outside of an app! "Generate plugin" command for complete plugin scaffolding Less error-prone and makes it easier to find help in the community for each specific platform
Registers and exports all JavaScript for each plugin based on the methods it detects at runtime	All methods available at runtime. No more need for "deviceready" event!
Capacitor CLI installed locally into each project	Easier to manage versions of Capacitor across apps

Explanations to these topics can be found in the following video post by Matt Netkow, Head of Developer Relations at the Ionic team:

▶ https://youtu.be/tDW2C6rcH6M

Now it's time to have a look at Capacitor in action.

Capacitor in action

We will now dare to migrate our BoB Tours app to Capacitor!

For this we open our current project (from chapter 12) in Visual Studio Code. In the terminal we enter the following:

```
$ ionic integrations enable capacitor
```

Ionic then installs `@capacitor/core` and `@capacitor/cli`.

```
> npm i --save -E @capacitor/core
...
 @capacitor/core@1.5.0
added 1 package from 1 contributor and audited 19285 packages in
14.052s
...
+ @capacitor/cli@1.5.0
added 19 packages from 16 contributors and audited 19370 packages in
6.052s
...


  Your Capacitor project is ready to go!  

Add platforms using "npx cap add":

  npx cap add android
  npx cap add ios
  npx cap add electron

Follow the Developer Workflow guide to get building:
https://capacitor.ionicframework.com/docs/basics/workflow

[OK] Integration capacitor added!
```

Now we can initialize our app with

```
$ npx cap init [appName] [appId]
```

where `appName` is the name of our app, and `appId` is the domain identifier of our app. For my app I type

```
$ npx cap init "BoB Tours" de.dormann.bobtours
```

Note: `npx` is a utility available in npm 5 or above that executes local binaries/scripts to avoid global installs.

A new configuration file called `capacitor.config.json` has been added to our app:

```
{} capacitor.config.json > ...
{
  "appId": "de.dormann.bobtours",
  "appName": "BoB Tours",
  "bundledWebRuntime": false,
  "npmClient": "npm",
  "webDir": "www"
}
```

Use the native IDEs to change these properties after initial configuration.

We must build our Ionic project at least once before adding any native platforms.

```
$ ionic build
```

This creates the `www` folder that Capacitor has been automatically configured to use as the `webDir` in `capacitor.config.json`.

As the very first success message after the `integrations` instruction reveals, we can now add, for example, the Android platform with the following terminal command:

```
$ npx cap add android
```

This installs the Android dependencies and a native Android project directly in the root of a project. These separate native project artifacts should be considered part of your Ionic app (i.e., check them into source control, edit them in their own IDEs, etc.).

After finishing the `add` process we can run

```
$ npx cap open android
```

to launch Android Studio.

In the same way you can create a native iOS project with

```
$ npx cap add ios
```

and open it in Xcode with

```
$ npx cap open ios
```

Note: Make sure you update CocoaPods using `pod repo update` before starting a new project, if you plan on building for iOS using a Mac.

Syncing an app with Capacitor

Every time you perform a build (e.g. ionic build) that changes your web directory (default: `www`), you'll need to copy those changes down to your native projects:

```
$ npx cap copy
```

Cordova and Ionic Native Plugins

You may have noticed the following hints during the `add` process:

```
4 Updating Android plugins in 14.30ms
[info] installing missing dependency plugin cordova-plugin-device
[info] installing missing dependency plugin cordova-plugin-badge
[info] installing missing dependency plugin es6-promise-plugin
4 Updating Android plugins in 25.24ms
  Found 0 Capacitor plugins for android:
  Found 6 Cordova plugins for android
    cordova-plugin-badge (0.8.8)
    cordova-plugin-device (2.0.3)
    cordova-plugin-geolocation (4.0.2)
    cordova-plugin-local-notification (0.9.0-beta.2)
    cordova-plugin-x-socialsharing (5.6.4)
    es6-promise-plugin (4.2.2)
4 update android in 9.53s
```

Our Cordova plugins for Keyboard, WebView Splash Screen and the Status Bar are no longer needed (and are therefore skipped) because the Capacitor app uses their native equivalents.

See the Using Cordova Plugins guide for more information:

► https://capacitor.ionicframework.com/docs/cordova/using-cordova-plugins/

Migrating from Cordova to Capacitor

Why should you migrate? Using Ionic and Capacitor together is the way to build an optimized app experience, since Ionic Framework provides UI and UX enhancements that Cordova doesn't have. Additionally, it works with Ionic's favorite web app framework, including Angular, React, and Vue. With the release of Capacitor, Ionic now controls almost all of its stack. When you build an Ionic app today, Ionic now controls the native runtime layer (Capacitor), the UI controls (Ionic Framework), and the "framework" used to build the controls (web components powered by Stencil). This is significant: If there's an issue in any part of the stack that Ionic controls, the Ionic team will fix it right away. So they promise. And I believe them.

We have already taken the first steps to migrate an Ionic 5 project to Capacitor. This is the beginning. You can continue to migrate from Cordova to Capacitor with this documentation here:

▶ https://capacitor.ionicframework.com/docs/cordova/migrating-from-cordova-to-capacitor

Starting a new Ionic project with capacitor

To create a new project directly with Capacitor, enter the following terminal command:

```
$ ionic start myApp tabs --capacitor
$ cd myApp
```

Well documented

As we know it from the Ionic team, Capacitor is well documented. It includes basics about the development workflow, building and running your app, guides about an Ionic Framework Camera App, Firebase Push Notifications, a variety of community guides and all important platform-specific stuff. You can find the entry point to the documentation here:

▶ https://capacitor.ionicframework.com/docs

Conclusion

Capacitor was released by the Ionic team in May 2019 with the ambition to become a modern successor to Cordova and the new official container for every new Ionic app. The work on it has already started in 2017. And it was worth it.

Meanwhile the Ionic team has developed numerous APIs: Accessibility, Background Task, Camera, Clipboard, Console, Device, Filesystem, Geolocation, Haptics, Local Notifications, Modal, Motion, Network, Push Notification, Share, Splash Screen, Status Bar, Storage , Toast.

And if that weren't enough, the community until now has contributed more than 30 (!) other APIs: AdMob, Data Storage SQLite, DatePicker, Downloader, Email, Facebook Login, Fancy Geo, Fancy Notifications, Filesharer, Fingerprint Auth, Firebase Analysis, Firebase Auth, Fused Location, Geofende Tracker, Google Sign-In, Heartland Form, Image Cache, Image Crop, Intercom, Media Operations, NFC, oAuth2, Single SignOn, SMS, Twilio iOS, Twitter Kit, Video Player, Video Recorder, YouTube, Zebra, Zip.

So there's almost no app that you can't do with Ionic and Capacitor.

With Capacitor Ionic's mission expanded to helping teams build great apps everywhere. And I say: Mission succeeded!

B3. Ionic and React

Before we look at the concrete implementation of Ionic with React by means of a small example, I would first like to give you an overview of the differences and similarities between React and Angular. Even though Ionic has always harmonized well with Angular since its creation, with Ionic 5 you have no need to use Angular any more. This clears the way to combine Ionic's merits with one of the increasingly popular framework alternatives.

React vs. Angular

Since the rise of React and Angular, there has been endless discussion on the Web, which is the "better" technology for developing web-based interfaces. Of course, both can each score with benefits, but of course they also have their respective disadvantages. Depending on your own requirements and needs, one can be better suited than the other or vice versa. Therefore, it is virtually impossible to choose a "winner". Since both are constantly being extended by new features, it makes little sense to determine a winner on the basis of the available functions, according to the motto: "X is better as Y, because X can do this and that and Y can't."

In fact, the only timeless aspect that can be compared is the paradigm underlying the two technologies: why do they each work the way they do it, and what does that mean for the users' productivity? So the following is an attempt to contrast React and Angular with their core concepts to provide the basis for an informed decision.

For the statistics

First, take a look at the "raw data" to be able to classify React and Angular somewhat React is originally a Facebook development from the year 2013. It was published from the beginning as open source and its code is available on GitHub:

- https://github.com/reactjs

React originally used the Apache 2.0 license with an additional patent clause, which led to some ambiguity. In 2017, Facebook changed the license from React and has since used the MIT license. At the beginning React used the version numbers 0.1 to 0.14, but then Facebook changed to 15.x. The current version line is 16.x.

Known React users are Airbnb, Asana, Atlassian, Codecademy, Dropbox, Facebook, Instagram, Intercom, Netflix, Microsoft, The New York Times, WhatsApp and Yahoo.

Angular saw the light of day three years later, in 2016, and was originally developed by Google. In fact, his story started six years earlier, in 2010, with a previous framework called AngularJS, but the similarity ends in the name. The concepts of Angular and AngularJS are quite different.

The framework uses the MIT license, and therefore the code was released as open source. It can also be found on GitHub:

- https://github.com/angular

Since AngularJS used versions 1.x, Angular started with number 2. Version 3 was skipped, but since version 4, Google is simply increasing the version number on each release. The current version is 7.

Some of the more popular users of Angular are AWS, Google, Freelancers, iStockphoto, Nike, PayPal, Telegram, Udemy, Upwork, Weather and YouTube.

Scope

React is a view library, while Angular is an UI framework.

React and Angular are very different in scope, dramatically affecting the way applications are written.

React is a library, not a framework. That means it's just a small building block for an application that you need to assemble and combine with many other low-level building blocks. The library is only responsible for the V in MVC, which means that it only takes care of the efficient rendering of a user interface.

There are only a few guidelines on how a React application should be structured or what additional services should be used. While this allows for a great deal of flexibility, it also means that you must first assemble a technology stack before you can start working on an application. On the other hand, if you want React to be replaced with something else at a later date, it's very easy because it doesn't have more than a dozen aspects attached to React. You could say React is like Lego for adults.

Angular is a framework, not a library. It includes many services besides the actual view management, such as dependency injection, routing, validation, an HTTP client, and so on.

Unlike React, Angular provides many guidelines on how to structure an application, which results in Angular applications following a common standard. This is a disadvantage if the developer wants to do something that Angular didn't anticipate, and therefore it's more difficult to leave the pre-trodden paths. If React is like Lego for adults, Angular is like Playmobil.

MV*

React uses the Model View Controller (MVC) pattern, Angular the Model View ViewModel (MVVM) pattern.

React and Angular have different concepts for managing an UI. They both follow an MV* pattern, but they ultimately use different variants.

React is committed to the classic MVC pattern and, as shown above, only looks after the V of MVC. It offers only one-sided data mining (referred to in React as "unidirectional data flow"). This means that React always controls the view. Changes made by the user must be explicitly performed via React before the view can be updated.

This makes UI changes very predictable and deterministic, and it also makes their behavior easy to understand: the UI always represents the state dictated by the React application, and the only one allowed to change that state is the React application.

In contrast, Angular follows the design pattern MVVM and provides the state of the view as a so-called ViewModel. While changes to the ViewModel change the interface, the reverse is true. This means that there is more than one way to change the state of the application: either programmatically or through user actions.

This makes UI changes difficult to predict and, in a sense, nondeterministic. In addition, this bidirectional data binding approach leads to situations with subtle nuances in state management, for example when the user clicks on a checkbox and runs an `onCheck()` handler: If you now access the value of the checkbox, it will contain the previous one or the new value? This makes it more difficult to think about UIs developed in Angular than in React.

DOM

React uses a virtual DOM for runtime, while Angular directly accesses the DOM.

As changes are made to the state of the application, React and Angular must somehow apply these changes to the DOM displayed in the browser.

React uses a virtual DOM and manages a copy of the current DOM in RAM, which it can access much faster than the actual DOM. Any changes to the state that cause re-rendering will go to the virtual DOM first. The library then transfers only changes in the virtual DOM to the current DOM in the browser. This makes updating the user interface extremely fast because React only needs to update those parts that have actually changed.

Angular accesses the DOM directly. Thus, if something has changed in the state of the application, the framework must either re-render the entire DOM (which is slow) or search the DOM for the component to be updated (which is also slow). Angular's approach is slower than that of React. And so Angular is less able to handle complex masks that may contain thousands of controls.

Paradigms

React and Angular use different paradigms, which leads to a different way the developer can handle them. React uses the functional paradigm, while Angular works with the object-oriented paradigm.

As described, React manages a virtual DOM. For React, it's important to be able to quickly find and compare elements in it. React uses the concept of immutability, so it only needs to compare references and not (nested) values.

However, this means that the developer must know the difference between the *stack* and the *heap*, and between *value* and *reference* types, as well as know how to update them. Strictly speaking, "update" is the wrong term, because existing values in React are always replaced by new ones because of the aforementioned immutability.

Immutability, along with the unidirectional flow of data, is a concept of functional programming and shows very clearly where React has its roots.

In contrast, Angular follows the object-oriented paradigm: it enables the definition of classes, it uses inheritance and dependency injection. All these things are known to developers who have already used object-oriented languages.

Unfortunately, object-oriented programming is reaching its limits, especially in terms of runtime behavior. Statements can't be optimized as well as expressions. Because object-oriented programming uses both (as opposed to functional programming that relies only on expressions), the object-oriented code is slower by comparison, such as when using a machine with multiple CPU cores. In other words: Functional code can be executed automatically in parallel; for object-oriented ones this isn't possible because of potential side effects.

Syntax

React uses primarily JavaScript native language features, Angular also introduces proprietary elements.

Angular and React have very different ideas about how to syntactically write code.

React uses JSX, which extends JavaScript with an XML data type. This way you can also use HTML in JavaScript, which becomes a part of the JavaScript code through JSX. Along with approaches like JSS (CSS in JavaScript), this results in a single JSX file containing the structure, styles, and behaviors of a component.

Because JSX is basically JavaScript, you can use all the tools that the JavaScript ecosystem knows about, including testing, "lints", and distributing components over `npm`.

It also means that existing JavaScript knowledge can be reused and you don't have to learn any additional concepts other than JSX syntax. For example, anyone who knows how to write a loop in JavaScript knows how to formulate a loop in JSX. This makes getting into JSX very easy.

In contrast, Angular emphasizes HTML and enriches HTML with its own elements and attributes. For example, if you want to loop through Angular, you need to know the Angular construct for loops, which is available in the form of its own `*ngFor` attribute (see "2 Angular Essentials", section "2.7 *ngFor", starting from page 40). This means that the developer can't reuse familiar things, but must re-learn them for Angular in an Angular-specific way. This makes getting into Angular harder than getting into React.

In addition, Angular uses TypeScript, a superset of JavaScript that fits well in the Angular object-oriented paradigm. This is for those who already work with TypeScript - but for everyone else it's an additional hurdle to take.

Native applications

React and Angular both have concepts on how to build native applications.

From time to time you don't need a web application, but a native application is sufficient. Both React and Angular have solutions.

React offers an implementation called React Native that lets you write native applications for iOS and Android using the library and JavaScript.

Angular also uses a similar approach with Native Script, which can also be used to write native applications for iOS and Android using Angular and JavaScript.

Update to new versions

Both React and Angular receive regular updates, but the way they treat each update is very different. React updates are usually backward compatible, while Angular updates are not compatible.

For example, Facebook is investing heavily to communicate legacy features early and to offer upgrade paths that sometimes even have automated tools. Updates are backward compatible with most aspects. This means that updating an application from one version of React to another is usually painless and can occur in a timely manner.

In contrast, new versions of Angular are usually incompatible with older ones and contain many major changes. This means that an application will remain with a certain Angular version over time, or the programmer will have to put some effort into updating each time a new Angular version is released. This makes updates - in connection with the fact that Angular code is usually more extensive than React code – annoying.

Use

After comparing concepts and paradigms up to now, one important aspect is the use of React and Angular. To get an honest and generally accepted impression of how the technologies are being used, there are several useful surveys. Let's take a closer look at the survey "The state of JavaScript 2018":

- https://2018.stateofjs.com/front-end-frameworks/overview/

The results for React indicate that the popularity of React has increased over time. 64.8 percent of the developers who participated in the survey used React and would use it again. 19.1 percent want to learn it; 9.2 percent are not interested in learning React. 6.7 percent have used the library before but would not do it again.

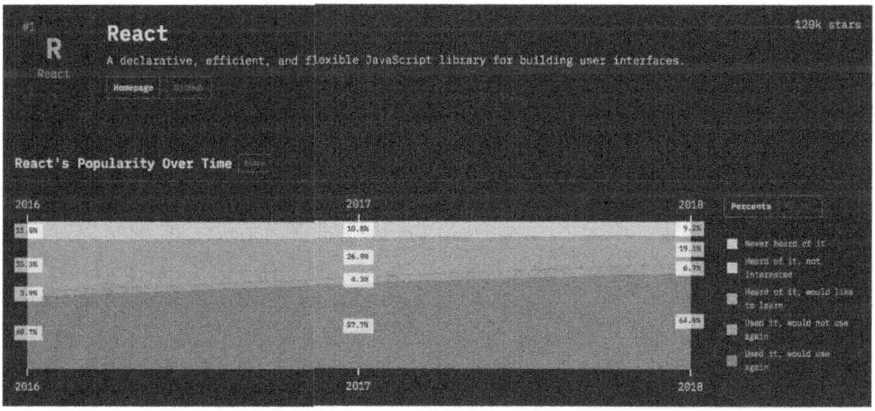

The results for Angular show that only 23.9 percent of the developers who participated in the survey and used Angular would use Angular again (again for comparison: the corresponding value for React is 64.8 percent). Even more impressively, a third (33.8 percent) of the developers who used Angular would not use it again (6.7 percent at React). The proportion of developers interested in Angular has fallen from 39.7 percent in 2016 to just 10.4 percent in 2018. If you put it all together, Angular seems to be on the decline. Today.

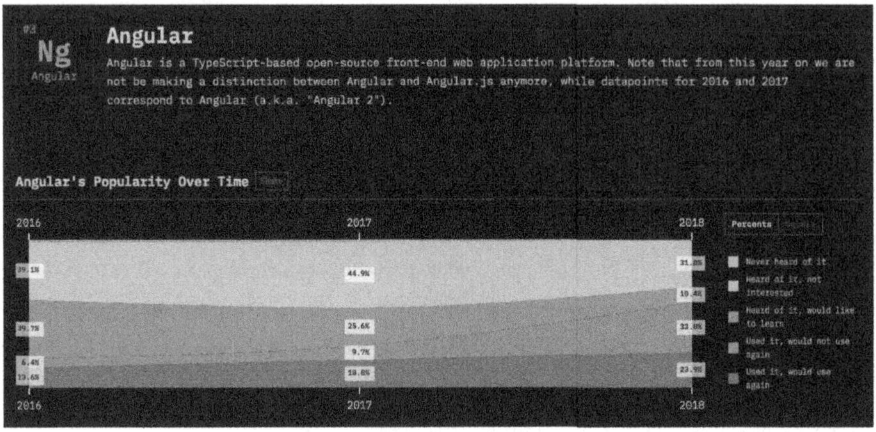

The country-specific development is interesting. When used per country shows that the world can be arranged by technology: the US, Scandinavia, China and Australia prefer React, Europe and South America prefer Angular.

In it's conclusion the survey says:

"Once again the front-end space is all about React and Vue.js. Vue's story in particular is worth considering: two years ago, 27% of respondents had never even heard of the library. Today, that fraction has fallen to just 1.3%! So while React still has a much larger share of the market, Vue's meteoric rise certainly shows no sign of stopping. In fact, Vue has already overtaken its rival for certain metrics such as total GitHub stars.

The other story of those past couple years is the fall of Angular. While it still ranks very high in terms of raw usage, it has a fairly disappointing 41% satisfaction ratio. So while it probably isn't going anywhere thanks to its large user base, it's hard to see how it will ever regain its place atop the front-end throne.

[..]

Update: many people have pointed out that Angular's poor satisfaction ratio is probably in part due to the confusion between Angular and the older, deprecated AngularJS (previous surveys avoided this issue by featuring both as separate items). So while Angular did "fall" –relatively speaking– from its dominance from a few years back, it might very well regain ground once the dust clears."

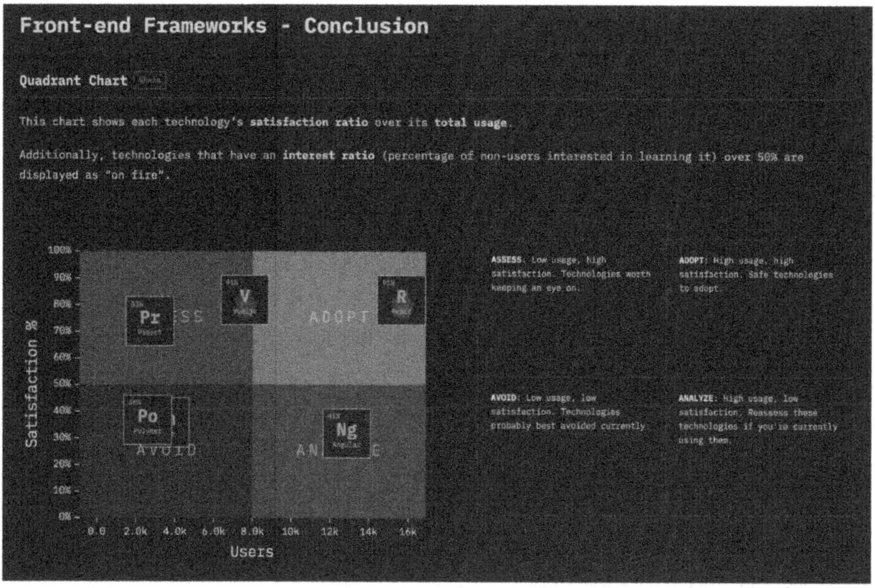

Summary

When comparing React and Angular, it makes sense not to focus on their functions as features can change very quickly over time. Instead, it makes more sense to compare React and Angular from a conceptual point of view, and many differences can be made here.

The main difference is that React follows the functional approach with all its consequences, and Angular follows the object-oriented approach. While object-oriented programming certainly had its time, it continues to struggle with modern demands such as automatically parallelized code.

Because React is based on functional concepts, it offers better performance in terms of speed, usability and maintainability. In addition, React is lighter weight than Angular and also results in much slimmer code. Besides, it doesn't enforce the use of TypeScript. Angular, on the other hand, is practically useless if you try to use it without TypeScript (which, as described, has its own complexity and involves a certain amount of effort).

Using React with Ionic

When I was almost finished writing this book, it came in time for the copy deadline: the first release candidate of `@ionic/react`. So the following first steps could be already a guide for you how to productively start an Ionic/React app project.

Let's start with the installation of the latest version of the Ionic CLI:

```
$ npm install -g @ionic/cli
```

Now we can create a blank React project with Ionic and all its dependencies with:

```
$ ionic start myReactIonicApp blank --type=react
$ cd  myReactIonicApp
```

This may take several minutes. After finishing this process we can run the app as usual with:

```
$ ionic serve
```

Let's get an overview of the new app project.

The entry point for our app is `src/index.tsx`:

```
import React from 'react';
import ReactDOM from 'react-dom';
import App from './App';
import * as serviceWorker from './serviceWorker';

ReactDOM.render(<App />, document.getElementById('root'));
```

The first three lines are pulling in some dependencies. The first being React itself. This allows us to write components in an HTML-like syntax called JSX. JSX stands for JavaScript XML or JavaScript Syntax Extension and is an extension of the usual JavaScript grammar for React.

The second import is for ReactDOM. The `ReactDOM.render` method is the browser/DOM specific way of taking our components and rendering it to a specified DOM node.

The third import is the root component for our app, simply named `App`. This is our first React component and will be used in the bootstrapping process for our React app.

The fourth import provides Service Worker functionalities.

Let's have a closer look at the root component. It's located in `src/app.tsx`;

```
import React from 'react';
import { Redirect, Route } from 'react-router-dom';
import { IonApp, IonRouterOutlet } from '@ionic/react';
import { IonReactRouter } from '@ionic/react-router';
import Home from './pages/Home';

/* Core CSS required for Ionic components to work properly */
import '@ionic/react/css/core.css';

/* Basic CSS for apps built with Ionic */
import '@ionic/react/css/normalize.css';
import '@ionic/react/css/structure.css';
import '@ionic/react/css/typography.css';

/* Optional CSS utils that can be commented out */
import '@ionic/react/css/padding.css';
import '@ionic/react/css/float-elements.css';
import '@ionic/react/css/text-alignment.css';
import '@ionic/react/css/text-transformation.css';
import '@ionic/react/css/flex-utils.css';
import '@ionic/react/css/display.css';

/* Theme variables */
import './theme/variables.css';

const App: React.FC = () => (
 <IonApp>
  <IonReactRouter>
    <IonRouterOutlet>
     <Route path="/home" component={Home} exact={true} />
     <Route exact path="/" render={() =>
                                 <Redirect to="/home" />} />
    </IonRouterOutlet>
  </IonReactRouter>
 </IonApp>
);

export default App;
```

As an attentive reader of my book and "co-developer" of the BoB Tours App, you will find some familiar, but not others. So here are a few explanations:

The first group of imports provide us with some React specific stuff: `React` itself in order to use JSX and `Route` from `react-router-dom`, a routing library built on top of React which is used to create the routing in react apps. Then follow `IonApp`, `IonReactRouter` and `IonRouterOutlet` as Ionic components we use in or app component. `IonReactRouter` wraps `ReactRouter's BrowserRouter` component. More informations about this topic you can find here:

► https://ionicframework.com/docs/react/navigation

The last import is `Home`. This component is our first page (a component with a route/URL) that we can navigate to.

Importing the `Core CSS` is required for the Ionic components to work properly.

We can optionally import the `CSS Utilities` (see "8.4 CSS Utilities", starting from page 350), if we want to use them.

The last import provides the `variables.css` we already know from Ionic/Angular apps as `variables.scss` (see "8.3 Local and global (S)CSS files", starting from page 341), which we can use to influence the theming of an app.

After reviewing all of the imports, we come to the React Component:

```
const App: React.FC = () => (
 <IonApp>
  <IonReactRouter>
    <IonRouterOutlet>
     <Route path="/home" component={Home} exact={true} />
     <Route exact path="/" render={() =>
                              <Redirect to="/home" />} />
    </IonRouterOutlet>
  </IonReactRouter>
 </IonApp>
);
```

This React component sets up the initial routing for our app, as well as include some core Ionic components for animations and layout (`IonRouterOutlet` and `IonApp`). One thing that stands out is that in React, to do data-binding, the value is passed in curly braces `{}`. So in the `Route` component, we can set the value of `component` to the `Home` component. This is how React will know that that value is not a string, but a reference to a component.

Let's take a look at this `Home` component and open the file `src/pages/Home.tsx`:

```
import { IonContent, IonHeader, IonPage, IonTitle,
IonToolbar } from '@ionic/react';
import React from 'react';
import ExploreContainer from '../components/ExploreContainer';
import './Home.css';

const Home: React.FC = () => {
  return (
    <IonPage>
      <IonHeader>
        <IonToolbar>
          <IonTitle>Blank</IonTitle>
        </IonToolbar>
      </IonHeader>
      <IonContent>
        <IonHeader collapse="condense">
          <IonToolbar>
            <IonTitle size="large">Blank</IonTitle>
          </IonToolbar>
        </IonHeader>
        <ExploreContainer />
      </IonContent>
    </IonPage>
  );
};

export default Home;
```

The code explained: For this Home page we again do some imports, the `React` component and some specific Ionic components (`IonContent`, `IonHeader`, `IonTitle`, `IonToolbar`). We also import a container element (`ExploreContainer`) and the corresponding CSS file for this page (`Home.css`). We use these quite similar to Ionic/Angular components (see chapter "6 UI Components", starting form page 151). This code should be easy to read and understand, right?

Let's rebuild `src/pages/Home.tsx` a bit to get a more app-typical UI:

```
import React from 'react';

import { IonContent, IonHeader, IonTitle, IonToolbar, IonList,
IonItem, IonCheckbox, IonLabel, IonRadioGroup, IonRadio,
IonRange, IonListHeader, IonIcon, IonPage }
         from '@ionic/react';
import { informationCircle } from 'ionicons/icons';

//import ExploreContainer
  from '../components/ExploreContainer';

import './Home.css';

const Home: React.FC = () => {

  const about = () => {
    alert('This is my 1st React/Ionic App!');
  }

  return (
    <IonPage>
      <IonHeader>
        <IonToolbar>
          <IonTitle>BoB Tours goes React</IonTitle>
        </IonToolbar>
      </IonHeader>
      <IonContent className="ion-padding">
        <IonList>
          <IonItem onClick={() => about()}>
            <IonIcon icon={informationCircle}
                     color="primary"
                     slot="start" />
            <IonLabel>About this app</IonLabel>
          </IonItem>
          <IonListHeader>Price Range</IonListHeader>
          <IonRange dualKnobs={true} snaps={true} step={20}
                   min={80} max={400} value={240}>
            <IonLabel slot="start">80</IonLabel>
            <IonLabel slot="end">400</IonLabel>
          </IonRange>
```

```
          <IonRadioGroup slot="end" value="azure">
            <IonItem>
              <IonLabel>Azure-Style</IonLabel>
              <IonRadio slot="end"
                        value="azure"
                        checked={true} />
            </IonItem>
            <IonItem>
              <IonLabel>Summer-Style</IonLabel>
              <IonRadio value="summer" slot="end" />
            </IonItem>
          </IonRadioGroup>
          <IonItem>
            <IonLabel>Allow messages</IonLabel>
            <IonCheckbox slot="end" />
          </IonItem>
        </IonList>
      </IonContent>
    </IonPage>
  );
};

export default Home;
```

As you can see, we now have some more Ionic component imports.

```
import { IonContent, IonHeader, IonTitle, IonToolbar, IonList,
IonItem, IonCheckbox, IonLabel, IonRadioGroup, IonRadio,
IonRange, IonListHeader, IonIcon } from '@ionic/react';
```

Every component we use here on the page must be explicitly imported in React. This also applies to the icon, which is also included as a component.

```
import { informationCircle } from 'ionicons/icons';
```

More about that right now.

Just after the `React.FunctionComponent` constructor and before the `return` part of our page we created a little function:

```
const about = () => {
  alert('This is my 1st React/Ionic App!');
}
```

This simply shows a browser alert. Nothing special (it's more interesting, in which way the function is called).

In the `IonContent` area we produce an `IonList` component with some `IonItem` elements. Does that look familiar?

Take a look at the first `IonItem` element:

```
<IonItem onClick={() => about()}>
  <IonIcon icon={informationCircle}
           color="primary"
           slot="start" />
  <IonLabel>About this app</IonLabel>
</IonItem>
```

`IonItem` can be clicked, because here we assign `onClick` our `about()` function.

This is followed by an `IonIcon` with the color `"primary"` (see its definition in `variables.css`) in the slot `"start"`, i.e. on the left in the `IonItem` element. Note that unlike Ionic/Angular, the icon is not set by the `name`, but the `icon` attribute, as reference to the previously imported icon component `informationCircle`! This topic has already caused many questions in community forums.

It shouldn't go unmentioned that in Ionic/React all XML tags without content can be formulated in the condensed XML special notation: `<IonIcon ... />`. That should be better not be done in Ionic/Angular.

The `IonIcon` is followed by an `IonLabel`.

Next, we use an `IonListHeader` as caption for the following `IonRange` component (see "6.21 Range", starting from page 250):

```
<IonListHeader>Price Range</IonListHeader>
<IonRange dualKnobs={true} snaps={true} step={20}
          min={80} max={400} value={240}>
  <IonLabel slot="start">80</IonLabel>
  <IonLabel slot="end">400</IonLabel>
</IonRange>
```

In most cases, the implementation works as described in the Ionic component documentation, of course with the React-compliant syntax.

In an `IonRadioGroup` we offer a selection by using two labeled `IonRadio` elements and pre-select it with the value `azure`:

```
<IonRadioGroup slot="end" value="azure">
  <IonItem>
    <IonLabel>Azure-Style</IonLabel>
    <IonRadio slot="end" value="azure" />
  </IonItem>
  <IonItem>
    <IonLabel>Summer-Style</IonLabel>
   <IonRadio slot="end" value="summer" />
  </IonItem>
</IonRadioGroup>
```

Last but not least we use a labeled `IonCheckbox` and set its `slot` attribute to `end` (the right end of the `IonItem` element) and its `checked` attribute to `{true}` to preselect it:

```
<IonItem>
  <IonLabel>Allow messages</IonLabel>
  <IonCheckbox slot="end" checked={true} />
</IonItem>
```

Here's our modified Ionic/React app in action:

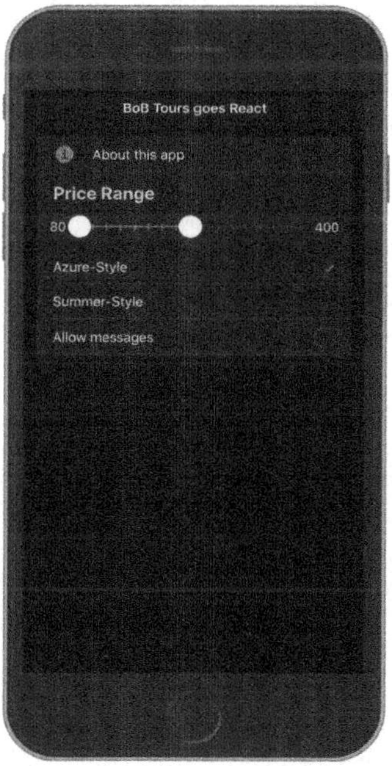

Let's expand this demo app. We'll now add a page component with some navigation functionality. First, we add little code to `Home.tsx`:

```
import React from 'react';
import { IonContent, IonHeader, IonTitle, IonToolbar, IonList,
IonItem, IonCheckbox, IonLabel, IonRadioGroup, IonRadio,
IonRange, IonListHeader, IonIcon, IonPage }
         from '@ionic/react';
import { informationCircle, play } from 'ionicons/icons';

const Home: React.FunctionComponent = () => {

  ...

  return (
    <IonPage>
      <IonHeader>
        <IonToolbar>
          <IonTitle>BoB Tours goes React</IonTitle>
        </IonToolbar>
      </IonHeader>
      <IonContent className="ion-padding">
        <IonList>
          <IonItem href="/slideshow">
            <IonIcon icon={play}
                     color="primary"
                     slot="start" />
            <IonLabel>Slideshow</IonLabel>
          </IonItem>
          <IonItem onClick={() => about()}>
            <IonIcon icon={informationCircle}
                     color="primary"
                     slot="start" />
            <IonLabel>About this app</IonLabel>
          </IonItem>
          ...
        </IonList>
      </IonContent>
    </IonPage>
  );
};
```

```
export default Home;
```

We add another `IonItem` with an icon and a label. The special here is the navigation instruction `href="/slideshow"`. This is to ensure that the user is guided to a `slideshow` page when clicking on the item.

Of course we still have to build this site. For this we create the file `src/pages/Slideshow.tsx`:

```
import React from 'react';
import { IonContent, IonHeader, IonTitle, IonToolbar,
IonButtons, IonBackButton, IonPage } from '@ionic/react';

const Slideshow: React.FunctionComponent = () => {

  return (
    <IonPage>
      <IonHeader>
        <IonToolbar>
          <IonTitle>Slideshow</IonTitle>
          <IonButtons slot="start">
            <IonBackButton defaultHref="/home" />
          </IonButtons>
        </IonToolbar>
      </IonHeader>
      <IonContent className="ion-padding ion-text-center">
        <h1>Slideshow page</h1>
        <p>This is a page component.</p>
      </IonContent>
    </IonPage>
  );
};

export default Slideshow;
```

This code is nearly self-explanatory, I think.

You should pay attention to the `IonBackButton` in the `IonHeader` area. Its navigation instruction `defaultHref="/home"` ensures that when you click on it the app always navigates you back to the `home` page.

What's missing? A route!

For our navigation to work, we have to specify a route for our new `slideshow` page in `App.tsx`:

```
import React from 'react';
...
import Slideshow from './pages/Slideshow';
...
const App: React.FunctionComponent = () => (
  <IonApp>
    <IonReactRouter>
      <IonPage>
        <IonRouterOutlet>
          <Route path="/home" component={Home} exact={true} />
          <Route path="/slideshow" component={Slideshow} />
          <Route exact path="/" render={() =>
                                        <Redirect to="/home" />} />
        </IonRouterOutlet>
      </IonPage>
    </IonReactRouter>
  </IonApp>
);

export default App;
```

Here's our app with navigation between the two pages in action:

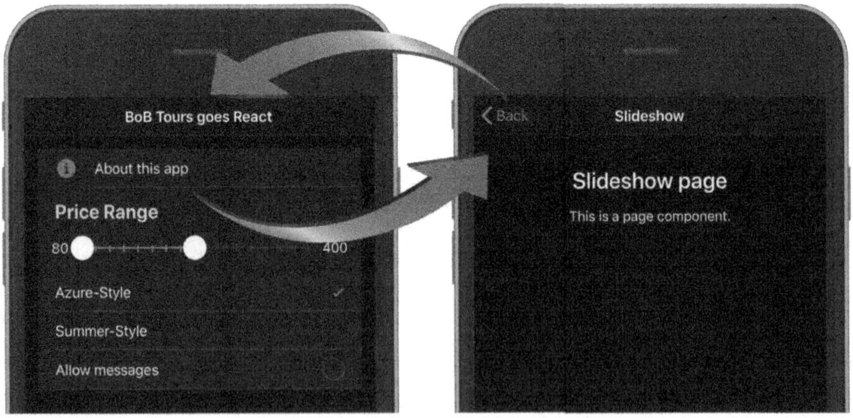

Conclusion

Our first adventure with Ionic/React wasn't that hard, was it?

Apart from a slightly different syntax, the way how to build Ionic UIs with React is very similar. Of course, apps are not just about surfaces and we didn't go deeper here. But in this bonus chapter I wanted to give you at least a first impression of maybe the new dream team Ionic and React.

I think, friends of React have no excuse any more not to combine their React skills with Ionic's excellent possibilities and its approximately 70 UI components to create awesome apps.

More about Ionic/React you can find here:

- https://ionicframework.com/docs/react/overview

B4. Ionic and Vue

Before we look at the concrete implementation of Ionic with Vue by means of a small example, I would first like to give you an overview of the differences and similarities between Vue and Angular. And here I repeat myself: Even though Ionic has always harmonized well with Angular since its creation, with Ionic 5 you have no need to use Angular any more. This clears the way to combine Ionic's merits with one of the increasingly popular framework alternatives like Vue.

Vue vs. Angular

Gladly Vue.js is called the simpler Angular. Let's look at why you can come to this assessment and whether the framework is also suitable for you.

Web frontend frameworks seem to pop up quickly and disappear very quickly. There are only a few exceptions. Starting with its initial release, AngularJS had taken the web frontend framework world by storm, and at the same time was largely responsible for the aforementioned fluctuation. At least with the successor, which is called only Angular (see chapter "2 Angular Essentials", starting from page 25), it referred many other frameworks on the siding. Only React (see "3. Ionic and React", starting from page 573) from Facebook came up with a completely different approach to the hype and spread of Google's giants. At first very small and inconspicuous, but in recent years increasingly self-confident Vue.js (pronounced as the view) as a third party in the league and is so many annoyed Angular developers ever suggested as the perfect alternative.

► https://github.com/vuejs/vue

I'll compare Angular and Vue.js on the basis of typical criteria that should generally be considered when using third-party components. It's therefore not only on the typical developer feeling, but also on hard facts such as the long-term usability. In doing so, attention should be paid to the most objective description, which feeds from the practical application of both frameworks in real projects. It is therefore important that you have some basic understanding of MVVM or MV* frameworks and can at least associate topics such as binding, routing, and the like.

Criteria

The use of foreign frameworks or libraries should be well thought out. Because in the long run, dependencies arise on things that you may not have any influence on. For example, what happens if the framework isn't developed further in the future because the original programmer simply doesn't feel like doing it anymore? What happens if the license terms change or contain errors that are simply not resolved? Going too blue-eyed at the choice of a framework can lead to serious problems and may even mean more work than you can save on the component.

This is even more true in the context of Vue.js and Angular, as they serve as application frameworks on the client side. Not only do they call our code like a test framework would do, but they provide the infrastructure to put all of the client's components together. So if you want to switch from one framework to another at a later time, this often means a complete rewrite.

For this reason, not only the handling of the frameworks is discussed below, but also the following criteria are considered:

- Business Conditions
- Architecture
- Rich Client Features
- Tooling
- Test Automation
- Documentation
- Ecosystem
- Learnability
- Scalability
- Future Security

Business Conditions

Let's start with a category that's usually not considered in such detail: the economic conditions. In this, it should be clarified to what extent the tools themselves incur costs in their use that are not caused by the actual programming with them anyway. These include, for example, acquisition costs, license fees, ongoing operating costs and the like. In the case of Vue.js and Angular, the category is at first very easy to estimate because both frameworks are very similar here. They are both under the MIT license and can be used free of charge. In addition, because they are available as open source at GitHub, have a vibrant community, and thus have the philosophy to work together to fix errors, lower economic risk can be expected in the event of misconduct. Furthermore, both frameworks are used comparatively frequently and also by large companies. At Angular this is of course Google, but also Microsoft. At Vue, for example, BMW and Apple are mentioned. Consequently, the chance of making serious mistakes is comparatively low as there are many users who are likely to spot such errors early on. In addition, planning for the next versions is easy to see in both cases, and you may even have the option to help yourself with the fix if something doesn't work as expected.

But there is a bigger difference in the organization. While behind Angular with Google is a large company that uses the framework itself in its own products, the operators of Vue.js are a grouping of individuals. Both have their own advantages and disadvantages.

With a large enterprise one can assume a certain financial strength and has the certainty that the investment security doesn't depend on the motivation of individual developers. Also in this case, typical team-internal problems, such as disputes or other discord, the product can't do so much harm, as it may be the case with pure hobby projects. On the other hand, however, one depends on the decisions of those large companies, and these decisions don't necessarily always have to be comprehensible. This can be seen, for example, in cooperation with the community, flexibility in proposing changes or when the operator decides to make the previously provided tool available at no cost.

But how does this actually work in the case of Vue.js? This doesn't purely build on the motivation of a small group of people. Because this group is very large with 20 active core members (as of June 2019), on the other hand the framework is financed by donations via Patreon or sponsoring of companies, which allows some of these developers a full-time job exclusively for Vue.js. Thus, the framework has reached a size and organization that distinguishes it from many other free projects.

Architecture

The basic architecture of both frameworks is quite similar. In their basic features, they represent component-oriented MV* frameworks, but they also offer many infrastructure components outside the pure representation. Accordingly, they severely separate the representation from the processing layer and offer possibilities for linking a backend or for outsourcing the processing in such a way that they are not necessarily linked to the representation of the component.

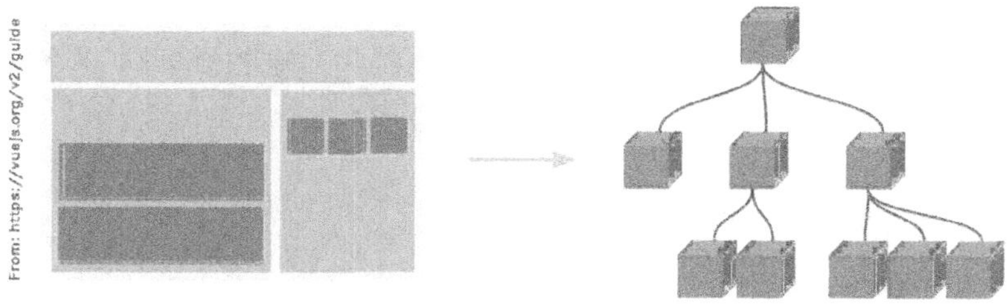

Component-oriented in this context also means that they no longer require thinking in the form of documents, as happens with jQuery (see “2. Ionic and ”, starting from page 565). Rather, they divide the components of the page into individual, self-contained units that can be nested at will.

A fundamental difference then shows up in the implementation. While Vue.js relies entirely on JavaScript, Angular made use of TypeScripts right from the start, allowing for more type-safe and object-oriented work. Neither one is necessarily better. However, it is noticeable during use, which is highlighted in other categories.

For the architecture is further pointed out that Vue can be used in two ways. So it can be used as an application framework for single page applications. On the other hand, it can just as well be used to realize only smaller components of an otherwise static website in a component-oriented way. Using Vue in this way is more like React rather than Angular.

Thus, there are already two reasons why Vue has a raison d'être besides Angular and React. On the one hand, unlike Angular and React, it relies on HTML and JavaScript, and thus on languages that Web developers are already familiar with, and on the other hand, web pages can be implemented step-by-step component-oriented and ultimately lead to a single page application. Not to be forgotten in this context is that the focus on JavaScript greatly simplifies the use of other JavaScript frameworks. Although the latter aspect has to be somewhat restricted, this is no longer a big problem with TypeScript and in the future Vue.js will also offer the direct use of TypeScript instead of JavaScript.

Components in detail

Of course, if components are so important, then the question arises of how these components are structured and how the two frameworks differ in their implementation. To explain this, we use the presentation from the documentation of Angular, as shown in the following figure and listings A and B:

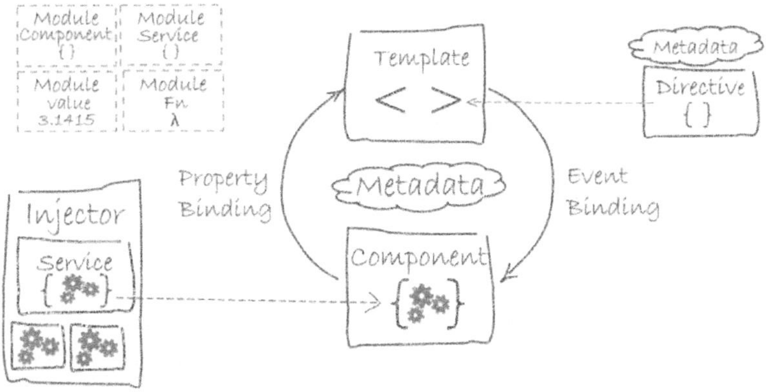

From: https://angular.io/guide/architecture

Listing A: A typical Angular component

```
@Component({
  selector:    'notification-hub',
  templateUrl: './notificationsHub.html',
  providers:   [ MessageBus ]
})
export class NotificationsHub {
  notificationText: "";

  constructor(private messages: MessageBus) { }
  publish() {
    messages.publishNotification(this.notificationText);
  }
}
```

Listing B: A typical Vue.js component

```
import {MessageBus} from "../plugins/MessageBus"
export default {
  name: "NotificationsHub",
  data: () => ({
    notificationText: ""
  }),
  methods: {
    publish {
      MessageBus.publish(this.notificationText)
    }
  }
}
```

In both frameworks, the template, i.e. the presentation layer, and the logic are usually stored in a file, although it is possible to provide each component in a separate file. For example, listings A and B make use of this feature, and therefore only compare the code of the logic layer of the same component while paging the representation for clarity. This offloading usually needs to be centrally configured or, as in the case of Angular, specified directly in the component. The communication then takes place via bindings, which are marked in the template by double curly brackets (see "2.6 Content Projection", starting from page 39).

Listings A and B therefore have the `notificationText` property. In both cases the template was bound to this property via a data binding and therefore via `{{notificationText}}`. The spelling is now almost standard and thus doesn't differ. An event binding also contains a reference to the `publish` function, with which the entered text is then transferred to another component or to a service. Not shown in the example, but implemented in almost the same way for both frameworks, there are features for displaying lists, manipulating the visibility of elements, and advanced input, such as mouse gestures or touch controls. Also, data binding doesn't necessarily have to be for a simple property or function. For example, these properties can also be compound: if a property changes, such as the year of birth, then they are automatically updated, for example, to calculate age. In addition, watchers can be defined, i.e. functions that are called automatically when the value of a property changes.

With that we are already at the differences. As the previous figure makes clear, Angular also offers the possibility to outsource business logic in the form of services. This is also necessary because Angular works object oriented and makes very strong use of Dependency Injection (see "2.4 Dependency Injection", starting from page 34). So if you want to use functionality in a component, you need to request that logic in the form of other components or services through its constructor. In order to avoid collisions and to allow code to be reused and even reloaded with delay, Angular offers the concept of the modules most likely to recall namespaces or packages in C#.

All this doesn't exist in Vue.js. Here we work mostly functional and based on JavaScript components, and even if TypeScript is configured as a language, it is rather the type system used, but not specifics such as Dependency Injection. Vue components react differently than their Angular equivalents and don't require constructors. Rather, just code is imported here, and then just that code is used. Different types of instances, as is the case with classes, don't have to be taken into account, and if you really want to provide services, then you just don't create a service, but simply create another function, which can possibly also work as an object with further sub functions. Again, Vue.js seems to be a lot easier than Angular, you don't have to worry about many things. Even in reality, this impression initially seems to be right; but with a growing amount of source code and a larger number of components you also want some more rules in Vue.js. Because in large projects, an error quickly arises, which is discovered only at runtime thanks to JavaScript, or it comes to collisions of identically named components.

While Angular is quite rigid in its architecture and the extensive use of various TypeScript features ago, Vue.js shines with freedom, which is also known from the use of JavaScript. However, this supposed advantage of Vue.js occasionally becomes detrimental in larger projects, as long as one doesn't have to apply the necessary discipline and order that Angular enforces right from the start.

Lifecycle hooks

Both Angular and Vue.js are more than just simple MV* frameworks. Rather, both can be used as application frameworks to map general requirements that arise in the context of single page applications. These include the previously noted binding and dependency injection, but also topics such as lifecycle hooks, which means that they can intervene in events that can occur during the lifetime of a component. Such events are, for example, the instantiation of the component, its integration into the DOM or the removal from it.

Both frameworks offer almost the same amount of possibilities. However, they differ again in the implementation. At Vue.js, the very easy way is to deposit appropriate methods in the component. So if there is a `mounted` function (see next figure), it will be called as soon as the component is inserted into the DOM, in the case of created you get a constructor and so on.

Angular gets the constructor as part of TypeScript and via the constructor keyword. All other hooks must be implemented based on interface definitions, for example with the method `ngOnInit` in which the initialization code is then stored. Whereby, this isn't true. Because it is one of the best practices to use the appropriate interfaces. In fact, Angular only needs to create the appropriate methods. The reason for this is in the transpilation: The TypeScript code of Angular is translated into normal JavaScript code and JavaScript knows no interfaces like those from TypeScript. That's why Angular uses the same approach as Vue.js at runtime, and so you would actually only need the `ngOnInit` function.

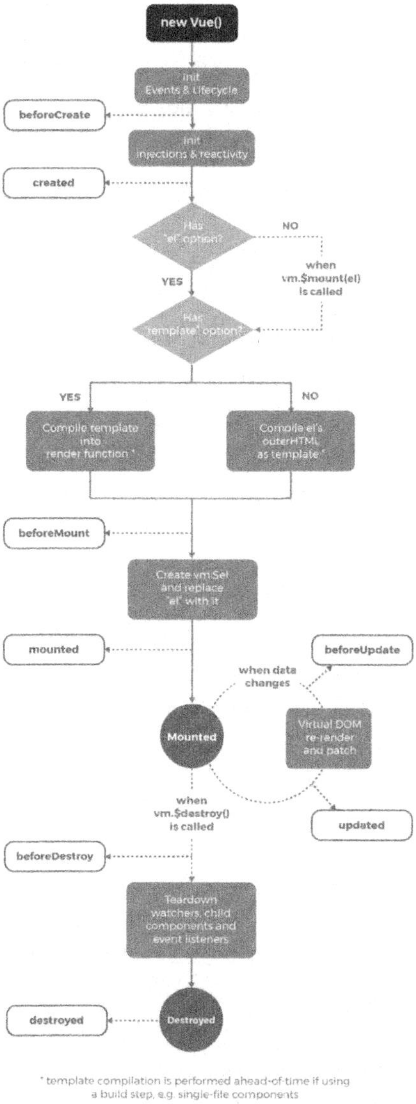

From: https://vuejs.org/v2/guide

Navigation and routing

Another important feature for single page applications is the routing or navigation between different UI components. In order to be able to implement all associated requirements, it must therefore be deposited in some way, from which views to which views can be navigated. This navigation must then also be carried out, with parameters to be passed between the views. If necessary, it should also be possible to navigate back to the previous view or to prevent navigational processes on the basis of status information (so-called navigation guards). The latter is used, for example, to allow no navigation, if the user isn't yet logged in.

All of these features translate both frameworks, with Vue.js using an additional package called *Vue Router*:

- https://router.vuejs.org/

The Vue router is maintained by the Vue core team, but it is deployed separately because it isn't needed, for example, if you only use Vue for individual components, not for entire applications. In the implementation, the two frameworks are so similar that these points should not be described in more detail here. What you need is there, works without problems, blends in well with the overall solution and leaves nothing to be desired.

State Management

If an application or a front-end consists of many individual components, the question soon arises as to how a common status can be shared between similar components. To understand this problem, let's just imagine a component that contains a list of user information and another that displays the data of the currently selected user. If you now change the data in the detail view, you should also update the contents of the list.

In Angular we would solve this by using services, which hold the respective status. You are notified when the data changes, and they then tell other components what they want to change. This also works for Angular because the framework merges its components into one environment. But this isn't necessary with Vue.js, since components can be integrated into the web pages completely decoupled from each other and thus exist without a surrounding framework that could take over administration of the services. Therefore, with the extension *Vuex* the Vue.js team also provides an implementation of the *Flux* architecture pattern, which was first known in connection with React:

► https://vuex.vuejs.org/

The next figure shows the basic sequence of an action as just described. At the center is the actual status, in this example the data that contains the list of all user objects. This status is stored in a store at Flux. The UI components or their views bind to the corresponding data fields in the store. This automatically updates them as those dates change.

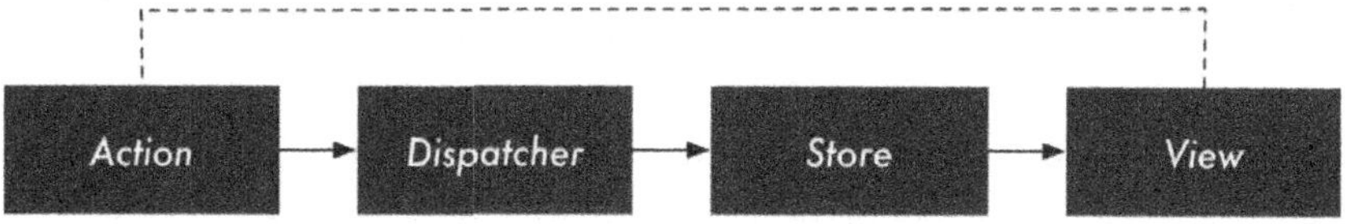

The change isn't made directly. Instead, actions are called that the store provides. These actions, in turn, synchronize via a dispatcher to the status in the store. If you change the user name in the detail view in the example, you would pass the changed data to an action, this action is directed to the dispatcher and tells him to update the corresponding data field in the store. The dispatcher makes the change and ensures that all views linked to the data field are subsequently updated.

The following listing shows how this is implemented within Vuex. Dispatching works through so-called mutations, but otherwise it isn't different:

```
Const store = new Vuex.Store({
  state: {
    users: []
  },
  mutations: {
    setUsers(state, users) {
      .users = users
    },
    updateUser(state, user) {
      ...
    }

  },
  getters: {
```

```
    getUserById: (state, id) => {
      ...
    },
  actions: {
    updateUser: function ({commit}, newData) {
      commit('updateUser', newData)
    },
    initialize: function({commit}) {
      fetch('[insert_url]')
      .then((response) =>
        commit('setUsers', response.json())
      )
    },
  }
})
export default store
```

Furthermore, there is the possibility to define filters in the form of getters. Accordingly, accesses to the actual backend are usually found in the actions. If they've this data, with which they have to adjust the internal status, they pass on the changes to the mutations, which in turn change the status in the store.

As interesting as the architectural pattern is and as helpful as it is in everyday life, it scales that much more difficult, at least for Vuex. The reason for this can already be seen in the listing above, because the names of the mutations are passed to the commit method as string parameters. These strings are also used for getters, actions, and possible namespaces. If one of the strings then needs to be changed at some point, one occasionally overlooks some of the places where they are used, and errors occur that are only discovered at runtime.

Although this can be compensated by string constants, the complexity nevertheless increases very quickly, making the handling of Vuex a challenge in larger projects. This is also the reason why the subject is treated so extensively at this point, as it indicates a common pattern in the context of Vue.js. Many things are much easier with this than with Angular. But as the amount of components increases, the reasons for this initial simplicity are negatively noticeable. That doesn't make Vue.js a bad framework, but it does suggest that you should consider the long-term purpose of the deployment.

I didn't make a direct comparison to Angular at this point, because Angular itself doesn't offer comparable services. Instead, you have to use external libraries such as *@ngrx/store*, which are not supported by the Angular team:

- https://ngrx.io/guide/store

Therefore we would have to face the same analysis as for Vue.js.

Other features

Let's have a look at common features of application frameworks like form handling, translation and backend connection.

As far as form handling is concerned, the question arises as to how forms are constructed and validated at runtime. Angular offers a very extensive library and various options for displaying error texts, for example (see chapter "7 Form validation", starting from page 307). Vue.js only has the ability to transfer data between the surface and the logic of a component using special model properties in the components. In addition, there is nothing that can't be done via HTML anyway. For validation, you usually have to either use a third-party library or just lend a hand. The same applies to the translation. While Angular provides an implementation for `i18n` on its own, Vue.js doesn't have its own solution.

When it comes to backend connectivity, Vue.js doesn't reinvent anything. Rather, it can be easily accessed again features such as the `fetch()` API or the `XMLHttpRequest` interface, which are provided by the browser. Google has built a separate capsule for Angular around the latter to simplify various functions and then inject them as a service into the components in which they are needed (see "5.2 An HTTPClient Service", starting from page 101). This procedure is particularly noticeable in the field of test automation.

Tooling

The "tooling" category concerns tool support for the frameworks that need to be compared. In the early days of Angular first-time developers came up with horror stories on how often the configuration has been changed. How hard the development environments did with TypeScript and how often you found yourself with bad error messages in situations that you yourself were not responsible for. That is passé, and so you hardly notice anything from tools like Webpack, NPM or others This is true not only on Angular, but also on Vue.js, the latter having the added benefit of being more deeply embedded in the overall ecosystem through the use of JavaScript.

Even with developer tools, both frameworks are quite similar. For Angular there's *Augury* (see "4.5 Pro Tip - Install the Augury Chrome Plugin" on page 94), even if it isn't from Google itself. For Vue.js, however, there are the *Vue-Devtools*:

► https://github.com/vuejs/vue-devtools

These two are extensions for common browsers, with which additional information can be determined, for example via routing, in the case of Angular Dependency Injection or, in the case of Vuex, the status of existing stores. Furthermore, both frameworks have their own command line interfaces, even if Google's CLI is clearly ahead of the pack and Vue.js spends a lot of work on NPM. A nice feature of the Vue.js CLI, though, is its plugin system. Thus, dedicated extensions of the core Vue components can be reloaded as plugins.

When installed, the developer is then conveniently guided through the various selection and configuration options. The actions that can be performed with the CLI need not be controlled by Vue.js. Because with the *Vue UI* Vue.js offers a user interface, as shown in the figure above. Dependencies can then be installed, analyzed and managed. The same applies to plugins, and not just to a project, but to all Vue projects that are set up on the same computer.

In general, the peculiarities of the frameworks are also covered by development environments such as Webstorm or Visual Studio, so in both cases the tooling can be rated as good and helpful. However, Angular also offers a bit more functionality in this area, for example by displaying error texts directly in the mentioned development environments and thanks to TypeScript also the context-sensitive support with IntelliSense works across the entire code base.

Test Automation

The subject of test automation has to be considered in two parts. On the one hand, it's important to understand the extent to which the framework supports automated testing itself, by preventing code that's difficult to test, and secondly, how well the framework's own components can be manipulated within tests.

In both cases, Vue.js had a relatively poor reputation until about mid-2019. Thus, there were no tools that replaced parts of the framework such as the router or the Vuex stores with test doubles or manipulated to query status information. Also, there wasn't enough documentation on how to do it all yourself. As a result, the test automation felt more like a loveless appendage, although it should actually have an even greater importance in the context of JavaScript. Because the dynamic typing and the general character of the ecosystem can easily mask mistakes and make them obvious only at runtime.

However, this disadvantage was alleviated now by publishing the *Vue Test Utils* in a stable and practicable state:

- https://vue-test-utils.vuejs.org/

Thus, with the greatly improved documentation and the general benefits of other frameworks like *Jest* or *Mocha*, the automation of unit testing is no longer a problem. The typical e2e tests can also be easily realized using tools such as *CypressJS* or the good old *Selenium*.

For Angular there is also the specialized tool *Protractor*, which in turn is based on *Selenium*. Otherwise, other common test tools can be used here as well. In a direct comparison, the automation of test cases with Angular applications is easier to implement overall and has a more mature tooling. Ionic takes advantage of this strength with immediate support for *Jasmine*, *TestBed* and *Karma* (see "11.6 Testing", starting from page 496). This is again due to the use of TypeScript and the associated better interface descriptions as well as the explicit visualization of external dependencies via constructor parameters. Most importantly, Dependency Injection, which is part of Angular rather than TypeScript, is a great help.

Documentation

The evaluation category for documentation is almost self-evident. Without documentation, the tools can't be used correctly and there's no indication of future development or breaking changes in newer versions. A good documentation therefore shows that it's up to date and has sufficient examples that are practical, but neither too simple nor too complex. It should also be stored centrally and visible to everyone. Furthermore, there must be evidence of where additional information can be found if it isn't found in the documentation.

With all these points, both frameworks are outstandingly good. This ranges from the described content to the actuality up to the used examples. In Vue.js I like that the respective functional modules such as routers, Vuex or similar are described on their own sub-web pages. This helps immensely to maintain the overview, because you are not confronted with too much information at the same time.

Of course, it can happen in both Angular and Vue.js in detail that one doesn't find information. But in these cases, the respective community is happy to help. At Vue.js you have to pay special attention to the forum and the corresponding chat. Because here's the actual music. It may be because Vue.js isn't as widely used as Angular, but it's already noticeable that questions are answered more slowly and less frequently on StackOverflow. Here Angular has a natural advantage as a top dog. Of course, where there are more people using the tools, there are also more people who can answer questions. It's therefore all the more important to know that there's a Discord chat for Vue.js, where the actual professionals are frolicking.

Ecosystem

We are already in the ecosystem, because that goes beyond the actual community. Here, it should be considered to what extent the frameworks are extended by additional tools, services and functionality that don't originate from the actual operator.

At the same time, it's also important to consider how much the framework depends on these things. After all, if you first have to load many different dependencies in order to be able to use the framework at all, then of course there are also many possible problem points. On the other hand, it makes sense, of course, if an application framework doesn't invent everything itself and instead accesses such standard solutions at points that can also be solved universally and independently of the framework. The framework should therefore provide a starting point for other services, where appropriate, and then, if possible, have a description of the use of those services.

The first place where these dependencies are already noticed is the test automation. By relying on external tools, one must, of course, be familiar with them as well, and the documentation, release cycles and general stability of these tools may differ significantly from those of the actual application framework.

Especially in the E2E testing of Vue.js applications, this is noticeable. Here you will usually only find descriptions for general web pages, and the peculiarities in the context of Vue won't be discussed further. This of course makes the training a little more difficult and can have serious disadvantages when changing the supported tools. While this scenario may sound unrealistic, both Angular and Vue.js have changed their recommendations for specific frameworks in recent years, and have changed the default application templates as well. This may not be earth-shattering in detail, but is proof of the susceptibility to interference and the effects of such dependencies.

It's better if the framework isn't based on other things, but these things are based on the framework. This is the case, for example, with component libraries. Optimizing those for Angular or Vue.js can greatly simplify developer life by allowing developers to design their applications without worrying too much about styling.

This is especially important in the context of single page applications and Progressive Web Apps (PWA) (see "12.8 Deploy & publish Progressive Web Apps", starting from page 546). Each is designed to look and feel like typical desktop or mobile applications, and it's just right when a component library provides all the components you've come to expect from the platform. This is why many manufacturers of component libraries such as Telerik or DevExpress offer optimized versions of their UI libraries. The fact that they support not only Angular and React but also Vue.js shows the importance of the framework meanwhile.

If you don't want to resort to commercial libraries, then you can also use the excellent *Vuetify* at Vue:

► https://vuetifyjs.com

This implements very extensively the material design specification of Google and has thereby even one or other component in stock, which doesn't even own Google material UI:

- https://material.angular.io/

But if you can't find everything at *Vuetify* or you are afraid to use such a large library, then take a look at *Awesome Vue*:

- https://github.com/vuejs/awesome-vue

This is basically a curated list of resources around Vue. This includes components, but also websites or Twitter accounts that deal with the framework.

That such things are of course also for Angular, is only briefly mentioned here. This is also because it is an integral part of almost every web development conference. At this point Vue.js has something to catch up with. Especially in German-speaking countries this is even more true. While Vue has enjoyed huge success in Version 1, it has only caused a stir with Version 2 in the US, and now, shortly before Version 3, it's spilling over to Europe on a much larger scale.

Learnability

Perhaps the fact that there's less visibility at conferences may be related to the fact that Vue.js doesn't have as much to explain as Angular does. This is partly because Vue just has less functionality and fewer core components. On the other hand, it's also learned very quickly. The structure of a component and the different forms of binding are understood by every person who has ever programmed JavaScript. The router and even Vuex have very similar structures to those found in the components, so these things are soon understood.

This leads directly to the exuberant eulogies in comparison to the sometimes heavyweight looking Angular. That's why Angular has a hard time with web developers because it threatens object orientation, static typing, and stateful work - all things that weren't found in Web front ends in the past. Although Vue.js has a certain form of "object orientation light" thanks to the latest ES6 features, it is still a long way from what's possible and necessary with TypeScript.

That's why many who have been more involved in JavaScript in the past are learning not just a framework like Angular, but also new concepts for them, and that can hurt. Just as people coming from languages like Java or C# can hurt to learn such a dynamic language as JavaScript. But in both cases, it pays off to really look at both frameworks and their approaches. Because with that you also learn a lot for your own work, no matter which of the two frameworks you decide on in the actual project.

Scalability and Future Security

Finally we come to the points scalability and future security.

The first is about how well processes can be parallelized and how well the frameworks work in larger teams. With the latter, the question is to clarify how the future prospects of both counter-parties, because nothing would be more wrong than to use a framework whose life cycle is about to end.

The latter point can be answered very quickly in both cases: there is no end in sight. Although Angular has lost some attention and benevolence since the initial hype, React and Vue.js have created two strong alternatives (see "3. Ionic and React", section "Use", starting from page 579). However, each of these frameworks has its intended use, and for each of these frameworks, there is a strong community and a strong team that works tirelessly to drive innovation.

The issue of scalability has already been addressed in various places. In a nutshell, thanks to typing and dependency injection, Angular scores higher, as both are early warning of a variety of errors. Further errors are then intercepted by the better testability, and thus more stable work is possible, especially in larger projects with many parallel participants. However, there are some requirements to be met, which can be very annoying, if you just want to build a website or a component. Therefore, Vue.js recommends itself for rather smaller front ends with fewer project participants, while Angular is especially suitable for larger projects. Nevertheless, both are very good and stable overall solutions that you can use at your own risk anyway, where you want.

Summary

Vue.js is a good alternative to Angular and especially suitable for smaller projects. It comes with all the features one would expect from an MV* and even application framework. It's easy to learn, and many negative points from the past, such as poor testability, have been consistently eliminated. The broad use of JavaScript also makes it very flexible and particularly popular with individual groups of people. However, this involves a number of risks in practical use. In order not to ignore these, Vue.js is already optimized for TypeScript and therefore even offers the option of static typing in newer versions.

It remains exciting how Vue.js will evolve. In any case, this framework is worth a look for newly launched projects, even if you are quite satisfied with Angular.

Using Vue with Ionic

At the completion of this book `@ioniv/vue` was still in the beta version, but despite of that I decided to go first steps with you to introduce this framework to you in this bonus chapter.

Let's start with the installation of the latest version of the Ionic CLI:

```
$ npm install -g @ionic/cli
```

Now we install Vue/CLI:

```
$ npm install -g @vue/cli
```

When that's done, we'll create a Vue app and go to its root directory:

```
$ vue create my-vue-ionic-app
$ cd my-vue-ionic-app
```

Now we can run the app with

```
$ npm run serve
```

Here is our first (pure) Vue app in action:

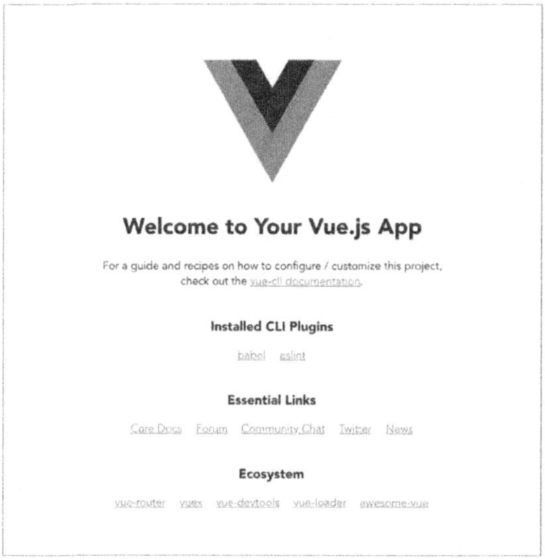

Let's get an overview of the new app project.

The entry point for our app is `src/main.js`:

```
import Vue from 'vue'
import App from './App.vue'

Vue.config.productionTip = false

new Vue({
  render: h => h(App),
}).$mount('#app')
```

As we can see, there's an import for the Vue framework itself and an import for a component called `App`. The underlying file for `App` is `src/App.vue`.

The `new Vue` method renders the app into an element with the id `#app`.

Tip: To introspect files with the ending `.vue` in Visual Studio Code I highly recommend the installation of the *Vetur* extension from Pine Wu:

▶ https://vuejs.github.io/vetur/

Let's have a look at `App.vue`:

```
<template>
  <div id="app">
    <img alt="Vue logo" src="./assets/logo.png">
    <HelloWorld msg="Welcome to Your Vue.js App"/>
  </div>
</template>

<script>
import HelloWorld from './components/HelloWorld.vue'

export default {
  name: 'app',
  components: {
    HelloWorld
  }
}
</script>
```

```
<style>
#app {
  font-family: 'Avenir', Helvetica, Arial, sans-serif;
  -webkit-font-smoothing: antialiased;
  -moz-osx-font-smoothing: grayscale;
  text-align: center;
  color: #2c3e50;
  margin-top: 60px;
}
</style>
```

`App.vue` is divided into three sections:

- template
- script
- style

This is the typical construction of a Vue component. The code in each section should be largely self-explanatory.

In the script section note the import of another component called `HelloWorld`, which can be found in the file `src/components/HelloWorld.vue`:

```
<template>
  <div class="hello">
    <h1>{{ msg }}</h1>
    <p>
      For a guide and recipes on how to configure / customize
      this project,
      <br />check out the
      <a
        href="https://cli.vuejs.org"
        target="_blank"
        rel="noopener"
      >vue-cli documentation</a>.
    </p>
    <h3>Installed CLI Plugins</h3>
    <ul>
      <li>
        <a
          href="https://github.com/vuejs/vue-cli/tree/
                dev/packages/%40vue/cli-plugin-babel"
          target="_blank"
```

```
        rel="noopener"
      >babel</a>
    </li>
    <li>
      <a
        href="https://github.com/vuejs/vue-cli/tree/
              dev/packages/%40vue/cli-plugin-eslint"
        target="_blank"
        rel="noopener"
      >eslint</a>
    </li>
  </ul>
  <h3>Essential Links</h3>
  <ul>
    <li>
      <a href="https://vuejs.org" target="_blank"
         rel="noopener">Core Docs</a>
    </li>
    <li>
      <a href="https://forum.vuejs.org" target="_blank"
         rel="noopener">Forum</a>
    </li>
    <li>
      <a href="https://chat.vuejs.org" target="_blank"
         rel="noopener">Community Chat</a>
    </li>
    <li>
      <a href="https://twitter.com/vuejs" target="_blank"
         rel="noopener">Twitter</a>
    </li>
    <li>
      <a href="https://news.vuejs.org" target="_blank"
         rel="noopener">News</a>
    </li>
  </ul>
  <h3>Ecosystem</h3>
  <ul>
    <li>
      <a href="https://router.vuejs.org" target="_blank"
         rel="noopener">vue-router</a>
    </li>
    <li>
```

```
        <a href="https://vuex.vuejs.org" target="_blank"
           rel="noopener">vuex</a>
      </li>
      <li>
        <a
          href="https://github.com/vuejs/vue-devtools
                #vue-devtools"
          target="_blank"
          rel="noopener"
        >vue-devtools</a>
      </li>
      <li>
        <a href="https://vue-loader.vuejs.org" target="_blank"
           rel="noopener">vue-loader</a>
      </li>
      <li>
        <a href="https://github.com/vuejs/awesome-vue"
           target="_blank" rel="noopener">awesome-vue</a>
      </li>
    </ul>
  </div>
</template>

<script>
export default {
  name: "HelloWorld",
  props: {
    msg: String
  }
};
</script>

<!-- Add "scoped" attribute to limit CSS to this component
only -->
<style scoped>
h3 {
  margin: 40px 0 0;
}
ul {
  list-style-type: none;
  padding: 0;
}
```

```
li {
  display: inline-block;
  margin: 0 10px;
}
a {
  color: #42b983;
}
</style>
```

Again, you can recognize the three sections `template`, `script` and `style`.

How the whole thing looks like, you have already seen in the figure before.

We now want to spice up this pure Vue app with Ionic. For this we install the `@ionic/vue` library:

```
$ npm install @ionic/vue
```

Once the install is finished we have access to the Ionic plugin and can add it to our `main.js`:

```
import Vue from 'vue';
import App from './App.vue';

import Ionic from '@ionic/vue';
import '@ionic/core/css/ionic.bundle.css';

Vue.use(Ionic);
Vue.config.productionTip = false;

new Vue({
  render: h => h(App),
}).$mount('#app')
```

You will probably get the following error message:

```
ERROR  Failed to compile with 1 errors

This dependency was not found:
* vue-router in ./node_modules/@ionic/vue/dist/ionic-vue.esm.js
To install it, you can run: npm install --save vue-router
```

If so, install the `vue-router`:

```
$ npm install --save vue-router
```

With the beta version of `@ionic/vue` there was a problem with using the `ionicons` library. This error occurred:

```
WARNING  Compiled with 1 warnings

warning  in ./node_modules/@ionic/vue/dist/ionic-vue.esm.js
"export 'ICON_PATHS' was not found in 'ionicons/icons'
```

And the app screen remained blank.

I could fix that with the following installation:

```
$ npm install ionicons@4.5.9-1 --save-dev
```

But this workaround only prevents the error. In order to display the icons, more workarounds had to be used. But since we can assume that a working release candidate for Ionic/Vue will be released shortly, I'll just drop icons in this example.

Now we have access to (nearly) all of Ionic's components. So let's redesign the `HelloWorld` component and put some Ionic UI elements into `src/components/HelloWorld.vue`:

```
<template>
  <div class="ion-page">
    <ion-header>
      <ion-toolbar>
        <ion-title>BoB Tours goes Vue</ion-title>
      </ion-toolbar>
    </ion-header>
    <ion-content class="ion-padding">
      <ion-list>
        <ion-item @click="about()">
          <ion-label>About this app</ion-label>
        </ion-item>
        <ion-list-header>Price Range</ion-list-header>
        <ion-range dualKnobs="true" snaps="true" step="20"
                   min="80" max="400" value="240">
          <ion-label slot="start">80</ion-label>
          <ion-label slot="end">400</ion-label>
        </ion-range>
        <ion-radio-group>
          <ion-item>
            <ion-label>Azure-Style</ion-label>
            <ion-radio value="azure" slot="end"
```

```
                             checked="true" />
          </ion-item>
          <ion-item>
            <ion-label>Summer-Style</ion-label>
            <ion-radio value="summer" slot="end" />
          </ion-item>
        </ion-radio-group>
        <ion-item>
          <ion-label>Allow messages</ion-label>
          <ion-checkbox slot="end" checked="true" />
        </ion-item>
      </ion-list>
    </ion-content>
  </div>
</template>

<script>
export default {
  name: "HelloWorld",
  //props: {
  //  msg: String
  //},
  methods: {
    about: () => {
      alert('This is my 1st Vue/Ionic App!');
    }
  }
};
</script>

<style scoped>
  ...
</style>
```

First we create an `ion-header` area with an `ion-toolbar` and an `ion-title`. In the following `ion-content` area we produce an `ion-list` component with some `ion-item` elements. Does that look familiar?

Take a look at the first `ion-item` element:

```
<ion-item @click="about()">
  <ion-label>About this app</ion-label>
</ion-item>
```

The item can be clicked, because here we assign `@click` to an `about()` function. We'll soon have a look at this function.

Next, we use an `ion-list-header` as caption for the following `ion-range` component (see "6.21 Range", starting from page 250):

```
<ion-list-header>Price Range</ion-list-header>
<ion-range dualKnobs="true" snaps="true" step="20"
          min="80" max="400" value="240">
  <ion-label slot="start">80</ion-label>
  <ion-label slot="end">400</ion-label>
</ion-range>
```

In most cases, the implementation works as described in the Ionic component documentation.

Within an `ion-radio-group` we offer a selection by using two labeled `ion-radio` elements:

```
<ion-radio-group>
  <ion-item>
    <ion-label>Azure-Style</ion-label>
    <ion-radio value="azure" slot="end"
               checked="true" />
  </ion-item>
  <ion-item>
    <ion-label>Summer-Style</ion-label>
    <ion-radio value="summer" slot="end" />
  </ion-item>
</ion-radio-group>
```

It shouldn't go unmentioned that in Ionic/Vue all XML tags without content can be formulated in the condensed XML special notation: `<IonIcon ... />`. That should be better not be done in Ionic/Angular.

Last but not least we use a labeled `ion-checkbox` and set its `slot` attribute to `"end"` (the right end of the item element) and its `checked` attribute to `"true"` to preselect it:

```
<ion-item>
  <ion-label>Allow messages</ion-label>
  <ion-checkbox slot="end" checked="true" />
</ion-item>
```

Within the `script` part of our page we create a `methods` block with a little function:

```
methods: {
  about: () => {
    alert('This is my 1st Vue/Ionic App!');
  }
}
```

This simply shows a browser alert. Nothing special.

Here's our modified Ionic/Vue app in action:

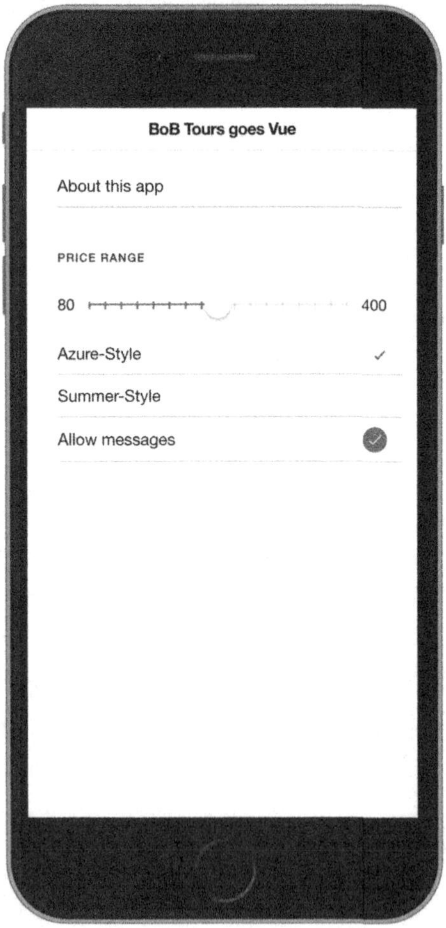

Let's rebuild our demo app and add some navigation functionality. In order to use navigation we need to install the Vue router with:

```
$ vue add router
```

If you are asked

```
? Use history mode for router? (Requires proper server setup
for index fallback in production) (Y/n)
```

you can answer with `Y` for `Yes`.

The command not only adds the router library, it also adds and modifies some files.

Let's have a look at `main.js`:

```
import Vue from 'vue'
import App from './App.vue'

import Ionic from '@ionic/vue';
import router from './router';
import '@ionic/core/css/ionic.bundle.css';

Vue.use(Ionic);
Vue.config.productionTip = false;

new Vue({
  router,
  render: h => h(App),
}).$mount('#app')
```

You should see the import of `router` and its injection in the Vue constructor.

We have a new folder/file in the `src` folder called `router/index.js`:

```
import Vue from 'vue'
import VueRouter from 'vue-router'
import Home from '../views/Home.vue'

Vue.use(VueRouter)

const routes = [
  {
    path: '/',
```

```
    name: 'Home',
    component: Home
  },
  {
    path: '/about',
    name: 'About',
    // route level code-splitting
    // this generates a separate chunk (about.[hash].js) for
this route
    // which is lazy-loaded when the route is visited.
    component:
      () => import(/* webpackChunkName: "about" */
                   '../views/About.vue')
  }
]

const router = new VueRouter({
  mode: 'history',
  base: process.env.BASE_URL,
  routes
})

export default router
```

Instead of the original Vue router we want to use `IonicVueRouter`. So let's replace the standard router in `src/router/index.js` as follows:

```
import Vue from 'vue'
import { IonicVueRouter } from '@ionic/vue'
import Home from './views/Home.vue'

Vue.use(IonicVueRouter)
  ...
})

const router = new IonicVueRouter({
  ...
})
```

We also have a modification in `App.vue`:

```
<template>
```

```
  <div id="app">
    <div id="nav">
      <router-link to="/">Home</router-link> |
      <router-link to="/about">About</router-link>
    </div>
    <router-view/>
  </div>
</template>
```

By the way - a short explanation to `Home` and `About`: As you may have seen, there is now a folder `src/views` that contains the files `Home.vue` and `About.vue`. We'll rebuild them soon.

We rebuild `App.vue` as follows:

```
<template>
  <div id="app">
    <ion-app>
      <ion-vue-router />
    </ion-app>
  </div>
</template>
```

What we have done is wrapping our entire app in an `ion-app` wrapper and using `ion-vue-router` now. `IonicVueRouter` requires the `ion-vue-router` element in order to render Ionic transitions.

You can get rid of the `style` area on this occasion. We don't need it.

Now we copy the `template` and `script` part from `src/components/HelloWorld.vue` into `src/views/Home.vue` (`HelloWorld.vue` can then be deleted.)

We rename `About.vue` to `Slideshow.vue` and code it like this:

```
<template>
  <div class="ion-page">
    <ion-header>
      <ion-toolbar>
        <ion-title>Slideshow</ion-title>
      </ion-toolbar>
    </ion-header>
    <ion-content class="ion-padding ion-text-center">
      <h1>Slideshow page</h1>
```

```
      <p>This is a page component.</p>
    </ion-content>
  </div>
</template>

<script>
export default {
  name: "Slideshow"
};
</script>

<style scoped>
h1 {
  margin: 48px 0 0;
}
</style>
```

For the app to work, `src/router/index.js` now needs to be customized:

```
import Vue from 'vue'
import { IonicVueRouter } from '@ionic/vue';
import Home from './views/Home.vue'

Vue.use(IonicVueRouter)

const router = new IonicVueRouter({
  mode: 'history',
  base: process.env.BASE_URL,
  routes: [
    {
      path: '/',
      name: 'home',
      component: Home
    },
    {
      path: '/slideshow',
      name: 'slideshow',
      component: () => import('./views/Slideshow.vue')
    }
  ]
})
```

What's missing, is a way for the user to navigate from the `Home` view (page) to the `Slideshow` view (page) and back.

Let's start with `Home.vue`:

```
<template>
  <div class="ion-page">
    <ion-header>
      <ion-toolbar>
        <ion-title>BoB Tours goes Vue</ion-title>
      </ion-toolbar>
    </ion-header>
    <ion-content class="ion-padding">
      <ion-list>
        <router-link to="/slideshow">
          <ion-item>
            <ion-label>Slideshow</ion-label>
          </ion-item>
        </router-link>
        <ion-item @click="about()">
          <ion-label>About this app</ion-label>
        </ion-item>
        <ion-list-header>Price Range</ion-list-header>
        <ion-range dualKnobs="true" snaps="true" step="20"
                   min="80" max="400" value="240">
          <ion-label slot="start">80</ion-label>
          <ion-label slot="end">400</ion-label>
        </ion-range>
        <ion-radio-group>
          <ion-item>
            <ion-label>Azure-Style</ion-label>
            <ion-radio value="azure" slot="end"
                       checked="true" />
          </ion-item>
          <ion-item>
            <ion-label>Summer-Style</ion-label>
            <ion-radio value="summer" slot="end" />
          </ion-item>
        </ion-radio-group>
        <ion-item>
          <ion-label>Allow messages</ion-label>
          <ion-checkbox slot="end" checked="true" />
```

```
        </ion-item>
      </ion-list>
    </ion-content>
  </div>
</template>

<script>
  ...
</script>
```

We simply create a `router-link`, give the `to` attribute the path to the desired page and wrap this around an `ion-item` element labeled `Slideshow`. Now this item can be clicked to navigate to the Slideshow page.

To come back from there we complete `Slideshow.vue`:

```
<template>
  <div class="ion-page">
    <ion-header>
      <ion-toolbar>
        <ion-title>Slideshow</ion-title>
        <ion-buttons slot="start">
          <router-link to="/home">
            <ion-back-button />
          </router-link>
        </ion-buttons>
      </ion-toolbar>
    </ion-header>
    <ion-content class="ion-padding ion-text-center">
      <h1>Slideshow page</h1>
      <p>This is a page component.</p>
    </ion-content>
  </div>
</template>

<script>
  ...
</script>
```

In the `ion-header` we add an `ion-buttons` area at the `start` slot. Within this area we place another `router-link` and wrap it around an `ion-back-button`. Now with this back button we are able to navigate back to our Home page.

We want to eliminate a small flaw: Since each `router-link` is rendered as `<a href="...">` tag, the `Slideshow` list item and the back button get underscores. This is unusual for apps. Of course they can be eliminated quickly with a little CSS. This is best done centrally with a little style snippet in `App.vue`:

```
<style>
  a {
      text-decoration: none;
    }
</style>
```

Here's our Ionic/Vue app with navigation in action:

Conclusion

As mentioned before, Vue.js is a good alternative to Angular and especially suitable for smaller projects. Ionic/Vue was in an early beta version at the time of writing this book. Not everything was perfect, like the support of the Ionicons. But still you should keep this combination of frameworks in view.

Summary

In this bonus chapter you got to know how to use Ionic without any other frameworks.

You met Ionic's Capacitor, the native bridge for cross-platform apps. With Capacitor you can build (web) apps that run equally well on iOS, Android, Electron, and as Progressive Web Apps.

You've learned some basic things about the popular React framework and how to build an app using Ionic and React.

Often considered as "the leaner Angular" Vue was finally our last trip and you've seen, that the combination of Ionic and Vue is also an interesting way to build apps.

This ends our journey through the universe of Ionic. I hope you've enjoyed it.

Now there is only one thing left to do for you:

Create awesome apps!

Made in United States
North Haven, CT
10 November 2026

22091242R00352